Microsoft® Official Academic Course

Windows Server® 2008
Enterprise Administrator (70-647)

Craig Zacker

WILEY

Credits

EXECUTIVE EDITOR	John Kane
DIRECTOR OF SALES	Mitchell Beaton
EXECUTIVE MARKETING MANAGER	Chris Ruel
MICROSOFT SENIOR PRODUCT MANAGER	Merrick Van Dongen of Microsoft Learning
DEVELOPMENT AND PRODUCTION	Custom Editorial Productions, Inc.
EDITORIAL PROGRAM ASSISTANT	Jennifer Lartz
CONTENT MANAGER	Micheline Frederick
PRODUCTION EDITOR	Amy Weintraub
CREATIVE DIRECTOR	Harry Nolan
COVER DESIGNER	Jim O'Shea
TECHNOLOGY AND MEDIA	Tom Kulesa/Wendy Ashenberg

Cover photo: Credit © Orbit/Masterfile

This book was set in Garamond by Aptara, Inc. and printed and bound by Bind Rite Robbinsville. The covers were printed by Bind Rite Robbinsville.

Founded in 1807, John Wiley & Sons, Inc. has been a valued source of knowledge and understanding for more than 200 years, helping people around the world meet their needs and fulfill their aspirations. Our company is built on a foundation of principles that include responsibility to the communities we serve and where we live and work. In 2008, we launched a Corporate Citizenship Initiative, a global effort to address the environmental, social, economic, and ethical challenges we face in our business. Among the issues we are addressing are carbon impact, paper specifications and procurement, ethical conduct within our business and among our vendors, and community and charitable support. For more information, please visit our website: www.wiley.com/go/citizenship.

ISBN 978-0-470-22516-5

Printed in the United States of America

10 9 8 7 6 5 4 3 2 1

www.wiley.com/college/microsoft or
call the MOAC Toll-Free Number: 1+(888) 764-7001 (U.S. & Canada only)

Foreword from the Publisher

Wiley's publishing vision for the Microsoft Official Academic Course series is to provide students and instructors with the skills and knowledge they need to use Microsoft technology effectively in all aspects of their personal and professional lives. Quality instruction is required to help both educators and students get the most from Microsoft's software tools and to become more productive. Thus our mission is to make our instructional programs trusted educational companions for life.

To accomplish this mission, Wiley and Microsoft have partnered to develop the highest quality educational programs for information workers, IT professionals, and developers. Materials created by this partnership carry the brand name "Microsoft Official Academic Course," assuring instructors and students alike that the content of these textbooks is fully endorsed by Microsoft, and that they provide the highest quality information and instruction on Microsoft products. The Microsoft Official Academic Course textbooks are "Official" in still one more way—they are the officially sanctioned courseware for Microsoft IT Academy members.

The Microsoft Official Academic Course series focuses on *workforce development*. These programs are aimed at those students seeking to enter the workforce, change jobs, or embark on new careers as information workers, IT professionals, and developers. Microsoft Official Academic Course programs address their needs by emphasizing authentic workplace scenarios with an abundance of projects, exercises, cases, and assessments.

The Microsoft Official Academic Courses are mapped to Microsoft's extensive research and job-task analysis, the same research and analysis used to create the Microsoft Certified Information Technology Professional (MCITP) exam. The textbooks focus on real skills for real jobs. As students work through the projects and exercises in the textbooks, they enhance their level of knowledge and their ability to apply the latest Microsoft technology to everyday tasks. These students also gain resume-building credentials that can assist them in finding a job, keeping their current job, or in furthering their education.

The concept of life-long learning is today an utmost necessity. Job roles, and even whole job categories, are changing so quickly that none of us can stay competitive and productive without continuously updating our skills and capabilities. The Microsoft Official Academic Course offerings, and their focus on Microsoft certification exam preparation, provide a means for people to acquire and effectively update their skills and knowledge. Wiley supports students in this endeavor through the development and distribution of these courses as Microsoft's official academic publisher.

Today educational publishing requires attention to providing quality print and robust electronic content. By integrating Microsoft Official Academic Course products, *WileyPLUS*, and Microsoft certifications, we are better able to deliver efficient learning solutions for students and teachers alike.

Bonnie Lieberman

General Manager and Senior Vice President

Welcome to the Microsoft Official Academic Course (MOAC) program for Microsoft Windows Server 2008. MOAC represents the collaboration between Microsoft Learning and John Wiley & Sons, Inc. publishing company. Microsoft and Wiley teamed up to produce a series of textbooks that deliver compelling and innovative teaching solutions to instructors and superior learning experiences for students. Infused and informed by in-depth knowledge from the creators of Windows Server 2008, and crafted by a publisher known worldwide for the pedagogical quality of its products, these textbooks maximize skills transfer in minimum time. Students are challenged to reach their potential by using their new technical skills as highly productive members of the workforce.

Because this knowledgebase comes directly from Microsoft, architect of the Windows Server operating system and creator of the Microsoft Certified Information Technology Professional and Microsoft Certified Professional exams (www.microsoft.com/learning/mcp/mcitp), you are sure to receive the topical coverage that is most relevant to your personal and professional success. Microsoft's direct participation not only assures you that MOAC textbook content is accurate and current; it also means that you will receive the best instruction possible to enable your success on certification exams and in the workplace.

▪ The Microsoft Official Academic Course Program

The *Microsoft Official Academic Course* series is a complete program for instructors and institutions to prepare and deliver great courses on Microsoft software technologies. With MOAC, we recognize that, because of the rapid pace of change in the technology and curriculum developed by Microsoft, there is an ongoing set of needs beyond classroom instruction tools for an instructor to be ready to teach the course. The MOAC program endeavors to provide solutions for all these needs in a systematic manner in order to ensure a successful and rewarding course experience for both instructor and student—technical and curriculum training for instructor readiness with new software releases; the software itself for student use at home for building hands-on skills, assessment, and validation of skill development; and a great set of tools for delivering instruction in the classroom and lab. All are important to the smooth delivery of an interesting course on Microsoft software, and all are provided with the MOAC program. We think about the model below as a gauge for ensuring that we completely support you in your goal of teaching a great course. As you evaluate your instructional materials options, you may wish to use this model for comparison purposes with available products:

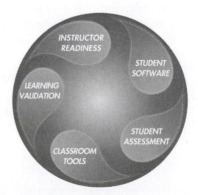

Illustrated Book Tour

■ Pedagogical Features

The MOAC textbook for Windows Server 2008 Enterprise Administrator is designed to cover all the learning objectives for that MCITP exam, which is referred to as its "objective domain." The Microsoft Certified Information Technology Professional (MCITP) exam objectives are highlighted throughout the textbook. Many pedagogical features have been developed specifically for *Microsoft Official Academic Course* programs.

Presenting the extensive procedural information and technical concepts woven throughout the textbook raises challenges for the student and instructor alike. The Illustrated Book Tour that follows provides a guide to the rich features contributing to *Microsoft Official Academic Course* program's pedagogical plan. Following is a list of key features in each lesson designed to prepare students for success on the certification exams and in the workplace:

- Each lesson begins with an **Objective Domain Matrix.** More than a standard list of learning objectives, the Domain Matrix correlates each software skill covered in the lesson to the specific MCITP "objective domain."

- Concise and frequent **step-by-step** Exercises teach students new features and provide an opportunity for hands-on practice. Numbered steps give detailed, step-by-step instructions to help students learn software skills. The steps also show results and screen images to match what students should see on their computer screens.

- **Illustrations**—in particular, screen images—provide visual feedback as students work through the exercises. The images reinforce key concepts, provide visual clues about the steps, and allow students to check their progress.

- Lists of **Key Terms** at the beginning of each lesson introduce students to important technical vocabulary. When these terms are used later in the lesson, they appear in bold italic type where they are defined.

- Engaging point-of-use **Reader Aids,** located throughout the lessons, tell students why this topic is relevant (*The Bottom Line*), provide students with helpful hints (*Take Note*), or show alternate ways to accomplish tasks (*Another Way*). Reader Aids also provide additional relevant or background information that adds value to the lesson.

- **Certification Ready** features throughout the text signal students where a specific certification objective is covered. They provide students with a chance to check their understanding of that particular MCITP objective and, if necessary, review the section of the lesson where it is covered. MOAC offers complete preparation for MCITP certification.

- **Knowledge Assessments** provide three progressively more challenging lesson-ending activities.

- **Case Scenarios** provide workplace-based situations that test students' ability to apply what they've learned in the lesson.

■ Lesson Features

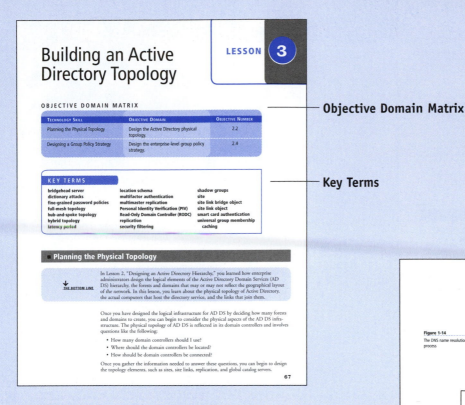

Objective Domain Matrix

Key Terms

X-Ref Reader Aid

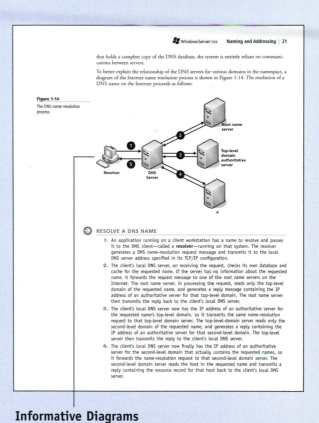

Informative Diagrams

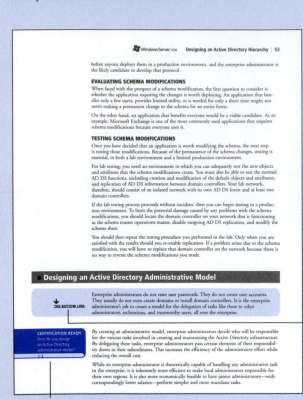

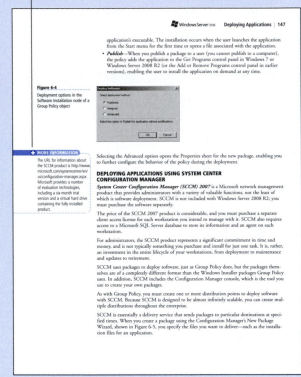

More Information Reader Aid

The Bottom Line Reader Aid

Certification Ready Alert

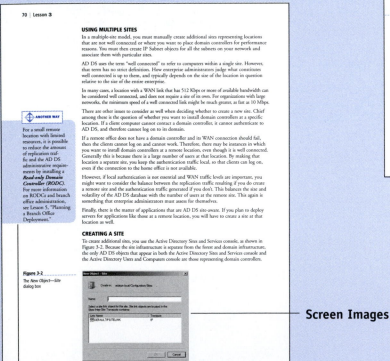

Screen Images

Another Way Reader Aid

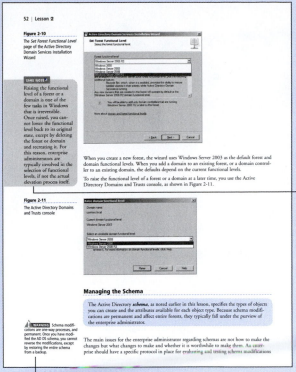

Figure 2-10

The *Set Forest Functional Level* page of the Active Directory Domain Services Installation Wizard

TAKE NOTE

Raising the functional level of a forest or a domain is one of the few tasks in Windows that is irreversible. Once raised, you cannot lower the functional level back to its original state, except by deleting the forest or domain and recreating it. For this reason, enterprise administrators are typically involved in the selection of functional levels, if not the actual elevation process itself.

When you create a new forest, the wizard uses Windows Server 2003 as the default forest and domain functional levels. When you add a domain to an existing forest, or a domain controller to an existing domain, the defaults depend on the current functional levels.

To raise the functional level of a forest or a domain at a later time, you use the Active Directory Domains and Trusts console, as shown in Figure 2-11.

Figure 2-11

The Active Directory Domains and Trusts console

WARNING Schema modifications are one-way processes, and permanent. Once you have modified the AD DS schema, you cannot reverse the modifications, except by restoring the entire schema from a backup.

Managing the Schema

The Active Directory *schema*, as noted earlier in this lesson, specifies the types of objects you can create and the attributes available for each object type. Because schema modifications are permanent and affect entire forests, they typically fall under the purview of the enterprise administrator.

The main issues for the enterprise administrator regarding schemas are not how to make the changes but what changes to make and whether it is worthwhile to make them. An enterprise should have a specific protocol in place for evaluating and testing schema modifications

Take Note Reader Aid

Warning Reader Aid

---

14 | Lesson 1

For the enterprise administrator, manual address allocation is even more impractical than in IPv4, because of the length of the addresses involved. Therefore, the other two options are more prevalent.

When a Windows computer starts, it initiates the stateless address autoconfiguration process, during which it assigns each interface a link-local unicast address. This assignment always occurs, even when the interface is to receive a global unicast address later. The link-local address enables the system to communicate with the router on the link, which provides additional instructions.

The steps of the stateless address autoconfiguration process are as follows:

PERFORM A STATELESS ADDRESS AUTOCONFIGURATION

1. Link-local address creation—The IPv6 implementation on the system creates a link-local address for each interface by using the fe80::/64 network address and generating an interface ID, using either the interface's MAC address or a pseudorandom generator.

2. Duplicate address detection—Using the IPv6 Neighbor Discovery (ND) protocol, the system transmits a Neighbor Solicitation message to determine if any other computer on the link is using the same address and listens for a Neighbor Advertisement message sent in reply. If there is no reply, then the system considers the address to be unique on the link. If there is a reply, the system must generate a new address and repeat the procedure.

3. Link-local address assignment—When the system determines that the link-local address is unique, it configures the interface to use that address. On a small network consisting of a single segment or link, this may be the interface's permanent address assignment. On a network with multiple subnets, the primary function of the link-local address assignment is to enable the system to communicate with a router on the link.

4. Router advertisement solicitation—The system uses the ND protocol to transmit Router Solicitation messages to the *all routers* multicast address. These messages compel routers to transmit the Router Advertisement messages more frequently.

5. Router advertisement—The router on the link uses the ND protocol to transmit Router Advertisement messages to the system that contain information on how the autoconfiguration process should proceed. The Router Advertisement messages typically supply a network prefix, which the system will use with its existing interface ID to create a global or unique local unicast address. The messages may also instruct the system to initiate a stateful autoconfiguration process by contacting a specific DHCPv6 server. If there is no router on the link, as determined by the system's failure to receive Router Advertisement messages, then the system must attempt to initiate a stateful autoconfiguration process.

6. Global or unique local address configuration—Using the information it receives from the router, the system generates a suitable address—one that is routable, either globally or within the enterprise—and configures the interface to use it. If so instructed, the system might also initiate a stateful autoconfiguration process by contacting the DHCPv6 server specified by the router and obtaining a global or unique local address from that server, along with other configuration settings.

For the enterprise administrator with a multi-segment network, it will be necessary to use unique local or global addresses for internetwork communication, so you will need either routers that advertise the appropriate network prefixes or DHCPv6 servers that can supply addresses with the correct prefixes. The Routing and Remote Access role service in Windows Server 2008 R2 and Windows Server 2008 supports IPv6 routing and advertising, and the DHCP role in those operating systems supports IPv6 address allocation.

Step-by-Step Exercises

---

72 | Lesson 3

If you have created sites but have not yet created subnets, the wizard enables you to select a site. If you have not yet created additional sites, the wizard automatically adds the domain controller to the Default-First-Site-Name site.

Designing a Replication Topology

AD DS uses a *multimaster replication* process, which means that you can modify the contents of the AD DS database on any domain controller and that domain controller will propagate the changes to all of the other domain controllers containing replicas of the modified partition. The exception to this is the Read-only Domain Controller, which only receives replication traffic; it does not send it.

As mentioned earlier, there are two kinds of AD DS replication traffic: intrasite and intersite. The differences between the two are listed in Table 3-1.

Table 3-1

Differences between Intrasite and Intersite Replication

INTRASITE REPLICATION	INTERSITE REPLICATION
Replication is initiated when an administrator makes a change to the AD DS database.	Replication events occur according to a schedule.
Replication traffic is not compressed.	Replication traffic is compressed.
Domain controllers transmit replication traffic to multiple replication partners.	Domain controllers at each site transmit replication traffic to a bridgehead server, which then transmits to a single bridgehead server at another site.
Rarely needs configuration.	Highly configurable.
Does not require the configuration of additional AD DS objects.	Requires the creation and configuration of site link objects, and possibly site link bridge objects.

Intrasite replication requires no effort from the enterprise administrator, whether the network has one site or many. The domain controllers in each site take care of their own interaction. However, an administrator must create and configure site link objects to provide the intersite connections.

SELECTING A REPLICATION MODEL

As part of the site design, enterprise administrators must decide on a topology for the intersite replication traffic. In other words, they must determine which sites will replicate with which. To some extent, this is dependent on the physical connections connecting the sites. You can create a replication topology that simply utilizes the entire WAN topology connecting the locations hosting separate sites, or designate a subset of the WAN topology to be used for replication.

In an AD DS installation with multiple sites, each site designates one domain controller as the *bridgehead server* for each partition with a replica at that site. The bridgehead servers are the only domain controllers that communicate with the other sites. Therefore, enterprise administrators create a replication model at the site level; they do not have to be concerned with selecting which domain controllers participate in intersite replication.

Easy-to-Read Tables

Skill Summary

Knowledge Assessment

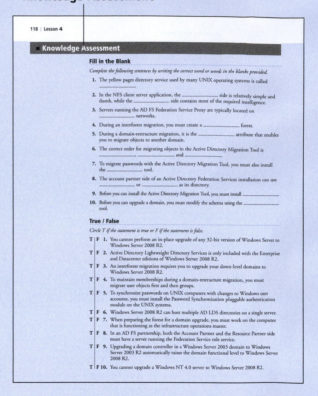

Case Scenarios

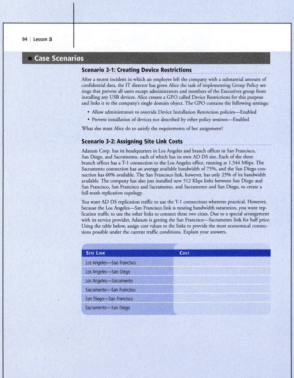

Conventions and Features Used in This Book

This book uses particular fonts, symbols, and heading conventions to highlight important information or to call your attention to special steps. For more information about the features in each lesson, refer to the Illustrated Book Tour section.

CONVENTION	MEANING
↓ THE BOTTOM LINE	This feature provides a brief summary of the material to be covered in the section that follows.
CLOSE	Words in all capital letters and in a different font color than the rest of the text indicate instructions for opening, saving, or closing files or programs. They also point out items you should check or actions you should take.
CERTIFICATION READY	This feature signals the point in the text where a specific certification objective is covered. It provides you with a chance to check your understanding of that particular MCITP objective and, if necessary, review the section of the lesson where it is covered.
TAKE NOTE*	Reader Aids appear in shaded boxes found in your text. *Take Note* provides helpful hints related to particular tasks or topics.
◆ ANOTHER WAY	*Another Way* provides an alternative procedure for accomplishing a particular task.
X REF	These notes provide pointers to information discussed elsewhere in the textbook or describe interesting features of Windows Server 2008 that are not directly addressed in the current topic or exercise.
Alt + Tab	A plus sign (+) between two key names means that you must press both keys at the same time. Keys that you are instructed to press in an exercise will appear in the font shown here.
A *shared printer* can be used by many individuals on a network.	Key terms appear in bold, italic font when they are defined.
Key My Name is.	Any text you are asked to key appears in color.
Click OK.	Any button on the screen you are supposed to click on or select will also appear in color.

Instructor Support Program

The *Microsoft Official Academic Course* programs are accompanied by a rich array of resources that incorporate the extensive textbook visuals to form a pedagogically cohesive package. These resources provide all the materials instructors need to deploy and deliver their courses. Resources available online for download include:

- The **MSDN Academic Alliance** is designed to provide the easiest and most inexpensive developer tools, products, and technologies available to faculty and students in labs, classrooms, and on student PCs. A free 3-year membership is available to qualified MOAC adopters.

  Note: Microsoft Windows Server 2008 can be downloaded from MSDN AA for use by students in this course.

- **Windows Server 2008 Evaluation Software.** DVDs containing an evaluation version of Windows Server 2008 are bundled inside the back cover of this text.

- The **Instructor's Guide** contains solutions to all the textbook exercises as well as chapter summaries and lecture notes. The Instructor's Guide and Syllabi for various term lengths are available from the Book Companion site (http://www.wiley.com/college/microsoft) and from *WileyPLUS*.

- The **Test Bank** contains hundreds of questions in multiple-choice, true-false, short answer, and essay formats and is available to download from the Instructor's Book Companion site (http://www.wiley.com/college/microsoft) and from *WileyPLUS*. A complete answer key is provided.

- **PowerPoint Presentations and Images.** A complete set of PowerPoint presentations is available on the Instructor's Book Companion site (http://www.wiley.com/college/micro-soft) and in *WileyPLUS* to enhance classroom presentations. Tailored to the text's topical coverage and Skills Matrix, these presentations are designed to convey key Windows Server concepts addressed in the text.

  All figures from the text are on the Instructor's Book Companion site (http://www.wiley.com/college/microsoft) and in *WileyPLUS*. You can incorporate them into your PowerPoint presentations, or create your own overhead transparencies and handouts.

  By using these visuals in class discussions, you can help focus students' attention on key elements of Windows Server and help them understand how to use it effectively in the workplace.

- When it comes to improving the classroom experience, there is no better source of ideas and inspiration than your fellow colleagues. The **Wiley Faculty Network** connects teachers with technology, facilitates the exchange of best practices, and helps to enhance instructional efficiency and effectiveness. Faculty Network activities include technology training and tutorials, virtual seminars, peer-to-peer exchanges of experiences and ideas, personal consulting, and sharing of resources. For details visit www.WhereFacultyConnect.com.

WileyPLUS

Broad developments in education over the past decade have influenced the instructional approach taken in the Microsoft Official Academic Course program. The way that students learn, especially about new technologies, has changed dramatically in the Internet era. Electronic learning materials and Internet-based instruction is now as much a part of classroom instruction as printed textbooks. *WileyPLUS* provides the technology to create an environment where students reach their full potential and experience academic success that will last them a lifetime!

WileyPLUS is a powerful and highly-integrated suite of teaching and learning resources designed to bridge the gap between what happens in the classroom and what happens at home and on the job. *WileyPLUS* provides instructors with the resources to teach their students new technologies and guide them to reach their goals of getting ahead in the job market by having the skills to become certified and advance in the workforce. For students, *WileyPLUS* provides the tools for study and practice that are available to them 24/7, wherever and whenever they want to study. *WileyPLUS* includes a complete online version of the student textbook, PowerPoint presentations, homework and practice assignments and quizzes, image galleries, test bank questions, gradebook, and all the instructor resources in one easy-to-use Web site.

Organized around the everyday activities you and your students perform in the class, *WileyPLUS* helps you:

- **Prepare and Present** outstanding class presentations using relevant PowerPoint slides and other *WileyPLUS* materials—and you can easily upload and add your own.

- **Create Assignments** by choosing from questions organized by lesson, level of difficulty, and source—and add your own questions. Students' homework and quizzes are automatically graded, and the results are recorded in your gradebook.

- **Offer Context-Sensitive Help to Students, 24/7.** When you assign homework or quizzes, you decide if and when students get access to hints, solutions, or answers where appropriate—or they can be linked to relevant sections of their complete, online text for additional help whenever—and wherever they need it most.

- **Track Student Progress** by analyzing students' results and assessing their level of understanding on an individual and class level using the *WileyPLUS* gradebook, or export data to your own personal gradebook.

- **Administer Your Course.** *WileyPLUS* can easily be integrated with another course management system, gradebook, or other resources you are using in your class, providing you with the flexibility to build your course, your way.

Please view our online demo at **www.wiley.com/college/wileyplus.** Here you will find additional information about the features and benefits of *WileyPLUS*, how to request a "test drive" of *WileyPLUS* for this title, and how to adopt it for class use.

MSDN ACADEMIC ALLIANCE—FREE 3-YEAR MEMBERSHIP AVAILABLE TO QUALIFIED ADOPTERS!

The Microsoft Developer Network Academic Alliance (MSDN AA) is designed to provide the easiest and most inexpensive way for universities to make the latest Microsoft developer tools, products, and technologies available in labs, classrooms, and on student PCs. MSDN AA is an annual membership program for departments teaching Science, Technology, Engineering, and Mathematics (STEM) courses. The membership provides a complete solution to keep academic labs, faculty, and students on the leading edge of technology.

Software available in the MSDN AA program is provided at no charge to adopting departments through the Wiley and Microsoft publishing partnership.

As a bonus to this free offer, faculty will be introduced to Microsoft's Faculty Connection and Academic Resource Center. It takes time and preparation to keep students engaged while giving them a fundamental understanding of theory, and the Microsoft Faculty Connection is designed to help STEM professors with this preparation by providing articles, curriculum, and tools that professors can use to engage and inspire today's technology students.

Contact your Wiley representative for details.

For more information about the MSDN Academic Alliance program, go to:

http://msdn.microsoft.com/academic/

Note: Microsoft Windows Server 2008 can be downloaded from MSDN AA for use by students in this course.

Important Web Addresses and Phone Numbers

To locate the Wiley Higher Education Representative in your area, go to the following Web address and click on the "*Who's My Rep?*" link at the top of the page:

http://www.wiley.com/college

Or call the MOAC toll-free number: 1 + (888) 764-7001 (U.S. & Canada only).

To learn more about becoming a Microsoft Certified Professional and exam availability, visit www.microsoft.com/learning/mcp.

Student Support Program

Book Companion Web Site (www.wiley.com/college/microsoft)

The students' book companion site for the MOAC series includes any resources, exercise files, and web links that will be used in conjunction with this course.

WileyPLUS

WileyPLUS is a powerful and highly-integrated suite of teaching and learning resources designed to bridge the gap between what happens in the classroom and what happens at home and on the job. For students, *WileyPLUS* provides tools for study and practice that are available 24/7, wherever and whenever they want to study. *WileyPLUS* includes a complete online version of the student textbook, PowerPoint presentations, homework and practice assignments and quizzes, image galleries, test bank questions, gradebook, and all the instructor resources in one easy-to-use Web site.

WileyPLUS provides immediate feedback on student assignments and a wealth of support materials. This powerful study tool will help your students develop their conceptual understanding of the class material and increase their ability to answer questions. It includes:

- A **Study and Practice** area links directly to text content, allowing students to review the text while they study and answer.

- An **Assignment** area keeps all the work you want your students to complete in one location, making it easy for them to stay on task. Students have access to a variety of interactive self-assessment tools, as well as other resources for building their confidence and understanding. In addition, all of the assignments and quizzes contain a link to the relevant section of the multimedia book, providing students with context-sensitive help that allows them to conquer obstacles as they arise.

- A **Personal Gradebook** for each student allows students to view their results from past assignments at any time.

Please view our online demo at www.wiley.com/college/wileyplus. Here you will find additional information about the features and benefits of *WileyPLUS*, how to request a "test drive" of *WileyPLUS* for this title, and how to adopt it for class use.

Wiley Desktop Editions

Wiley MOAC Desktop Editions are innovative, electronic versions of printed textbooks. Students buy the desktop version for 50% off the U.S. price of the printed text, and get the added value of permanence and portability. Wiley Desktop Editions provide students with numerous additional benefits that are not available with other e-text solutions.

Wiley Desktop Editions are NOT subscriptions; students download the Wiley Desktop Edition to their computer desktops. Students own the content they buy to keep for as long as they want. Once a Wiley Desktop Edition is downloaded to the computer desktop, students have instant access to all of the content without being online. Students can also print out the sections they prefer to read in hard copy. Students also have access to fully integrated resources within their Wiley Desktop Edition. From highlighting their e-text to taking and sharing notes, students can easily personalize their Wiley Desktop Edition as they are reading or following along in class.

Windows Server 2008 Evaluation Edition

All MOAC Windows Server 2008 textbooks are packaged with an evaluation edition of Windows Server 2008 on the companion DVDs. Installing the Windows Server Evaluation Edition provides students with the state-of-the-art system software, enabling them to use a full version of Windows Server 2008 for the course exercises. This also promotes the practice of learning by doing, which can be the most effective way to acquire and remember new computing skills.

Evaluating Windows Server 2008 software does not require product activation or entering a product key. The Windows Server 2008 Evaluation Edition provided with this textbook may be installed without activation and evaluated for an initial 60 days. If you need more time to evaluate Windows Server 2008, the 60-day evaluation period may be reset (or re-armed) three times, extending the original 60-day evaluation period by up to 180 days for a total possible evaluation time of 240 days. After this time, you will need to uninstall the software or upgrade to a fully licensed version of Windows Server 2008.

System Requirements

The following are estimated system requirements for Windows Server 2008. If your computer has less than the minimum requirements, you will not be able to install this product correctly. Actual requirements will vary based on your system configuration and the applications and features you install.

PROCESSOR

Processor performance depends not only on the clock frequency of the processor, but also on the number of processor cores and the size of the processor cache. The following are the processor requirements for this product:

TAKE NOTE*

An Intel Itanium 2 processor is required for Windows Server 2008 for Itanium-Based Systems.

- Minimum: 1 GHz (for x86 processors) or 1.4 GHz (for x64 processors)
- Recommended: 2 GHz or faster

RAM

The following are the RAM requirements for this product:

- Minimum: 512 MB
- Recommended: 2 GB or more

- Maximum (32-bit systems): 4 GB (for Windows Server 2008 Standard) or 64 GB (for Windows Server 2008 Enterprise or Windows Server 2008 Datacenter)
- Maximum (64-bit systems): 32 GB (for Windows Server 2008 Standard) or 2 TB (for Windows Server 2008 Enterprise, Windows Server 2008 Datacenter, or Windows Server 2008 for Itanium-Based Systems)

Disk Space Requirements

The following are the approximate disk space requirements for the system partition. Itanium-based and x64-based operating systems will vary from these estimates. Additional disk space may be required if you install the system over a network. For more information, see http://www.microsoft.com/windowsserver2008.

- Minimum: 10 GB
- Recommended: 40 GB or more
- DVD-ROM drive
- Super VGA (800 x 600) or higher-resolution monitor
- Keyboard and Microsoft mouse (or other compatible pointing device)

Important Considerations for Active Directory Domain Controllers

The upgrade process from Windows Server 2003 to Windows Server 2008 requires free disk space for the new operating system image, for the Setup process, and for any installed server roles.

For the domain controller role, the volume or volumes hosting the following resources also have specific free disk space requirements:

- Application data (%AppData%)
- Program files (%ProgramFiles%)
- Users' data (%SystemDrive%\Documents and Settings)
- Windows directory (%WinDir%)

The free space on the %WinDir% volume must be equal or greater than the current size of the resources listed above and their subordinate folders when they are located on the %WinDir% volume. By default, dcpromo places the Active Directory database and log files under %Windir%—in this case, their size would be included in the free disk space requirements for the %Windir% folder.

However, if the Active Directory database is hosted outside of any of the folders above, then the hosting volume or volumes must only contain additional free space equal to at least 10% of the current database size or 250 MB, whichever is greater. Finally, the free space on the volume that hosts the log files must be at least 50 MB.

A default installation of the Active Directory directory service in Windows Server 2003 has the Active Directory database and log files under %WinDir%\NTDS. With this configuration, the NTDS .DIT database file and all the log files are temporarily copied over to the quarantine location and then copied back to their original location. This is why additional free space is required for those resources. However, the SYSVOL directory, which is also under %WinDir% (%WinDir%\SYSVOL), is moved and not copied. Therefore, it does not require any additional free space.

After the upgrade, the space that was reserved for the copied resources will be returned to the file system.

Installing and Re-Arming Windows Server 2008

Evaluating Windows Server 2008 software does not require product activation. The Windows Server 2008 Evaluation Edition may be installed without activation, and it may be evaluated for 60 days. Additionally, the 60-day evaluation period may be reset (re-armed) three times. This action extends the original 60-day evaluation period by up to 180 days for a total possible evaluation time of 240 days.

How to Install Windows Server 2008 Without Activating It

1. Run the Windows Server 2008 Setup program.
2. When you are prompted to enter a product key for activation, do not enter a key. Click No when Setup asks you to confirm your selection.
3. You may be prompted to select the edition of Windows Server 2008 that you want to evaluate. Select the edition that you want to install.
4. When you are prompted, read the evaluation terms in the Microsoft Software License Terms, and then accept the terms.
5. When the Windows Server 2008 Setup program is finished, your initial 60-day evaluation period starts. To check the time that is left on your current evaluation period, run the Slmgr.vbs script that is in the System32 folder. Use the **-dli** switch to run this script. The **slmgr.vbs -dli** command displays the number of days that are left in the current 60-day evaluation period.

How to Re-Arm the Evaluation Period

This section describes how to extend, or re-arm, the Windows Server 2008 evaluation period. The evaluation period is also known as the "activation grace" period.

When the initial 60-day evaluation period nears its end, you can run the Slmgr.vbs script to reset the evaluation period. To do this, follow these steps:

1. Click **Start**, and then click **Command Prompt**.
2. Type **slmgr.vbs -dli**, and then press **ENTER** to check the current status of your evaluation period.
3. To reset the evaluation period, type **slmgr.vbs –rearm**, and then press **ENTER**.
4. Restart the computer.

This resets the evaluation period to 60 days.

How to Automate the Extension of the Evaluation Period

You may want to set up a process that automatically resets the evaluation period every 60 days. One way to automate this process is by using the Task Scheduler. You can configure the Task Scheduler to run the Slmgr.vbs script and to restart the server at a particular time. To do this, follow these steps:

1. Click **Start**, point to **Administrative Tools**, and then click **Task Scheduler**.
2. Copy the following sample task to the server, and then save it as an .xml file. For example, you can save the file as **Extend.xml**.

```
<?xml version="1.0" encoding="UTF-16"?> <Task version="1.2"
xmlns="http://schemas.microsoft.com/windows/2004/02/mit/task">
```

```
<RegistrationInfo> <Date>2007-09-17T14:26:04.433</Date>
<Author>Microsoft Corporation</Author> </RegistrationInfo>
<Triggers> <TimeTrigger id="18c4a453-d7aa-4647-916b-
af0c3ea16a6b"> <Repetition> <Interval>P59D</Interval>
<StopAtDurationEnd>false</StopAtDurationEnd> </Repetition>
<StartBoundary>2007-10-05T02:23:24</StartBoundary>
<EndBoundary>2008-09-17T14:23:24.777</EndBoundary>
<Enabled>true</Enabled> </TimeTrigger> </Triggers>
<Principals> <Principal id="Author">
<UserId>domain\alias</UserId>
<LogonType>Password</LogonType>
<RunLevel>HighestAvailable</RunLevel> </Principal>
</Principals> <Settings> <IdleSettings>
<Duration>PT10M</Duration> <WaitTimeout>PT1H</WaitTimeout>
<StopOnIdleEnd>true</StopOnIdleEnd>
<RestartOnIdle>false</RestartOnIdle> </IdleSettings>
<MultipleInstancesPolicy>IgnoreNew</MultipleInstancesPolicy>
<DisallowStartIfOnBatteries>true</DisallowStartIfOnBatteries>
<StopIfGoingOnBatteries>true</StopIfGoingOnBatteries>
<AllowHardTerminate>true</AllowHardTerminate>
<StartWhenAvailable>false</StartWhenAvailable>
<RunOnlyIfNetworkAvailable>false</RunOnlyIfNetworkAvailable>
<AllowStartOnDemand>true</AllowStartOnDemand>
<Enabled>true</Enabled> <Hidden>false</Hidden>
<RunOnlyIfIdle>false</RunOnlyIfIdle>
<WakeToRun>true</WakeToRun>
<ExecutionTimeLimit>P3D</ExecutionTimeLimit>
<DeleteExpiredTaskAfter>PT0S</DeleteExpiredTaskAfter>
<Priority>7</Priority> <RestartOnFailure>
<Interval>PT1M</Interval> <Count>3</Count>
</RestartOnFailure> </Settings> <Actions Context="Author">
<Exec> <Command>C:\Windows\System32\slmgr.vbs</Command>
<Arguments>-rearm</Arguments> </Exec> <Exec>
<Command>C:\Windows\System32\shutdown.exe</Command>
<Arguments>/r</Arguments> </Exec> </Actions> </Task>
```

3. In the sample task, change the value of the following "UserID" tag to contain your domain and your alias:

```
<UserId>domain\alias</UserId>
```

4. In the Task Scheduler, click **Import Task** on the **Action** menu.

5. Click the sample task .xml file. For example, click **Extend.xml**.

6. Click **Import**.

7. Click the **Triggers** tab.

8. Click the **One Time** trigger, and then click **Edit**.

9. Change the start date of the task to a date just before the end of your current evaluation period.

10. Click **OK**, and then exit the Task Scheduler.

The Task Scheduler will now run the evaluation reset operation on the date that you specified.

Preparing to Take the Microsoft Certified Information Technology Professional (MCITP) Exam

The Microsoft Certified Information Technology Professional (MCITP) certifications enable professionals to target specific technologies and to distinguish themselves by demonstrating in-depth knowledge and expertise in their specialized technologies. Microsoft Certified Information Technology Professionals are consistently capable of inplementing, building, troubleshooting, and debugging a particular Microsoft Technology.

For organizations, the new generation of Microsoft certifications provides better skills verification tools that help with assessing not only in-demand skills on Windows Server, but also the ability to quickly complete on-the-job tasks. Individuals will find it easier to identify and work towards the certification credential that meets their personal and professional goals.

To learn more about becoming a Microsoft Certified Professional and exam availability, visit www.microsoft.com/learning/mcp.

Microsoft Certifications for IT Professionals

The new Microsoft Certified Technology Specialist (MCTS) and Microsoft Certified IT Professional (MCITP) credentials provide IT professionals with a simpler and more targeted framework to showcase their technical skills in addition to the skills that are required for specific developer job roles.

The Microsoft Certified Database Administrator (MCDBA), Microsoft Certified Desktop Support Technician (MCDST), Microsoft Certified System Administrator (MCSA), and Microsoft Certified Systems Engineer (MCSE) credentials continue to provide IT professionals who use Microsoft SQL Server 2000, Windows XP, and Windows Server 2003 with industry recognition and validation of their IT skills and experience.

Microsoft Certified Technology Specialist

The new Microsoft Certified Tehnology Specialist (MCTS) credential highlights your skills using a specific Microsoft technology. You can demonstrate your abilities as an IT professional or developer with in-depth knowledge of the Microsoft technology that you use today or are planning to deploy.

The MCTS certifications enable professionals to target specific technologies and to distinguish themselves by demonstrating in-depth knowledge and expertise in their specialized technologies. Microsoft Certified Technology Specialists are consistently capable of implementing, building, troubleshooting, and debugging a particular Microsoft technology.

You can learn more about the MCTS program at www.microsoft.com/learning/mcp/mcts.

Microsoft Certified IT Professional

The new Microsoft Certified IT Professional (MCITP) credential lets you highlight your specific area of expertise. Now, you can easily distinguish yourself as an expert in database administration, database development, business intelligence, or support.

By becoming certified, you demonstrate to employers that you have achieved a predictable level of skill not only in the use of the Windows Server operating system, but with a comprehensive set of Microsoft technologies. Employers often require certification either as a condition of employment or as a condition of advancement within the company or other organization.

You can learn more about the MCITP program at www.microsoft.com/learning/mcp/mcitp.

The certification examinations are sponsored by Microsoft but administered through Microsoft's exam delivery partner Prometric.

Preparing to Take an Exam

Unless you are a very experienced user, you will need to use a test preparation course to prepare to complete the test correctly and within the time allowed. The *Microsoft Official Academic Course* series is designed to prepare you with a strong knowledge of all exam topics, and with some additional review and practice on your own, you should feel confident in your ability to pass the appropriate exam.

After you decide which exam to take, review the list of objectives for the exam. You can easily identify tasks that are included in the objective list by locating the Objective Domain Matrix at the start of each lesson and the Certification Ready sidebars in the margin of the lessons in this book.

To take the MCITP test, visit www.microsoft.com/learning/mcp/mcitp to locate your nearest testing center. Then call the testing center directly to schedule your test. The amount of advance notice you should provide will vary for different testing centers, and it typically depends on the number of computers available at the testing center, the number of other testers who have already been scheduled for the day on which you want to take the test, and the number of times per week that the testing center offers MCITP testing. In general, you should call to schedule your test at least two weeks prior to the date on which you want to take the test.

When you arrive at the testing center, you might be asked for proof of identity. A driver's license or passport is an acceptable form of identification. If you do not have either of these items of documentation, call your testing center and ask what alternative forms of identification will be accepted. If you are retaking a test, bring your MCITP identification number, which will have been given to you when you previously took the test. If you have not prepaid or if your organization has not already arranged to make payment for you, you will need to pay the test-taking fee when you arrive.

About the Author

Craig Zacker is a writer, editor, and networker whose computing experience began in the days of teletypes and paper tape. After making the move from minicomputers to PCs, he worked as an administrator of Novell NetWare networks and as a PC support technician while operating a freelance desktop publishing business. After earning a Master's Degree in English and American Literature from New York University, Craig worked extensively on integrating Microsoft Windows operating systems into existing internetworks, supported fleets of Windows workstations, and was employed as a technical writer, content provider, and webmaster for the online services group of a large software company. Since devoting himself to writing and editing full-time, Craig has authored or contributed to dozens of books on networking topics, operating systems, and PC hardware, including Microsoft Official Academic Course titles *Windows(R) 7 Configuration, Exam 70-680; Windows Server(R) 2008 Applications Infrastructure Configuration, Exam 70-643; and Windows Server(R) 2008 Administrator, Exam 70-646.* He has developed educational texts for college courses, designed online training courses for the web, and published articles in top industry publications.

Acknowledgments

MOAC Instructor Advisory Board

We would like to thank our Instructor Advisory Board, an elite group of educators who has assisted us every step of the way in building these products. Advisory Board members have acted as our sounding board on key pedagogical and design decisions leading to the development of these compelling and innovative textbooks for future Information Workers. Their dedication to technology education is truly appreciated.

Charles DeSassure, Tarrant County College

Charles DeSassure is Department Chair and Instructor of Computer Science & Information Technology at Tarrant County College Southeast Campus, Arlington, Texas. He has had experience as a MIS Manager, system analyst, field technology analyst, LAN Administrator, microcomputer specialist, and public school teacher in South Carolina. Charles has worked in higher education for more than ten years and received the Excellence Award in Teaching from the National Institute for Staff and Organizational Development (NISOD). He currently serves on the Educational Testing Service (ETS) iSkills National Advisory Committee and chaired the Tarrant County College District Student Assessment Committee. He has written proposals and makes presentations at major educational conferences nationwide. Charles has served as a textbook reviewer for John Wiley & Sons and Prentice Hall. He teaches courses in information security, networking, distance learning, and computer literacy. Charles holds a master's degree in Computer Resources & Information Management from Webster University.

Kim Ehlert, Waukesha County Technical College

Kim Ehlert is the Microsoft Program Coordinator and a Network Specialist instructor at Waukesha County Technical College, teaching the full range of MCSE and networking courses for the past nine years. Prior to joining WCTC, Kim was a professor at the Milwaukee School of Engineering for five years where she oversaw the Novell Academic Education and the Microsoft IT Academy programs. She has a wide variety of industry experience including network design and management for Johnson Controls, local city fire departments, police departments, large church congregations, health departments, and accounting firms. Kim holds many industry certifications including MCDST, MCSE, Security+, Network+, Server+, MCT, and CNE.

Kim has a bachelor's degree in Information Systems and a master's degree in Business Administration from the University of Wisconsin Milwaukee. When she is not busy teaching, she enjoys spending time with her husband Gregg and their two children—Alex, 14, and Courtney, 17.

Penny Gudgeon, Corinthian Colleges, Inc.

Penny Gudgeon is the Program Manager for IT curriculum at Corinthian Colleges, Inc. Previously, she was responsible for computer programming and web curriculum for twenty-seven campuses in Corinthian's Canadian division, CDI College of Business, Technology and Health Care. Penny joined CDI College in 1997 as a computer programming instructor at one of the campuses outside of Toronto. Prior to joining CDI College, Penny taught productivity software at another Canadian college, the Academy of Learning, for four years. Penny has experience in helping students achieve their goals through various learning models from instructor-led to self-directed to online.

Before embarking on a career in education, Penny worked in the fields of advertising, marketing/sales, mechanical and electronic engineering technology, and computer programming. When not working from her home office or indulging her passion for lifelong learning, Penny likes to read mysteries, garden, and relax at home in Hamilton, Ontario, with her Shih-Tzu, Gracie.

Margaret Leary, Northern Virginia Community College

Margaret Leary is Professor of IST at Northern Virginia Community College, teaching Networking and Network Security Courses for the past ten years. She is the Co-Principal Investigator on the CyberWATCH initiative, an NSF-funded regional consortium of higher education institutions and businesses working together to increase the number of network security personnel in the workforce. She also serves as a Senior Security Policy Manager and Research Analyst at Nortel Government Solutions and holds a CISSP certification.

Margaret holds a B.S.B.A. and MBA/Technology Management from the University of Phoenix, and is pursuing her Ph.D. in Organization and Management with an IT Specialization at Capella University. Her dissertation is titled "Quantifying the Discoverability of Identity Attributes in Internet-Based Public Records: Impact on Identity Theft and Knowledge-based Authentication." She has several other published articles in various government and industry magazines, notably on identity management and network security.

Wen Liu, ITT Educational Services, Inc.

Wen Liu is Director of Corporate Curriculum Development at ITT Educational Services, Inc. He joined the ITT corporate headquarters in 1998 as a Senior Network Analyst to plan and deploy the corporate WAN infrastructure. A year later he assumed the position of Corporate Curriculum Manager supervising the curriculum development of all IT programs. After he was promoted to the current position three years ago, he continued to manage the curriculum research and development for all the programs offered in the School of Information Technology in addition to supervising the curriculum development in other areas (such as Schools of Drafting and Design and Schools of Electronics Technology). Prior to his employment with ITT Educational Services, Wen was a Telecommunications Analyst at the state government of Indiana working on the state backbone project that provided Internet and telecommunications services to the public users such as K-12 and higher education institutions, government agencies, libraries, and healthcare facilities.

Wen has an M.A. in Student Personnel Administration in Higher Education and an M.S. in Information and Communications Sciences from Ball State University, Indiana. He used to be the Director of Special Projects on the board of directors of the Indiana Telecommunications User Association, and used to serve on Course Technology's IT Advisory Board. He is currently a member of the IEEE and its Computer Society.

Jared Spencer, Westwood College Online

Jared Spencer has been the Lead Faculty for Networking at Westwood College Online since 2006. He began teaching in 2001 and has taught both on-ground and online for a variety of institutions, including Robert Morris University and Point Park University. In addition to his academic background, he has more than fifteen years of industry experience working for companies including the Thomson Corporation and IBM.

Jared has a master's degree in Internet Information Systems and is currently ABD and pursuing his doctorate in Information Systems at Nova Southeastern University. He has authored several papers that have been presented at conferences and appeared in publications such as the Journal of Internet Commerce and the Journal of Information Privacy and Security (JIPC). He holds a number of industry certifications, including AIX (UNIX), A+, Network+, Security+, MCSA on Windows 2000, and MCSA on Windows 2003 Server.

MOAC Windows Server Reviewers

We also thank John Blackwood at Umpqua Community College, Brian Caton at El Centro College in the Dallas County Community College District, Gralan Gilliam at Kaplan Career Institute—ICM Campus, James Herbert at Fountainhead College of Technology, and Jeff Riley for their diligent review and for providing invaluable feedback in the service of quality instructional materials.

Focus Group and Survey Participants

Finally, we thank the hundreds of instructors who participated in our focus groups and surveys to ensure that the Microsoft Official Academic Courses best met the needs of our customers.

Jean Aguilar, Mt. Hood Community College

Konrad Akens, Zane State College

Michael Albers, University of Memphis

Diana Anderson, Big Sandy Community & Technical College

Phyllis Anderson, Delaware County Community College

Judith Andrews, Feather River College

Damon Antos, American River College

Bridget Archer, Oakton Community College

Linda Arnold, Harrisburg Area Community College–Lebanon Campus

Neha Arya, Fullerton College

Mohammad Bajwa, Katharine Gibbs School–New York

Virginia Baker, University of Alaska Fairbanks

Carla Bannick, Pima Community College

Rita Barkley, Northeast Alabama Community College

Elsa Barr, Central Community College–Hastings

Ronald W. Barry, Ventura County Community College District

Elizabeth Bastedo, Central Carolina Technical College

Karen Baston, Waubonsee Community College

Karen Bean, Blinn College

Scott Beckstrand, Community College of Southern Nevada

Paulette Bell, Santa Rosa Junior College

Liz Bennett, Southeast Technical Institute

Nancy Bermea, Olympic College

Lucy Betz, Milwaukee Area Technical College

Meral Binbasioglu, Hofstra University

Catherine Binder, Strayer University & Katharine Gibbs School–Philadelphia

Terrel Blair, El Centro College

Ruth Blalock, Alamance Community College

Beverly Bohner, Reading Area Community College

Henry Bojack, Farmingdale State University

Matthew Bowie, Luna Community College

Julie Boyles, Portland Community College

Karen Brandt, College of the Albemarle

Stephen Brown, College of San Mateo

Jared Bruckner, Southern Adventist University

Pam Brune, Chattanooga State Technical Community College

Sue Buchholz, Georgia Perimeter College

Roberta Buczyna, Edison College

Angela Butler, Mississippi Gulf Coast Community College

Rebecca Byrd, Augusta Technical College

Kristen Callahan, Mercer County Community College

Judy Cameron, Spokane Community College

Dianne Campbell, Athens Technical College

Gena Casas, Florida Community College at Jacksonville

Jesus Castrejon, Latin Technologies

Gail Chambers, Southwest Tennessee Community College

Jacques Chansavang, Indiana University–Purdue University Fort Wayne

Nancy Chapko, Milwaukee Area Technical College

Rebecca Chavez, Yavapai College

Sanjiv Chopra, Thomas Nelson Community College

Greg Clements, Midland Lutheran College

Dayna Coker, Southwestern Oklahoma State University–Sayre Campus

Tamra Collins, Otero Junior College

Janet Conrey, Gavilan Community College

www.wiley.com/college/microsoft *or*
call the MOAC Toll-Free Number: 1+(888) 764-7001 (U.S. & Canada only)

Carol Cornforth, West Virginia Northern Community College

Gary Cotton, American River College

Edie Cox, Chattahoochee Technical College

Rollie Cox, Madison Area Technical College

David Crawford, Northwestern Michigan College

J.K. Crowley, Victor Valley College

Rosalyn Culver, Washtenaw Community College

Sharon Custer, Huntington University

Sandra Daniels, New River Community College

Anila Das, Cedar Valley College

Brad Davis, Santa Rosa Junior College

Susan Davis, Green River Community College

Mark Dawdy, Lincoln Land Community College

Jennifer Day, Sinclair Community College

Carol Deane, Eastern Idaho Technical College

Julie DeBuhr, Lewis-Clark State College

Janis DeHaven, Central Community College

Drew Dekreon, University of Alaska–Anchorage

Joy DePover, Central Lakes College

Salli DiBartolo, Brevard Community College

Melissa Diegnau, Riverland Community College

Al Dillard, Lansdale School of Business

Marjorie Duffy, Cosumnes River College

Sarah Dunn, Southwest Tennessee Community College

Shahla Durany, Tarrant County College–South Campus

Kay Durden, University of Tennessee at Martin

Dineen Ebert, St. Louis Community College–Meramec

Donna Ehrhart, State University of New York–Brockport

Larry Elias, Montgomery County Community College

Glenda Elser, New Mexico State University at Alamogordo

Angela Evangelinos, Monroe County Community College

Angie Evans, Ivy Tech Community College of Indiana

Linda Farrington, Indian Hills Community College

Dana Fladhammer, Phoenix College

Richard Flores, Citrus College

Connie Fox, Community and Technical College at Institute of Technology West Virginia University

Wanda Freeman, Okefenokee Technical College

Brenda Freeman, Augusta Technical College

Susan Fry, Boise State University

Roger Fulk, Wright State University–Lake Campus

Sue Furnas, Collin County Community College District

Sandy Gabel, Vernon College

Laura Galvan, Fayetteville Technical Community College

Candace Garrod, Red Rocks Community College

Sherrie Geitgey, Northwest State Community College

Chris Gerig, Chattahoochee Technical College

Barb Gillespie, Cuyamaca College

Jessica Gilmore, Highline Community College

Pamela Gilmore, Reedley College

Debbie Glinert, Queensborough Community College

Steven Goldman, Polk Community College

Bettie Goodman, C.S. Mott Community College

Mike Grabill, Katharine Gibbs School–Philadelphia

Francis Green, Penn State University

Walter Griffin, Blinn College

Fillmore Guinn, Odessa College

Helen Haasch, Milwaukee Area Technical College

John Habal, Ventura College

Joy Haerens, Chaffey College

Norman Hahn, Thomas Nelson Community College

Kathy Hall, Alamance Community College

Teri Harbacheck, Boise State University

Linda Harper, Richland Community College

Maureen Harper, Indian Hills Community College

Steve Harris, Katharine Gibbs School–New York

Robyn Hart, Fresno City College

Darien Hartman, Boise State University

Gina Hatcher, Tacoma Community College

Winona T. Hatcher, Aiken Technical College

BJ Hathaway, Northeast Wisconsin Tech College

Cynthia Hauki, West Hills College – Coalinga

Mary L. Haynes, Wayne County Community College

www.wiley.com/college/microsoft *or*
call the MOAC Toll-Free Number: 1+(888) 764-7001 (U.S. & Canada only)

Marcie Hawkins, Zane State College

Steve Hebrock, Ohio State University Agricultural Technical Institute

Sue Heistand, Iowa Central Community College

Heith Hennel, Valencia Community College

Donna Hendricks, South Arkansas Community College

Judy Hendrix, Dyersburg State Community College

Gloria Hensel, Matanuska-Susitna College University of Alaska Anchorage

Gwendolyn Hester, Richland College

Tammarra Holmes, Laramie County Community College

Dee Hobson, Richland College

Keith Hoell, Katharine Gibbs School–New York

Pashia Hogan, Northeast State Technical Community College

Susan Hoggard, Tulsa Community College

Kathleen Holliman, Wallace Community College Selma

Chastity Honchul, Brown Mackie College/ Wright State University

Christie Hovey, Lincoln Land Community College

Peggy Hughes, Allegany College of Maryland

Sandra Hume, Chippewa Valley Technical College

John Hutson, Aims Community College

Celia Ing, Sacramento City College

Joan Ivey, Lanier Technical College

Barbara Jaffari, College of the Redwoods

Penny Jakes, University of Montana College of Technology

Eduardo Jaramillo, Peninsula College

Barbara Jauken, Southeast Community College

Susan Jennings, Stephen F. Austin State University

Leslie Jernberg, Eastern Idaho Technical College

Linda Johns, Georgia Perimeter College

Brent Johnson, Okefenokee Technical College

Mary Johnson, Mt. San Antonio College

Shirley Johnson, Trinidad State Junior College–Valley Campus

Sandra M. Jolley, Tarrant County College

Teresa Jolly, South Georgia Technical College

Dr. Deborah Jones, South Georgia Technical College

Margie Jones, Central Virginia Community College

Randall Jones, Marshall Community and Technical College

Diane Karlsbraaten, Lake Region State College

Teresa Keller, Ivy Tech Community College of Indiana

Charles Kemnitz, Pennsylvania College of Technology

Sandra Kinghorn, Ventura College

Bill Klein, Katharine Gibbs School–Philadelphia

Bea Knaapen, Fresno City College

Kit Kofoed, Western Wyoming Community College

Maria Kolatis, County College of Morris

Barry Kolb, Ocean County College

Karen Kuralt, University of Arkansas at Little Rock

Belva-Carole Lamb, Rogue Community College

Betty Lambert, Des Moines Area Community College

Anita Lande, Cabrillo College

Junnae Landry, Pratt Community College

Karen Lankisch, UC Clermont

David Lanzilla, Central Florida Community College

Nora Laredo, Cerritos Community College

Jennifer Larrabee, Chippewa Valley Technical College

Debra Larson, Idaho State University

Barb Lave, Portland Community College

Audrey Lawrence, Tidewater Community College

Deborah Layton, Eastern Oklahoma State College

Larry LeBlanc, Owen Graduate School– Vanderbilt University

Philip Lee, Nashville State Community College

Michael Lehrfeld, Brevard Community College

Vasant Limaye, Southwest Collegiate Institute for the Deaf–Howard College

Anne C. Lewis, Edgecombe Community College

Stephen Linkin, Houston Community College

Peggy Linston, Athens Technical College

Hugh Lofton, Moultrie Technical College

Donna Lohn, Lakeland Community College

Jackie Lou, Lake Tahoe Community College

Donna Love, Gaston College

Curt Lynch, Ozarks Technical Community College

www.wiley.com/college/microsoft *or*
call the MOAC Toll-Free Number: 1+(888) 764-7001 (U.S. & Canada only)

Sheilah Lynn, Florida Community College–Jacksonville

Pat R. Lyon, Tomball College

Bill Madden, Bergen Community College

Heather Madden, Delaware Technical & Community College

Donna Madsen, Kirkwood Community College

Jane Maringer-Cantu, Gavilan College

Suzanne Marks, Bellevue Community College

Carol Martin, Louisiana State University–Alexandria

Cheryl Martucci, Diablo Valley College

Roberta Marvel, Eastern Wyoming College

Tom Mason, Brookdale Community College

Mindy Mass, Santa Barbara City College

Dixie Massaro, Irvine Valley College

Rebekah May, Ashland Community & Technical College

Emma Mays-Reynolds, Dyersburg State Community College

Timothy Mayes, Metropolitan State College of Denver

Reggie McCarthy, Central Lakes College

Matt McCaskill, Brevard Community College

Kevin McFarlane, Front Range Community College

Donna McGill, Yuba Community College

Terri McKeever, Ozarks Technical Community College

Patricia McMahon, South Suburban College

Sally McMillin, Katharine Gibbs School–Philadelphia

Charles McNerney, Bergen Community College

Lisa Mears, Palm Beach Community College

Imran Mehmood, ITT Technical Institute–King of Prussia Campus

Virginia Melvin, Southwest Tennessee Community College

Jeanne Mercer, Texas State Technical College

Denise Merrell, Jefferson Community & Technical College

Catherine Merrikin, Pearl River Community College

Diane D. Mickey, Northern Virginia Community College

Darrelyn Miller, Grays Harbor College

Sue Mitchell, Calhoun Community College

Jacquie Moldenhauer, Front Range Community College

Linda Motonaga, Los Angeles City College

Sam Mryyan, Allen County Community College

Cindy Murphy, Southeastern Community College

Ryan Murphy, Sinclair Community College

Sharon E. Nastav, Johnson County Community College

Christine Naylor, Kent State University Ashtabula

Haji Nazarian, Seattle Central Community College

Nancy Noe, Linn-Benton Community College

Jennie Noriega, San Joaquin Delta College

Linda Nutter, Peninsula College

Thomas Omerza, Middle Bucks Institute of Technology

Edith Orozco, St. Philip's College

Dona Orr, Boise State University

Joanne Osgood, Chaffey College

Janice Owens, Kishwaukee College

Tatyana Pashnyak, Bainbridge College

John Partacz, College of DuPage

Tim Paul, Montana State University–Great Falls

Joseph Perez, South Texas College

Mike Peterson, Chemeketa Community College

Dr. Karen R. Petitto, West Virginia Wesleyan College

Terry Pierce, Onandaga Community College

Ashlee Pieris, Raritan Valley Community College

Jamie Pinchot, Thiel College

Michelle Poertner, Northwestern Michigan College

Betty Posta, University of Toledo

Deborah Powell, West Central Technical College

Mark Pranger, Rogers State University

Carolyn Rainey, Southeast Missouri State University

Linda Raskovich, Hibbing Community College

Leslie Ratliff, Griffin Technical College

Mar-Sue Ratzke, Rio Hondo Community College

Roxy Reissen, Southeastern Community College

Silvio Reyes, Technical Career Institutes

Patricia Rishavy, Anoka Technical College

Jean Robbins, Southeast Technical Institute

Carol Roberts, Eastern Maine Community College and University of Maine

**www.wiley.com/college/microsoft or
call the MOAC Toll-Free Number: 1+(888) 764-7001 (U.S. & Canada only)**

Teresa Roberts, Wilson Technical Community College

Vicki Robertson, Southwest Tennessee Community College

Betty Rogge, Ohio State Agricultural Technical Institute

Lynne Rusley, Missouri Southern State University

Claude Russo, Brevard Community College

Ginger Sabine, Northwestern Technical College

Steven Sachs, Los Angeles Valley College

Joanne Salas, Olympic College

Lloyd Sandmann, Pima Community College–Desert Vista Campus

Beverly Santillo, Georgia Perimeter College

Theresa Savarese, San Diego City College

Sharolyn Sayers, Milwaukee Area Technical College

Judith Scheeren, Westmoreland County Community College

Adolph Scheiwe, Joliet Junior College

Marilyn Schmid, Asheville-Buncombe Technical Community College

Janet Sebesy, Cuyahoga Community College

Phyllis T. Shafer, Brookdale Community College

Ralph Shafer, Truckee Meadows Community College

Anne Marie Shanley, County College of Morris

Shelia Shelton, Surry Community College

Merilyn Shepherd, Danville Area Community College

Susan Sinele, Aims Community College

Beth Sindt, Hawkeye Community College

Andrew Smith, Marian College

Brenda Smith, Southwest Tennessee Community College

Lynne Smith, State University of New York–Delhi

Rob Smith, Katharine Gibbs School–Philadelphia

Tonya Smith, Arkansas State University–Mountain Home

Del Spencer, Trinity Valley Community College

Jeri Spinner, Idaho State University

Eric Stadnik, Santa Rosa Junior College

Karen Stanton, Los Medanos College

Meg Stoner, Santa Rosa Junior College

Beverly Stowers, Ivy Tech Community College of Indiana

Marcia Stranix, Yuba College

Kim Styles, Tri-County Technical College

Sylvia Summers, Tacoma Community College

Beverly Swann, Delaware Technical & Community College

Ann Taff, Tulsa Community College

Mike Theiss, University of Wisconsin–Marathon Campus

Romy Thiele, Cañada College

Sharron Thompson, Portland Community College

Ingrid Thompson-Sellers, Georgia Perimeter College

Barbara Tietsort, University of Cincinnati–Raymond Walters College

Janine Tiffany, Reading Area Community College

Denise Tillery, University of Nevada Las Vegas

Susan Trebelhorn, Normandale Community College

Noel Trout, Santiago Canyon College

Cheryl Turgeon, Asnuntuck Community College

Steve Turner, Ventura College

Sylvia Unwin, Bellevue Community College

Lilly Vigil, Colorado Mountain College

Sabrina Vincent, College of the Mainland

Mary Vitrano, Palm Beach Community College

Brad Vogt, Northeast Community College

Cozell Wagner, Southeastern Community College

Carolyn Walker, Tri-County Technical College

Sherry Walker, Tulsa Community College

Qi Wang, Tacoma Community College

Betty Wanielista, Valencia Community College

Marge Warber, Lanier Technical College–Forsyth Campus

Marjorie Webster, Bergen Community College

Linda Wenn, Central Community College

Mark Westlund, Olympic College

www.wiley.com/college/microsoft or
call the MOAC Toll-Free Number: 1+(888) 764-7001 (U.S. & Canada only)

Carolyn Whited, Roane State Community College

Winona Whited, Richland College

Jerry Wilkerson, Scott Community College

Joel Willenbring, Fullerton College

Barbara Williams, WITC Superior

Charlotte Williams, Jones County Junior College

Bonnie Willy, Ivy Tech Community College of Indiana

Diane Wilson, J. Sargeant Reynolds Community College

James Wolfe, Metropolitan Community College

Marjory Wooten, Lanier Technical College

Mark Yanko, Hocking College

Alexis Yusov, Pace University

Naeem Zaman, San Joaquin Delta College

Kathleen Zimmerman, Des Moines Area Community College

We also thank Lutz Ziob, Merrick Van Dongen, Bruce Curling, Joe Wilson, Rob Linsky, Jim Clark, Scott Serna, Ben Watson, David Bramble, and Dan Weis at Microsoft for their encouragement and support in making the Microsoft Official Academic Course program the finest instructional materials for mastering the newest Microsoft technologies for both students and instructors.

Brief Contents

Contents

Lesson 11: Securing Infrastructure Services 260

Lesson 12: Ensuring Business Continuity 288

Naming and Addressing

OBJECTIVE DOMAIN MATRIX

TECHNOLOGY SKILL	OBJECTIVE DOMAIN	OBJECTIVE NUMBER
Designing an IP Addressing Strategy	Plan for name resolution and IP addressing.	1.1

KEY TERMS

6to4
Berkeley Internet Name Daemon (BIND)
bubbles
Classless Inter-Domain Routing (CIDR)
format prefix (FP)
forwarder
GlobalNames zone
global unicast address

Intra-Site Automatic Tunnel Addressing Protocol (ISATAP)
iterative query
link-local unicast address
network address translation (NAT)
organizationally unique identifier (OUI)
proxy server
recursive query
referral

scope
site-local unicast address
stateless address autoconfiguration
Teredo
tunneling
unique local unicast address
Windows Internet Name System (WINS)
zone transfer

■ Designing an IP Addressing Strategy

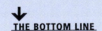

THE BOTTOM LINE

Many enterprise administrators are so comfortable working with IPv4 addresses that they are hesitant to change. Network Address Translation (NAT) and Classless Inter-Domain Routing (CIDR) have been excellent stopgaps to the depletion of the 32-bit IP address space for years, and many would like to see them continue as such. However, the IPv6 transition, long a specter on the distant horizon, is now suddenly approaching at frightening speed, and it is time for administrators not familiar with the new technologies to catch up—or be left behind.

The networking industry, and particularly the Internet, has made huge investments in IPv4 technologies, and replacing them with IPv6 must be a gradual process. In fact, it is a gradual process that was supposed to have begun in earnest over ten years ago. However, many people treat their IPv4 equipment like household appliances; unless they stop working, there is no need to replace them. Unfortunately, the day on which that equipment stops working might be approaching.

Estimates vary, but several reliable sources predict that depletion of the IPv4 address space will occur as early as 2011. One report that is automatically updated on a daily basis states (on the date of this writing) that exhaustion of the Internet Assigned Numbers Authority (IANA) unallocated address pool will occur on July 1, 2011, and that the regional Internet registries will deplete their available addresses on January 28, 2012.

So, while it might not yet be time to embrace IPv6 exclusively, enterprise administrators should have the transition in mind as they design their networks and make their purchasing decisions.

IPv4 Addressing Review

Enterprise administrators are no doubt familiar with the basic principles of the IPv4 address space. This section reviews those principles, and describes the usual process for designing an IPv4 addressing strategy.

CERTIFICATION READY
How do you plan for name resolution and IP addressing?
1.1

The IPv4 address space, as you should already know, consists of 32-bit addresses, notated as four 8-bit decimal values from 0 to 255, separated by periods, as in the example 192.168.43.100. This is known as dotted decimal notation, and the individual 8-bit decimal values are called octets, bytes, or quads.

Each address consists of network bits, which identify a network, and host bits, which identify a particular device on that network. To differentiate the network bits from the host bits, each address must have a subnet mask.

A subnet mask is another 32-bit value consisting of binary 1 bits and 0 bits. When compared to an IP address, the bits corresponding to the 1s in the mask are the network bits, while the bits corresponding to the 0s are the host bits. Thus, if the 192.168.43.100 address mentioned earlier has a subnet mask of 255.255.255.0 (which in binary form is 11111111.11111111. 11111111.00000000), the first three octets (192.168.43) identify the network and the last octet (100) identifies the host.

IPV4 CLASSFUL ADDRESSING

Because the subnet mask associated with IP addresses can vary, so can the number of bits used to identify the network and the host. The original Internet Protocol (IP) standard defines three address classes for assignment to networks, as shown in Table 1-1, which support different numbers of networks and hosts.

Table 1-1

IPv4 Address Classes

IP Address Class	Class A	Class B	Class C
Number of network identifier bits	8	16	24
Number of host identifier bits	24	16	8
Number of possible networks	128	16,384	2,097,152
Number of possible hosts	16,777,216	65,536	256

TAKE NOTE *

In addition to Classes A, B, and C, the IP standard also defines two additional classes, Class D, which was reserved for multicast identifiers, and class E, which was labeled as experimental.

At the time when IP was developed, no one imagined that the 32-bit address space would ever be exhausted. In the early 1980s, there were no networks that had 65,536 computers, never mind 16 million, but no one worried about the wastefulness of assigning IP addresses based on these classes.

CLASSLESS INTER-DOMAIN ROUTING

Because of its wastefulness, classful addressing was gradually obsolesced by a series of subnetting methods, including variable-length subnet masking (VLSM) and eventually *Classless Inter-Domain Routing (CIDR)*. CIDR is a subnetting method that enables administrators to place the division between the network bits and the host bits anywhere in the address, not just between octets. This makes it possible to create networks of almost any size.

CIDR also introduces a new notation for network addresses. A standard dotted-decimal address representing the network is followed by a forward slash and a numeral specifying the size of the network-identifying prefix. For example, 192.168.43.0/24 represents a single Class C address that uses a 24-bit network identifier, leaving the other 8 bits for up to 254 host identifiers. Each of those hosts would receive an address from 192.168.43.1 to 192.168.43.254, using the subnet mask 255.255.255.0.

TAKE NOTE*

To calculate the number of subnets or hosts provided by a given length identifier, one raises to the power representing the number of bits and subtracts two, resulting in the formula $2^n - 2$, where n is the number of bits. Thus, an 8-bit host identifier would provide $2^8 - 2$ or 254 hosts. The host identifier consisting of all 0 bits on every subnet is typically used to identify the network itself, and the host identifier consisting of all 1 bits is reserved for use as a broadcast address. This is the reason for subtracting 2 from 2^n.

However, using CIDR, an administrator can subnet this address further, by allocating some of the host bits to create subnets. To create subnets for four offices, for example, the administrator can take two of the host identifier bits, changing the network address in CIDR notation to 192.168.43.0/26. Because the network identifier is now 26 bits, the subnet masks for all four networks will now be 11111111.11111111.11111111.11000000 in binary form, or 255.255.255.192 in standard decimal form. Each of the four networks will have up to 62 hosts, using the IP address ranges shown in Table 1-2.

Table 1-2

Sample CIDR 192.168.43.0/26 Networks

NETWORK ADDRESS	STARTING IP ADDRESS	ENDING IP ADDRESS	SUBNET MASK
192.168.43.0	192.168.43.1	192.168.43.62	255.255.255.192
192.168.43.64	192.168.43.65	192.168.43.126	255.255.255.192
192.168.43.128	192.168.43.129	192.168.43.190	255.255.255.192
192.168.43.192	192.168.43.193	192.168.43.254	255.255.255.192

If the administrator needs more than four subnets, changing the address to 192.168.43.0/28 adds two more bits to the network address, for a maximum of 16 subnets, each of which can support up to 14 hosts. The subnet mask for these networks would therefore be 255.255.255.240.

PUBLIC AND PRIVATE IPv4 ADDRESSING

For a computer to be accessible from the Internet, it must have an IP address that is both registered and unique. All of the web servers on the Internet have registered addresses, as do all of the other types of Internet servers.

The Internet Assigned Numbers Authority (IANA) is the ultimate source for all registered addresses; managed by the Internet Corporation for Assigned Names and Numbers

(ICANN), IANA allocates blocks of addresses to regional Internet registries (RIR), which allocate smaller blocks in turn to Internet service providers (ISPs). An organization that wants to host a server on the Internet typically obtains a registered address from an ISP.

Registered IP addresses are not necessary for workstations that merely access resources on the Internet. If organizations used registered addresses for all their workstations, the IPv4 address space would have been depleted long ago. Instead, organizations typically use private IP addresses for their workstations. Private IP addresses are blocks of addresses that are allocated specifically for private network use. Anyone can use these addresses without registering them, but they cannot make computers using private addresses accessible from the Internet.

The three blocks of addresses allocated for private use are as follows:

- 10.0.0.0/8
- 172.16.0.0/12
- 192.168.0.0/16

Most enterprise networks use addresses from these blocks for their workstations. It doesn't matter if other organizations use the same addresses also, because the workstations are never directly connected to the same network.

USING NETWORK ADDRESS TRANSLATION

The question of how workstations with unregistered private addresses communicate with registered servers on the Internet still remains, however. An unregistered workstation can conceivably send messages to an Internet web server, but how can the web server respond when the workstation is using an address that is not visible from the Internet, and also might be shared by dozens of other computers? The answer is by using a technology called *network address translation (NAT)* or a slightly different mechanism called a *proxy server.*

NAT is a network-layer routing technology that enables a group of workstations to share a single registered address. A NAT router is a device with two network interfaces, one connected to a private network and one to the Internet. When a workstation on the private network wants to access an Internet resource, it sends a request to the NAT router.

Normally, a router passes traffic from one network to another without modifying the data. However, in this case, the NAT router substitutes its own registered IP address for the workstation's private address, and sends the request on to the Internet server. The server responds to the NAT router, thinking that the router generated the original request. The router then performs the same substitution in reverse and forwards the response back to the original unregistered workstation. The router, in essence, functions as an intermediary between the client and the server.

A single NAT router can perform this same service for hundreds of private workstations, by maintaining a table of the address substitutions it has performed. In addition to conserving the IPv4 address space, NAT also provides a certain amount of protection to the network workstations. Because the workstations are functionally invisible to the Internet, attackers cannot readily probe them for open ports and other common exploits.

USING A PROXY SERVER

Because NAT routers function at the network layer of the protocol stack, they can handle any kind of traffic, regardless of the application that generated it. A proxy server is another type of intermediary—functioning at the application layer—that is designed to forward specific types of traffic to destinations on the Internet. In most cases, the primary function of a proxy server is to provide workstations with web access through a browser, such as Internet Explorer.

Like a NAT router, a proxy server receives requests from clients on a private network, and forwards those requests to the destination on the Internet, using its own registered address to identify itself. The primary difference between a proxy server and a NAT router is that the

proxy server interposes additional functions into the forwarding process. These functions can include the following:

- Filtering—Administrators can configure proxy servers to limit user access to the Internet by filtering out requests to undesirable sites.
- Logging—A proxy server can maintain logs of user Internet activity, for later evaluation and reporting.
- Caching—A proxy server can store frequently accessed Internet data in a local cache, which it can then use to satisfy subsequent requests for the same data at greater speeds.
- Scanning—A proxy server can scan incoming data from the Internet for various types of malware and outgoing data for confidential company information.

Unlike a NAT router, which is invisible to the workstation, applications must be configured to use a proxy server, a process that can be manual or automatic.

IPV4 SUBNETTING

In most cases, enterprise administrators use addresses in one of the private IP address ranges to create the subnets they need. If you are building a new enterprise network from scratch, you can choose any one of the private address blocks and make things easy on yourself by subnetting along the octet boundaries.

For example, you can take the 10.0.0.0/8 private IP address range and use the entire second octet as a subnet ID. This enables you to create up to 256 subnets with as many as 65,536 hosts on each one. The subnet masks for all of the addresses on the subnets will be 255.255.0.0 and the network addresses will proceed as follows:

- 10.0.0.0/16
- 10.1.0.0/16
- 10.2.0.0/16
- 10.3.0.0/16
- …
- 10.255.0.0/16

Of course, when you are working on an existing network, the subnetting process is likely to be more difficult. You may, for example, be given a relatively small range of addresses and be asked to create a certain number of subnets out of them. To do this, you use the following procedure.

 CALCULATE IPv4 SUBNETS

1. Determine how many subnet identifier bits you need to create the required number of subnets.
2. Subtract the subnet bits you need from the host bits and add them to the network bits.
3. Calculate the subnet mask by adding the network and subnet bits in binary form and converting the binary value to decimal.
4. Take the least significant subnet bit and the host bits, in binary form, and convert them to a decimal value.
5. Increment the network identifier (including the subnet bits) by the decimal value you calculated to determine the network addresses of your new subnets.

Using the example from earlier in this lesson, if you take the 192.168.43.0/24 address and allocate two extra bits for the subnet ID, you end up with a binary subnet mask value of 11111111.11111111.11111111.11000000 (255.255.255.192 in decimal form, as noted earlier).

X REF

Enterprise administrators should already be familiar with the subnetting process. For more extensive coverage of IP addressing and subnetting, see MOAC 70-642: Windows Server 2008 Network Infrastructure Configuration.

The least significant subnet bit plus the host bits gives you a binary value of 1000000, which converts to a decimal value of 64. Therefore, if we know that the network address of your first subnet is 192.168.43.0, the second subnet must be 192.168.43.64, the third 192.168.43.128, and the fourth 192.168.43.192, as shown in the earlier table.

Using IPv6 Addressing

As most administrators know, IPv6 is designed to increase the size of the IP address space, thus providing addresses for many more devices than IPv4. The 128-bit address size of IPv6 allows 2^{128} possible addresses, an enormous number that works out to over 54 million addresses for each square meter of the Earth's surface.

TAKE NOTE*

IPv6 was designed to provide a permanent solution for the IP address-space depletion problem. Of course, at the time IP was conceived, in the late 1970s, no one involved in the project imagined that the 32-bit IPv4 address space would ever be exhausted either. These people had no idea that every home, every car, and nearly every pocket or purse in America would have at least one computer in it. One can only wonder what the world will look like if there ever comes a time when the IPv6 address space is approaching depletion.

In addition to providing more addresses, IPv6 will also reduce the size of the routing tables in the routers scattered around the Internet. This is because the size of the addresses provides for more than the two levels of subnetting currently possible with IPv4.

INTRODUCING IPv6

IPv6 addresses are different from IPv4 addresses in many ways other than length. Instead of the four 8-bit decimal numbers separated by periods that IPv4 uses, IPv6 addresses use a notation called colon-hexadecimal format, which consists of eight 16-bit hexadecimal numbers, separated by colons, as follows:

`XX:XX:XX:XX:XX:XX:XX:XX`

TAKE NOTE*

Hexadecimal notation is another name for Base 16, which means that each digit can have sixteen possible values. To express hexadecimal numbers, you use the numerals 0 to 9 and the letters A to F to represent those 16 values. In binary (Base 2) notation, an 8-bit (one-byte) number can have 256 possible values, but to express those 256 possible values in hexadecimal form, two characters are required. This is why some of the 2-byte XX values in the sample IPv6 address require four digits in hexadecimal notation.

Each X represents eight bits (or one byte), which in hexadecimal notation is represented by two characters, as in the following example:

`21cd:0053:0000:0000:e8bb:04f2:003c:c394`

CONTRACTING IPv6 ADDRESSES

When an IPv6 address has two or more consecutive 8-bit blocks of zeros, you can replace them with a double colon, as follows (but only once in any given address):

`21cd:0053::e8bb:04f2:003c:c394`

You can also remove the leading zeros in any block where they appear, as follows:

`21cd:53::e8bb:4f2:3c:c394`

EXPRESSING IPv6 NETWORK ADDRESSES

There are no subnet masks in IPv6. Network addresses use the same slash notation as CIDR to identify the network bits. In the example specified here, the network address is notated as follows:

`21cd:53::/64`

This is the contracted form for the following network address:

`21cd:0053:0000:0000/64`

UNDERSTANDING IPv6 ADDRESS TYPES

There are no broadcast transmissions in IPv6, and therefore no broadcast addresses, as in IPv4. IPv6 supports three address types as follows:

- Unicast—Provides one-to-one transmission service to individual interfaces, including server farms sharing a single address. IPv6 supports several types of unicast addresses, including global, link-local, and unique local, which are terms that identify the scope of the address. Each type of unicast has a different *format prefix (FP)*, a sequence of bits that identifies the type, just as an IPv4 address uses a sequence of bits to identify its class.
- Multicast—Provides one-to-many transmission service to groups of interfaces identified by a single multicast address.
- Anycast—Provides one-to-one-of-many transmission service to groups of interfaces, only the nearest of which (measured by the number of intermediate routers) receives the transmission.

GLOBAL UNICAST ADDRESSES

A *global unicast address* is the equivalent of a registered IPv4 address, routable worldwide and unique on the Internet. The original format of the address, as shown in Figure 1-1, consists of the following elements:

- Format prefix (FP)—An FP value of 001 identifies the address as a global unicast.

> **TAKE NOTE***
>
> In IPv6, the *scope* of an address refers to the size of its functional area. For example, the scope of a global unicast is unlimited, the entire Internet. The scope of a link-local unicast is the immediate link, that is, the local network. The scope of a unique local unicast is all the subnets within an organization.

Figure 1-1

The original IPv6 global unicast address format

Bit	Field
	001
16	Top Level Aggregator (TLA)
	Reserved
32	
	Next Level Aggregator (NLA)
48	
64	Site Level Aggregator (SLA)
80	
96	Extended Unique Identifier (EUI-64)
112	
128	

- Top-Level Aggregator (TLA)—A 13-bit globally unique identifier allocated to regional internet registries by the IANA.
- Reserved—An 8-bit field that is currently unused.
- Next-Level Aggregator (NLA)—A 24-bit field that the TLA organization uses to create a multilevel hierarchy for allocating blocks of addresses to its customers.
- Site-Level Aggregator (SLA)—A 16-bit field that organizations can use to create an internal hierarchy of sites or subnets.
- Extended Unique Identifier (EUI-64) (64 bits)—A 64-bit field, derived from the network interface adapter's MAC address, identifying a specific interface on the network.

These original field descriptions still appear in many IPv6 descriptions, but the standard was actually modified in 2003 to eliminate the separate TLA and NLA fields and rename the SLA field. The current official format for global unicast addresses, as shown in Figure 1-2, consists of the following elements:

- Global routing prefix—A 48-bit field beginning with the 001 FP value, the hierarchical structure of which is left up to the RIR.
- Subnet ID—Formerly known as the SLA, a 16-bit field that organizations can use to create an internal hierarchy of sites or subnets.
- Interface ID—A 64-bit field identifying a specific interface on the network.

Figure 1-2

The current IPv6 global unicast address format

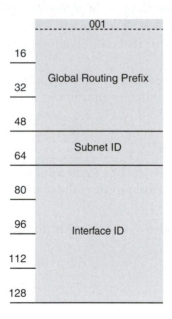

Theoretically, the global routing prefix and subnet ID fields can be any size. They are represented in the IPv6 standard by the letters "n" and "m," with the size of the interface ID specified as "128-n-m." In practice, however, organizations obtaining an address from an RIR or ISP are usually supplied with a 48-bit prefix, known colloquially as a "/48."

The organization then has the 16-bit subnet ID with which to create an internal subnet hierarchy, if desired. Some of the possible subnetting options are as follows:

- One-level subnet—By setting all of the subnet ID bits to 0, all of the computers in the organization are part of a single subnet. This option is only suitable for smaller organizations.
- Two-level subnet—By creating a series of 16-bit values, you can split the network into as many as 65,536 subnets. This is the functional equivalent of IPv4 subnetting, but with a much larger subnet address space.

- Multi-level subnet—By allocating specific numbers of subnet ID bits, you can create multiple levels of subnets, sub-subnets, and sub-sub-subnets, suitable for an enterprise of almost any size.

In one example, designed to support a large international enterprise, you could split the subnet ID as follows:

- Country (4 bits)—Creates up to 16 subnets representing countries in which the organization has offices.
- State (6 bits)—Creates up to 64 sub-subnets within each country, representing states, provinces, or other geographical divisions.
- Office (2 bits)—Creates up to four sub-sub-subnets within each state or province, representing offices located in various cities.
- Department (4 bits)—Creates up to 16 sub-sub-sub-subnets within each office, representing the various departments or divisions.

To create a subnet ID for a particular office, it is up to the enterprise administrators to assign values for each of the fields. To use the value 1 for the United States, the Country bits would be as follows:

```
0001------------
```

To create a subnet for an office in Alaska, you can use a value of 49 in the State field, which in binary form would appear as follows:

```
----110001------
```

For the second office in Alaska, use the value 2 for Office bits, as follows:

```
----------10----
```

For the Sales department in the office, use the value 9 for the Department bits, as follows:

```
------------1001
```

The resulting value for the subnet ID, in binary form, would therefore be as follows:

```
0001110001101001
```

In hexadecimal form, that would be 1c69.

Because the subnet ID is wholly controlled by the organization that owns the prefix, enterprise administrators can adjust the number of levels in the hierarchy and the number of bits dedicated to each level as needed.

Finally, the last field, the interface ID, contains a unique identifier for a specific interface on the network. The Institute for Electrical and Electronics Engineers (IEEE) defines the format for the 48-bit MAC address assigned to each network adapter by the manufacturer, as well as the EUI-64 identifier format derived from it.

A MAC address consists of two 24-bit values, which are usually already expressed in hexadecimal notation. The first 24 bits, an ***organizationally unique identifier (OUI)***, identifies the company that made the adapter. The second 24 bits is a unique value for each individual device.

To derive the 64-bit interface ID for an interface, an IPv6 implementation takes the two 24-bit values and adds a 16-bit value between them: *11111111 11111110* in binary or *fffe* in hexadecimal. Then, it changes the seventh bit in the OUI—called the universal/local bit—from a 0 to a 1. This changes the hexadecimal value of the first byte in the address from 00 to 02.

Therefore, as shown in Figure 1-3, a computer with a network adapter that has a MAC address of *00-1a-6b-3c-ba-1f* would have an IPv6 global unicast address with the following interface ID:

```
021a:6bff:fe3c:ba1f
```

Figure 1-3

Converting a MAC address to an IPv6 interface ID

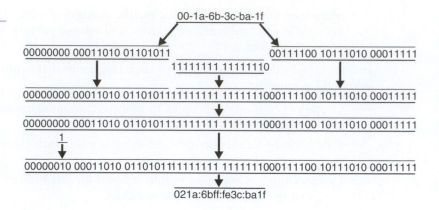

One perceived problem with this method of deriving interface IDs from the computer's hardware is that the location of a mobile computer might be tracked based on its IPv6 address. This raises privacy concerns. Instead of using MAC addresses, Windows operating systems generate random interface IDs by default. Figure 1-4 demonstrates this, showing a system with a randomly generated IPv6 address that does not match the Physical Address value.

Figure 1-4

A randomly generated IPv6 address

```
Administrator: Command Prompt                                          _ □ ×

Ethernet adapter Local Area Connection:

   Connection-specific DNS Suffix   . : adatum.local
   Description . . . . . . . . . . . : Intel(R) PRO/1000 MT Network Connection
   Physical Address. . . . . . . . . : 00-0C-29-5B-29-D2
   DHCP Enabled. . . . . . . . . . . : Yes
   Autoconfiguration Enabled . . . . : Yes
   Link-local IPv6 Address . . . . . : fe80::e8bb:f2f2:372c:c394%11(Preferred)
   IPv4 Address. . . . . . . . . . . : 10.0.0.51(Preferred)
   Subnet Mask . . . . . . . . . . . : 255.255.255.0
   Lease Obtained. . . . . . . . . . : Thursday, July 22, 2010 8:04:22 PM
   Lease Expires . . . . . . . . . . : Friday, July 30, 2010 8:04:15 PM
   Default Gateway . . . . . . . . . : 10.0.0.1
   DHCP Server . . . . . . . . . . . : 10.0.0.2
   DHCPv6 IAID . . . . . . . . . . . : 234884137
   DHCPv6 Client DUID. . . . . . . . : 00-01-00-01-13-D3-B1-E4-00-0C-29-5D-EC-17

   DNS Servers . . . . . . . . . . . : 10.0.0.2
   NetBIOS over Tcpip. . . . . . . . : Enabled

Tunnel adapter isatap.adatum.local:

   Media State . . . . . . . . . . . : Media disconnected
   Connection-specific DNS Suffix   . : adatum.local
   Description . . . . . . . . . . . : Microsoft ISATAP Adapter #2
```

To modify this default behavior, you can type the following at an elevated command prompt:

```
netsh interface ipv6 set global
randomizeidentifiers=disabled
```

With this feature disabled, the system reverts to the standard practice of creating an interface ID from the MAC address, as shown in Figure 1-5.

Figure 1-5

An IPv6 address generated from the MAC address

```
Administrator: Command Prompt                                          _ □ ×

Ethernet adapter Local Area Connection:

   Connection-specific DNS Suffix   . : adatum.local
   Description . . . . . . . . . . . : Intel(R) PRO/1000 MT Network Connection
   Physical Address. . . . . . . . . : 00-0C-29-5B-29-D2
   DHCP Enabled. . . . . . . . . . . : Yes
   Autoconfiguration Enabled . . . . : Yes
   Link-local IPv6 Address . . . . . : fe80::20c:29ff:fe5b:29d2%11(Preferred)
   IPv4 Address. . . . . . . . . . . : 10.0.0.51(Preferred)
   Subnet Mask . . . . . . . . . . . : 255.255.255.0
   Lease Obtained. . . . . . . . . . : Thursday, July 22, 2010 8:04:22 PM
   Lease Expires . . . . . . . . . . : Friday, July 30, 2010 8:04:14 PM
   Default Gateway . . . . . . . . . : 10.0.0.1
   DHCP Server . . . . . . . . . . . : 10.0.0.2
   DHCPv6 IAID . . . . . . . . . . . : 234884137
   DHCPv6 Client DUID. . . . . . . . : 00-01-00-01-13-D3-B1-E4-00-0C-29-5D-EC-17

   DNS Servers . . . . . . . . . . . : 10.0.0.2
   NetBIOS over Tcpip. . . . . . . . : Enabled

Tunnel adapter isatap.adatum.local:

   Media State . . . . . . . . . . . : Media disconnected
   Connection-specific DNS Suffix   . : adatum.local
```

LINK-LOCAL UNICAST ADDRESSES

In IPv6, systems that assign themselves an address automatically create a *link-local unicast address*, which is essentially the equivalent of an Automatic Private IP Addressing (APIPA) address in IPv4. All link local addresses have the same network identifier: a 10-bit FP of 11111110 010 followed by 54 zeros, resulting in the following network address:

```
fe80:0000:0000:0000/64
```

In its more compact form, the link-local network address is as follows:

```
fe80::/64
```

Because all link-local addresses are on the same network, they are not routable and systems possessing them can only communicate with other systems on the same link.

UNIQUE LOCAL UNICAST ADDRESSES

Unique local unicast addresses are the IPv6 equivalent of the 10.0.0.0/8, 172.16.0.0/12, and 192.168.0.0/16 private network addresses in IPv4. Like the IPv4 private addresses, unique local addresses are routable within an organization. Administrators can also subnet them as needed to support an organization of any size.

The format of a unique local unicast address, as shown in Figure 1-6, is as follows:

- Global ID—A 48-bit field beginning with an 8-bit FP of 11111101 in binary, or fd00::/8 in hexadecimal. The remaining 40 bits of the global ID are randomly generated.
- Subnet ID—A 16-bit field that organizations can use to create an internal hierarchy of sites or subnets.
- Interface ID—A 64-bit field identifying a specific interface on the network.

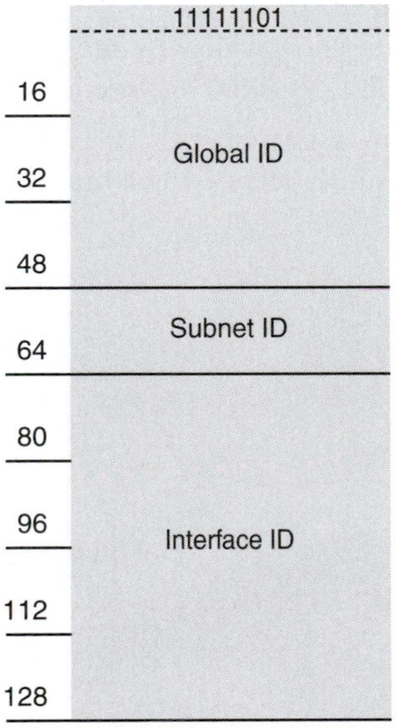

Figure 1-6

The IPv6 unique local unicast address format

```
              11111101
16
              Global ID
32

48
              Subnet ID
64

80

96
              Interface ID
112

128
```

Because unique local addresses are not routable outside the organization, it is in most cases not essential for the global ID to be unique. In fact, because part of the global ID value is randomly generated, there is a remote possibility that two organizations might end up using the same value. However, the IPv6 standards make every attempt short of creating a central register to keep these identifiers unique. This is so that there are unlikely to be addressing conflicts when organizations merge, when virtual private network (VPN) address spaces overlap, or when mobile computers connect to different enterprise networks.

TAKE NOTE *

Many sources of IPv6 information continue to list *site-local unicast addresses* as a valid type of unicast, with a function similar to that of the private IPv4 network addresses. Site-local addresses have an FP of 11111110 11 in binary, or fec0::/10 in hexadecimal. For various reasons, site-local unicast addresses have been deprecated, and while their use is not forbidden, their functionality has been replaced by unique local unicast addresses.

SPECIAL ADDRESSES

There are two other IPv6 unicast addresses with special purposes that correspond to equivalents in IPv4. The loopback address causes any messages sent to it to be returned to the sending system. In IPv6, the loopback address is 0:0:0:0:0:0:0:1, more commonly notated as follows:

::1

The other special address is 0:0:0:0:0:0:0:0, also known as the unspecified address. This is the address a system uses while requesting an address assignment from a DHCP server.

MULTICAST ADDRESSES

Multicast addresses always begin with an FP value of 11111111, in binary, or ff in hexadecimal. The entire multicast address format, as shown in Figure 1-7, is as follows:

- FP—An 8-bit field that identifies the message as a multicast.
- Flags (4 bits)—A 4-bit field that specifies whether the multicast address contains the address of a rendezvous point (0111), is based on a network prefix (0010), and is permanent (0000) or transient (0001).
- Scope—A 4-bit field that specifies how widely routers can forward the address. Values include interface-local (0001), link-local (0010), site-local (0101), organization-local (1000), and global (1110).
- Group ID—A 112-bit field uniquely identifying a multicast group.

Figure 1-7

The IPv6 multicast address format

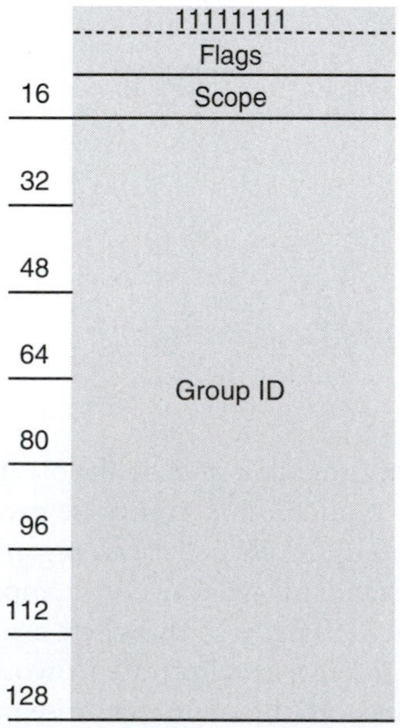

IPv6 can simulate the functionality of a broadcast transmission with a transmission to the *all hosts* multicast group, when necessary. However, the elimination of the broadcast traffic generated by the Address Resolution Protocol (ARP) is one of the advantages of IPv6.

ARP resolves IPv4 addresses into the media access control (MAC) address coded into network adapters by transmitting broadcasts containing addresses and waiting for the computers with those addresses to reply. However, every computer on the local network must process all of the broadcast messages, which increases the burden on the computers as well as the network traffic levels. IPv6 replaces ARP with a protocol called Neighbor Discovery (ND), which performs the same function without using broadcast messages.

ANYCAST ADDRESSES

The function of an anycast address is to identify the routers within a given address scope and send traffic to the nearest router, as determined by the local routing protocols. Organizations can use anycast addresses to identify a particular set of routers in the enterprise, such as those that provide access to the Internet. To use anycasts, the routers must be configured to recognize the anycast addresses as such.

Anycast addresses do not have a special network identifier format; they are derived from any of the standard unicast formats and consist of the entire subnet identifier and an interface identifier set to all 0s. Thus, the scope of an anycast address is the same as that of the unicast address from which it is derived.

As an example, the anycast address for the sample network used earlier in this lesson would be as follows, with the first 64 bits serving as the subnet ID:

```
21cd:0053:0000:0000:0000:0000:0000:0000
```

UNDERSTANDING IPv6 ADDRESS ASSIGNMENT

As with IPv4, a Windows computer can obtain an IPv6 address by three possible methods:

- Manual allocation—A user or administrator manually types an address and other information into the Internet Protocol Version 6 (TCP/IPv6) Properties sheet shown in Figure 1-8.
- Self-allocation—The computer creates its own address using a process called *stateless address autoconfiguration.*
- Dynamic allocation—The computer solicits and receives an address from a Dynamic Host Configuration Protocol (DHCPv6) server on the network.

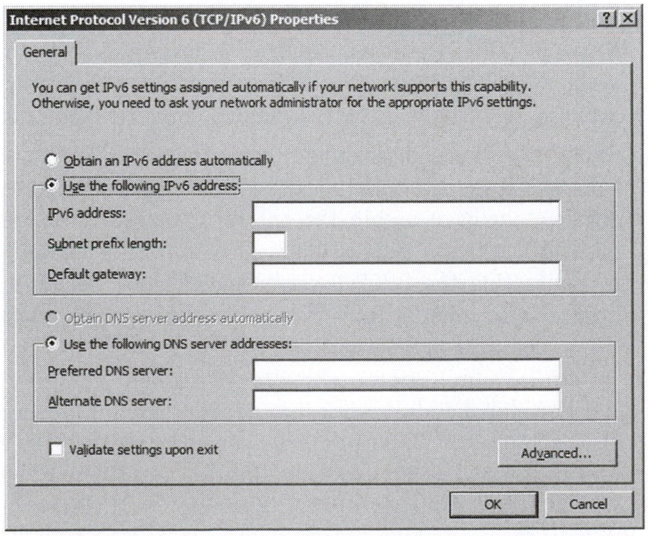

Figure 1-8

The Internet Protocol Version 6 (TCP/IPv6) Properties sheet

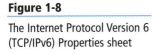

For the enterprise administrator, manual address allocation is even more impractical than in IPv4, because of the length of the addresses involved. Therefore, the other two options are more prevalent.

When a Windows computer starts, it initiates the stateless address autoconfiguration process, during which it assigns each interface a link-local unicast address. This assignment always occurs, even when the interface is to receive a global unicast address later. The link-local address enables the system to communicate with the router on the link, which provides additional instructions.

The steps of the stateless address autoconfiguration process are as follows:

 PERFORM A STATELESS ADDRESS AUTOCONFIGURATION

1. Link-local address creation—The IPv6 implementation on the system creates a link-local address for each interface by using the fe80::/64 network address and generating an interface ID, using either the interface's MAC address or a pseudorandom generator.

2. Duplicate address detection—Using the IPv6 Neighbor Discovery (ND) protocol, the system transmits a Neighbor Solicitation message to determine if any other computer on the link is using the same address and listens for a Neighbor Advertisement message sent in reply. If there is no reply, then the system considers the address to be unique on the link. If there is a reply, the system must generate a new address and repeat the procedure.

3. Link-local address assignment—When the system determines that the link-local address is unique, it configures the interface to use that address. On a small network consisting of a single segment or link, this may be the interface's permanent address assignment. On a network with multiple subnets, the primary function of the link-local address assignment is to enable the system to communicate with a router on the link.

4. Router advertisement solicitation—The system uses the ND protocol to transmit Router Solicitation messages to the *all routers* multicast address. These messages compel routers to transmit the Router Advertisement messages more frequently.

5. Router advertisement—The router on the link uses the ND protocol to transmit Router Advertisement messages to the system that contain information on how the autoconfiguration process should proceed. The Router Advertisement messages typically supply a network prefix, which the system will use with its existing interface ID to create a global or unique local unicast address. The messages may also instruct the system to initiate a stateful autoconfiguration process by contacting a specific DHCPv6 server. If there is no router on the link, as determined by the system's failure to receive Router Advertisement messages, then the system must attempt to initiate a stateful autoconfiguration process.

6. Global or unique local address configuration—Using the information it receives from the router, the system generates a suitable address—one that is routable, either globally or within the enterprise—and configures the interface to use it. If so instructed, the system might also initiate a stateful autoconfiguration process by contacting the DHCPv6 server specified by the router and obtaining a global or unique local address from that server, along with other configuration settings.

For the enterprise administrator with a multi-segment network, it will be necessary to use unique local or global addresses for internetwork communication, so you will need either routers that advertise the appropriate network prefixes or DHCPv6 servers that can supply addresses with the correct prefixes. The Routing and Remote Access role service in Windows Server 2008 R2 and Windows Server 2008 supports IPv6 routing and advertising, and the DHCP role in those operating systems supports IPv6 address allocation.

Planning an IP Transition

Technologies such as CIDR and NAT have prolonged the useful life of IPv4, and at the same time, they have become comfortable shelters for network administrators. IPv6 makes redundant many of the tools and skills that have served these administrators well for years, and many are not happy to lose them. However, the transition from IPv4 to IPv6 is undoubtedly coming, and it is not a transition that you can perform overnight.

Enterprise administrators can do as they wish within the enterprise itself. If all of the network devices in the organization support IPv6, they can begin to use IPv6 at any time. However, the Internet is still firmly based on IPv4, and will continue to be so for several years. Therefore, an IPv4-to-IPv6 transition must be a gradual project that includes some period of support for both IP versions.

At the present time and for the immediate future, administrators must work under the assumption that the rest of the world is using IPv4, and that you must implement a mechanism for transmitting your IPv6 traffic over an IPv4 connection. Eventually, the situation will be reversed. Most of the world will be running IPv6, and the remaining IPv4 technologies will have to transmit their older traffic over new links.

USING A DUAL IP STACK

The simplest and most obvious method for transitioning from IPv4 to IPv6 is to run both, and this is what all current versions of Windows do, including Windows 7, Windows Vista, Windows Server 2008 R2, and Windows Server 2008.

By default, these operating systems install both IP versions and use them simultaneously. In fact, even if you have never heard of IPv6 until today, your computers are likely already using it, and have IPv6 link-local addresses that you can see by running the *ipconfig /all* command.

TAKE NOTE*

Windows Server 2003 and Windows XP both include support for IPv6, but they do not install it by default. To configure these operating systems to use IPv6, you must install the Microsoft TCP/IP version 6 protocol driver in the Local Area Connection Properties sheet. In this IPv6 implementation, the two networking stacks are completely separate, except for the physical layer. The IPv4 and IPv6 drivers each have a separate implementation of the upper-layer protocols. Later versions of Windows have separate IPv4 and IPv6 implementations, but they share the same stack at the upper layers.

The network-layer implementations in Windows are separate, so you configure them separately. For both IPv4 and IPv6, you can choose to configure the address and other settings manually or use autoconfiguration.

Because Windows supports both IP versions, the computers can communicate with TCP/IP resources running IPv4 or IPv6. However, an enterprise network includes other devices also, most particularly routers, that may not yet support IPv6. The Internet also is nearly all still based on IPv4.

Beginning right now, enterprise administrators should make sure that any network-layer equipment they buy includes support for IPv6. Failure to do so will almost certainly cost them later.

TUNNELING

Right now, there are many network services that are IPv4-only, and comparatively few that require IPv6. Those IPv6 services are coming, however. The new DirectAccess remote networking feature in Windows Server 2008 R2 and Windows 7 is an example of an IPv6-only technology, and much of its complexity is due to the need to establish IPv6 connections over the IPv4 Internet.

The primary method for transmitting IPv6 traffic over an IPv4 network is called tunneling. *Tunneling*, in this case, is the process by which a system encapsulates an IPv6 datagram within an IPv4 packet, as shown in Figure 1-9. The system then transmits the IPv4 packet to its destination, with none of the intermediate systems aware of the packet's contents.

Figure 1-9

IPv6 traffic encapsulated inside an IPv4 datagram

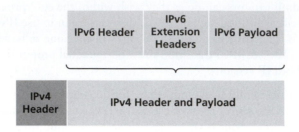

Tunneling can work in a variety of configurations, depending on the network infrastructure, including router-to-router, host-to-host, router-to-host, and host-to-router. However, the most common configuration is router-to-router, as in the case of a IPv4-only connection between an IPv6 branch office and an IPv6 home office, as shown in Figure 1-10.

Figure 1-10

Two IPv6 networks connected by an IPv4 tunnel

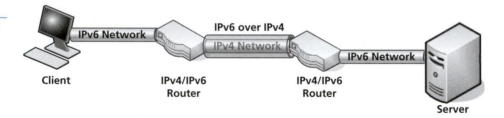

The two routers support both IPv4 and IPv6, and the local networks at each site use IPv6. However, the link connecting the two sites is IPv4-only. By creating a tunnel between the routers in the two offices using their IPv4 interfaces, they can exchange IPv6 traffic as needed. Computers at either site can send IPv6 traffic to the other site, and the routers are responsible for encapsulating the IPv6 data in IPv4 packets for the trip through the tunnel.

Windows supports several different tunneling methods, both manual and automatic, as described in the following sections.

CONFIGURING TUNNELS MANUALLY

It is possible to manually create semi-permanent tunnels that carry IPv6 traffic through an IPv4-only network. When a computer running Windows Server 2008 R2 or Windows 7 is functioning as one end of the tunnel, you can use the following command:

```
netsh interface ipv6 add v6v4tunnel "interface"
localaddress remoteaddress
```

In this command, *interface* is a friendly name you want to assign to the tunnel you are creating and *localaddress* and *remoteaddress* are the IPv4 addresses forming the two ends of the tunnel. An example of an actual command would be as follows:

```
netsh interface ipv6 add v6v4tunnel "tunnel" 206.73.118.19 157.54.206.43
```

CONFIGURING TUNNELS AUTOMATICALLY

There are also a number of mechanisms that automatically create tunnels over IPv4 connections. These are technologies designed to be temporary solutions during the transition from IPv4 to IPv6. All of them include a mechanism for expressing an IPv4 address in the IPv6 format. The IPv4-to-IPv6 transition technologies that Windows supports are described in the following sections.

6TO4

The *6to4* mechanism essentially incorporates the IPv4 connections in a network into the IPv6 infrastructure by defining a method for expressing IPv4 addresses in IPv6 format and encapsulating IPv6 traffic into IPv4 packets.

To enable IPv4 links to function as part of the IPv6 infrastructure, 6to4 translates public IPv4 addresses into IPv6 using the following format, as shown in Figure 1-11:

- FP—The 3-bit format prefix is 001 in binary, the standard global unicast value.
- TLA—A 13-bit TLA value that, for a 6to4 address, is always 0002 in hexadecimal.
- V4ADDR—A 32-bit V4ADDR value containing the IPv4 dotted decimal address, split into four separate octets and converted into hexadecimal form.
- SLA ID—A 16-bit SLA ID (or subnet ID) field that organizations can use to create an internal hierarchy of sites or subnets.
- Interface ID—A 64-bit field identifying a specific interface on the network.

Figure 1-11

The 6to4 address format

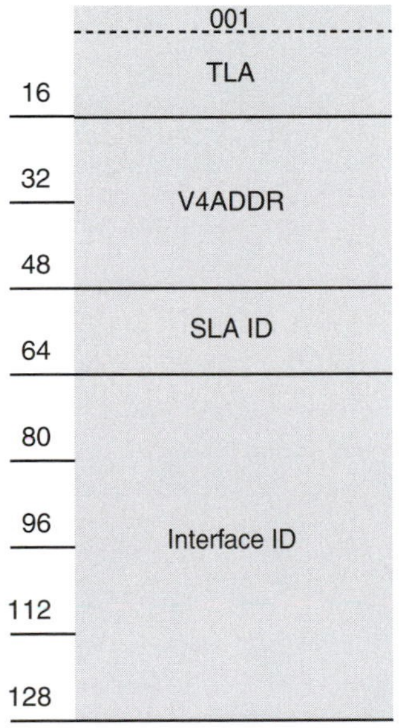

```
                        001
          ┌─────────────────────────────┐
          │            TLA               │
     16   ├─────────────────────────────┤
          │                             │
     32   │          V4ADDR             │
          │                             │
     48   ├─────────────────────────────┤
          │          SLA ID             │
     64   ├─────────────────────────────┤
          │                             │
     80   │                             │
          │                             │
     96   │        Interface ID         │
          │                             │
    112   │                             │
          │                             │
    128   └─────────────────────────────┘
```

For example, to convert the IPv4 address 157.54.176.7 into a 6to4 IPv6 address, you begin with 2002 for the FP and TLA fields, and then convert the four decimal values from the IPv4 address into hexadecimal, as follows:

- 157 = 9d
- 54 = 36
- 176 = b0
- 7 = 07

Therefore, you end up with the following IPv6 address:

`2002:9d36:b007:subnetID:interfaceID`

The subnet and interface identifiers use the same values as any other IPv6 link on the network. The encapsulation method is the same as that for a manually created tunnel, with a standard IPv4 header and containing the IPv6 data as the payload. A 6to4 router examines incoming packets and, if it detects the 2002 value in the first block, knows to transmit the packet over the IPv4 interface, using the 32 bits following the 2002 block as the IPv4 address.

ISATAP

Intra-Site Automatic Tunnel Addressing Protocol (ISATAP) is an automatic tunneling protocol used by the Windows workstation operating systems that emulates an IPv6 link using an IPv4 network. ISATAP also converts IPv4 addresses into IPv6 link-layer address format, but it uses a different method than 6to4. An ISATAP address uses the following format, as shown in Figure 1-12:

- The first 64 bits consist of the standard link-local network identifier, the value fe80 following by 48 bits of 0s.
- The first 16-bit block of the interface identifier consists of all 0s, except for the seventh bit, which is set to 1 when the IPv4 address is globally unique, and the eighth bit, which is set to 1 when the IPv4 address identifies a multicast group. In most cases, this block consists of all 0s.
- The second 16-bit block of the interface ID consists of the value 5efe, which represents the concatenated OUI for ISATAP (5e) and the standardized value fe.
- The final 32 bits of the interface identifier consist of the IPv4 address, in hexadecimal form.

Figure 1-12

The ISATAP address format

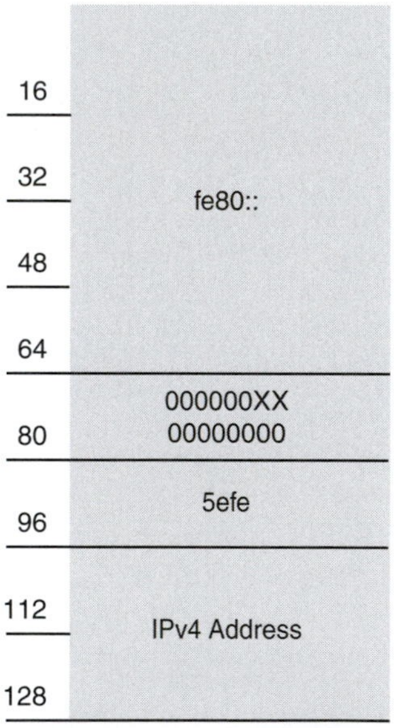

Therefore, the IPv4 address 157.54.176.7 would have the following as its ISATAP address:

`fe80:0000:0000:0000:0000:5efe:9d36:b007`

In compressed form, the address appears as follows:

`fe80::5efe:9d36:b007`

ISATAP does not support multicasting, so it cannot locate routers in the usual manner, using the Neighbor Discovery protocol. Instead, the system compiles a potential routers list (PRL) using DNS queries and sends Router Discovery messages to them on a regular basis, using Internet Control Message Protocol version 6 (ICMPv6).

TEREDO

To use 6to4 tunneling, both endpoints of the tunnel must have registered IPv4 addresses. However, on many networks, the system that would function as the endpoint is located behind a NAT router, and therefore has an unregistered address. In such a case, the only registered address available is assigned to the NAT router itself, and unless the router supports 6to4 (which many don't), it is impossible to establish the tunnel.

Teredo is a mechanism that addresses this shortcoming by enabling devices behind non-IPv6 NAT routers to function as tunnel endpoints. To do this, Teredo encapsulates IPv6 packets within transport-layer User Datagram Protocol (UDP) datagrams, rather than network-layer IPv4 datagrams, as 6to4 does.

For a Teredo client to function as a tunnel endpoint, it must have access to a Teredo server, with which it exchanges Router Solicitation and Router Advertisement messages to determine whether the client is located behind a NAT router.

Teredo clients have the most complicated form of IPv6 address yet, which uses the following format, as shown in Figure 1-13:

- Prefix—A 32-bit field that identifies the system as a Teredo client. Windows clients use the prefix value 2001:0000, or 2001::/32.

- Server IPv4—A 32-bit field containing the IPv4 address of the Teredo server the client uses.

- Flags—A 16-bit field, the first bit of which is the Cone flag, set to 1 when the NAT device providing access to the Internet is a cone NAT, which stores the mappings between internal and external addresses and port numbers. The second bit is reserved for future use. The seventh and eighth bits are the Universal/Local and Individual/Group flags, which are both set to 0. The Teredo standard calls for the remaining 12 bits to be set to 0, but Windows assigns a random number to these bits, to prevent attackers from attempting to discover the Teredo address.

- Port—A 16-bit field that specifies the external UDP port that the client uses for all Teredo traffic, in obscured form. The obscuration of the port number (and the following IPv4 address) is to prevent the NAT router from translating the port as it normally would as part of its packet processing. To obscure the port, the system runs an exclusive OR (XOR) with the value ffff.

- Client IPv4—A 32-bit field that specifies the external IPv4 address that the client uses for all Teredo traffic, in obscured form. As with the Port field, the obscuration is the result of converting the IPv4 address to hexadecimal and running an XOR with the value ffffffff.

Figure 1-13

The Teredo address format

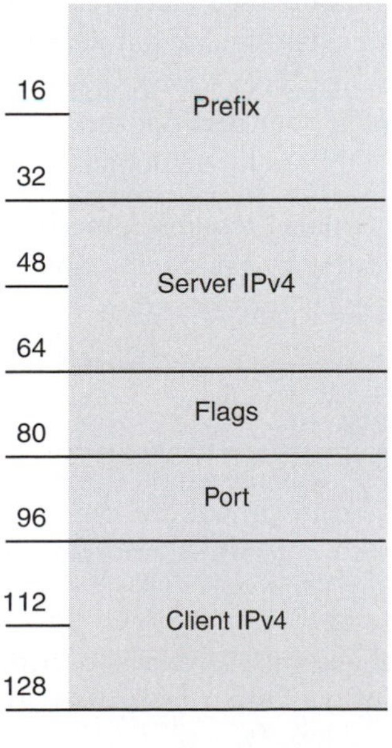

16	
	Prefix
32	
48	
	Server IPv4
64	
80	Flags
96	Port
112	
	Client IPv4
128	

If, for example, the IPv4 address and port of the Teredo client are 192.168.31.243:32000, the Teredo server uses the address 157.54.176.7, and the client is behind a cone NAT router, the Teredo address, in standard format, would consist of the following elements:

- 2001:0000—Standard Teredo prefix
- 9d36:b007—Server IPv4 address (157.54.176.7) converted to hexadecimal
- 8000—Flags field with first bit set to 1 and all others 0
- 82ff—Client UDP port number (32000), converted to hexadecimal (7d00) and XORed with ffff
- 3f57:e00c—Client IPv4 address (192.168.31.243), converted to hexadecimal (C0a8:1ff3) and XORed with ffffffff

Thus, the final Teredo address is as follows:

`2001:0000:9d36:b007:8000:82ff:3f57:e00c`

To initiate communications, a Teredo client exchanges null packets called *bubbles* with the desired destination, using the Teredo servers at each end as intermediaries. The function of the bubble messages is to create mappings for both computers in each other's NAT routers.

■ Creating a Naming and Name-Resolution Strategy

THE BOTTOM LINE

As all enterprise administrators know, network devices typically have names, because names are easier to remember and work with than addresses. The length and hexadecimal notation of IPv6 addresses only makes this more true. When designing an enterprise network, administrators must develop policies for creating effective names and also plan for the implementation of name-resolution mechanisms such as Domain Name System (DNS).

Name resolution is the process of locating the IP address equivalent for a given name. All TCP/IP communication is based on IP addresses, though users rarely see them. When you access a network resource by name, one of the first things the system does is resolve that name into an IP address.

As you probably know, the most commonly used name-resolution mechanism today is DNS, which is a distributed database of names and their equivalent IP addresses. If your users access the Internet, they use a global network of DNS servers that is able to resolve any public server name in the world into an IP address. If your network uses Active Directory Domain Services (AD DS), the AD DS clients all use DNS to locate domain controllers.

Some legacy networks still use another name-resolution mechanism called Windows Internet Name Service (WINS). This complicates the name-resolution environment, but there are ways for the two services to work together and cooperate.

DNS Name-Resolution Review

Enterprise administrators should be familiar with the process by which the DNS resolves names into IP addresses, but this section provides a brief review of the process.

DNS is essentially a distributed database, with servers all over the Internet functioning as authoritative sources for small parts of the DNS namespace. Because there is no one server that holds a complete copy of the DNS database, the system is entirely reliant on communications between servers.

To better explain the relationship of the DNS servers for various domains in the namespace, a diagram of the Internet name resolution process is shown in Figure 1-14. The resolution of a DNS name on the Internet proceeds as follows:

Figure 1-14

The DNS name resolution process

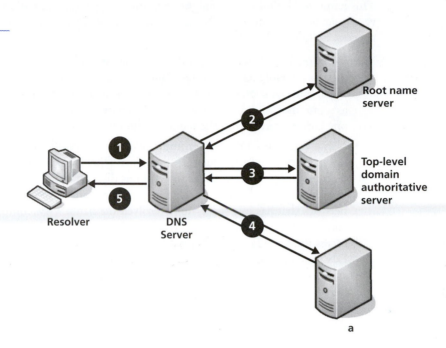

RESOLVE A DNS NAME

1. An application running on a client workstation has a name to resolve and passes it to the DNS client—called a **resolver**—running on that system. The resolver generates a DNS name-resolution request message and transmits it to the local DNS server address specified in its TCP/IP configuration.

2. The client's local DNS server, on receiving the request, checks its own database and cache for the requested name. If the server has no information about the requested name, it forwards the request message to one of the root name servers on the Internet. The root name server, in processing the request, reads only the top-level domain of the requested name, and generates a reply message containing the IP address of an authoritative server for that top-level domain. The root name server then transmits the reply back to the client's local DNS server.

3. The client's local DNS server now has the IP address of an authoritative server for the requested name's top-level domain, so it transmits the same name-resolution request to that top-level domain server. The top-level-domain server reads only the second-level domain of the requested name, and generates a reply containing the IP address of an authoritative server for that second-level domain. The top-level server then transmits the reply to the client's local DNS server.

4. The client's local DNS server now finally has the IP address of an authoritative server for the second-level domain that actually contains the requested names, so it forwards the name-resolution request to that second-level domain server. The second-level domain server reads the host in the requested name and transmits a reply containing the resource record for that host back to the client's local DNS server.

5. The client's local DNS server receives the resource record from the second-level domain server and forwards it to the resolver on the client computer. The resolver then supplies the IP address associated with the requested name to the original application, after which direct communication between the client and the intended destination can begin.

This name-resolution process might seem incredibly long and tedious, but it actually proceeds very quickly. There are also DNS server mechanisms that help to shorten the name-resolution process, including the following:

- Combined DNS Servers—In the DNS name-resolution process just described, the process of resolving the top-level and second-level domain names is portrayed in separate steps, but this is often not the case. The most commonly used top-level domains, such as .com, .net, and .org, are actually hosted by the root name servers, which eliminates one entire referral from the name-resolution process.

- Name Caching—DNS server implementations typically maintain a cache of information they receive from other DNS servers. When a server possesses information about a requested FQDN in its cache, it responds directly using the cached information, rather than sending a referral to another server. Therefore, if you have a DNS server on your network that has just successfully resolved the name www.contoso.com for a client by contacting the authoritative server for the contoso.com domain, a second user trying to access the same host a few minutes later will receive an immediate reply from the local DNS server's cache, rather than having to wait for the entire referral process to repeat, as shown in Figure 1-15. Caching is a critical part of the DNS, as it reduces the amount of network traffic generated by the name-resolution process and reduces the burden on the root name and top-level domain servers.

Figure 1-15

Name caching enables the second name-resolution request for the same name to bypass the referral process

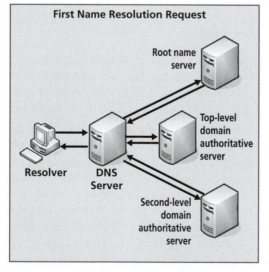
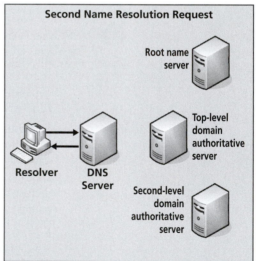

Designing a Domain-Naming Strategy

One of the primary functions of an enterprise administrator is to establish policies that can be applied throughout a large organization without consulting the policy makers. When it comes to naming things, such as domains, computers, and AD DS objects, you do not want to receive a phone call from every branch office each time someone creates a new subdomain or installs a new server, asking you what name to give it, nor do you want to have to call them to find out what name they have chosen.

A domain-naming strategy for an enterprise is a set of rules that administrators at any level can apply both when they have to create a new name and when they are attempting to locate a particular resource. For example, when a user from a branch office calls the help desk to report a problem accessing a server, the support staff should know immediately what server the user is talking about and be able to find it in the AD DS hierarchy. A good top-to-bottom naming policy also includes server names that identify the location of the computer, and perhaps its function.

SELECTING INTERNAL AND EXTERNAL DOMAIN NAMES

Working from the top down, the first issue to consider is that of naming the domains your organization will use. This process is obviously associated with the Active Directory design process, which is covered in Lesson 2, "Designing an Active Directory Hierarchy;" this section concerns only the names you will use for the domains.

The term domain refers to an organizational division, but it has two distinct uses in enterprise networking. Internally, a domain refers to an AD DS domain, but externally, it refers to an Internet domain.

Internally, AD DS domains can enable administrators to emulate geographical or departmental divisions in the AD DS hierarchy. Users look in particular domains to find the network resources they need, such as servers and printers. On the Internet, domains enable users to locate your organization's Web servers and other public resources.

There must, of course, be a boundary between these two types of domains. You want internal users to be able to access resources on the Internet, but you absolutely do not want Internet users to be able to access your internal resources.

With these necessities in mind, there are three possible strategies you can use when creating your internal and external domains, as follows:

- Use the same domain internally and externally—It is possible to use the same second-level domain, such as *adatum.com,* for both internal and external resources. The domain name you choose must be registered in a top-level domain, such as .com or .org, so that it is accessible from the Internet. Using a single domain name provides a unified experience and corporate identity for all users. However, administrators must maintain separate DNS zones with the same name for internal and external records, which can be confusing. This solution also leads to problems when internal users must access the organization's external servers, because the internal DNS zone resolves the domain name to internal, not external, resources. For this reason, administrators must duplicate the external zone on the internal DNS servers. From an administrative and security perspective, this is the least desirable of the naming options. However, if you are working with an existing DNS namespace, this might be the most expedient option.

- Create separate domains in the same hierarchy—Once you register a second-level domain, such as *adatum.com*, for use on the public Internet, you also gain the right to create additional subdomain levels beneath that domain. Therefore, you can conceivably use *adatum.com* for your external resources and create a third-level domain, such as *internal.adatum.com*, for your internal resources. The biggest problem with this solution is that the fully qualified domain names (FQDNs) of your internal resources can be unmanageably long.

- Create separate internal and external domains—Creating entirely separate domains for your internal and external resources, such as *adatum.local* and *adatum.com*, respectively, is generally considered to be the optimum solution, for administrative and security reasons. The internal domain can be, but does not have to be, registered. In this case, *.local* is not a valid top-level domain, so it is not possible for Internet users to resolve the names associated with your internal resources, which provides additional security. Because the domain names are different, internal users do not have any problems accessing external resources. For organizations in which a particular domain name is intimately associated with a corporate branding effort, there may be nontechnical objections to using another domain name, even internally. However, administrators can use aliases and other techniques to keep the internal domain name almost completely hidden, even from internal users.

TAKE NOTE*

An internal domain name can use either a valid or an invalid top-level domain name. If you elect to create an internal domain using a valid top-level domain name, such as .com or .org, you are not required to register the domain for use on the Internet. However, registering the name is still a good idea, because if someone else on the Internet registers the name, your internal users' attempts to resolve that name will direct them to the Internet domain, and not the internal one.

Whichever naming strategy you elect to use, keeping the internal DNS records separated from the external ones is imperative. In most cases, enterprise networks maintain separate DNS servers for this purpose. For example, Figure 1-16 illustrates a simple network with two DNS servers on either side of the corporate firewall.

Figure 1-16

DNS servers for separate internal and external domains

Internal   External

TAKE NOTE*

Figure 1-16 illustrates a simple domain model that does not take into account the need for additional DNS servers in a typical enterprise network design. Enterprise networks usually have multiple DNS servers, for domain-delegation and fault-tolerance purposes.

The external server is responsible for the *adatum.com* domain and is the authoritative source for information about that domain on the Internet. This DNS server should contain only the records for Internet-accessible resources, such as web and mail servers.

The internal server is responsible for the *adatum.local* domain, and contains records for internal resources only. This includes the AD DS domain controller records and possibly records for all of the computers on the network, which is why they must be secured. When internal users attempt to access resources on the Internet, the internal DNS server is configured to forward those Internet name-resolution requests to the external DNS server.

This arrangement is basically the same if you elect to use a single domain name or separate domain in the same hierarchy. Only the names of the zones are different. You still must make the external records available to the Internet, while protecting the internal records from Internet access.

CREATING AN INTERNAL DOMAIN-NAMING HIERARCHY

The external DNS namespace is usually quite simple, often consisting of only a single domain name with a few resource records. If your organization consists of several companies, you might have multiple second-level domain names registered, and different content associated with each one. In that case, you might have multiple zones on your external DNS server, or perhaps even separate DNS servers for each domain name.

The internal naming hierarchy, however, can often be more complex in a large enterprise. In most cases, the domain namespace for an enterprise is based—at least in part—on the design of its AD DS hierarchy. The same circumstances that can lead to the creation of multiple AD DS domains should lead administrators to create separate DNS domains as well.

Most enterprise administrators design their domain hierarchies along geographic or departmental lines, or sometimes a combination of both. For example, the *adatum.local* internal domain mentioned earlier might have child domains named for the cities in which branch offices are located, as shown in Figure 1-17. In this example, the child DNS domains correspond to the AD DS domain tree, and the same servers that perform AD DS name resolution also enable users to access Internet resources.

Figure 1-17

DNS servers for child domains in an AD DS tree

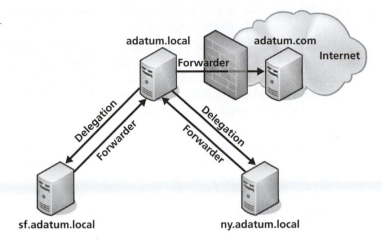

ADDING AD DS DOMAINS TO AN EXISTING DNS HIERARCHY

The previous example assumes an enterprise built around Active Directory Domain Services. But what about an enterprise with an existing DNS namespace to which you are adding AD DS? The existing DNS infrastructure might consist of non-Windows DNS servers that provide users with name-resolution services for Internet resources and UNIX servers on the network.

To introduce AD DS domain onto a network with an existing DNS namespace, you once again have three options:

- Use the existing domains for AD DS—You can use the existing internal domain names for AD DS, either by using the existing non-Windows DNS servers or by replacing them with Windows Server 2008 R2.
- Create new domains for AD DS—You can create a new second-level domain, such as adadatum.local, to function as the root domain for your AD DS tree.
- Create child domains for AD DS—You can leave the existing namespace intact and add a third-level child domain, such as ad.adatum.local, to function as the root domain for your AD DS tree.

Administrators generally base this decision on the enterprise's physical DNS infrastructure, as discussed later in this lesson.

Designing a Physical DNS Infrastructure

The DNS naming strategy you devise for your enterprise network does not necessarily have to correspond to your DNS server infrastructure. As you probably know, to host a domain on a DNS server, you create a zone, and a single DNS server can host multiple zones. In each zone, you create resource records that contain information about the computers on the network. When a DNS server hosts a zone, it becomes an authoritative source for information about the resources in that zone.

Each resource record on a Microsoft DNS server consumes 100 bytes of memory. At that rate, 10,000 records require 1 million bytes, or 1 megabyte (MB). A single DNS server can therefore support a network of almost any conceivable size, theoretically. Thus, there must be factors other than record capacity that compel administrators to install multiple DNS servers on their networks, such as the following:

- Security—To prevent users on the Internet from accessing records for internal DNS resources, they must be stored on a separate server from the external resource records, not just a separate zone. This is true even if you are using the same domain name for your internal and external resources.

- Fault tolerance—DNS is a critical service that must be available at all times. For external services, a DNS failure can mean that Internet users cannot access your Web sites and incoming email bounces back to the sender. For internal users, without DNS, all AD DS authentication and authorization stops. Therefore, the recommended practice is to have at least two copies of every zone on at least two different servers.

- Performance—Although one single DNS server could probably handle all the name-resolution requests for your entire enterprise, this is usually not a practical solution, especially if you have offices at remote locations connected by wide-area network (WAN) links. Nearly every network operation that a user performs begins with a DNS name-resolution request, and delays as these requests pass over relatively slow WAN links can cause performance to degrade noticeably. Therefore, whenever possible, you should provide users with access to a local DNS server.

TAKE NOTE*

DNS servers installed in branch offices or other locations for performance reasons do not have to be an authoritative source for a zone. They can function as caching-only DNS servers, which simply provide name-resolution services to clients on the network.

As a result of these factors, a typical enterprise network will have a minimum of two DNS servers on the perimeter network with the servers that are accessible to the Internet, and two on the internal network. Larger branch offices might also have their own DNS servers, possibly coupled with a read-only domain controller (RODC).

In many cases, enterprise administrators install one external DNS server of their own on the perimeter network, and contract with an ISP to maintain a replica. Because the two servers are located at different sites and often use different backbones to connect to the Internet, this arrangement can provide a greater degree of fault tolerance than two servers located in the same data center.

SELECTING ZONE TYPES

DNS servers traditionally store their resource records in text files. This is the method that Microsoft DNS Server uses when you create a primary or secondary zone. To create multiple copies of a zone, you first create a primary zone, and then one or more secondary zones. Then you configure zone transfers to occur on a regular schedule. A *zone transfer* simply copies the records from the primary zone to a secondary zone.

A Windows Server 2008 R2 DNS server can host both primary and secondary zones on the same server, so you don't have to install additional servers just to create secondary zones. You can configure each of your DNS servers to host a primary zone, and then create secondary zones on each server for one or more of the primaries on other servers. Each primary can have multiple secondaries located on servers throughout the network. This not only provides fault tolerance, but also prevents all the traffic for a single zone from flooding a single subnet.

On networks using AD DS, however, it is more common for administrators to create Active Directory-integrated zones, which store their resource records in the Active Directory database. The advantages of this option are as follows:

- Fault tolerance—The DNS data is stored on domain controllers throughout the network.
- Security—Using Windows permissions, you can control access to the DNS zones.

- Compatibility—You can perform zone transfers of AD-integrated zones to standard secondary zones, if desired.
- Replication—AD DS replicates the DNS data along with the rest of its information. Unlike zone transfers, AD DS replication is multiple master, meaning that you can modify the data on any server, and compressed, for better traffic utilization on slow WAN links.

TAKE NOTE*

By default, Windows Server 2008 R2 replicates the database for a primary zone stored in Active Directory to all the other domain controllers running the DNS Server role in the AD DS domain where the primary is located. You can also modify the scope of zone database replication to keep copies on all domain controllers throughout the enterprise, or on all domain controllers in the Active Directory domain, whether or not they are running the DNS server. You can also create a custom replication scope that copies the zone database to the domain controllers you specify.

However, while Active Directory-integrated zones provide definite advantages, you will not want to use them everywhere. For example, for the external DNS servers on your perimeter network, you will not want to expose your AD DS information to the Internet, so you should create standard file-based primary or secondary zones on these servers.

USING FORWARDERS

As mentioned earlier, the DNS relies heavily on communication between servers, especially in the form of referrals. A *referral* is the process by which one DNS server sends a name resolution request to another DNS server.

DNS servers recognize two types of name resolution requests, as follows:

- Recursive query—In a *recursive query*, the DNS server receiving the name-resolution request takes full responsibility for resolving the name. If the server possesses information about the requested name, it replies immediately to the requester. If the server has no information about the name, it sends referrals to other DNS servers until it obtains the information it needs. TCP/IP client resolvers always send recursive queries to their designated local DNS servers.
- Iterative query—In an *iterative query*, the server that receives the name-resolution request immediately responds with the best information it possesses at the time. This information could be cached or authoritative, and it could be a resource record containing a fully resolved name or a reference to another DNS server. DNS servers generally use iterative queries when communicating with each other.

In most cases, it would be improper to configure one DNS server to send a recursive query to another DNS server. For example, if DNS servers started sending recursive queries to the root name servers instead of iterative queries, the additional burden on the root name servers would be immense, and probably cause the entire Internet to grind to a halt.

The only time a DNS server does send recursive queries to another server is in the case of a special type of server called a *forwarder,* which is specifically intended to interact with other servers in this way. For example, in the DNS server arrangement described earlier, with external servers on the perimeter network and internal servers on the other side of the firewall, the external DNS servers typically function as forwarders for the internal servers, as shown in Figure 1-18.

Figure 1-18

Using a forwarder

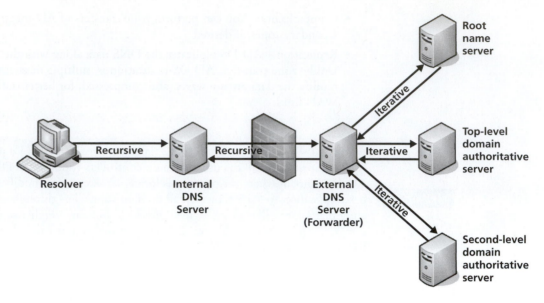

When the clients on the internal network attempt to access Internet resources, they send a recursive name-resolution query to their local DNS server, on the internal network. This DNS server is not directly accessible from the Internet, so you configure it to forward the name-resolution query to the external DNS server on the perimeter network.

This will be a recursive query because you want the external DNS server to handle all of the individual queries to the authoritative root name, top-level, and second-level servers. Only when the external DNS server is able to actually resolve the name requested by the client does it return a response to the internal DNS server, which responds in turn to the client resolver.

The difference in a forwarder arrangement is in the nature of the query, so you don't have to modify the configuration of the server that will act as the forwarder. However, you do have to configure the other server to use a specific computer as a forwarder.

To configure a Microsoft DNS server to use a forwarder, you open the server's Properties sheet in the DNS Manager console and click the Forwarders tab, as shown in Figure 1-19. On this tab, you specify the IP addresses of the DNS servers you want to use as forwarders, if the server is not able to resolve a requested name on its own.

Figure 1-19

The Forwarders tab of a DNS server's Properties sheet

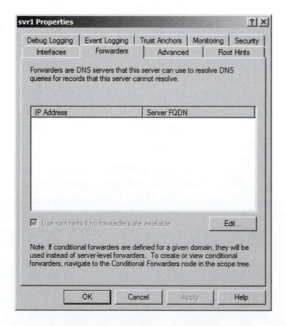

There are other situations in which you might want to use forwarders as well. For example, if a branch office has a slow link to the Internet, you might want to configure its local DNS server to use the DNS server at the home office as a forwarder. This would enable the home office server to use its faster Internet connection to perform the interim resolution steps, only returning the final resolved name to the branch office server over the slow link.

INTEGRATING AD DS DOMAINS INTO AN EXISTING DNS INFRASTRUCTURE

Earlier in this lesson, you learned about three options for integrating AD DS into an enterprise network with an existing DNS infrastructure. Whichever of the three domain-naming options you choose, you can continue to use your existing DNS servers in most cases, deploy Microsoft DNS servers instead, or maintain a combination.

In an enterprise with an existing DNS infrastructure to which you want to add AD DS, you are likely to have non-Microsoft DNS servers currently in service. The most common DNS server is the **Berkeley Internet Name Daemon (BIND)**, also known as named (pronounced name-dee), which is supplied with many UNIX and Linux distributions.

The only special requirement for a DNS server to function with AD DS is support for the Service (SRV) resource record, which enables client to use a DNS query to locate domain controllers on the network. The current version of BIND, version 9.x, supports the SRV record, as do most other DNS server implementations.

If you choose to create new domains or child domains for AD DS, whichever DNS server versions you elect to use, you can create forwarders to make sure that queries for AD DS resources are referred to the correct servers.

Using WINS

Before the introduction of Active Directory in Windows 2000, Windows used simple 15-character NetBIOS names to identify computers on the network. The NetBIOS namespace is flat, not hierarchical like that of DNS, and is designed only for use on private networks, not the Internet. To use these names with TCP/IP—a combination called NetBIOS over TCP/IP (NetBT)—a name-resolution service is needed, but DNS is not suitable for these types of names.

Windows can use a variety of NetBIOS name-resolution mechanisms, but the one most suited for the enterprise is the **Windows Internet Name System (WINS)**. WINS is a client/server application that registers NetBIOS names and IP addresses as computers connect to the network, and fulfills requests for the addresses associated with those names.

If you have computers on your network running versions of Windows earlier than Windows 2000, then they are reliant on NetBIOS names for identification, and you are probably running a WINS server to provide them with NetBIOS name-resolution services. WINS is more advanced than the original DNS service in that it registers computer names automatically and stores its information in a database rather than a text file.

If all the Windows computers on your network are running Windows 2000 or later with AD DS, the network is not using NetBIOS names, and you don't have to run WINS servers for NetBIOS name resolution. You can also disable the NetBIOS Over TCP/IP (NetBT) protocol on your computers by using the controls in the NetBIOS Setting box, which is located on the WINS tab in the Internet Protocol Version 4 (TCP/IPv4) Properties/Advanced TCP/IP Settings dialog box, as shown in Figure 1-20.

Figure 1-20

The WINS tab on the *Advanced TCP/IP Settings* dialog box

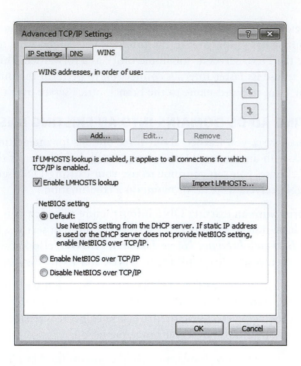

If you do have pre-Windows 2000 computers on your network, you are using NetBIOS names and NetBT, and while WINS is not essential, it provides more efficient name resolution than other methods.

CREATING A WINS REPLICATION STRATEGY

WINS is designed for use on large internetworks. You can run multiple WINS servers to provide fault tolerance and service thousands of clients. WINS servers can also communicate with one another to replicate their database information. This enables you to maintain a composite picture of your entire NetBIOS namespace on all of your WINS servers.

WINS servers can replicate their databases by pushing data to other servers, pulling data from them, or both. When you configure a WINS server as a push partner, the server sends messages to all its pull partners whenever the database changes. The pull partners then respond by requesting an update, and the push partner transmits any new database records. A WINS server that you configure as a pull partner issues requests to its push partners for database records with version numbers higher than the last record it received during the previous replication.

The basic difference between push and pull partnerships is that push partners trigger replication events when a specific number of database changes have occurred, while pull partners initiate replication according to a predetermined schedule. Therefore, push partnerships are preferable when the WINS servers are connected by a fast link and you don't mind if replication occurs at any time. Pull partnerships are preferable for servers connected by slower links, such as WAN connections, because you can schedule replication to occur during off hours, when traffic is low.

Because the records on any WINS server can change, it is important for each server to replicate its data to all the other servers. This way, every WINS server has a complete listing of the NetBIOS names on the network. For the replication process to function properly, you must configure each WINS server to be both a push and a pull partner, but the two partnerships don't necessarily have to be with the same server.

Obviously, if you have only two WINS servers on your network, they must be partners with each other. You configure each server to be a push/pull partner with the other in the WINS console. After creating the replication partner, you click the Advanced tab in that partner's Properties dialog box, shown in Figure 1-21. For the pull partnership, you specify when the pull replication should occur and the interval between pull replications. For the push partnership, you specify the number of updates to the WINS database that must occur before the next replication event.

Figure 1-21

The Advanced tab in a WINS
replication partner's *Properties*
dialog box

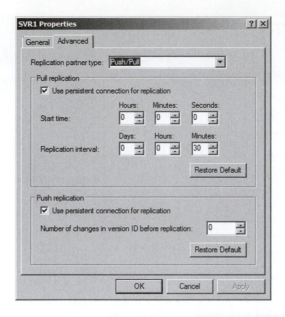

When you have more than two WINS servers on your network, you have greater flexibility
in designing a replication topology. When all the WINS servers are connected by fast links,
one common solution is to configure them in the form of a ring, with each server acting as
the push partner to its downstream neighbor and the pull partner to its upstream neighbor, as
shown in Figure 1-22. To configure the replication for this topology, you create two partnerships on each WINS server, making one a push partner and one a pull partner.

Figure 1-22

A WINS ring replication
topology

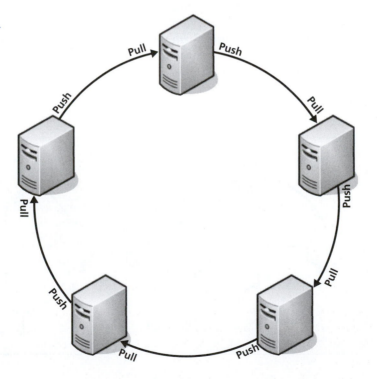

One problem with a ring topology is that a failure of any one connection between two WINS
servers prevents all the servers from being updated properly. To address this problem, you can
create redundant partnerships traveling in the other direction, to form a double ring topology,
as shown in Figure 1-23. The only additional cost is the amount of network traffic generated
by the replication process.

Figure 1-23

A WINS double ring replication topology

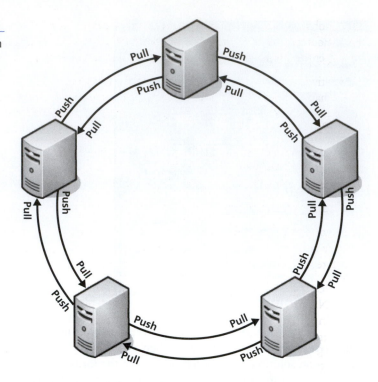

If your network consists of multiple sites connected by WAN links, you probably want to minimize the WINS replication traffic passing over those links. The strategy for this is to create only a single push/pull partnership over each link, with replication scheduled to occur during low-traffic hours. For example, in Figure 1-24, the WINS servers at each site all replicate among themselves, using high-speed LAN connections for push partnerships in a mesh replication topology. The administrator then chooses one server at each site to act as a pull partner to a server at the other site. This way, only the two pull connections use the WAN link, instead of two or more, and the administrator can configure the replication to occur during low-traffic hours.

Figure 1-24

Minimizing WINS traffic over WAN links

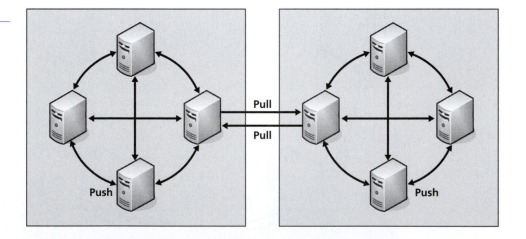

REPLACING WINS WITH THE DNS GLOBALNAMES ZONE

WINS is a technology that is all but obsolete, and it is entirely possible that Microsoft will choose to drop it from future versions of Windows. Fortunately, Windows Server 2008 and Windows Server 2008 R2 include a new DNS feature called the *GlobalNames zone*, which can resolve single-label names like those used in the NetBIOS namespace.

The GlobalNames zone is not a complete replacement for WINS. It does not support the dynamic registration of names, as WINS does, nor is it intended to provide name resolution for the entire NetBIOS namespace, just for selected servers.

For relatively small enterprise networks, DNS is capable of resolving single-label names by applying domain suffixes to them until it finds the domain in which the name is located. However, in large enterprises with many domain names, or with multiple forests, maintaining the list of domain suffixes can be a problem. The GlobalNames zone provides a more scalable solution.

Before you can create a GlobalNames zone, all the DNS servers on your network must be running Windows Server 2008 or later, and you must enable GlobalNames support by running the following command from an elevated command prompt on each DNS server:

```
dnscmd <server_name> /config /enablesglobalnamessupport 1
```

Once you have done this, you can use the DNS Manager console to create a forward-lookup primary zone called GlobalNames. Configure the zone to be stored in Active Directory and set the replication scope to all DNS servers running on domain controllers in the forest.

After creating the GlobalNames zone, you can begin to create resource records in it. GlobalNames does not support dynamic updates. You must create CNAME records manually, specifying the single-label equivalent for the desired server's DNS name, using the interface shown in Figure 1-25. If you have multiple forests in your enterprise network, you must also create SRV records in the _msdcs zone of each other forest, pointing to the domain controller/DNS servers hosting the GlobalNames zone.

Figure 1-25

The *New CNAME Resource Record* dialog box

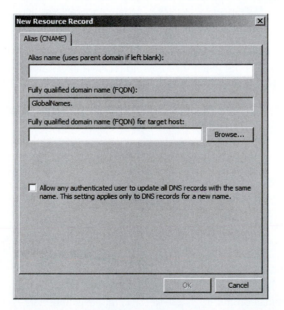

SKILL SUMMARY

IN THIS LESSON YOU LEARNED:

- The IPv4 address space consists of 32-bit addresses, notated as four 8-bit decimal values from 0 to 255, separated by periods, as in the example 192.168.43.100. This is known as dotted decimal notation, and the individual 8-bit decimal values are called octets, bytes, or quads.

- Because the subnet mask associated with IP addresses can vary, so can the number of bits used to identify the network and the host. The original Internet Protocol (IP) standard defines three address classes for assignment to networks, which support different numbers of networks and hosts.

- Because of its wastefulness, classful addressing was gradually made obsolete by a series of subnetting methods, including variable-length subnet masking (VLSM) and eventually Classless Inter-Domain Routing (CIDR). CIDR is a subnetting method that enables administrators to place the division between the network bits and the host bits anywhere in the address, not just between octets.

- In IPv6, a global unicast address is the equivalent of a registered IPv4 address, routable worldwide and unique on the Internet.

- In IPv6, systems that assign themselves an address automatically create a link-local unicast address, which is essentially the equivalent of an Automatic Private IP Addressing (APIPA) address in IPv4.

- Unique local unicast addresses are the IPv6 equivalent of the 10.0.0.0/8, 172.16.0.0/12, and 192.168.0.0/16 private network addresses in IPv4.

- The function of an anycast address is to identify the routers within a given address scope and send traffic to the nearest router, as determined by the local routing protocols.

- When a Windows computer starts, it initiates the stateless address autoconfiguration process, during which it assigns each interface a link-local unicast address.

- The simplest and most obvious method for transitioning from IPv4 to IPv6 is to run both, and this is what all current versions of Windows do.

- The primary method for transmitting IPv6 traffic over an IPv4 network is called tunneling. Tunneling is the process by which a system encapsulates an IPv6 datagram within an IPv4 packet.

- A domain-naming strategy for an enterprise is a set of rules that administrators at any level can apply both when they have to create a new name and when they are attempting to locate a particular resource.

- DNS servers traditionally store their resource records in text files. This is the method that Microsoft DNS Server uses when you create a primary or secondary zone. To create multiple copies of a zone, you first create a primary zone, and then one or more secondary zones. Then you configure zone transfers to occur on a regular schedule. A zone transfer simply copies the records from the primary zone to a secondary zone.

- In an enterprise with an existing DNS infrastructure to which you want to add AD DS, you are likely to have non-Microsoft DNS servers currently in service. The most common DNS server is the Berkeley Internet Name Daemon (BIND), also known as named, which is supplied with many UNIX and Linux distributions.

- Windows can use a variety of NetBIOS name-resolution mechanisms, but the one most suited for the enterprise is the Windows Internet Name System (WINS). WINS is a client/server application that registers NetBIOS names and IP addresses as computers connect to the network, and fulfills requests for the addresses associated with those names.

■ Knowledge Assessment

Fill in the Blank

Complete the following sentences by writing the correct word or words in the blanks provided.

1. For a computer to be accessible from the Internet, it must have an IP address that is both _____ and _____.

2. A _____ is the process by which one DNS server sends a name-resolution request to another DNS server.

3. The _____ manages IANA, the ultimate source for all registered addresses.

4. IANA allocate blocks of addresses to _____, which allocate smaller blocks in turn to Internet service providers (ISPs).

5. Windows Server 2008 and Windows Server 2008 R2 include a new DNS feature called the _____, which can resolve single-label names like those used in the NetBIOS namespace.

6. A DNS server can function as a _____, which simply provides name-resolution services to clients on the network.

7. Windows can use a variety of NetBIOS name-resolution mechanisms, but the one most suited for the enterprise is the _____.

8. _____ is an automatic tunneling protocol used by Windows workstation operating systems that are located behind NAT routers.

9. A special type of DNS server specifically intended to send recursive queries to another server is called a _____.

10. The primary method for transmitting IPv6 traffic over an IPv4 network is called _____.

True / False

Circle T if the statement is true or F if the statement is false.

T | F 1. Windows Server 2003 and Windows XP both include support for IPv6, and install it by default.

T | F 2. Push partnerships are preferable for WINS servers connected by slower links, such as WAN connections, because you can schedule replication to occur during off hours, when traffic is low.

T | F 3. The IP standard included Class D, which was reserved for experimental use, and Class E, which was reserved for use as multicast identifiers.

T | F 4. Name resolution is the process of locating the IP address equivalent for a given name.

T | F 5. Zone transfers are not necessary when you configure a primary zone to be stored in Active Directory.

T | F 6. If you have computers running Windows versions prior to Windows 2000 on your network, then you must have a WINS server to provide NetBIOS name-resolution services.

T | F 7. The ISATAP tunneling protocol incorporates the workstation's IPv4 address into the interface ID field of an IPv6 address.

T | F 8. Classless Inter-Domain Routing (CIDR) is a subnetting method that enables administrators to place the division between the network bits and the host bits anywhere in the address, not just between octets.

T | F 9. In IPv6, link-local unicast addresses always begin with fd00 as the value of the first block.

T | F 10. Using the same domain name for internal and external networks is usually not recommended, because it can make it difficult for internal users to access external resources.

Review Questions

1. List the three blocks of IPv4 addresses allocated by the Internet Engineering Task Force for private network use.

2. In the DNS, describe the difference between a recursive query and an iterative query.

■ Case Scenarios

Scenario 1-1: Calculating IPv4 Subnets

The enterprise administrator has assigned Arthur the network address 172.16.85.0/25 for the branch office network that he is constructing. Arthur calculates that this gives him 126 (2^7) IP addresses, which is enough for his network, but he has determined that he needs six subnets with at least ten hosts on each one. How can Arthur subnet the address he has been given to satisfy his needs? What IP addresses and subnet masks will the computers on his branch office network use?

Scenario 1-2: Regulating DNS Traffic

Ralph is an enterprise administrator for Wingtip Toys, which has recently expanded its customer service division by adding 100 workstations. All of the workstations on the company network are configured to use a server on the perimeter network as their primary DNS server and a server on their ISP's network as a secondary. As a result of the expansion, Internet performance has slowed down perceptibly, and a Network Monitor trace indicates that there is a disproportionate amount of DNS traffic on the link between the perimeter network and the ISP's network. What are two ways that Ralph can reduce the amount of DNS traffic passing over the Internet connection?

Designing an Active Directory Hierarchy

OBJECTIVE DOMAIN MATRIX

TECHNOLOGY SKILL	OBJECTIVE DOMAIN	OBJECTIVE NUMBER
Creating a Forest and Domain Design	Design Active Directory forests and domains.	2.1
Designing an Active Directory Administrative Model	Design the Active Directory administrative model.	2.3

KEY TERMS

administrative autonomy
administrative isolation
data management
forest root domain

functional level
organizational forest model
perimeter network
resource forest model

restricted-access forest
   model
schema
service management

■ Creating a Forest and Domain Design

THE BOTTOM LINE

Creating Active Directory Domain Services (AD DS) objects, such as forests and domains, is easy. Windows Server 2008 R2 provides wizards that walk you through the process in a few simple steps. However, understanding why you should create a forest or domain is not so simple.

Every AD DS infrastructure starts with a single forest containing a single domain, as shown in Figure 2-1. There are a great many organizations—even very large ones—that this simple structure can service perfectly well.

CERTIFICATION READY
How do you design Active Directory forests and domains?
2.1

However, many administrators feel compelled to create additional domains or additional forests simply because they can. A competent enterprise administrator is an individual who, when designing an Active Directory hierarchy, adds domains and forests only when the organization's requirements call for them.

Designing an AD DS hierarchy is a high-level process that is concerned with business and management issues as much as it is with technical ones. The enterprise administrator must know what Active Directory can do and also what the organization needs it to do. The design process is a matter of finding a common ground between those AD DS capabilities and the organization's requirements.

The first part of the design process consists of gathering information about the infrastructure of the organization and the existing technical resources. Then the enterprise administrator creates a

Figure 2-1

The simplest Active Directory hierarchy

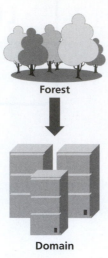

design for a forest structure and, within each forest, a domain structure. Finally, the administrator considers any modifications that might be necessary to satisfy the organization's requirements.

Using Microsoft Operations Framework

Depending on the size and nature of the organization, designing an Active Directory hierarchy can be an extremely large and complex project. To organize and define projects of this type, Microsoft has created a collection of documents called the Microsoft Operations Framework (MOF).

Now in version 4.0, the MOF defines the entire lifecycle of an IT service, such as Active Directory, by splitting it into three distinct phases, as follows:

- Plan—An agreement between IT and management on a set of business requirements to be provided by the service, a mechanism to monitor the service's reliability, and a budget to support the service.
- Deliver—The actual planning, testing, and deployment of the service.
- Operate—Procedures for the operation, support, and eventual retirement of the service.

The three phases of the project are all supervised by a Manage layer.

The MOF does not contain instructions for specific project types; instead, it is an organization and planning tool that consists of a series of white papers called service management functions (SMFs). SMFs define processes for specific elements of each phase and management reviews that are to occur at specific milestones.

TAKE NOTE*

The Microsoft Operations Framework 4.0 package is available free of charge from the Microsoft Download Center at http://www.microsoft.com/downloads/details .aspx?FamilyId=457ED61D-27B8-49D1-BACA-B175E8F54C0C.

Gathering Information

Before you can actually begin to design the forest and domain structure for your enterprise network, you must assemble a body of information about the organization that AD DS will service and about the infrastructure on which you will build.

The information-gathering process falls into two categories: business and technical. In both cases, there are certain types of information that a well-run organization should have readily available, and there is other information that you might have to discover yourself or wheedle out of colleagues who may or may not be cooperative.

ASCERTAINING THE ROLE OF AD DS

Arguably the most important question you have to answer is what role the AD DS database will play in your organization. More specifically, what kind of information will be stored in the AD DS database?

In your server administrator training, you learned about the default network operating system (NOS) functions of Active Directory. AD DS is a directory service. In its basic form, it is essentially the digital equivalent of a telephone book. The AD DS database contains information about users, computers, printers, and services that enables users to access those resources and administrators to control access to them.

Some enterprises limit their use of AD DS to these basic NOS functions. However, as a directory service, AD DS is almost infinitely expandable, capable of storing a great deal more information about its existing objects, and of supporting additional object types as well.

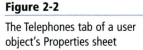

Despite its apparent complexity in large enterprise installations, AD DS is still just a database that has two basic elements: objects and attributes. Network or company resources are represented in AD DS by objects. Objects can represent physical resources, such as users and computers, or virtual ones, such as domains and groups. Each object, whatever it represents, is just a collection of attributes. A user object has as its attributes various types of information about the user, such as names and addresses. A group object has as its attributes a list of its members. The structure of an AD DS database—that is, the types of objects it can contain and the attributes allowed for each object type—is dictated by the Active Directory schema. Administrators can modify the schema to create new object types or new attributes for existing objects. This is what gives AD DS almost unlimited scalability.

By consulting with management, you and your organization may decide to use AD DS as a full-fledged enterprise directory. An enterprise directory is a repository for more extensive information about an organization's resources that users consult on a daily basis.

The default AD DS schema defines a variety of informational attributes for user objects, including telephone numbers, as shown in Figure 2-2.

Figure 2-2

The Telephones tab of a user object's Properties sheet

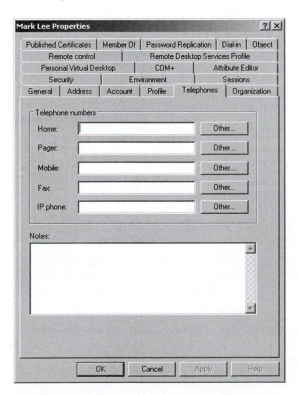

These attributes do not serve any NOS function; they are a means for storing enterprise directory information. When administrators keep these fields updated, users can search for staff telephone numbers using AD DS as a "white-pages" directory, replacing whatever other telephone directory list or application the organization would otherwise use.

The potential for AD DS as an enterprise directory goes far beyond simple white-pages information, however. By altering the directory schema, an organization can use AD DS to store all kinds of information about its resources. For example, user objects can include employee records and payroll information. Computer and printer objects can include maintenance records and technical support contacts.

Another potential use for AD DS is as an external directory that stores customer data, including contact information and order histories.

Using AD DS as an enterprise or external directory can present the enterprise administrator with factors that complicate the AD DS design process. Security is the most obvious factor, because, by default, all domain users have read access to the entire AD DS database. If that database contains confidential user information, such as payroll data, or customer information that must be protected by law, then the administrator must include security considerations in the AD DS design.

While it might at first seem that these security considerations are a matter of modifying permission assignments to specific object attributes—a process that occurs much later in the AD DS deployment—many administrators find it easier to create a separate forest for the storage of confidential information. In addition, because of certain legal statutes, such as the Health Insurance Portability and Accountability Act (HIPAA), it may be necessary to create a separate storehouse for external data, such as customer or client information. These factors require consideration at the very beginning of the AD DS design process, when you are deciding how many forests to create.

DIAGRAMMING THE CURRENT INFRASTRUCTURE

Enterprise AD DS deployments are not usually created out of nothing. There might be an existing AD DS infrastructure in place, but even if there is not, there is nearly always some existing business and technical infrastructure you must consider in your design.

Before you can begin designing your forests and domain, you must collect the following information:

- Organizational infrastructure—The political divisions of your organization, including companies, divisions, and departments.
- Geographical infrastructure—The locations of the organization's various elements, on both large and small scale, including continents, countries, states, and counties or cities.
- Network infrastructure—The network facilities at each of the organization's locations, including all of the links between them and their speeds.

All three of these elements can take the form of a diagram. In most large organizations, these should already exist. If not, management should most likely be responsible for creating the first two and IT the last.

In addition to these three elements, you should also consider other IT-related infrastructures that might already exist within the organization, including the following:

- IT administration—The current IT administration paradigm is likely to be the model for future AD DS designs. For example, if each of the organization's offices maintains its own autonomous IT staff, you might have to establish barriers between the offices as they are represented in the new AD DS hierarchy.
- IP addressing—What IP versions do your network devices support and what progress has been made in the transition to IPv6? How is the enterprise network subnetted and what addresses are they using?

- Name resolution—What DNS names is the organization currently using for its domains and hosts, and what is the policy for creating those names? What DNS server software is the network using and how are the zones and zone replication configured?
- Active Directory—How many forests and domains does the current AD DS hierarchy have? What trusts are there among the forests? What are the current forest and domain functional levels? How many domain controllers and global catalog servers are there?

DETERMINING BUSINESS REQUIREMENTS

As a business decision, implementing or extending an Active Directory infrastructure must yield some palpable benefits to the organization—benefits beyond the satisfaction and convenience of the IT staff. Any type of service deployment in a large organization is liable to be expensive—in terms of time, manpower, and lost productivity—and those expenses must be justified.

As a result, there will usually be a list of business requirements that the project must meet before management approves it. These requirements obviously can vary widely, but might include elements like the following:

- Functional requirements—Stipulations of services that the project will be able to provide, capabilities that the project will enhance, or problems that the project will solve.
- Legal stipulations—Compliance with specific codes governing areas such as information storage and data confidentiality. For international organizations, there may be different legal requirement for different countries.
- Service level agreements—Stipulations that the service, when complete, will meet specified levels of performance and availability.
- Security requirements—Specifications for system, data, network, and application security.
- Project constraints—Agreements that the project will be completed according to a specified schedule and budget.

Designing a Forest Structure

The first question in Active Directory design is whether to use one forest or multiple forests. The main reason why this question comes first is that it is difficult to split one forest into two or join two forests into one. Therefore, it is best to consider the possible reasons for creating multiple forests at the beginning of the design process.

Active Directory forests are designed to keep things separated, things like directory information and administrative permissions. Within a single forest, the default behavior is to share information unless an administrator expressly prohibits that sharing.

If your organization consists mostly of individuals, departments, and divisions that are accustomed to working together in a cooperative and trustworthy manner, then they can very likely coexist within a single forest. If, on the other hand, elements of your organization's business model typically operate independently and have different business requirements, then multiple forests might be the better choice.

To create the simplest possible example, consider an organization that consists of two separate companies. Perhaps they were independent companies that have now merged. The companies have different names, separate facilities, separate computer networks, separate IT staffs, and separate management infrastructures, except for the executives at the very top of the corporate tree.

In a case like this, creating two separate forests makes sense. This is because, if you used one forest, the AD DS administrators would probably spend more time erecting barriers between the companies than they would creating connections between them if there were two forests. Forests are separated by nature. The only changes needed in this situation are a few connections between the two forests at the top of the hierarchy.

The converse example is also true. If you have two companies that share many of the same resources, such as one IT staff and one computer network, erecting the necessary barriers in a single forest would be easier than creating many connections between two separate forests.

SHARED FOREST ELEMENTS

To fully understand the circumstances under which it is preferable to create multiple forests, it is necessary to comprehend the differences between them. A single forest shares each of the following elements:

- Global catalog—A forest has a single global catalog that enables computers and users to locate objects in any domain in the forest.
- Configuration directory partition—All of the domain controllers in a forest share a single partition in which AD DS stores configuration data for AD-enabled applications.
- Trust relationships—All of the domains in a forest are connected by two-way transitive trust relationships, enabling users and computers in one domain to access resources in other domains.
- Schema—The domains in a forest all share a single schema. If modifications to the schema are required by one business element, they affect all of the other elements in the forest.
- Trustworthy administrators—Any individual with the permissions needed to administer an AD DS domain controller can make changes that affect the entire forest. Therefore, a certain level of trustworthiness is necessary for all administrators in a forest.

If your business requirements call for any of these elements to be separated for part of your network, then additional forests might be in order.

WHY CREATE MULTIPLE FORESTS?

As a general rule of Active Directory design, enterprise administrators should stick to one forest, unless they have an explicit reason to create more. Some of the most common reasons are described in the following sections.

PERIMETER NETWORKS

Many organizations create separate networks—called *perimeter networks*—for their Internet servers, such as those hosting Web sites and email services. Because these servers are accessible from the Internet, they are isolated from the internal network by a firewall and are usually not part of the internal AD DS hierarchy.

However, administrators sometimes find that the services provided by AD DS are too useful to forego on these servers, so they create a separate forest for the perimeter network, isolated from the internal network.

INCOMPATIBLE SCHEMA

AD-enabled applications often make changes to the schema, adding their own objects and attributes. If administrators must deploy two such applications for different pools of users, and the schema modifications those applications make are not compatible with each other, then the only solution is to deploy the applications in separate forests.

TRUST RELATIONSHIPS

As mentioned earlier, all of the domains in a forest have two-way transitive trusts to the other domains. It is not possible to break these trusts. If, for any reason, administrators must restrict the inter-domain access and collaboration that these trusts provide, the only way to do so is to create separate forests.

INFORMATION PROTECTION

In some cases, legal or contractual requirements force administrators to keep information generated by a particular business unit completely separate from that from other business units. The only way to do this is by creating separate forests.

ADMINISTRATIVE ISOLATION

In Active Directory, it is important to distinguish between two conditions of administrative separation. *Administrative autonomy* is when an individual is granted complete administrative control over some part of a forest—an organizational unit (OU), a domain, or the entire forest. However, that individual does not have exclusive control over that element. There are still enterprise administrators who also have control and can rescind the individual autonomy.

By contrast, *administrative isolation* is when an individual has complete and exclusive control over some part of a forest. No one can rescind the individual's control, and no one else can exercise control unless the individual grants them permission.

It is possible to grant someone administrative autonomy within a forest, but the only way to provide administrative isolation is to create a separate forest.

TAKE NOTE ✻   There is almost never sufficient technical reason to create multiple forests. A single forest can have multiple domains, with each domain containing hundreds of thousands of objects, so it is unlikely that any enterprise network in existence is too big for a single forest.

CHOOSING A FOREST MODEL

Once you have decided to create multiple forests, there are several models you can use to separate the enterprise resources, as described in the following sections.

ORGANIZATIONAL FOREST MODEL

In the *organizational forest model*, the divisions between the forests are based on organizational or political divisions within the enterprise. Administrators frequently use this model when an enterprise consists of distinctly separate business units, due to acquisitions, mergers, or geographical separation.

For example, Figure 2-3 depicts an enterprise network with three forests representing isolated divisions on three continents. Trusts among the forests in this model are optional, but by creating them, administrators and users can still gain access to resources throughout the enterprise.

Figure 2-3

The organizational forest model

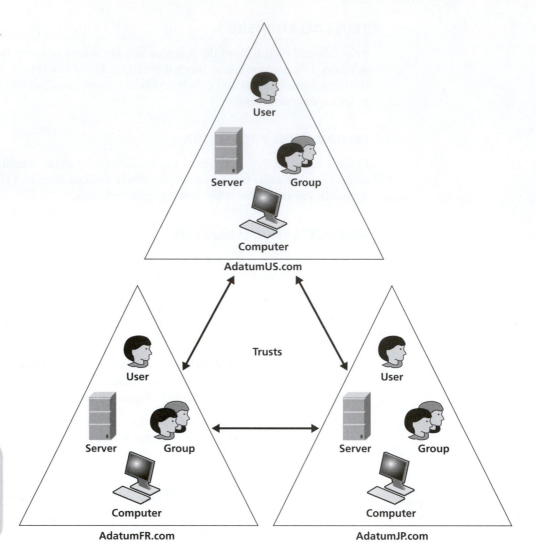

AdatumUS.com

AdatumFR.com

AdatumJP.com

TAKE NOTE＊

An enterprise that consists of a single forest is still considered to be using the organizational forest model.

RESOURCE FOREST MODEL

In the *resource forest model*, as shown in Figure 2-4, administrators create one or more forests containing users and group objects, and one or more separate forests containing the resources that the users and groups will access, such as servers and applications. By separating the users from the resources, it is possible to give each administrative isolation.

Figure 2-4

The resource forest model

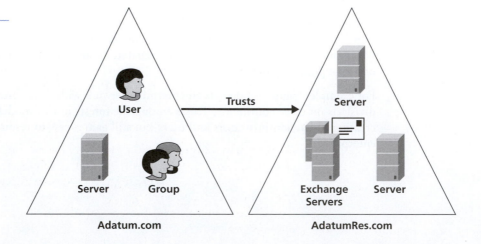

Adatum.com

AdatumRes.com

For this model to function, administrators must create trust relationships between the forests. The most common arrangement is to create one-way trusts running from the forests containing the users to the forests containing the resources. The trusts can be one-way because the users must access the resources, but the resources don't have to access the users.

RESTRICTED-ACCESS FOREST MODEL

The *restricted-access forest model* is intended for an enterprise with a business unit that must remain completely isolated from the rest of the network. This forest arrangement is like the organizational forest model, except that there are no trust relationships among the forests, as shown in Figure 2-5.

Figure 2-5

The restricted-access forest model

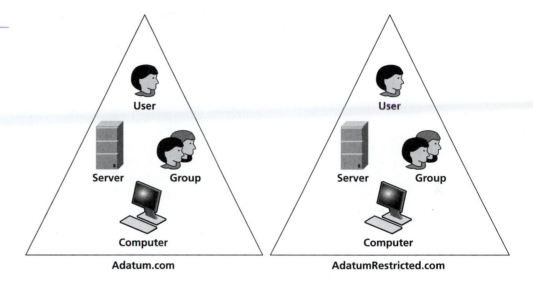

This means that for users to access resources in both forests, they must have a separate user account in each one and separate workstations joined to each forest.

Designing a Domain Structure

Once you have determined how many forests you will create in your enterprise, the next step is to move down one level in the AD DS hierarchy and populate each forest with one or more domains. The question here is the same one you asked about forests: should you create multiple domains in each forest or is one sufficient?

The default configuration is to have one domain per forest, and as before, you should only create multiple domains if you have specific reasons for doing so. A single AD DS domain can support over a million objects, so the sheer size of your network is not sufficient reason for creating multiple domains.

The most common reasons for creating more than one domain in a forest are as follows:

- Security—Certain key security policies, such as password and account lockout policies, are domain-level settings. While it is ultimately possible to create fine-grained password policies for individual groups within a domain, the administrative effort involved when you have many groups with different security requirements can be excessive. Creating separate domains enables administrators to create separate security policy settings.

- Administration—Domains do not provide administrative isolation as forests do, but they can provide administrative autonomy. However, organizational units (OUs) can provide administrative autonomy as well, so enforcing administrative boundaries need not be the sole reason to create multiple domains. Many administrators do use multiple domains for this purpose, though.

- Namespaces—Sometimes the different business units in a single enterprise must maintain different namespaces, for branding purposes or because mergers and acquisitions have brought businesses together. Different domains in a single forest can maintain different namespaces without affecting their inter-domain access.

- Replication—All of the domain controllers in a domain replicate the domain directory partition and the contents of the SYSVOL folder among themselves, which can generate a lot of network traffic. By comparison, replication traffic between domains is relatively light. When parts of a network are connected by relatively slow wide-area network (WAN) links, or when relatively little bandwidth is available between sites, creating separate domains can be preferable.

TAKE NOTE*

Planning for AD DS replication traffic is not just a matter of comparing the speeds of the WAN links connecting the organization's sites. Administrators must also consider the bandwidth available on those links. Two sites might have a high-speed link connecting them, but if that link is already saturated with traffic, adding more by creating an AD DS domain that encompasses both sites can degrade performance in other areas. Conversely, a relatively slow link that is underused may be able to support the addition of domain-replication traffic. Network traffic conditions tend to change over time, so a major AD DS deployment project should always include a reassessment of the traffic levels on all of the enterprise's WAN links.

Enterprise administrators should consider also some of the disadvantages of creating multiple domains, including the following:

- Group Policy—Group Policy application is limited by domain boundaries. Therefore you must create separate Group Policy objects for each domain.

- Moving objects—It is much easier to move objects between OUs than between domains. If your organization tends to reorganize frequently, this might be a factor worthy of consideration.

- Domain controllers—Each domain you create should have at least two domain controllers, for fault-tolerance purposes. An enterprise network with multiple domains will therefore most likely require more servers than a single domain.

- Administration policies—Even when domains are autonomous, there will always be enterprise administration policies to be disseminated, implemented, and enforced.

- Access control—For users that require access to resources in other domains, administrators must assign permission across domain boundaries and rely on inter-domain trusts for reliable access.

- Global catalog—With multiple domains, administrators must be conscious of which domain controllers they designate as global catalog servers, so that users throughout the enterprise have adequate access to the catalog.

CREATING A FOREST ROOT DOMAIN

When you create a new forest and assign it a name, that name becomes the name of the first domain in the forest, called the *forest root domain*. The forest root domain performs critical forest-level functions that make it vital to the operation of the other domains in the forest, including the following:

- Forest-level administration groups—The forest root domain contains the Enterprise Admins and Schema Admins groups, membership in which should be limited to only the most trustworthy administrators.
- Forest-level operations masters—The forest root domain contains the domain controllers that function as the domain-naming master and the schema master. These roles are vital to the creation of new domains and the modification of the schema for the forest.
- Inter-domain authentication and authorization—Users throughout the enterprise must have access to the forest root domain when they log on to other domains and when they access resources in other domains.

The first step in designing a domain structure for a forest is deciding whether to use the forest root domain as part of the domain hierarchy or to create a dedicated root domain. A dedicated root domain is a forest root domain that performs only critical forest-level functions; it contains no users or resources other than those needed to manage the forest. When you create your domain hierarchy, you build it off the dedicated root domain, as shown in Figure 2-6.

Figure 2-6

A forest with a dedicated root domain

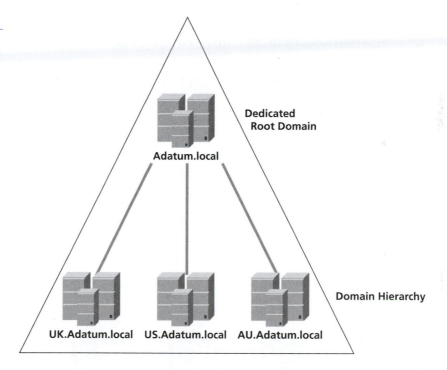

There are a number of benefits to creating a dedicated root domain, including the following:

- Forest-level group security—Creating a dedicated root domain can minimize the number of users in the Enterprise Admins and Schema Admins groups and prevent Domain Admins members from modifying those group memberships.
- Simplified replication—A dedicated root domain contains very few objects and therefore generates little replication traffic. It is therefore easy to scatter domain controllers around the enterprise without overburdening WAN links.
- Easy backup—The small size of the domain database makes it fast and simple to back up and restore.

CREATING A DOMAIN HIERARCHY

Once you have made the decision to create multiple domains within an AD DS forest, the question remains of what divisions to use as the model for the domain hierarchy. The most common models that enterprise administrators use to create multiple domains are as follows:

- Geographical divisions—Divisions across geographical lines, such as countries, cities, or even buildings on a campus, are typically the result of the need to limit AD DS replication traffic on WAN links between sites.

- Business unit divisions—Divisions based on company or departmental lines are usually the result of the desire for administrative autonomy in specific areas of the enterprise, or the need to maintain separate namespaces. In some cases, business unit divisions are combined with geographical divisions.

- Account and resource divisions—Creating separate domains for user accounts and shared resources was a common practice in Windows NT 4.0, and some administrators still adhere to it. However, in AD DS, the ability to delegate administrative autonomy to individual OUs and the virtually unlimited scalability of a domain eliminates the need for this practice.

When creating domains within a forest, you can create one domain tree in which all of the domains share the same namespace, or different trees. The geographical domain model typically uses a single tree, with each domain forming a branch off a second-layer domain name. For domains created along business unit divisions, however, it is more common for administrators to create multiple trees with separate namespaces, as shown in Figure 2-7.

Figure 2-7

A forest with multiple domain trees

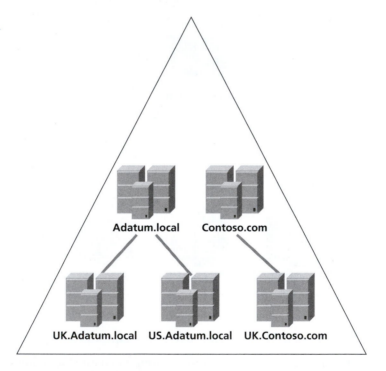

Functionally, the question of whether to use one domain tree or multiple trees has little bearing on the operation of a forest. The trust relationships that AD DS automatically creates between domains in the same forest enable users in any domain to log on to any other domain and access its resources, regardless of whether they are in the same tree or not.

However, in a large forest with multiple trees and multiple domain levels in each tree, the default trust relationships can conceivably result in performance delays.

By default, every parent domain in a tree has a trust relationship with its child domains. In addition, the root domain of every tree has a trust relationship with the root domains of the other trees. Therefore, in a large complex forest, the network of trust relationships can look like the diagram on Figure 2-8.

Figure 2-8

Trust relationships in a forest with multiple domain trees

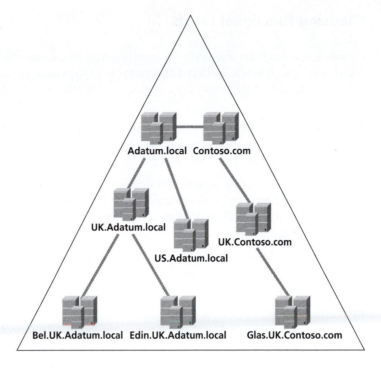

The potential problem with this arrangement occurs when a user from a domain at the bottom of a tree attempts to log on to a domain at the bottom of another tree, as in the figure if an Edinburgh user in the Edin.UK.Adatum.local domain tries to access a server in the Glasgow domain of the company's other division (Glas.UK.Contoso.com). Access is possible, but the logon request must be referred all the way up one tree to its root, over to the root of the other tree, and then down through the levels to the desired domain. This can be a lengthy process. To improve the situation, administrators can create shortcut trusts between domains at the lower levels of the trees, as shown in Figure 2-9.

Figure 2-9

Shortcut trusts in a forest with multiple domain trees

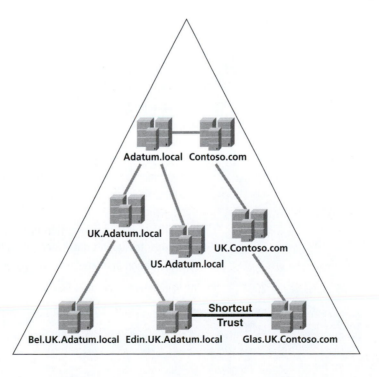

Choosing Functional Levels

Functional levels are essentially a version-control mechanism for Active Directory forests and domains. When you select a functional level for a domain or a forest, you activate features that Microsoft introduced in successive versions of Windows Server.

Active Directory Domain Services, in all but the smallest installations, requires multiple servers to function as domain controllers. In a large enterprise installation, there can be dozens of domain controllers.

The domain controllers in a particular domain can run different versions of Windows Server, because it would be utterly impractical to have it any other way. An organization can hardly be expected to upgrade all its domain controllers at the same time, leaving the entire network idle until the upgrades are complete.

However, the problem with having domain controllers running different Windows Server versions is that the older domain controllers do not support the newer AD DS features Microsoft introduced in later versions of Windows. This is where the concept of functional levels comes in.

By raising the functional level of a domain or a forest, you enable certain new AD DS features. To raise a functional level, all of the domain controllers involved must be running a certain Windows Server version or later.

For example, to raise a forest to the Windows Server 2003 forest functional level, all of the domain controllers in the forest must be running at least Windows Server 2003. Thus, the functional level available for a particular forest or domain is equivalent to the oldest Windows Server version running on one of its domain controllers.

The Active Directory features provided by each of the forest functional levels are listed in Table 2-1.

Table 2-1

Forest Functional Level Features

FOREST FUNCTIONAL LEVEL	FEATURES
Windows 2000	All default Active Directory features
Windows Server 2003	All default Active Directory features plus the following: • Forest trusts • Domain renaming • Linked value replication • Read-only domain controllers running Windows Server 2008 • Improved Knowledge Consistency Checker (KCC) algorithms and scalability • Ability to create dynamic auxiliary class instances called *dynamicObjects* in a domain directory partition • Ability to convert an *inetOrgPerson* object instance into a *User* object instance • Ability to create application basic groups and LDAP query groups, to support role-based authorization • Deactivation and redefinition of schema attributes and classes
Windows Server 2008	All Windows Server 2003 features
Windows Server 2008 R2	All Windows Server 2008 features plus the following: • Active Directory Recycle Bin

The Active Directory features provided by each of the domain functional levels are listed in Table 2-2.

Table 2-2

Domain Functional Level Features

DOMAIN FUNCTIONAL LEVEL	FEATURES
Windows 2000 Native	All default Active Directory features plus the following: • Universal groups • Group nesting • Group conversion • Security identifier (SID) history
Windows Server 2003	All Windows 2000 Native features plus the following: • Domain renaming • Updated logon timestamp • The *userPassword* attribute on the *inetOrgPerson* object and *User* objects • Redirectable Users and Computers containers • Storage of Authorization Manager policies • Constrained delegation, allowing Kerberos authentication for applications • Selective authentication for users accessing resources in a trusting forest
Windows Server 2008	All Windows Server 2003 features plus the following: • Support for SYSVOL in Distributed File System Replication • Advanced Encryption Services for Kerberos • Information about the last interactive logon • Fine-grained password policies
Windows Server 2008 R2	All Windows Server 2008 features plus the following: • Authentication assurance

When you create a new domain controller, the Active Directory Domain Services Installation Wizard provides the opportunity to set the forest and domain functional levels, as shown in Figure 2-10.

Figure 2-10

The *Set Forest Functional Level* page of the Active Directory Domain Services Installation Wizard

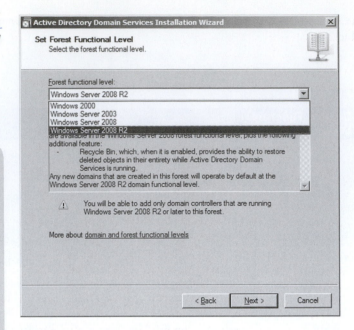

Raising the functional level of a forest or a domain is one of the few tasks in Windows that is irreversible. Once raised, you cannot lower the functional level back to its original state, except by deleting the forest or domain and recreating it. For this reason, enterprise administrators are typically involved in the selection of functional levels, if not the actual elevation process itself.

When you create a new forest, the wizard uses Windows Server 2003 as the default forest and domain functional levels. When you add a domain to an existing forest, or a domain controller to an existing domain, the defaults depend on the current functional levels.

To raise the functional level of a forest or a domain at a later time, you use the Active Directory Domains and Trusts console, as shown in Figure 2-11.

Figure 2-11

The Active Directory Domains and Trusts console

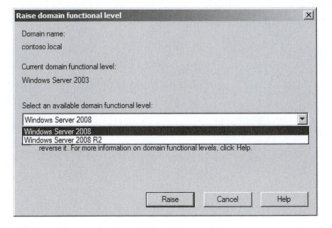

Managing the Schema

> The Active Directory *schema*, as noted earlier in this lesson, specifies the types of objects you can create and the attributes available for each object type. Because schema modifications are permanent and affect entire forests, they typically fall under the purview of the enterprise administrator.

⚠ **WARNING** Schema modifications are one-way processes, and permanent. Once you have modified the AD DS schema, you cannot reverse the modifications, except by restoring the entire schema from a backup.

The main issues for the enterprise administrator regarding schemas are not how to make the changes but what changes to make and whether it is worthwhile to make them. An enterprise should have a specific protocol in place for evaluating and testing schema modifications

before anyone deploys them in a production environment, and the enterprise administrator is the likely candidate to develop that protocol.

EVALUATING SCHEMA MODIFICATIONS

When faced with the prospect of a schema modification, the first question to consider is whether the application requiring the changes is worth deploying. An application that benefits only a few users, provides limited utility, or is needed for only a short time might not merit making a permanent change to the schema for an entire forest.

On the other hand, an application that benefits everyone would be a viable candidate. As an example, Microsoft Exchange is one of the most commonly used applications that requires schema modifications because everyone uses it.

TESTING SCHEMA MODIFICATIONS

Once you have decided that an application is worth modifying the schema, the next step is testing those modifications. Because of the permanence of the schema changes, testing is essential, in both a lab environment and a limited production environment.

For lab testing, you need an environment in which you can adequately test the new objects and attributes that the schema modifications create. You must also be able to test the normal AD DS functions, including creation and modification of the default objects and attributes, and replication of AD DS information between domain controllers. Your lab network, therefore, should consist of an isolated network with its own AD DS forest and at least two domain controllers.

If the lab testing process proceeds without incident, then you can begin testing in a production environment. To limit the potential damage caused by any problems with the schema modifications, you should locate the domain controller on your network that is functioning as the schema master operations master, disable outgoing AD DS replication, and modify the schema there.

You should then repeat the testing procedure you performed in the lab. Only when you are satisfied with the results should you re-enable replication. If a problem arises due to the schema modification, you will have to replace that domain controller on the network because there is no way to reverse the schema modifications you made.

■ Designing an Active Directory Administrative Model

THE BOTTOM LINE

Enterprise administrators do not reset user passwords. They do not create user accounts. They usually do not even create domains or install domain controllers. It is the enterprise administrator's job to create a model for the delegation of tasks like these to other administrators, technicians, and trustworthy users, all over the enterprise.

CERTIFICATION READY
How do you design an Active Directory administrative model?
2.3

By creating an administrative model, enterprise administrators decide who will be responsible for the various tasks involved in creating and maintaining the Active Directory infrastructure. By delegating these tasks, enterprise administrators pass certain elements of their responsibility down to their subordinates. This increases the efficiency of the administrative effort while reducing the overall cost.

While an enterprise administrator is theoretically capable of handling any administrative task in the enterprise, it is inherently more efficient to make local administrators responsible for their own regions. It is also more economically feasible to have junior administrators—with correspondingly lower salaries—perform simpler and more mundane tasks.

In addition to designating who will be responsible for certain tasks, the administrative model also specifies how those individuals will receive the rights and permissions they need to perform those tasks. This aspect of delegation is one of the most critical, because to maintain a secure environment, it is necessary to make sure that individuals have the administrative capabilities they need to perform certain tasks, and little or none more than that. You do not want to grant a junior administrator complete control over a domain so that he can reset user passwords.

Understanding Administrative Tasks

Before you can construct a model for the delegation of Active Directory administrative tasks, you must be conscious of what tasks are involved.

The administrative tasks required to maintain an Active Directory infrastructure can be divided into two categories. *Service management* tasks are those that maintain the efficient and reliable delivery of the directory service throughout the enterprise. *Data management* tasks are those concerned with the creation and management of the information stored in the directory service. The most common tasks in these two categories are listed in Table 2-3.

Table 2-3

Active Directory Administration Tasks

SERVICE MANAGEMENT	DATA MANAGEMENT
Creation and deletion of domains	Creating, maintaining, and removing user and computer accounts
Installing, maintaining, and removing domain controllers	Creating and managing security groups
Configuring functional levels	Creating, linking, and removing Group Policy objects
Managing the schema	Managing servers and workstations
Configuring operations master roles	Managing resources hosted by servers
Backing up and restoring the AD DS database	Managing data for AD-enabled applications
Managing replication	
Managing security policies	

As part of the process of designing an administrative model, enterprise administrators should compile a detailed list of the tasks they intend to delegate. The tasks listed in the table are general in scope, and do not usually reflect complete administrative roles.

For example, managing user accounts consists of many distinct tasks requiring varying levels of expertise. You might delegate the task of creating accounts for new users to a single individual in each domain, but you might also need several people in each department who are capable of resetting forgotten passwords. Your task list should therefore reflect, to some degree, the number of people to whom you intend to delegate each task and the differences in skills and experience each task requires.

Creating an Administrative Model

The process of designing a model by which your organization will delegate Active Directory administrative tasks will be based on many of the same factors that you considered when designing your forest and domain hierarchies. The same business requirements that led you to create separate forests or separate domains may lead you to provide those forests or domains with administrative autonomy or isolation.

This type of high-level delegation is relatively simple to model and equally simple to implement. If, for example, your organization has recently merged with another company that already has its own IT staff and Active Directory infrastructure, incorporating their forests and/or domains into your existing enterprise is not difficult if they are going to continue to manage their own infrastructure. The only major decision you have to make regarding delegation is whether they will remain completely isolated or be an autonomous division with enterprise administration over them.

In most enterprises, however, the delegation model is not this simple. Enterprise administrators must consider the size of the organization and the distribution of both network hardware resources and IT staff throughout the various sites before they can craft an appropriate model.

As with forest and domain hierarchies, administrative delegation is often based on geographic or business-unit divisions. However, it is also possible to create a task-based distribution of labor. Microsoft defines three types of administrative models, which help to define how enterprise administrators will delegate tasks. These three models are as follows:

- Centralized—In a centralized model, a single staff manages all administrative tasks from a single location, usually the organization's headquarters. For this to be practical, most, if not all, of the organization's mission critical servers must be located at or near the same central location. The AD DS hierarchy often consists of a single forest with a single domain, and tasks are more likely to be distributed among the central IT staff by type, rather than by geographic or business unit divisions. This model is most effective in organizations maintaining small branch offices that do not merit their own IT personnel.

- Distributed—In a distributed model, enterprise administrators delegate administrative tasks among IT staff members and senior non-IT personnel scattered around the enterprise. This model is most suitable for an organization with relatively large regional or branch offices that maintain their own IT staffs and their own servers and other network resources. The AD DS hierarchy might include multiple forest and/or domains. Task delegation to IT staffers is typically based on geography, but administrators may delegate low-level tasks to non-IT personnel.

- Mixed—The mixed model calls for a combination of centralized and distributed delegation. Generally, regional and branch offices have their own IT staff, but they receive a lesser degree of autonomy than in a true distributed model. For example, the central IT staff might define the security policies and server configurations to be used throughout the enterprise, but delegate administrative tasks, such as implementing those policies, to IT staffers at regional offices.

It should be no surprise to experienced administrators that large organizations often end up with a situation that combines elements of all three of these models. A large regional office with an IT staff might receive relative autonomy, while small branch offices have less or no administrative control.

Delegating Administrative Tasks

Enterprise administrators are not likely to be involved in the actual physical delegation of AD DS administrative tasks, except possibly at the very top of the hierarchy, but it is still essential for them to understand the mechanics of the delegation process.

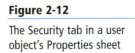

The Active Directory permission system is virtually identical in function to, but completely separate from, the other Windows permission systems, such as those protecting the NTFS file system and the registry. Like NTFS, Active Directory uses standard permissions, which are composed of combinations of special permissions. The rules of permission inheritance, inheritance blocking, and effective permissions are the same, as well.

There are two basic elements that individuals need to be able to delegate: Active Directory permissions and user rights.

USING PERMISSIONS

As with file system elements, such as files and folders, every object in an Active Directory Domain Service installation has an access control list (ACL), and every ACL consists of a list of access control entries (ACEs). These ACLs and ACEs make up the system of Active Directory permissions, which provide users with access to the AD DS infrastructure.

By default, all authenticated users receive various Active Directory read permissions that enable them to see most of the attributes for the objects in the AD DS hierarchy. For example, each user object grants the Authenticated Users special identity the following permissions:

- Allow Read General Information
- Allow Read Personal Information
- Allow Read Public Information
- Allow Read Web Information
- Allow Read Permissions

By granting permissions to the SELF special identity, users are allowed to modify certain informational attributes of their own user objects, but users cannot modify other people's user objects or—with very few exceptions—any other objects in the AD DS database. Therefore, the process of delegating administrative tasks involves assigning permissions to certain users.

By default, the Active Directory Users and Computers console does not display Active Directory permission assignments. To view the Active Directory permissions assigned to objects, you first must select View → Advanced Features. This causes the Security tab to appear in every object's Properties sheet, as shown in Figure 2-12.

Figure 2-12

The Security tab in a user object's Properties sheet

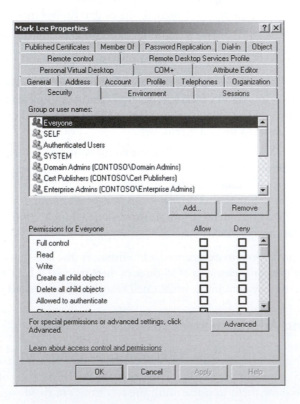

While it is possible to use the controls on an object's Security tab to grant a user specific permissions for that object, administrators almost never do this. Instead, they are more likely to use the Delegation of Control Wizard, which enables them to assign permissions to multiple users or groups simultaneously, and assign permissions based on tasks, as shown in Figure 2-13.

Figure 2-13

The *Tasks to Delegate* page in the Delegation of Control Wizard

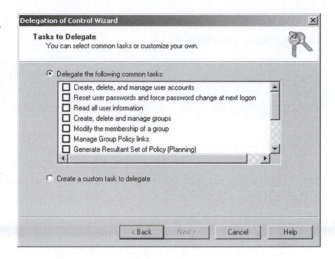

USING USER RIGHTS

The other means by which AD DS administrators receive their special privileges is through user rights. User rights are assignments that enable recipients to perform specific system tasks. For example, the *Backup files and directories* user right enables the individuals possessing that right to perform backups, even if they do not have the permissions needed to access the files and directories in the normal manner. In fact, the *Backup files and directories* right is an excellent way to delegate backup privileges without giving the administrator the ability to open and read the files.

To assign user rights, you use Group Policy objects (GPOs), as shown in Figure 2-14. There are 44 user rights that can provide individuals with a variety of system privileges, ranging from remote access to changing the system time.

Figure 2-14

Default user rights assignments in the Default Domain Controllers Policy GPO

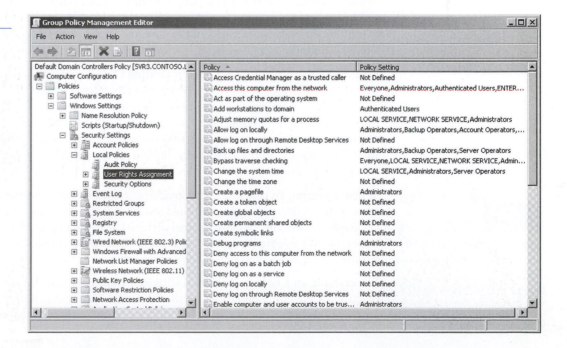

Although it is possible to assign user rights to individual users, professional administrators never do this; they assign rights to groups instead. When you look at the default user rights assignments in the Default Domain Controllers Policy GPO, you can see how the Administrators group obtains it privileges, as do the other built-in domain local groups.

Using Delegation Strategies

Active Directory permissions and user rights are the mechanisms by which you can delegate AD DS administrative tasks, but an administrative model also must specify how those mechanisms are to be used throughout the enterprise.

In a large enterprise environment, it's a general rule never to assign permissions, rights, or anything else to individual users. Users come and go, and configuring them individually just means more work for the administrators. Instead, you assign permissions and rights to groups, so that the assignments remain, and you can simply adjust the group memberships as needed.

The same policy holds true when it comes to delegating access to the Active Directory hierarchy. Administrators never assign permissions to individual leaf objects, such as computers and users. Instead, they assign permissions to container objects, such as domains and organizational units, and let the leaf objects inherit the permissions from their parent containers.

To implement an Active Directory administrative model, enterprise administrators must devise a strategy for using groups and containers effectively, as discussed in the following sections.

CREATING AN ORGANIZATIONAL STRUCTURE

Earlier in this lesson, you learned about creating a forest and domain structure for your enterprise network. The next level below the domain in the Active Directory hierarchy is the organizational unit. Compared with forests and domains, OUs are relatively easy to create and destroy, and administrators can readily move objects between them.

While creating a forest is a comparatively momentous decision, and creating a domain somewhat less so, creating an OU is almost trivial by comparison. However, even though enterprise administrators might not be involved in the actual design of an OU infrastructure, they should be the guiding hand in creating the policies that govern the creation of OUs.

One of the most common reasons for creating OUs is to delegate administrative control over them. OUs are the means by which you can delegate low-level tasks on a departmental basis, or give administrators autonomy over a relatively small part of the AD DS hierarchy. Administrators can assign permissions to an OU using the Delegation of Control Wizard, to provide specific user and groups with the ability to perform specific administrative tasks. More importantly, administrators can link GPOs to an OU, so that all of the settings in those GPOs will be inherited by all of the objects in the OU (including subordinate OUs).

When designing an organizational structure, you can choose among the same options as when you considered creating multiple forests and domains. You can create OUs based on geographical divisions or departmental divisions, even mixing the two as needed, but it is important to understand that the organizational structure should be based on the organization's administrative needs, and not on an arbitrary adherence to the company organization chart.

For example, in a large organization with well-connected regional sites, you might use a single domain for the entire enterprise. In that case, your first inclination might be to use the first level of OUs in the domain to reflect the geography of the regional offices, as shown in Figure 2-15.

X REF

For more information on the role of Group Policy in enterprise administration, see Lesson 3, "Building an Active Directory Topology."

Figure 2-15

Organizational units based on
geographical divisions

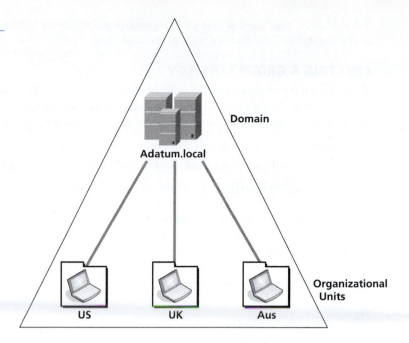

This might be a viable solution if you are going to be delegating administrative tasks to IT staff or senior users at the regional offices. However, in an enterprise where the regional offices are small and IT administration is centralized, creating a separate OU for each office would not be necessary when each one is going to receive exactly the same set of policies.

You might instead create a first level of OUs that reflect the business units in the organization, because each business unit has a different set of administrative requirements. The business units can span all of the regional offices, and you can use a second layer of OUs or site objects to reflect the geographical divisions, if necessary, as shown in Figure 2-16.

Figure 2-16

Organizational units based on
business unit divisions and
then geographical divisions

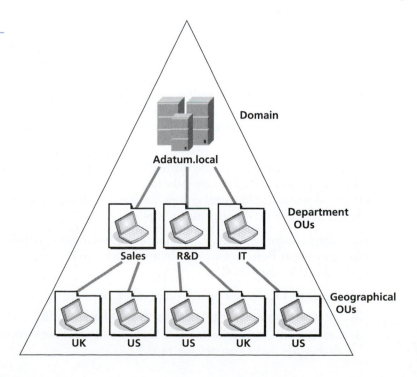

What is most important is that your organizational structure reflects the administrative needs of the enterprise, not that it draws an accurate map.

CREATING A GROUP STRATEGY

With a hierarchy of organizational units in place, you must create a group strategy before you can use the OUs to delegate control and assign user rights. Experienced server administrators should be aware of the standard Windows three-step policy for creating groups, which is as follows:

1. Create domain local groups and grant them access to resources.
2. Create global groups and add users (or other global groups) to them.
3. Add the global groups as members of the domain-local groups.

This same policy applies to your administrative model as well. If you look at the Builtin container in the Active Directory Users and Computers console, as shown in Figure 2-17, you can see how the default domain-local groups are based on administrative tasks.

Figure 2-17

Built-in domain-local groups

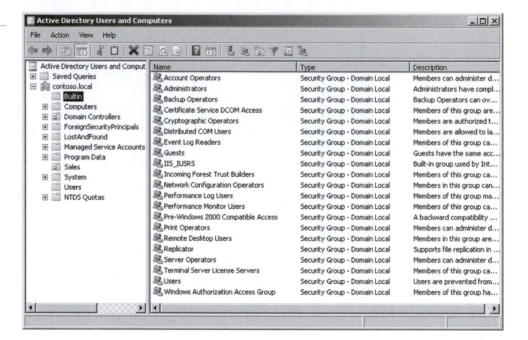

For example, the Backup Operators group enables members to perform backups on the computers in the domain. This is because the Backup Operators group receives the *Backup files and directories* user right through the Default Domain Controllers Policy and Local Security Policy GPOs.

Administrators can use the same method to create their own domain-local groups, to which they will delegate administrative tasks and user rights for particular OUs. Then, after creating global groups (or universal groups, for forest-wide assignments) and adding them to the domain local groups, the structure is in place.

For a simple example, if you are running a single-domain enterprise and want to grant the manager of your Boston office the ability to back up the computers at that site, you could use a procedure like the following:

1. Create an OU for the branch office called Boston.
2. Create a domain-local group called Boston Backup.
3. Create a GPO called Boston OU Backup and grant the Boston Backup group the *Backup files and directories* user right.

4. Link the GPO to the Boston OU.

5. Create a global group called Boston Office Managers.

6. Add the Boston Office Managers group to the Boston Backup group as a member.

All that remains is to add the user account for the Boston branch manager to the Boston Office Managers global group. If the manager should go on vacation or leave the company, the only thing an administrator at the central office has to do to grant someone else the rights to perform backups is to add another user from the Boston office to the Boston Office Managers group.

This procedure grants one user the rights needed to perform one task at one site. Obviously, it would not be efficient to delegate every task individually this way. A more efficient method would be for enterprise administrators to organize their lists of tasks into groups, which they or others will assign to IT staffers. Microsoft refers to these groups as management roles and has published lists of recommended roles for service management and data management tasks, as shown in Table 2-4.

Table 2-4

Active Directory Management Roles

SERVICE MANAGEMENT ROLES	DATA MANAGEMENT ROLES
Forest Configuration Operators	Business Unit Administrators
Domain Configuration Operators	Account Administrators
Security Policy Administrators	Workstation Administrators
Service Administration Managers	Server Operators
Domain Controller Administrators	Resource Administrators
Backup Operators	Security Group Administrators
Schema Administrators	Help Desk Operators
Replication Management Administrators	Application-Specific Administrators
Replication Monitoring Operators	
DNS Administrators	

Auditing Administrator Compliance

Delegating a task to others does not absolve you of responsibility for it. Enterprise administrators must still see to it that the tasks they assign are completed, even if the individuals they delegate tasks to delegate them in turn to someone else.

The best way to monitor Active Directory administrative procedures is to use auditing, which records the success and/or failure of specific activities in the Windows Security event log. However, auditing is a Windows feature that you must configure carefully, as it is capable of recording vast amounts of information. In some cases, too much information can be as bad as no information at all.

To audit AD DS activity, you must enable the *Audit directory service access* policy in the Default Domain Controllers Policy GPO. You can elect to audit only successful accesses, only failed accesses, or both. When enabled, the *Audit directory service access* policy logs accesses to all Active Directory objects that have system access control lists (SACLs) specified for them.

By default, domain objects have various SACLs defined, which the objects in the domain inherit. You can regulate the amount of information that the policy gathers by modifying the SACLs to specify which objects you want to audit. To alter the default SACLs, you open an object's Properties sheet, select the Security tab, click Advanced to open the Advanced Security Settings dialog box, and select the Auditing tab, as shown in Figure 2-18.

Figure 2-18

The Auditing tab of an AD DS object's Advanced Security Settings dialog box

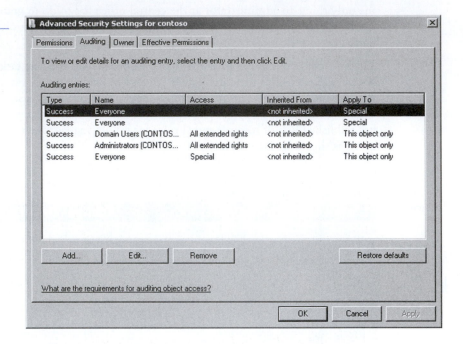

In Windows Server 2008 or later, it is also possible to exercise more detailed control over directory-service access auditing by using the settings in the Advanced Audit Policy Configuration folder of a GPO, as shown in Figure 2-19. These settings, instead of auditing all access to an object, enable you to audit only elements such as object modifications and replication activities.

Figure 2-19

The Advanced Audit Policy Configuration settings

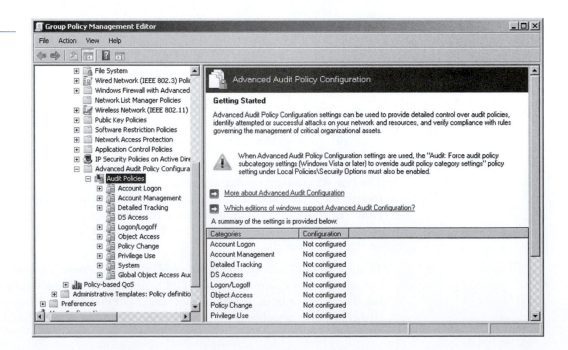

SKILL SUMMARY

IN THIS LESSON YOU LEARNED:

- A competent enterprise administrator is an individual who, when designing an Active Directory hierarchy, adds domains and forests only when the organization's requirements call for them.

- Designing an AD DS hierarchy is a high-level process that is concerned with business and management issues as much as with technical ones. The enterprise administrator must know what Active Directory can do and also what the organization needs it to do. The design process is a matter of finding a common ground between those AD DS capabilities and the organization's requirements.

- The most important question you have to answer is what role the AD DS database will play in your organization. More specifically, what kind of information will be stored in the AD DS database?

- The first question in Active Directory design is whether to use one forest or multiple forests.

- The default configuration is to have one domain per forest; you should only create multiple domains if you have specific reasons for doing so.

- The main issues for the enterprise administrator regarding schemas are not how to make the changes but what changes to make and whether it is worthwhile to make them.

- It is the enterprise administrator's job to create a model for the delegation of tasks like these to other administrators, technicians, and trustworthy users all over the enterprise.

- There are two basic elements that individuals need to be able to perform AD DS service-management and data-management tasks: Active Directory permissions and user rights.

- One of the most common reasons for creating OUs is to delegate administrative control over them. OUs are the means by which you can delegate low-level tasks on a departmental basis, or give administrators autonomy over a relatively small part of the AD DS hierarchy.

- With a hierarchy of organizational units in place, you must create a group strategy before you can use the OUs to delegate control and assign user rights.

■ Knowledge Assessment

Fill in the Blank

Complete the following sentences by writing the correct word or words in the blanks provided.

1. An AD DS database that contains information about users, computers, printers, and services that enables users to access those resources and administrators to control access to them, is called a _____ directory.

2. The three phases of an IT service's lifecycle, as defined by the Microsoft Operations Framework, are _____, _____, and _____.

3. To assign user rights with a graphical interface, you use the _____ tool.

4. Only the _____ forest model never includes trust relationships.

5. Creating and maintaining user accounts is an Active Directory _____ management task.

6. To raise the forest functional level on an existing AD DS installation with a graphical environment, you use the _____ tool.

7. The first domain you create in a new Active Directory domain Services installation is called the _____.

8. The _____ administrative model is most effective in organizations maintaining small branch offices that do not merit their own IT personnel.

9. The Backup Operators group receives the *Backup files and directories* user right from the _____ GPO.

10. The _____ domain model was a common practice in Windows NT 4.0, but the ability in AD DS to delegate administrative autonomy to individual OUs has largely eliminated the need for this practice

True / False

Circle T if the statement is true or F if the statement is false.

T | F 1. In Active Directory administration, data management tasks are those that maintain the efficient and reliable delivery of the directory service throughout the enterprise.

T | F 2. Organizational units are easier to create and destroy than domains or forests.

T | F 3. The Active Directory Recycle Bin is a feature implemented in the Windows Server 2008 R2 domain functional level.

T | F 4. When deploying schema modifications on a production network, you should first disable Active Directory replication and then modify the schema on the domain controller performing the domain-naming master operations master role.

T | F 5. Most users are able to read the attributes of AD DS objects due to permissions assigned by default to the Authenticated Users special identity.

T | F 6. The functional level available for a particular forest or domain is equivalent to the newest Windows Server version running on one of its domain controllers.

T | F 7. Like NTFS, Active Directory uses standard permissions, which are composed of combinations of special permissions.

T | F 8. The Advanced Audit Policy Configuration settings are only available on servers running Windows Server 2003 or later.

T | F 9. Stipulations that the service, when complete, will meet specified levels of performance and availability are called project constraints.

T | F 10. Administrative autonomy is when an individual is granted complete and exclusive administrative control over some part of a forest.

Review Questions

1. The general rule for an AD DS design is to create just one forest, unless you have specific reasons to create more than one. List three reasons why you might want to create multiple forests in your enterprise network.

2. List the three steps of the standard Windows policy for creating groups.

■ Case Scenarios

Scenario 2-1: Creating Forests

The Adatum Corporation of Washington, DC, has recently acquired a small company called Fabrikam, Inc. Fabrikam's offices are located in nearby Baltimore, and there are currently no plans to move them.

Adatum is currently using Active Directory Domain Services in a single-forest configuration. It has a centralized IT department that administers the networks at the headquarters and at four small branch offices. Fabrikam is running Microsoft Windows on all of its computers, but it is not using AD DS. They have a three-person IT staff, none of whom have Active Directory experience.

In a meeting with the management of both companies, Adatum's enterprise administrator was instructed to bring Fabrikam into the company's AD DS infrastructure.

1. Based on the information provided thus far, should the enterprise administrator create a separate AD DS forest for the Fabrikam network or add them to the existing Adatum forest? Explain your answer.

2. What additional information might the enterprise administrator discover that could affect his forest design decision?

Scenario 2-2: Raising Functional Levels

You are the enterprise administrator for Contoso, Ltd., a company with an Active Directory Domain Services network that includes two forests, one called contoso.com for the main company network and one called contosogov.com for a special project under government contract. The contoso.com forest has three domains and the contosogov.com forest one, as shown in Figure 2-20 (on the next page). The domain controllers in the domains are running various Windows versions, including Windows Server 2003, Windows Server 2008, and Windows Server 2008 R2.

Figure 2-20

Contoso, Ltd. Active Directory
Domain Services infrastructure

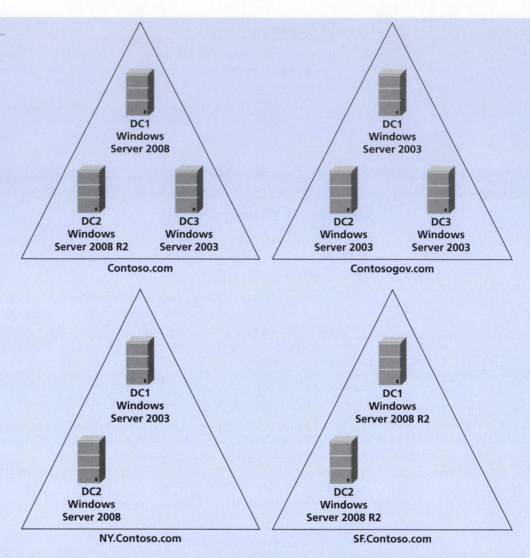

After testing the Active Directory Recycle bin feature on a lab network, you are ready to use it in production in the contoso.com domain. Which of the following tasks must you complete before you can use the Active Directory Recycle Bin?

  a. Upgrade DC1 in Contoso.com to Windows Server 2008 R2.

  b. Upgrade DC3 in Contoso.com to Windows Server 2008 R2.

  c. Raise the domain functional level in Contoso.com to Windows Server 2008 R2.

  d. Upgrade DC1 in NY.Contoso.com to Windows Server 2008 R2.

  e. Upgrade DC2 in NY.Contoso.com to Windows Server 2008 R2.

  f. Raise the domain functional level in NY.Contoso.com to Windows Server 2008 R2.

  g. Upgrade DC1 in Contosogov.com to Windows Server 2008 R2.

  h. Upgrade DC2 in Contosogov.com to Windows Server 2008 R2.

  i. Upgrade DC3 in Contosogov.com to Windows Server 2008 R2.

  j. Raise the domain functional level in Contosogov.com to Windows Server 2008 R2.

  k. Raise the forest functional level in Contoso.com to Windows Server 2008 R2.

  l. Raise the forest functional level in Contosogov.com to Windows Server 2008 R2.

Building an Active Directory Topology

OBJECTIVE DOMAIN MATRIX

TECHNOLOGY SKILL	OBJECTIVE DOMAIN	OBJECTIVE NUMBER
Planning the Physical Topology	Design the Active Directory physical topology.	2.2
Designing a Group Policy Strategy	Design the enterprise-level group policy strategy.	2.4

KEY TERMS

bridgehead server
dictionary attacks
fine-grained password policies
full-mesh topology
hub-and-spoke topology
hybrid topology
latency period

location schema
multifactor authentication
multimaster replication
Personal Identity Verification (PIV)
Read-Only Domain Controller (RODC)
replication
security filtering

shadow groups
site
site link bridge object
site link object
smart card authentication
universal group membership
 caching

■ Planning the Physical Topology

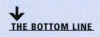

THE BOTTOM LINE

In Lesson 2, "Designing an Active Directory Hierarchy," you learned how enterprise administrators design the logical elements of the Active Directory Domain Services (AD DS) hierarchy, the forests and domains that may or may not reflect the geographical layout of the network. In this lesson, you learn about the physical topology of Active Directory, the actual computers that host the directory service, and the links that join them.

Once you have designed the logical infrastructure for AD DS by deciding how many forests and domains to create, you can begin to consider the physical aspects of the AD DS infrastructure. The physical topology of AD DS is reflected in its domain controllers and involves questions like the following:

- How many domain controllers should I use?
- Where should the domain controllers be located?
- How should be domain controllers be connected?

Once you gather the information needed to answer these questions, you can begin to design the topology elements, such as sites, site links, replication, and global catalog servers.

CERTIFICATION READY
How do you design an
Active Directory physical
topology?
2.2

Gathering Network Information

Much of the same information you gathered when considering your forest and domain hierarchy can also affect the physical topology design. However, there are other elements you need to know as well.

Replication is one of the most critical aspects of the physical AD DS topology. If your entire enterprise network is located in a single office building, your topology design could not be simpler. All of your domain controllers can be located in the same site, and you can let them replicate at will because they are all connected to the same high-speed network.

This is rarely the case, however. Whether you are constructing a new AD DS infrastructure or upgrading an existing one, most enterprise networks have computers in a variety of different locations, and those locations could well be connected by different technologies, running at different speeds, and with different traffic conditions.

Therefore, as in the forest design process, a diagram of the enterprise network is essential, and should include the types and speeds of all wide-area network (WAN) links connecting remote locations. The link speeds help you determine whether and how well the connections can handle replication traffic generated by domain controllers. Therefore, the diagram should include not only the raw speeds of the WAN links, but an indication of their current traffic conditions as well, as shown in Figure 3-1.

Figure 3-1

Diagram of enterprise network locations

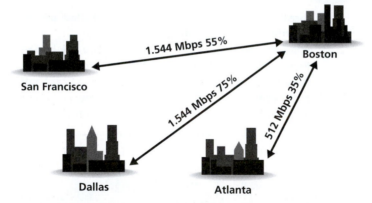

Network traffic levels are a subject that many administrators ignore until a communication problem arises. You may have taken baseline measurements of your WAN links' bandwidth utilization at the time they were installed, but if your figures are more than a year old, you should repeat those measurements when planning for a major update to your AD DS replication infrastructure.

In addition to the information about the internetwork links, you must also compile information about each individual remote network as well, including the following:

- Number of domains
- Number of domain controllers per domain
- Number of servers per domain
- Number of workstations per domain
- Number of users per domain
- IP network addresses in use

This information is necessary to help you create a site infrastructure and determine where to locate your domain controllers and global catalog servers. The network addresses are required because when Windows computers authenticate to Active Directory, they discover the nearest domain controller based on their IP subnet addresses.

Designing a Site Topology

> In Active Directory terminology, a site is a special type of AD DS container object that provides the connection between the logical AD DS infrastructure—forests, domains, and organizational units—and the physical network infrastructure—cables, routers, and WAN links.

The strict definition of a *site* is an area of an AD DS network in which all of the domain controllers are well connected—that is, connected by a fast and reliable network link. The site topology is completely independent of forests and domain; you can have one domain that encompasses many sites or a single site that includes multiple domains.

Unlike the forest and domain design decisions you made in Lesson 2, site divisions are based exclusively on physical network conditions. You do not create a site topology based on business units, contractual requirements, or political decisions. In fact, you do not even necessarily create sites based on geographical divisions. If, sometime in the future, it becomes practical to create a global network in which the links between locations are as fast as the links within a location, there will be no need for multiple sites.

However, in the current state of the technology, intranetwork connections run at much faster speeds than internetwork links. Local-area networks (LANs) today typically run at 100 or 1,000 megabits per second (Mbps), while the typical WAN connections used by most companies rarely exceed T-1 speed (1.544 Mbps). This is a vast difference in available bandwidth, and you must also consider that other applications are already using the WAN connections.

The primary reason for creating multiple AD DS sites is to conserve the bandwidth on those relatively slow and expensive WAN connections. Such sites can do this in three ways, as follows:

- Replication—AD DS domain controllers have two different ways of replicating their data: intrasite and intersite. Intersite replication is compressed and schedulable, so that it can use a minimum of bandwidth.

- Authentication—Windows client computers always attempt to authenticate themselves using a domain controller on the same site, which prevents the authentication traffic from consuming WAN bandwidth.

- Applications—Certain AD-aware applications and services, such as the Distributed File System (DFS) and Microsoft Exchange, are conscious of the sites in which their servers reside and make efforts to minimize intersite traffic. DFS clients connect to replicas in their own sites whenever possible and Exchange servers minimize the message traffic they transmit over intersite WAN links.

USING A SINGLE SITE

When you create a new forest, the Active Directory Domain Services Installation Wizard automatically creates a first site object, which it calls Default-First-Site-Name. Until you create additional sites manually, AD DS adds all of the computers in the forest to the Default-First-Site-Name site, so there is no need to distinguish among the IP subnets on which the computers are located.

<aside>
TAKE NOTE*

You can rename the Default-First-Site-Name site object to reflect the actual location of the site.
</aside>

In a single-site configuration, all domain controllers replicate on demand and do not compress their replication traffic. The objective is to update each domain controller as rapidly as possible, regardless of the amount of bandwidth the replication process consumes.

The single-site model assumes that all of the domain controllers are well connected and that the available bandwidth is not limited. In most cases, a single site requires no configuration and no maintenance.

USING MULTIPLE SITES

In a multiple-site model, you must manually create additional sites representing locations that are not well connected or where you want to place domain controllers for performance reasons. You must then create IP Subnet objects for all the subnets on your network and associate them with particular sites.

AD DS uses the term "well connected" to refer to computers within a single site. However, that term has no strict definition. How enterprise administrators judge what constitutes well connected is up to them, and typically depends on the size of the location in question relative to the size of the entire enterprise.

In many cases, a location with a WAN link that has 512 Kbps or more of available bandwidth can be considered well connected, and does not require a site of its own. For organizations with large networks, the minimum speed of a well connected link might be much greater, as fast as 10 Mbps.

There are other issues to consider as well when deciding whether to create a new site. Chief among these is the question of whether you want to install domain controllers at a specific location. If a client computer cannot contact a domain controller, it cannot authenticate to AD DS, and therefore cannot log on to its domain.

If a remote office does not have a domain controller and its WAN connection should fail, then the clients cannot log on and cannot work. Therefore, there may be instances in which you want to install domain controllers at a remote location, even though it is well connected. Generally this is because there is a large number of users at that location. By making that location a separate site, you keep the authentication traffic local, so that clients can log on, even if the connection to the home office is not available.

However, if local authentication is not essential and WAN traffic levels are important, you might want to consider the balance between the replication traffic resulting if you do create a remote site and the authentication traffic generated if you don't. This balances the size and volatility of the AD DS database with the number of users at the remote site. This again is something that enterprise administrators must assess for themselves.

Finally, there is the matter of applications that are AD DS site-aware. If you plan to deploy servers for applications like those at a remote location, you will have to create a site at that location as well.

ANOTHER WAY

For a small remote location with limited resources, it is possible to reduce the amount of replication traffic and the AD DS administrative requirements by installing a *Read-only Domain Controller (RODC)*. For more information on RODCs and branch office administration, see Lesson 5, "Planning a Branch Office Deployment."

CREATING A SITE

To create additional sites, you use the Active Directory Sites and Services console, as shown in Figure 3-2. Because the site infrastructure is separate from the forest and domain infrastructure, the only AD DS objects that appear in both the Active Directory Sites and Services console and the Active Directory Users and Computers console are those representing domain controllers.

Figure 3-2

The *New Object—Site* dialog box

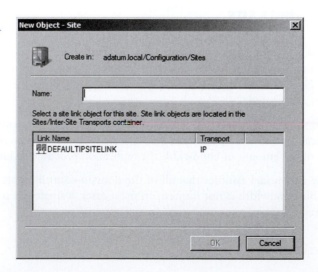

When creating a new site, you must specify the site link that it uses to connect to at least one other site. By default, there is only one site link object, called DEFAULTIPSITELINK, but you will likely be creating others during the replication topology design process.

After you create a site, you must create subnet objects, as shown in Figure 3-3, and associate them with the sites in which they are located. Assigning subnets to sites ensures that new domain controllers are placed in the correct sites and that clients access the domain controller closest to them.

Figure 3-3

The *New Object—Subnet* dialog box

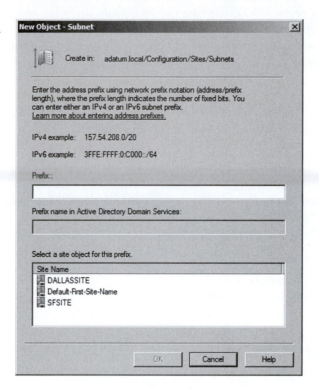

After creating sites and subnets, when you install a new domain controller, the Active Directory Domain Services Installation Wizard automatically places it in the correct site, based on the subnet where its IP address is located, as shown in Figure 3-4.

Figure 3-4

The *Select a Site* page in the Active Directory Domain Services Installation Wizard

If you have created sites but have not yet created subnets, the wizard enables you to select a site. If you have not yet created additional sites, the wizard automatically adds the domain controller to the Default-First-Site-Name site.

Designing a Replication Topology

AD DS uses a *multimaster replication* process, which means that you can modify the contents of the AD DS database on any domain controller and that domain controller will propagate the changes to all of the other domain controllers containing replicas of the modified partition. The exception to this is the Read-only Domain Controller, which only receives replication traffic; it does not send it.

As mentioned earlier, there are two kinds of AD DS replication traffic: intrasite and intersite. The differences between the two are listed in Table 3-1.

Table 3-1

Differences between Intrasite and Intersite Replication

INTRASITE REPLICATION	INTERSITE REPLICATION
Replication is initiated when an administrator makes a change to the AD DS database.	Replication events occur according to a schedule.
Replication traffic is not compressed.	Replication traffic is compressed.
Domain controllers transmit replication traffic to multiple replication partners.	Domain controllers at each site transmit replication traffic to a bridgehead server, which then transmits to a single bridgehead server at another site.
Rarely needs configuration.	Highly configurable.
Does not require the configuration of additional AD DS objects.	Requires the creation and configuration of site link objects, and possibly site link bridge objects.

Intrasite replication requires no effort from the enterprise administrator, whether the network has one site or many. The domain controllers in each site take care of their own interaction. However, an administrator must create and configure site link objects to provide the intersite connections.

SELECTING A REPLICATION MODEL

As part of the site design, enterprise administrators must decide on a topology for the intersite replication traffic. In other words, they must determine which sites will replicate with which. To some extent, this is dependent on the physical connections connecting the sites. You can create a replication topology that simply utilizes the entire WAN topology connecting the locations hosting separate sites, or designate a subset of the WAN topology to be used for replication.

In an AD DS installation with multiple sites, each site designates one domain controller as the *bridgehead server* for each partition with a replica at that site. The bridgehead servers are the only domain controllers that communicate with the other sites. Therefore, enterprise administrators create a replication model at the site level; they do not have to be concerned with selecting which domain controllers participate in intersite replication.

For example, in a forest with two domains, the headquarters site might have four domain controllers, two for each domain, as shown in Figure 3-5. A branch office functioning as a separate site also has two domain controllers for each domain. At each of the two sites, one domain controller for each domain is designated as the bridgehead server. The communication between the sites occurs between the two pairs of bridgehead servers.

Figure 3-5

Bridgehead servers for two domains replicating between two sites

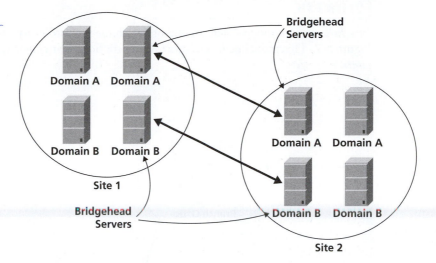

If you expand the example to include two more branch offices, the replication topology becomes more complicated. Assuming that each branch office is a separate site, with at least one domain controller for each of the two domains, there are several models the enterprise administrator can use to build a replication topology, as shown in the following sections.

HUB AND SPOKE

In one model, the *hub-and-spoke topology* shown in Figure 3-6, one site, in this case the headquarters, is designated as the hub and communicates with each of the other sites. The branch office sites do not communicate with one another. Separate links for each domain are still required.

Figure 3-6

The hub-and-spoke replication topology model

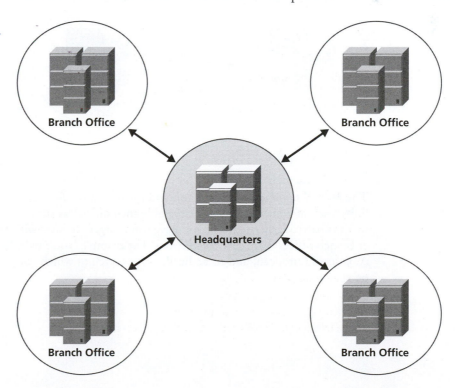

This is a particularly useful arrangement if the links to the headquarters site are faster than those between the branch offices. However, the replication *latency period*—that is, the time it takes for changes to propagate to all the domain controllers in the enterprise—can be relatively large.

FULL MESH

In a *full-mesh topology*, each site maintains connections to every other site, as shown in Figure 3-7. This model generates more WAN traffic, but it generally reduces replication latency.

Figure 3-7

The full-mesh replication topology model

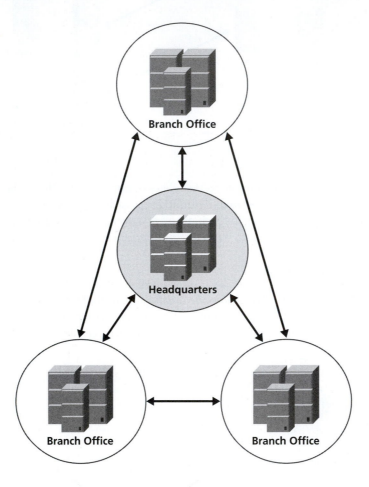

HYBRID

The *hybrid topology* mixes the hub and spoke and the full mesh by using two connected hubs, each of which connects to several branch offices, as shown in Figure 3-8. This arrangement is particularly suitable if you have some larger facilities with fast connections and smaller branch offices with slow connections. For example, you might have hubs in your North American, European, and Asian headquarters, each of which connects to the branch offices on that continent.

Figure 3-8

The hybrid replication topology model

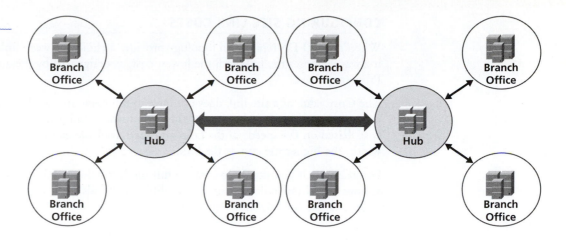

CREATING SITE LINKS

To enable replication between two sites, you must have a site link object associated with both of them. A *site link object* represents the physical connection between remote sites. The purpose of the site link is to indicate which sites are connected and to provide details about the cost and availability of the physical connection.

By default, the Active Directory Domain Services Installation Wizard creates a site link object called DEFAULTIPSITELINK. If all of your sites are connected using WAN links running at the same speed and with the same available bandwidth, then you can use this default site link for all of your connections. However, if you have WAN connections running at different speeds, or with different amounts of bandwidth utilization, then you must create additional site link objects and configure them to reflect the physical capabilities of the connections.

Each site link object must have at least two site objects associated with it, representing both ends of the connection. When you add sites to a new site link, as shown in Figure 3-9, do not forget to remove them from the DEFAULTIPSITELINK site link, if AD DS has added them to it.

TAKE NOTE⁎

As with the Default-First-Site-Name site object, you can rename the DEFAULTIPSITELINK object to reflect its actual function.

Figure 3-9

A site link's Properties sheet

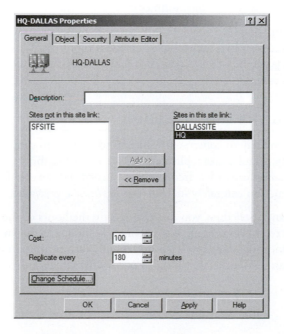

CONFIGURING SITE LINK COSTS

When the AD DS replication topology provides a choice between links connecting two sites, it always chooses the link with the lowest cost, as designated by the administrator on the link's Properties sheet.

The Cost value of a site link does not have to represent an actual monetary value; it is significant only in relation to the costs of the other links. Administrators often calculate site link costs based on the speeds of the links and their available bandwidth. The lower the bandwidth, the higher the cost of the link.

For example, if you decide to create a full-mesh topology and your sites are connected by various WAN technologies running at different speeds, you might create a list of designated link costs like the one shown in Table 3-2.

Table 3-2

Sample Site Link Costs for Various Connection Speeds

CONNECTION SPEED	SITE LINK COST
1.544 Mbps	100
512 Kbps	300
256 Kbps	600
128 Kbps	1200
64 Kbps	2400

TAKE NOTE*

The numbers you use for the site link costs are not relevant; only the relationships between them are. You can just as easily drop the trailing zeros and use the values 1, 3, 6, 12, and 24 for your costs.

By selecting appropriate cost values for your site links, you can make sure that replication traffic takes the route you want it to take under normal conditions. However, be sure to consider the possibility of a link failure as well, and make sure that traffic takes the route you want it to take when the optimum path is not available.

It is important to remember that site link costs are only important when there are multiple links available between two sites, as in a full-mesh topology. If, as in a hub-and-spoke topology, there is only one link connecting each pair of sites, then AD DS must use that link, regardless of its cost.

CONFIGURING SITE LINK SCHEDULES

The most efficient way to conserve intersite bandwidth is to specify when AD DS replication should occur. By default, sites replicate every 180 minutes, but you can configure site link objects to replicate more or less frequently as needed. For an AD DS infrastructure that does not change often, you can safely increase the *Replicate every* value.

By clicking Change Schedule, you can also specify the hours of the day and the days of the week on which replication should occur, using the interface shown in Figure 3-10. If you have WAN connections that approach peak bandwidth utilization during business hours, for example, you can configure replication to occur only when both sites are closed.

Figure 3-10

The *Schedule* dialog box for a site link object

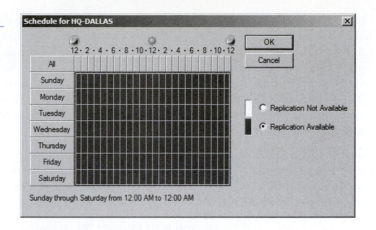

CREATING SITE LINK BRIDGES

By default, site link bridging is enabled for all of your site links, rendering all of the links transitive. This means that if there is a site link connecting your North American hub with your European hub, and another site link connecting your European hub to your Asian hub, then your North American site can replicate with your Asian site, as shown in Figure 3-11.

Figure 3-11

Site link bridging in effect

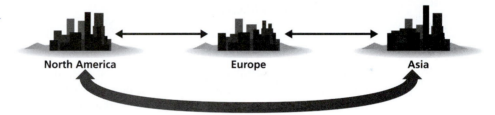

North America   Europe   Asia

In some cases, you might want to turn off the default bridging for all of your site links and create your own site link bridge objects instead. A ***site link bridge object*** is a connection between two site links that renders them transitive.

To change the site link bridging default, you expand the Sites\Inter-Site Transports folder, right-click IP, and open the IP Properties sheet, as shown in Figure 3-12. Clearing the *Bridge all site links* checkbox disables bridging.

Figure 3-12

The *IP Properties* dialog box

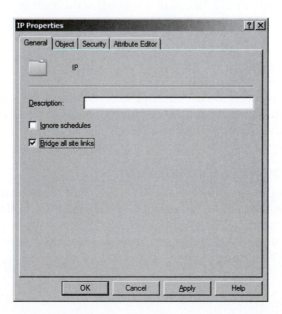

One reason why you might want to change the site link bridging default would be if you have a hybrid replication topology with links between hub sites that are relatively slow or have little available bandwidth. For example, if bridging is enabled for all of your sites, then the transitive nature of the links means that the branch offices connected to the New York hub will replicate not only with the Paris hub but also with all of the other three European branch offices. This means that the NY-Paris link will have to carry multiple copies of the same replication traffic. If the site link between New York and Paris is heavily trafficked already, this could be a problem.

To prevent this behavior, you can disable the default site bridging, and then create individual site link bridge objects for each path between a North American branch office and the Paris hub. In the same way, you will have to create site link bridges from the European branch offices to the New York hub.

For this example, therefore, you will need to create the following six site link bridges:

- Philadelphia-NY/NY-Paris
- Baltimore-NY/NY-Paris
- Boston-NY/NY-Paris
- NY-Paris/Paris-Brussels
- NY-Paris/Paris-Zurich
- NY-Paris/Paris-Marseille

The result of this arrangement is that the NY-Paris link will only have to carry one copy of the replication traffic for each branch office.

You can also use site link bridge objects to control replication traffic on networks that are not fully routed, such as those using dial-up or demand-dial links, or to control replication traffic routes in a failover situation, such as a malfunction at one of the hub sites.

> **TAKE NOTE** *
>
> Each site link bridge must contain at least two site objects with one common site between them. This enables AD DS to calculate the total cost of the route by adding the costs of the individual site links.

Selecting Domain Controller Locations

To some degree, the designs you have already created for your AD DS infrastructure dictate the basic placement of domain controllers throughout your enterprise. The decisions to create additional forests, domains, and sites all must include the monetary costs and administrative considerations of additional domain controllers in the enterprise administrator's calculations.

Every forest needs domain controllers for its forest-root domain, and every additional domain in a forest needs its own domain controllers. In addition, every site you create must have domain controllers for the domains with resources at that site. However, there are still further elements of the domain controller deployment process to consider, including the number and type of domain controllers to install at the enterprise's various locations.

HOW MANY DOMAIN CONTROLLERS?

Several rules for enterprise domain controller deployment are discussed in this lesson and Lesson 2. Every domain must have at least two domain controllers, for fault-tolerance purposes. Every site must have at least one—and preferably two—domain controllers for each domain with resources at that site. However, there are conditions in which you might want additional domain controllers.

If you have one domain controller at a remote site and that domain controller fails, then users at that site must authenticate using a domain controller at another site. This could be undesirable for several reasons, including the following:

- The link to the other site might be slow or congested.
- The domain controller at the other site might be overburdened with local traffic.
- Business requirements might dictate that all users at the remote site authenticate locally.

In any of these cases, you might want to consider installing multiple domain controllers for each domain at a remote site.

DEPLOYING FOREST-ROOT DOMAIN CONTROLLERS

The computer on which you create a forest becomes the first domain controller for the forest-root domain. Because anyone able to physically access a forest-root domain controller can conceivably damage the entire forest, whether deliberately or not, the physical security of this domain controller is critical. Most forest-root domain controllers are deployed in locked server closets or data centers for that reason.

The primary responsibility of the forest-root domain is to establish trust paths that enable users in one domain to access resources in other domains. Therefore, if you have a remote site with domain controllers for two domains, a user in one domain accessing the other still has to go through the forest-root domain controller in the home office's data center.

Depending on how frequently your users must access other domains and how fast the link is between the sites, you may find it necessary to deploy additional forest-root domain controllers at remote sites. If you elect to do this, the security of this domain controller is paramount.

 **ANOTHER WAY**   To prevent having to deploy additional forest-root domain controllers at remote sites, you can create shortcut trusts between domains lower down in the hierarchy at the remote site.

DEPLOYING READ-ONLY DOMAIN CONTROLLERS

Security considerations are not limited to forest-root domain controllers. All domain controllers are susceptible to physical attacks that can affect the entire domain they service. For branch offices, this has long been a considerable problem, because these locations often lack the facilities needed to secure domain controllers.

To address this problem, Windows Server 2008 introduced the ability to create a read-only domain controller (RODC). RODCs only receive replication traffic; they do not send it, so it is not possible for an attacker to compromise the AD DS database and replicate it to the rest of the domain.

To install an RODC, the computer must be running Windows Server 2008 or Windows Server 2008 R2. In addition, the nearest read/write domain controller for the same domain— that is, the domain controller with the lowest link cost—must also be running Windows Server 2008 or newer.

DEPLOYING GLOBAL CATALOG SERVERS

When you promote a server to a domain controller using the Active Directory Domain Services Installation Wizard, you have the option of making the computer a global catalog server as well, as shown in Figure 3-13. Client computers require access to a global catalog server to log on to another domain or search the AD DS database.

Figure 3-13

The *Additional Domain Controller Options* page in the Active Directory Domain Services Installation Wizard

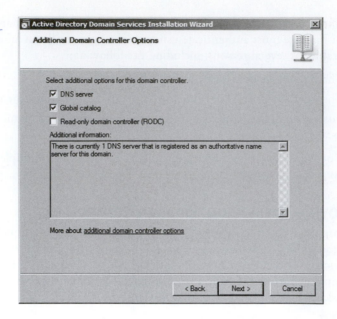

Installing a global catalog server at every site improves performance, but on a large enterprise network with multiple domains, the amount of network traffic resulting from the global catalog replication can be significant. Generally speaking, a site with 100 users or more should definitely have one of its domain controllers functioning as a global catalog server.

One way to avoid creating a global catalog server at a particular site is to enable universal group membership caching instead. ***Universal group membership caching*** is a feature introduced in Windows Server 2003 that enables a domain controller to store users' group memberships in a cache, which it refreshes from a global catalog server every eight hours.

To enable universal group membership caching, you open the NTDS Site Settings Properties sheet for a particular site, as shown in Figure 3-14. Select the Enable Universal Group Membership Caching check box and, in the Refresh cache from drop-down list, select the site with the nearest global catalog server.

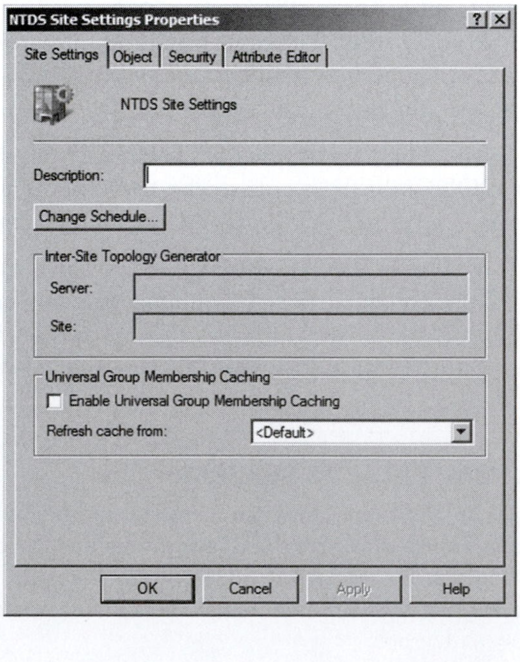

Figure 3-14

The *NTDS Site Settings Properties* sheet

Locating Printers

Publishing printers in AD DS makes it possible for users to locate them by running a search. When you create a printer location schema and assign locations to the subnets you created in the Active Directory Sites and Services console, AD DS automatically associates printers with specific locations, based on the subnet to which you connect them.

A *location schema* is a hierarchical system for designating physical locations of printers and other devices. A location consists of a series of names separated by slashes, indicating successively granular location names.

For example, a location schema for a global organization might have five levels, beginning with a continent and narrowing down locations to countries, cities, buildings, and specific rooms, as follows:

- Continent
- Country
- City
- Building
- Room

An example of a location using this schema would be as follows:

- North America/US/Boston/Adatum/1725

For a more localized organization, you can use fewer than five levels and begin with states or cities at the top level, if desired. Once you create a location schema, you can open the Properties sheets for the subnet objects you created and specify their locations, as shown in Figure 3-15.

TAKE NOTE*

The schema you create can have as many as 256 levels, with names up to 260 characters long, but only 32 characters fit in the user interface.

Figure 3-15

The *Properties* sheet for a subnet object

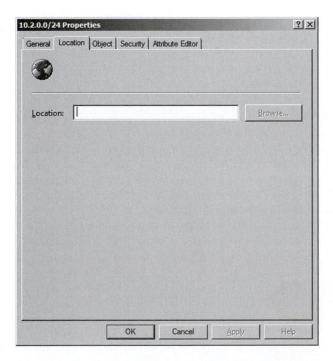

Finally, you must enable the *Pre-populate printer search location text* policy, found in the Computer Configuration\Policies\Administrative Templates\Printers folder of any Group Policy object. This setting enables Location Tracking, which enables users to browse locations in the Find Printers dialog box.

■ Designing a Group Policy Strategy

In a perfect world, you would be hired as an enterprise administrator and given the opportunity to build up a huge network from nothing. You would create policies and your staff would adhere to those policies from the start. The network would grow in a logical, orderly manner, with every aspect of its administration conforming to your directives.

CERTIFICATION READY
How do you design an enterprise-level group policy strategy?
2.4

But the world is not perfect. In nearly all cases, enterprise administrators must take charge of networks that have evolved in a decidedly messy manner. Your typical IT administrator is usually too busy putting out the fires that are burning right now to worry about policies to prevent future problems.

Group Policy is one of the areas where a new enterprise administrator is most likely to find evidence of this messy growth. When, in the course of performing a task or addressing a problem, administrators have to deploy a new Group Policy setting, they have two choices: they can add the setting to an existing Group Policy object (GPO) or create a new GPO for each setting. As a result, a new enterprise administrator examining a network for the first time might encounter one of the following:

- A single GPO with a vast number of settings
- A vast number of GPOs, each with one setting

In reality, a network with no set Group Policy strategy is likely to have a combination of these two results. The enterprise administrator's job is to create a strategy for Group Policy application, so that when other administrators have settings to deploy, they do so in a controlled and predictable manner. The objective is for other administrators to know intuitively where to look for Group Policy settings and how to deploy their own settings effectively.

The other—and arguably more difficult—part of the exercise is to apply the enterprise administrator's strategy to the existing Group Policy objects currently deployed on the network. This requires the administrators to review the settings currently in use and the methods previous administrators used to deploy them. Depending on the efficiency of the previous administrations, the current settings may or may not be properly documented or logically implemented.

Establishing a Group Policy Hierarchy

You learned in Lesson 2 and earlier in this lesson that the designs of the logical elements and the physical topology of your AD DS hierarchy are intimately related. The same is true of your Group Policy hierarchy, which you build on the AD DS objects you have already created.

As an enterprise administrator, you will already have put out your share of fires, and will be familiar with the various ways of deploying group policy settings. You can link group policy objects to domain objects, organizational units, or, in the physical topology, sites. You can also control the deployment of Group Policy settings by blocking inheritance, regulating enforcement, applying security filters, and adjusting GPO precedence.

When administrators are left to their own devices, you might find Group Policy settings deployed on the network using any of these techniques in various combinations. The result can be a barely controlled chaos in which administrators, concerned only about the settings they are currently deploying, unknowingly sabotage the settings previously created by others.

One of the most common reasons for creating organizational units in AD DS domains in the first place is to facilitate the deployment of Group Policy settings to specific sets of users and computers. Even if a domain includes a top level of OUs based on geographical or business divisions, lower-level OU creation is likely to be more directly influenced by the need to deploy the same Group Policy settings to certain recipients.

As with all AD DS design efforts, simplicity is best whenever possible, so the recommended course of action for the enterprise administrator is to create an OU hierarchy that enables administrators to link GPOs to domains or OUs and allow the default Group Policy inheritance rules to carry the settings downwards.

TAKE NOTE*

Group Policy is similar to the NTFS permission system in that it gives administrators a large number of different deployment techniques. However, just because these techniques are available to you doesn't mean you have to use them. When assigning permissions, most administrators only use Allow permissions and rarely modify the default inheritance properties. The same should be true with Group Policy. Link GPOs to OUs in the normal manner and don't block inheritance or disable enforcement except in special instances when it is absolutely necessary.

CREATING GPOs STRATEGICALLY

Some of the rules you should observe when creating a GPO strategy are as follows:

- Create GPOs for specific purposes—From an administrative perspective, a larger number of GPOs containing a few settings each is preferable to a single GPO with a great many settings. Group settings according to purpose or function, so that other administrators can locate them easily.

- Give GPOs descriptive names—Create names for your GPOs that reflect the purpose of the settings inside and/or the users and computers that will receive the settings. This also enables other administrators to locate existing Group Policy settings more easily.

- Do not deploy the same GPO to multiple sites—If you have to deploy the same settings to domains or OUs in different sites, create duplicate copies of the GPO rather than link it to multiple objects. This improves client performance and reduces WAN traffic.

- Disable unused Group Policy elements—If a GPO contains only user settings, then disable the computers settings in the GPO, to speed up client logons and minimize resource utilization.

- Use blocking and enforcement sparingly—If possible, link GPOs to multiple OUs lower in the hierarchy, rather than linking to higher-level GPOs and using blocking or enforcement to control inheritance.

USING SECURITY FILTERING

By default, all of the AD DS objects in an organizational unit to which you have linked a GPO receive the settings contained in that GPO. However, there are occasions in which you might want to apply Group Policy settings in a more granular way, and the best way of doing that is to use security filtering.

Security filtering enables you to restrict the application of GPO settings in an OU only to the members of security groups you specify in the Group Policy Management console, as shown in Figure 3-16.

Figure 3-16

Security filtering in the Group Policy Management console

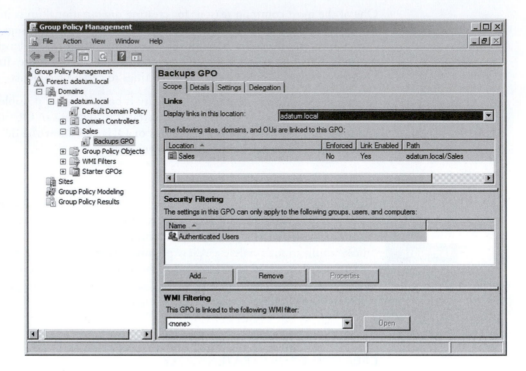

Security filtering is actually enabled on all GPOs, by default, with the Authenticated Users group configured to receive the GPO settings. When you modify the default by adding other groups to the Security Filtering box, be sure to remove the Authenticated Users group, or everyone will continue to receive the settings.

Authenticating and Authorizing Users

When you use Active Directory Domain Services on an enterprise network, the directory service becomes a critical component in two of the most important security mechanisms in networking: authentication and authorization.

Enterprise administrators should be intimately familiar with these mechanisms, and even though they are no longer involved in the day-to-day tasks by which other administrators maintain them, they are responsible for setting the policies that other people implement throughout the organization.

UNDERSTANDING AUTHENTICATION

To authenticate a user on a network with reasonable certainty that the individual is who he or she claims to be, the user needs to provide two pieces of information: identification and proof of identity. On most networks, users identify themselves with an account name or an email address. The proof of identity can vary, however, depending on the amount of security the network requires.

Proof of identity typically takes one of three forms:

- Something you know—Most commonly, proof of identity takes the form of a password. A password is a type of shared secret. The user knows the password, and the server authenticating the user either has the password stored, or has some information that it can use to validate the password.

- Something you have—Many modern computer networks requiring greater security authenticate users by reading information from a smart card. A smart card is a credit-card-sized device containing memory and embedded circuitry that enables it to store data, such as a digital certificate or a public encryption key. Running the card through an electronic card reader provides an electronic equivalent of a password.

- Something you are—For even greater security, some networks require you to provide proof of identify by confirming a physical attribute using biometrics. A biometric system proves a user's identity by scanning a unique part of the body such as fingerprints, the retina of the eye, or facial features.

Passwords can be guessed, and smart cards can be stolen. One form of authentication alone might not meet your organization's security requirements. ***Multifactor authentication*** combines two or more authentication methods, and significantly reduces the likelihood that an attacker will be able to impersonate a user during the authentication process. The most common example of multifactor authentication is combining a smart card with a password. Typically, the user supplies a password to retrieve a key stored on the smart card.

NETWORK PLANNING AND AUTHENTICATION

Many organizations have to provide seamless network access for multiple types of users, such as office workers, employees who are traveling, business partners, and customers. At the same time, organizations must protect network resources from potential intruders. A network designed with an eye towards authentication can help you to achieve this complex balance between reliable access for users and strong network security for your organization.

As with other AD DS design tasks, when establishing an authentication strategy, you must be conscious of the physical and virtual topology of your network. As mentioned earlier in this lesson, authentication is one of the factors you must consider when creating site and site link objects. Authentication is a viable reason for adding more domain controllers to a site, or for creating a separate site in the first place.

TAKE NOTE*

Many administrators express concern about whether they have enough bandwidth between sites, but it is actually latency (the time it takes for a packet to travel from a source to a destination) that's more likely to cause authentication problems across WAN links. Authentication requires very little bandwidth. However, packets must go back and forth across the link several times. If latency causes a significant delay for each round trip, authentication will seem slow.

REQUIRING SMART CARDS

As an enterprise administrator, it is up to you to evaluate the security requirements for your organization, as well as other factors, such as budget constraints, when designing an authentication strategy for your network. Smart cards are more secure than passwords, because there is no practical way to duplicate the information they contain by guessing or brute-force attack. It is possible for users to have their smart cards lost or stolen, but in most cases, they know when this occurs and can report the loss. An administrator can then revoke the certificate on the card, rendering it invalid and useless.

Windows has supported *smart-card authentication* for some time, but until Windows 7, you had to install a third-party device driver along with the card-reader hardware. By including support for the *Personal Identity Verification (PIV)* standard, published by the National Institute of Standards and Technology (NIST), Windows 7 can now obtain drivers for PIV smart cards from Windows Update or use a PIV minidriver included with the operating system.

Enterprise administrators can require passwords and smart cards for all the organization's users, but this represents a substantial investment in cards and card-reader hardware, as well as education for users and administrators. Biometric systems require even more of an investment, in every way.

To limit these expenses, you can design a policy that requires only certain individuals to use smart cards or biometrics. For example, you might require network administrators to use smart cards because their privileges provide attackers with a more significant opportunity than those of a common user.

TAKE NOTE *

Requiring smart cards for authentication can cause problems with existing applications. However, if an application includes the Certified for Windows Server 2008 logo, the application has been tested to ensure that it meets Microsoft security standards for Windows Server 2008. One of the security requirements for the Certified for Windows Server 2008 logo is that the application "support smart card login and secure credential management."

For organizations that are committed to the use of smart cards for authentication, there are two smart-card-related Group Policy settings that Windows 7 supports. These settings, located in the Computer Configuration\Policies\Windows Settings\Security Settings\Local Policies\Security Options node, are as follows:

- Interactive Logon: Require Smart Card—Configures Windows 7 to allow only smart-card user authentications.
- Interactive Logon: Smart Card Removal Behavior—Specifies how Windows 7 should behave when a user removes the smart card from the reader while logged on to the computer. The possible values are as follows:
  - No action—Enables the user to remove the smart card without affecting the session. This is the default setting.
  - Lock Workstation—Disables the workstation while leaving the session open until the user reinserts the smart card. This enables the user to leave the workstation temporarily without leaving the smart card and without having to log off.
  - Force Logoff—Causes the workstation to log the user off as soon as the smart card is removed.
  - Disconnect if a Remote Desktop Services session—Disconnects the computer from the Remote Desktop Services server without logging the user off from the session. The user can then resume the session by reinserting the smart card at the same or another computer.

USING STRONG PASSWORDS

The encryption systems that Windows uses when working with passwords limit an organization's vulnerability to interception and misuse of user credentials. Specifically, password encryption is designed to make it extremely difficult for unauthorized users to decrypt captured passwords. Ideally, when accounts use strong passwords, it should take an attacker months, years, or decades to extract a password after capturing the encrypted or hashed data. During that time, the user should have changed the password—rendering the cracked password useless.

Weak passwords, on the other hand, can be cracked in a matter of hours or days, even when encrypted. Encryption also cannot protect against passwords that are easily guessable, because weak passwords are vulnerable to ***dictionary attacks***. Dictionary attacks encrypt a list of common passwords and compare the results with the captured cyphertext. If the password appears in the password dictionary, the attacker can identify the password quickly. Administrators can defend against this vulnerability by implementing a strong password policy throughout the enterprise.

A strong password is one that a user can easily remember but which is also too complex for a stranger to guess. For example, **&_I5y#<.h* might appear to be a good password, but few users would be able to remember it without writing it down, creating a significant security vulnerability. Fortunately, there are techniques for creating strong passwords that humans can remember more easily. For example, you can take a password that is easy to remember (and easy to guess), such as *99Butterflies*, and add an easy-to-remember suffix to it to make it more secure: *99Butterflies@complexpassword.com*. You now have a password that is 33 characters long, uses uppercase, lowercase, and symbols, is easy to remember, and that, because of its length, is harder than the **&_I5y#<.h* password to crack.

In the example above, an email type suffix was added to the end of the password to make it complex. You can also require the addition of phone numbers, addresses, and file-path locations (like c:\winnt\system32) to make a password complex.

TAKE NOTE*

The Microsoft definition of a complex password is one that is at least six characters long and uses at least three of the following four types of characters: uppercase, lowercase, numerals, and symbols.

USING PASSWORD POLICIES

When devising a password policy, consider users' inability to remember passwords that are too complex, change too often, and are too long. When passwords are too complex or too long, the eventuality that users will use other methods to remember their passwords, such as writing them down, is more likely.

To implement a strong password strategy, Windows Server 2008 R2 provides a series of password settings that you can deploy using Group Policy. An effective combination of password policies compels users to select appropriate passwords and change them at regular intervals.

The Group Policy settings that dictate password policies are located in the Computer Configuration\Policies\Windows Settings\Security Settings\Account Policies\Password Policy container, as shown in Figure 3-17.

Figure 3-17

Password Policy settings in the Group Policy Management Editor

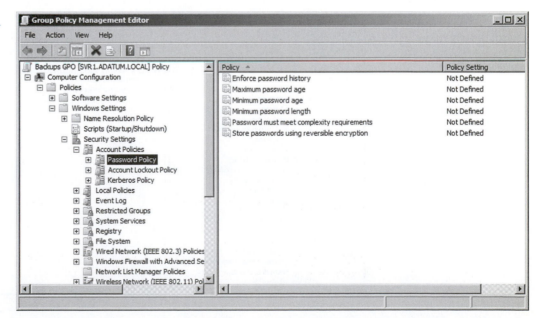

Although enterprise administrators do not usually work with GPOs and Group Policy settings themselves, they do create strategies that dictate how other administrators will use the settings. The strategic functions of the Password Policy settings are as follows:

- Enforce password history—Prevents users from defeating password change requirements by reusing the same passwords.

- Maximum password age—Compels users to change their passwords at regular intervals. Higher values increase the likelihood that passwords can be cracked, while lower values can increase the number of support calls relating to forgotten passwords.

- Minimum password age—Prevents users from defeating password uniqueness requirements by changing their passwords and then immediately changing them back again.

- Minimum password length—Longer passwords provide greater security, but can also be more difficult for users to remember.

- Password must meet complexity requirements—Complex passwords have a minimum length requirement and use a larger character set, and are therefore mathematically harder to crack.

Although you can enforce strong passwords in Windows Server 2008 Active Directory using password policies, employee education is the only way to keep users from writing down passwords in public locations or using discoverable personal information in passwords.

USING ACCOUNT LOCKOUT POLICIES

Account lockout policies can limit your network's vulnerability to password-guessing attacks, but they also expose you to a denial-of-service vulnerability. A malicious attacker with access to user names can guess incorrect passwords and lock everyone's accounts, which denies legitimate users access to network resources. Lockouts also increase the burden on the help desk, branch office supervisors, or whoever else is responsible for accounts locked due to forgotten passwords.

Windows Server 2008 R2 does not enable account lockouts by default. You should only enable them in environments where the threat from guessed passwords is greater than the threat of a denial-of-service attack. Like password policies, you define account lockout policy settings using Group Policy, as shown in Figure 3-18. When configuring these settings, you should select values that are sufficiently lax to allow for user input error, but are also stringent enough to prevent attacks on user accounts.

Figure 3-18

Account Lockout Policy settings in the Group Policy Management Editor

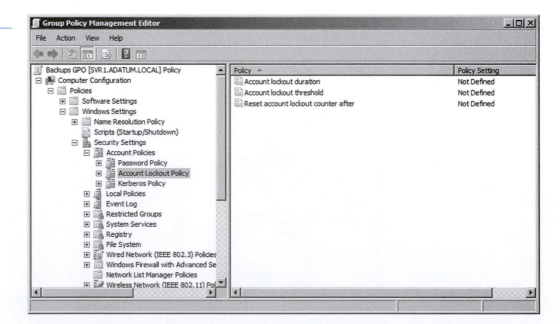

USING FINE-GRAINED PASSWORD POLICIES

Unlike other Group Policy settings, you can only apply the Password Policy and Account Lockout Policy settings in a GPO to an entire AD DS domain, not to an individual OU. Administrators have complained about this limitation for years, and Windows Server 2008 finally introduced a mechanism that provides *fine-grained password policies* that you can apply to individual groups within a domain.

The primary reason for fine-grained password policies is that administrators have long recognized that some users should have more stringent policies than others. To adequately protect administrative passwords providing privileges that could be extremely damaging in the wrong hands, administrators have had to impose password length requirements and frequent password changes on all users.

Using fine-grained password policies, enterprise administrators can create different sets of policies for different classes of users. For example, a typical use of this feature might call for three sets of password policies, as follows:

- Administrators—Because administrators have more privileges than regular users, they should have more stringent password and account-lockout policy settings, including longer passwords and more frequent password changes.
- Service accounts—Because no one has to type service account passwords on a regular basis, they can be much longer than any other passwords, and have much longer expiration dates.
- Users—Passwords for regular user accounts can be shorter than those of administrators, and change less frequently. Depending on the privileges granted to the users, you might also disable password complexity.

If you have users with varying degrees of access to the network, you might want to create additional sets of policies.

To implement fine-grained password policies, Windows Server 2008 expanded the AD DS schema to create a password settings container and an object type called password settings object (PSO). To use these schema modifications, you must raise the domain functional level for your domains to Windows Server 2008.

Microsoft has not integrated these new objects into the Group Policy Management console interface. Instead, you can only access them graphically using the ADSI Edit console, as shown in Figure 3-19, to modify the object attributes directly.

Figure 3-19

The ADSI Edit console

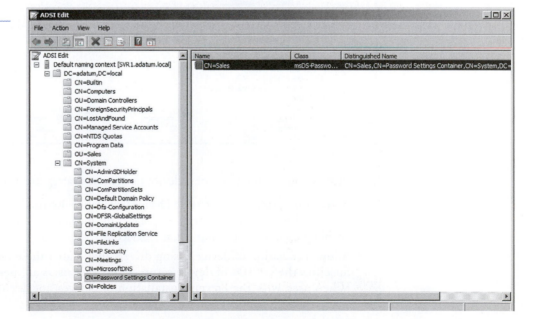

Unlike GPOs, you cannot link PSOs to organizational units. You can only link them to global security groups. Some administrators create *shadow groups*, which are simply global groups that contain all of the users found in a particular OU, and use them to deploy PSOs.

Controlling Device Installation

Protecting the organization's data is one of the chief responsibilities of the enterprise administrator, and Group Policy provides the means to do this by controlling what devices users are permitted to install on their computers.

In some situations, administrators want to prevent users from removing data from their computers, and today that typically means preventing users from inserting USB flash drives or other writable data storage devices.

However, as usual, there are likely to be exceptions. You might want to deny regular users the ability to insert devices, but allow administrators to do so. You might want to allow users to insert particular devices, but deny them the use of all others. You might even want to deny the use of specific devices and allow all others. By combining Group Policy settings, you can achieve nearly any configuration.

The Group Policy settings that control device installation are located in the Computer Configuration\Policies\Administrative Templates\System\Device Installation\Device Installation Restrictions container, as shown in Figure 3-20.

Figure 3-20

Device Installation Restriction settings in the Group Policy Management Editor

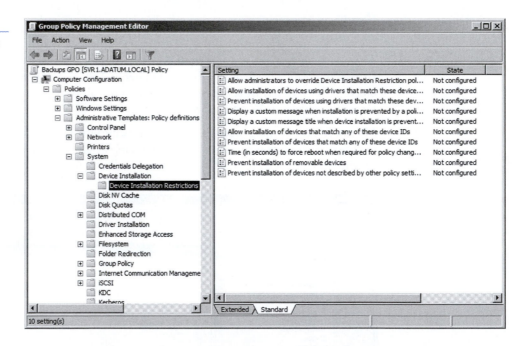

The settings you can use to create a device restriction strategy are as follows:

- Allow administrators to override Device Installation Restriction policies—Overrides all other device installation restriction policies for members of the Administrators group, enabling them to install and use any device.
- Allow installation of devices using drivers that match these device setup classes— Specifies the GUIDs of device setup classes that users are permitted to install. When used with the Prevent installation of devices not described by other policy

sessions setting, users are able to install only the devices specified by the GUIDs you supply.

- Prevent installation of devices using drivers that match these device setup classes—Specifies the GUIDs of device setup classes that users are not permitted to install. Users are permitted to install devices not specified by the GUIDs you supply.

- Allow installation of devices that match any of these device IDs—Specifies the hardware IDs or compatible IDs of devices that users are permitted to install. When used with the Prevent installation of devices not described by other policy sessions setting, users are able to install only the devices specified by the IDs you supply.

- Prevent installation of devices that match any of these device IDs—Specifies the hardware IDs or compatible IDs of devices that users are not permitted to install. Users are permitted to install devices not specified by the IDs you supply.

- Prevent installation of removable devices—Denies users the ability to install removable devices, overriding all other settings allowing device installation.

- Prevent installation of devices not described by other policy sessions—Denies users the ability to install any devices not specified by other policy settings.

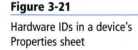

The Device Installation Restriction policies do not affect the use of USB flash drives for the Windows ReadyBoost feature. This is because ReadyBoost is a System installation.

One of the most common combinations is to enable the Prevent installation of devices not described by other policy sessions and allow administrators to override Device Installation Restriction policies settings. This prevents regular users from installing devices, but allows administrators to override that policy.

For the settings that enable you to create a list of devices to allow or prevent installation, you can use a number of identifiers to reference specific hardware components. To discover the identifiers for a particular device, you install it in the normal manner and examine the properties that the installation creates.

Hardware IDs and compatible IDs are values that you determine by opening a device's Properties sheet in Device Manager and looking at the Details tab, as shown in Figure 3-21. GUIDs for device setup classes are located in the Windows registry in the HKLM\CurrentControlSet\Control\Class\ClassGUID key.

Figure 3-21

Hardware IDs in a device's Properties sheet

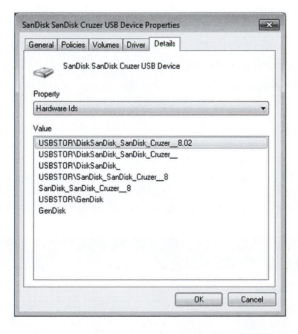

SKILL SUMMARY

IN THIS LESSON YOU LEARNED:

- Once you have designed the logical infrastructure for AD DS by deciding how many forests and domains to create, you can begin to consider the physical aspects of the AD DS infrastructure.

- A site is a special type of AD DS container object that provides the connection between the logical AD DS infrastructure—forests, domains, and organizational units—and the physical network infrastructure—cables, routers, and WAN links.

- In an AD DS installation with multiple sites, each site designates one domain controller as the bridgehead server for each partition with a replica at that site. The bridgehead servers are the only domain controllers that communicate with the other sites.

- In one model, the hub-and-spoke topology, one site, in this case the headquarters, is designated as the hub and communicates with each of the other sites. The branch office sites do not communicate with each other. Separate links for each domain are still required.

- In a full-mesh topology, each site maintains connections to every other site. This model generates more WAN traffic, but it generally reduces replication latency.

- To enable replication between two sites, you must have a site link object associated with both of them. A site link object represents the physical connection between remote sites. The purpose of the site link is to indicate which sites are connected and to provide details about the cost and availability of the physical connection.

- In some cases, you might want to turn off the default bridging for all of your site links and create your own site link bridge objects instead. A site link bridge object is a connection between two site links that renders them transitive.

- The enterprise administrator's job is to create a strategy for Group Policy application, so that when other administrators have settings to deploy, they do so in a controlled and predictable manner.

- As with all AD DS design efforts, simplicity is best whenever possible, so the recommended course of action for the enterprise administrator is to create an OU hierarchy that enables administrators to link GPOs to domains or OUs and allow the default Group Policy inheritance rules to carry the settings downwards.

- Scope filtering enables you to restrict the application of GPO settings in an OU only to the members of security groups you specify in the Group Policy Management console.

- Unlike other Group Policy settings, you can only apply the Password Policy and Account Lockout Policy settings in a GPO to an entire AD DS domain, not to an individual OU. Administrators have complained about this limitation for years, and Windows Server 2008 finally introduced a mechanism that provides fine-grained password policies that you can apply to individual groups within a domain.

■ Knowledge Assessment

Fill in the Blank

Complete the following sentences by writing the correct word or words in the blanks provided.

1. An area of an Active Directory Domain Services network in which all of the domain controllers are well connected is known as a _____.

2. The domain controller at a particular site that is responsible for communicating with domain controllers at other sites is called a _____.

3. To avoid installing additional domain controllers for the forest-root domain, you can create _____ instead.

4. For users in a particular site to be able to search in other domains, they must have access to a _____.

5. You can restrict the deployment of Group Policy settings to member of specific groups by using _____.

6. The amount of time it takes for AD DS changes to propagate to all of the domain controllers in the enterprise is called the _____.

7. To create password settings objects, you must use the _____ tool.

8. A security system that scans a part of the body to confirm a user's identity is called a _____ system.

9. The single-site model assumes that all the domain controllers on the network are _____.

10. When you create multiple site objects for your network, you must also create _____ objects.

True / False

Circle T if the statement is true or F if the statement is false.

T | F 1. The name of the first site created in every new forest is Default-First-Site-Name.

T | F 2. The AD DS object type that connects two sites together is called a site link bridge object.

T | F 3. A shadow group is an AD DS object that has global groups as members.

T | F 4. To install a read-only domain controller, you must have at least two computers running Windows Server 2008 or Windows Server 2008 R2 functioning as domain controllers on your network.

T | F 5. To use fine-grained password policies, you must raise your forest functional level to Windows Server 2008.

T | F 6. One viable alternative to installing a global catalog server at a branch office site is to enable universal group membership caching.

T | F 7. When designing a Group Policy strategy, it is preferable to create a single GPO with a large number of settings rather than many GPOs with a few settings each.

T | F 8. The Prevent installation of devices not described by other policy sessions setting overrides all other Device Installation restriction settings.

T | F 9. You cannot apply fine-grained password policies to organizational unit objects, only to security groups.

T | F 10. Replication traffic between sites is always compressed.

Review Questions

1. List three differences between the intersite and intrasite replication processes in an Active Directory Domain Services network.

2. Explain the difference between site link objects and site link bridge objects.

■ Case Scenarios

Scenario 3-1: Creating Device Restrictions

After a recent incident in which an employee left the company with a substantial amount of confidential data, the IT director has given Alice the task of implementing Group Policy settings that prevent all users except administrators and members of the Executives group from installing any USB devices. Alice creates a GPO called Device Restrictions for this purpose and links it to the company's single domain object. The GPO contains the following settings:

- Allow administrators to override Device Installation Restriction policies—Enabled
- Prevent installation of devices not described by other policy sessions—Enabled

What else must Alice do to satisfy the requirements of her assignment?

Scenario 3-2: Assigning Site Link Costs

Adatum Corp. has its headquarters in Los Angeles and branch offices in San Francisco, San Diego, and Sacramento, each of which has its own AD DS site. Each of the three branch offices has a T-1 connection to the Los Angeles office, running at 1.544 Mbps. The Sacramento connection has an average available bandwidth of 75%, and the San Diego connection has 60% available. The San Francisco link, however, has only 25% of its bandwidth available. The company has also just installed new 512 Kbps links between San Diego and San Francisco, San Francisco and Sacramento, and Sacramento and San Diego, to create a full-mesh replication topology.

You want AD DS replication traffic to use the T-1 connections wherever practical. However, because the Los Angeles—San Francisco link is nearing bandwidth saturation, you want replication traffic to use the other links to connect these two cities. Due to a special arrangement with its service provider, Adatum is getting the San Francisco—Sacramento link for half price. Using the table below, assign cost values to the links to provide the most economical connections possible under the current traffic conditions. Explain your answers.

SITE LINK	COST
Los Angeles—San Francisco	
Los Angeles—San Diego	
Los Angeles—Sacramento	
Sacramento—San Francisco	
San Diego—San Francisco	
Sacramento—San Diego	

Planning for Migration and Interoperability

OBJECTIVE DOMAIN MATRIX

TECHNOLOGY SKILL	OBJECTIVE DOMAIN	OBJECTIVE NUMBER
Migrating to Windows Server 2008 R2	Plan for domain or forest migration, upgrade, and restructuring.	3.1
Planning for Interoperability	Plan for interoperability.	3.4

KEY TERMS

Active Directory Federation
  Services (AD FS)
Active Directory Lightweight
  Directory Services (AD LDS)
Active Directory Migration Tool
  (ADMT)
domain-restructure migration
domain-upgrade migration

domain upgrade-then-
  restructure migration
federation claims
identity federation
Identity Management for UNIX
interforest migration
intraforest migration
Network File System (NFS)

Network Information Service (NIS)
Password Synchronization
pristine forest
security identifier (SID)
Server Message Blocks (SMB)
Services for Network File
  System
sIDHistory attribute

■ Migrating to Windows Server 2008 R2

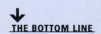
THE BOTTOM LINE

For many enterprise administrators, deploying Windows Server 2008 R2 will be a matter of integrating the new operating system into a network that already has servers running earlier Windows versions. As with the other aspects of Active Directory Domain Services administration discussed in previous lessons, a migration to Windows Server 2008 R2 requires careful planning to ensure successful completion without any interruption of services.

CERTIFICATION READY
How do you plan for domain or forest migration, upgrade, and restructuring
3.1

Adding computers running Windows Server 2008 R2 to an existing Windows Server 2003 or Windows 2000 Server network as member servers does not require any special planning or preparation. However, if you are planning to upgrade existing servers to Windows Server 2008 R2, there are certain limitations.

TAKE NOTE *

Because Microsoft no longer supports Windows NT 4.0, you cannot upgrade a Windows NT 4.0 server to Windows Server 2008 R2.

In-place upgrades to Windows Server 2008 R2 are permissible from Windows Server 2003 SP2, Windows Server 2003 R2, or Windows Server 2008, as long as the platform, architecture, edition, and language are the same.

Generally speaking, you cannot upgrade across platforms or architectures, but you can upgrade across editions if the Windows Server 2008 R2 edition is the same or higher than its predecessor. For example, you can upgrade Windows Server 2003 R2 Standard to Windows Server 2008 R2 Enterprise, but you cannot upgrade an Enterprise edition to Standard. You also cannot upgrade a full installation to Server Core, or vice versa.

TAKE NOTE *

Whenever it is practical, a clean installation is always preferable to an in-place upgrade.

Understanding Migration Paths

Upgrading member servers is a relatively simple matter, but migrating domain controllers is considerably more complicated. You can't add a domain controller running Windows Server 2008 or Windows Server 2008 R2 to a Windows 2000 Server or Windows Server 2003 Active Directory domain without upgrading it to Active Directory Domain Services (AD DS).

A directory service migration is the process that takes you from a *source* directory, that is, your current Active Directory infrastructure, to a *target* directory, which is a Windows Server 2008 R2 AD DS infrastructure. There are three possible migration paths from the source to the target, as follows:

- Domain upgrade—In a ***domain-upgrade migration***, you either upgrade one of the existing domain controllers in your source domain to Windows Server 2008 R2 or install a new domain controller running Windows Server 2008 R2 into the domain. In this model, the process upgrades all of the objects in your source domain at the same time, leaving you with the same domain structure as before the migration. Once the upgrade is completed, the target is created and the source ceases to exist.

- Domain restructure—In a ***domain-restructure migration***, you create an entirely new Windows Server 2008 R2 domain on a newly installed domain controller, and then you copy or move objects from your original source domain to the new target. With this model, the source domain remains operational throughout the migration process, and administrators have the opportunity to redesign the domain as they migrate the objects. It is also possible to migrate objects selectively, eliminating those that are no longer needed and moving others to different domains or forests.

- Upgrade-then-restructure—An ***upgrade-then-restructure migration*** is a two-phase process in which you first upgrade your existing forest and domains to Windows Server 2008 R2 and then restructure the AD DS database by migrating objects into other domains within the same forest.

SELECTING A MIGRATION PATH

Like nearly every activity in the enterprise administrator's job description, migrating to AD DS involves a great deal of planning and decision making before the hands-on part of the project even begins. One of the first steps in the planning process is to decide which migration path you want to use. Some of the criteria you should use to make that decision are as follows:

- Design—If you are satisfied with the design of your Active Directory infrastructure—the forests, domains, and organizational units (OUs) that make up your directory—then you might want to consider the domain-upgrade migration path. A domain upgrade leaves everything where it is, and is by far the simplest and most expedient of the migration paths. If, on the other hand, you feel that your existing domain infrastructure is not

satisfactory—perhaps because it is outdated, or because you have inherited a directory that was badly designed to begin with—a domain-restructure migration to Windows Server 2008 R2 provides an opportunity to redesign your domains.

- Time—The domain-upgrade migration path is much faster and requires less planning and interaction than a domain-restructure migration. Domain restructure migrations are often long-term projects that occur gradually in phases, while a domain upgrade must be completed all at once. The time required for the upgrade depends on the size and number of objects in the Active Directory database.

- Budget—A domain-upgrade migration is usually less expensive than a domain-restructure migration because in many cases it can use the same domain controller hardware. However, if your existing domain controllers cannot run Windows Server 2008 R2 and you have to replace them anyway, you might want to consider incorporating a domain structure into your migration.

- Productivity—One advantage of a domain-restructure migration is that it requires no downtime and therefore no loss of productivity from network users. The source directory remains continuously operative throughout the process, while administrators construct and test the target domains. Then, the transition from source to target can be seamless. By contrast, the source domains are offline during a domain-upgrade process, the length of which is dependent on the size of the database.

- Manpower—The domain-upgrade migration process is largely automated, so in most cases the manpower demands for the project are minimal. This can change, however, if the upgrade requires the installation of new servers. A domain-restructure migration requires considerably more effort, both for planning and for the actual deployment of the new domains, which is largely a manual process.

MIGRATING OBJECTS

All migrations that include a domain restructuring require administrators to copy or move objects between domains, or possibly between forests. Although the native Windows Server tools are not capable of doing this, a variety of other products can, both from Microsoft and from third parties.

Active Directory Migration Tool (ADMT) is a free package from Microsoft that can migrate objects with or between forests, and includes a modeling mode that enables you to try out sample designs before committing to them.

Upgrading a Domain

Upgrading a Windows 2000 Server or Windows Server 2003 domain is basically a matter of introducing a Windows Server 2008 R2 domain controller onto the network. However, there are some steps that you must perform first.

To prepare the forest and the domain for the upgrade, you must modify the schema of your existing Active Directory installation. Then you can upgrade one of the domain controllers to Windows Server 2008 R2 or install a new Windows Server 2008 R2 domain controller.

Before you begin, be conscious of the Windows Server 2008 R2 upgrade limitations. You cannot upgrade a domain controller to Windows Server 2008 R2 if any of the following conditions are true:

- Your domain controller is running a 32-bit or Itanium version of a Windows Server operating system.

- Your domain controller is running a Windows Server edition different from that of the Windows Server 2008 R2 product you purchased.

In either of these cases, you can upgrade your domain by installing a new Windows Server 2008 R2 domain controller instead of upgrading your existing ones. The down-level domain controllers can then remain in the domain indefinitely, or until you find it necessary to raise the functional level of the domain or the forest.

It is impossible to upgrade a domain by using either of the upgrade-migration path options if any of the following are true:

- Your existing domain is running at the Windows 2000 mixed or Windows Server 2003 interim functional level.
- Any of your domain controllers are running Windows NT 4.0.

In these cases, you must upgrade your domain to Windows 2000 Server or Windows Server 2003 before you can upgrade it to Windows Server 2008 R2.

PREPARING THE FOREST

To prepare the forest for the upgrade, you must modify the schema of the existing Active Directory database using the Adprep.exe utility included with Windows Server 2008 R2. Only one domain controller—the schema operations master—is capable of writing changes to the schema, so you must perform this procedure on that domain controller.

To locate the domain controller that is functioning as the schema operations master, open the Active Director Schema console, right-click Active Directory Schema, and, from the context menu, select Operations Master. The Change Schema Master dialog box appears, as shown in Figure 4-1.

Figure 4-1

The *Change Schema Master dialog box*

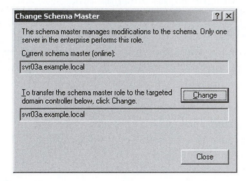

The Active Directory Schema console does not appear in the Administrative tools program group, nor does the Active Directory Schema snap-in appear in the Add Standalone Snap-in dialog box in Microsoft Management Console (MMC) by default. Before you can add the snap-in, you must register the schema management library on your computer using the following command at a command prompt:

TAKE NOTE*

```
regsvr32 schmmgmt.dll
```

To prepare the forest for an upgrade to Windows Server 2008 R2, use the following procedure.

 PREPARE A FOREST

GET READY. Log on to the down-level domain controller that is the schema operations master for the forest, using an account with Enterprise Admins and Schema Admins privileges.

1. Disconnect the schema operations master computer from the network by disabling the Local Area Connection or disconnecting the network cable. This prevents the

system from replicating the changes you will make to the schema to other domain controllers until you are sure the changes are completed successfully.

2. Insert the Windows Server 2008 R2 installation DVD into the computer's drive.

3. Open a Command Prompt window and switch to the support\adprep folder on the DVD.

4. Type the command adprep /forestprep and press Enter. A warning appears, prompting you to confirm that all of the domain controllers in the forest are running Windows 2000 Server SP4 or later.

5. To continue, type C and press Enter. The program displays a series of results like those in Figure 4-2 as it imports and modifies individual Active Directory elements.

Figure 4-2

Results of the adprep /forestprep command

6. Open the Event Viewer console and check the System log for any errors that may have occurred during the schema upgrade. If any errors have occurred that you cannot correct with normal troubleshooting procedures, you should restore the schema operations master computer from your backup without reconnecting it to the network.

7. If the command completes successfully and no errors have occurred, reconnect the computer to the network to allow the schema changes to replicate to the other domain controllers.

Before you proceed to prepare the domain for the upgrade, as described in the next section, you must wait for the forest schema changes you have made to replicate to the other domain controllers throughout the forest, in particular to the infrastructure operations master for the domain you intend to upgrade. If the forest consists of multiple sites, you may have to wait for some time.

PREPARING THE DOMAIN

The process of preparing individual domains for an upgrade is similar to that of preparing a forest, except that you must perform the procedure on the infrastructure operations master instead of the schema operation master.

To locate the domain controller that is functioning as the infrastructure operations master, open the Active Director Users and Computers console, right-click the domain and, from the context menu, select Operations Master. In the Operations Masters dialog box, click the Infrastructure tab, as shown in Figure 4-3.

Figure 4-3

The *Operations Masters* dialog box

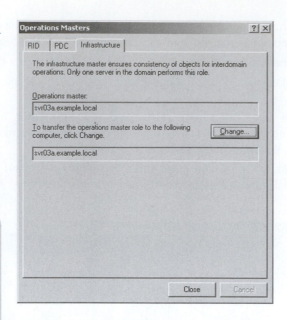

If the domain is using the Windows 2000 mixed domain functional level, you must raise it to Windows 2000 native or Windows Server 2003 before you can perform the following procedure.

To prepare a domain for an upgrade to Windows Server 2008 R2, use the following procedure.

 PREPARE A DOMAIN

GET READY. Log on to the down-level domain controller that is the infrastructure operations master for the domain, using an account with Enterprise Admins and Domain Admins privileges.

1. Insert the Windows Server 2008 R2 installation DVD into the computer's drive.
2. Open a Command Prompt window and switch to the support\adprep folder on the DVD.
3. Type the command adprep /domainprep /gpprep and press Enter. The program updates the domain and the permissions on the Group Policy objects in the directory, as shown in Figure 4-4.

Figure 4-4

Results of the adprep /domainprep /gpprep command

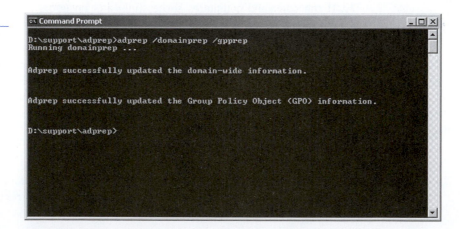

4. Open the Event Viewer console and check the System log for any errors that may have occurred during the schema upgrade.
5. If the command completes successfully and no errors have occurred, the preparation for the domain upgrade is complete.

As with the forest preparation, you must wait for the changes you have made to replicate throughout the enterprise before you proceed to upgrade the operating system on the domain controllers.

UPGRADING A DOMAIN

Once you have completed the controller preparation procedures for your forest and domain, you can proceed to upgrade one of the domain controllers to Windows Server 2008 R2 or install a new computer running Windows Server 2008 R2 and promote it to a domain controller. This will complete the upgrade of Windows 2000 Server or Windows Server 2003 Active Directory to Windows Server 2008 R2 Active Directory Domain Services.

As long as down-level domain controllers remain, you will not be able to raise the forest or domain functional levels to Windows Server 2008 R2, but deploying a single domain controller running Windows Server 2008 R2 upgrades the entire directory.

Restructuring a Domain

> A domain restructure enables the enterprise administrator to alter the existing Active Directory hierarchy by creating a new directory infrastructure using the same objects.

As mentioned earlier, in a domain restructure migration, you create at least one new Windows Server 2008 R2 domain and copy or move your existing objects into it. Because you are moving objects individually, you can place them in different domains and organizational units, creating an entirely different AD DS hierarchy for your network.

There are two basic types of domain restructure: interforest or intraforest. In an ***interforest migration***, you create a new Windows Server 2008 R2 forest—called a ***pristine forest*** because it is in no way an upgrade from your existing directory—and copy or move objects from your source domain into it. In this model, the source domain remains unmodified because the only connection between the source and the target domains is a trust relationship, and trusts can exist between forests using different versions of Windows Server.

In an ***intraforest migration***, you create a new domain in the same forest as your source domain and copy or move objects between the two. However, you cannot create a Windows Server 2008 R2 domain in an existing Windows Server 2003 or Windows 2000 Server forest. Therefore, you must upgrade your existing forest to Windows Server 2008 R2 first, and then perform the restructure. This is the upgrade-then-restructure migration process mentioned earlier in this lesson.

PERFORMING AN INTERFOREST MIGRATION

An interforest domain restructure migration does not require the schema preparation that a domain upgrade does, because you are not adding to or modifying the source domain in any way. However, while the process may seem simple on paper, you must remember that when creating your new forest, you must consider all the design issues discussed in Lesson 2, "Designing an Active Directory Hierarchy," and Lesson 3, "Building an Active Directory Topology."

The steps involved in performing the migration are discussed in the following sections.

CREATING A PRISTINE FOREST

The target domain in an interforest restructure migration is a new—or pristine—forest that you create from scratch on a computer running Windows Server 2008 R2. The procedure for planning and implementing this forest is the same as that for a new network. You must decide what and how many domains to create, build a hierarchy of organizational units, and plan a group policy strategy, just as you learned in the previous lessons.

This is the part of the process where the actual domain restructuring takes place. Depending on the circumstances, you may want to make only slight modifications to the domain hierarchy—largely recreating the infrastructure on your source directory—or you may create a completely new design for your network.

One of the advantages of this type of migration is that you can correct errors in judgment you might have made earlier. If you have determined that there is no real need to create two separate domains on your source directory, you can consolidate them into one domain in the target. In the same way, if you have organizational units in your source domain that need autonomy or isolation, you can restructure them into separate domains, or even separate forests.

CREATING INTERFOREST CONNECTIONS

Once you have created your pristine forest, you will have two separate Active Directory installations. The next step in the migration process is to establish connections between your two forests, so that a tool such as ADMT can move objects between them.

Your first concern is that the domain controllers in the two forests know of each other's existence. This means that the forests must share Domain Name System (DNS) information about each other. If, when creating your pristine forest, you configure your first domain controller to function as a DNS server, it will have no knowledge of your source directory until you provide it with access to the DNS information from your existing servers.

The simplest way to provide each forest with access to the other is to create a secondary zone on each DNS server that contains the primary zone from the other server. That is, create a zone for the target domain on the DNS server for your source forest and a zone for the source domain on your target DNS server, as shown in Figure 4-5.

Figure 4-5

DNS secondary zones for inter-forest communication

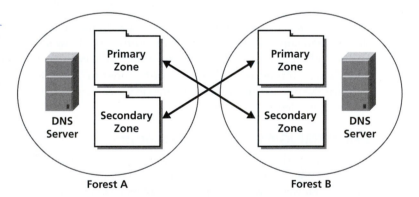

Once the DNS zones are in place, you must create trust relationships between the source and target domains. These trusts are necessary for the systems to grant administrative permissions to accounts from a different forest.

Using the Active Directory Domains and Trusts console on your source domain controller, use the New Trust Wizard to create a one-way outgoing trust to the target domain in your pristine forest, as shown in Figure 4-6.

Figure 4-6

Create trusts between your source and target forests

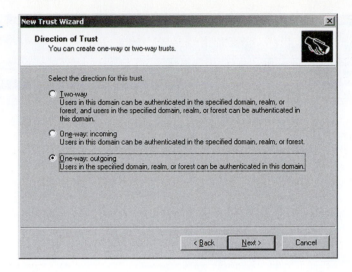

If you plan to be migrating objects from more than one source domain or to more than one target, then you must create trusts from each source to each target that will receive objects.

INSTALLING ACTIVE DIRECTORY MIGRATION TOOL

Active Directory Migration Tool (ADMT) is a wizard-based utility that enables you to perform both interforest and intraforest migrations. Once you have your trusts in place, you can download and install ADMT on a computer in your target domain.

ADMT version 3.2 is available as a free download from the Microsoft Download Center at http://www.microsoft.com/downloads/details.aspx?familyid=20C0DB45-DB16-4D10-99F2-539B7277CCDB&displaylang=en.

The computer on which you install ADMT must be running Windows Server 2008 R2, but it does not have to be your target domain controller. In fact, it might be better to use a member server because ADMT requires access to a SQL Server database. You can use an existing Microsoft SQL Server installation or download the free SQL Server Express 2008 package from http://www.microsoft.com/downloads/details.aspx?displaylang=en&FamilyID=01af61e6-2f63-4291-bcad-fd500f6027ff.

ENABLING AUDITING

To ensure that operations complete successfully, it is strongly recommended that you enable the auditing of account management operations in both the source and target domains. You do this by opening the Group Policy Management console, editing the Default Domain Controllers Policy, and enabling the Audit Account Management Policy setting for both successes and failures in the Computer Configuration\Policies\Windows Settings\Security Settings\Local Policies\Audit Policy container, as shown in Figure 4-7.

Figure 4-7

The Audit Policy container

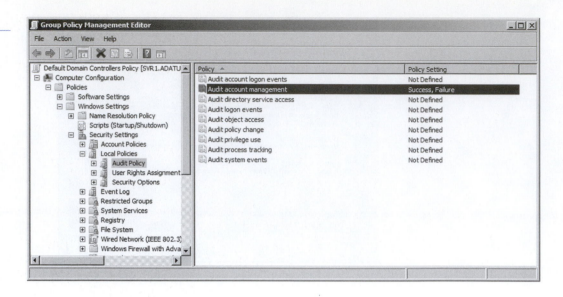

UNDERSTAND THE ORDER OF MIGRATION

With all of the components in place, you can begin to migrate objects from your source domain to your target domain. However, to preserve all of the object attributes and to place all of the objects in the appropriate destinations, you must migrate the objects in the correct order, as follows:

1. Groups
2. Users
3. Computers

MIGRATING GROUPS

You must migrate global and domain local groups before you migrate users, so that when ADMT adds the users to the target domain, their group memberships are preserved. ADMT has individual wizards for the migration of various object types, and the Group Account Migration Wizard enables you to select the groups that you want to migrate, as shown in Figure 4-8.

Figure 4-8

The *Group Selection* page of the Group Account Migration Wizard

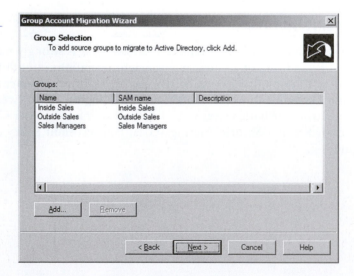

After selecting the target OU for the groups you selected, you can specify what information is migrated in great detail, selecting options and even specific group object attributes, as shown in Figure 4-9.

Figure 4-9

The *Object Property Exclusion* page of the Group Account Migration Wizard

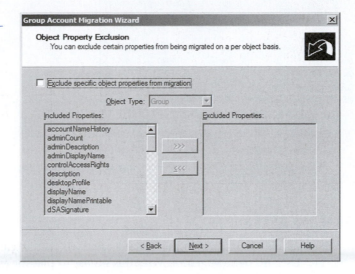

Finally, you specify what the wizard should do in the case of a conflict—that is, if a group with the same name already exists in the target OU. You can opt not to migrate the conflicting group, or merge the groups together in a number of ways, as shown in Figure 4-10.

Figure 4-10

The *Conflict Management* page of the Group Account Migration Wizard

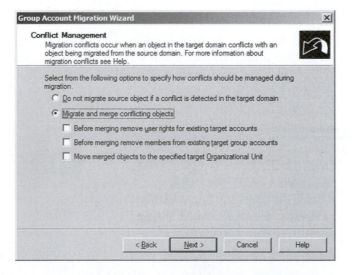

When the process is completed, a Migration Progress dialog box appears indicating the results, as shown in Figure 4-11.

Figure 4-11

The *Migration Progress* page of the Group Account Migration Wizard

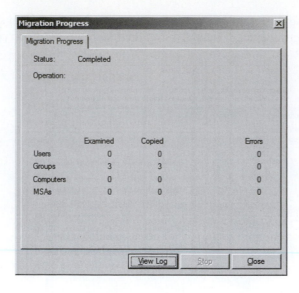

MIGRATING USERS

With the group objects in place in the target domain, you can begin to migrate the user objects. The User Account Migration Wizard is similar to that for groups, enabling you to select the user objects and the object attributes you want to migrate.

You can select users for migration from anywhere in the source domain, but the wizard migrates them all to a single target OU. Therefore, you may want to migrate your users in stages, based on the design of your target domain and selecting the users destined for one particular OU in each run of the wizard.

As with a group migration, after you select the users you want to migrate and the target out, the wizard presents a variety of options. One particularly important issue with user account migration is that of passwords.

ADMT by itself cannot migrate the passwords associated with user accounts. The wizard's *Password Options* page, shown in Figure 4-12, enables you to generate new complex passwords for the migrated users and store them in a text file, so that you can supply them to the users later.

Figure 4-12

The *Password Options* page of the User Account Migration Wizard

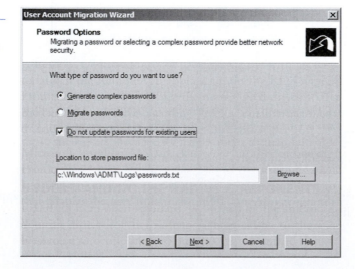

This page also has a Migrate Passwords option, but this option is not functional unless you have installed Microsoft Password Export Server (PES) on your source domain controller. PES enables ADMT to migrate user passwords through a secure channel between the source and target domain, providing users with a seamless transition to the new domain.

PES is available in two versions, for domain controllers running 32-bit and 64-bit versions of Windows Server 2003. The x86 version is available at http://www.microsoft.com/downloads/details.aspx?familyid=F0D03C3C-4757-40FD-8306-68079BA9C773&displaylang=en and the x64 version at http://www.microsoft.com/downloads/details.aspx?familyid=5B4E5C61-1C00-4DA7-9C0D-130200AED21A&displaylang=en.

UNDERSTANDING CROSS-FOREST AUTHENTICATION

Every object in an Active Directory or Active Directory Domain Services database has a unique *security identifier (SID)*. Just as TCP/IP networks rely on IP addresses to identify hosts, providing names only for the convenience of human operators, AD DS uses SIDs internally to identify objects.

No matter what migration tool or mechanism you use, when AD DS creates new objects in your target domain, it assigns new SIDs to them. So, despite having many of the same attributes as their counterparts in the source domain, they are really not the same objects.

How then can the target domain retain all of the object relationships that are critical to AD DS operations, such as group memberships and permissions? In other words, how can a new user object in the pristine forest continue to access network resources that know the user by another SID?

The answer is a special attribute in all AD DS security principals—such as user, group, and computer objects—called *sIDHistory*. The ***sIDHistory attribute*** contains all of the former SIDs by which the object has been known. Therefore, a user object migrated to your target domain receives a new SID in the *objectSID* attribute as the User Account Migration Wizard creates it, and still retains its former SID from the source domain in the *sIDHistory* attribute.

When a user, after logging on to the new target domain, attempts to access a protected resource, such as a folder on an NTFS drive on a file server, the authorization process always includes the contents of the *sIDHistory* attribute as well as the *objectSID* attribute. Therefore, while the access control list (ACL) for the NTFS folder might not contain an entry for the user's new SID in the target domain, it will find an entry containing the old SID from the source domain, enabling it to associate the user with the permissions stored with the folder.

MIGRATING COMPUTERS

After migrating your users and groups, you can proceed to migrate the computers other than the domain controllers in your source domain. Because the member servers and workstations in your source domain are actual physical resources, the migration process is somewhat more complicated than it is for logical objects, such as users and groups.

When you run the Computer Migration Wizard, you begin by identifying your source and target domains and selecting the objects you want to migrate, as usual. Then, in the *Translate Objects* page, as shown in Figure 4-13, you select the elements whose ACLs you want to migrate to the target domain as well. For the elements you select, the wizard updates its ACLs by substituting the source SID of each security principal that has permission to access the element with the new SID assigned to the user or group in the target domain.

Figure 4-13

The *Translate Objects* page of the Computer Migration Wizard

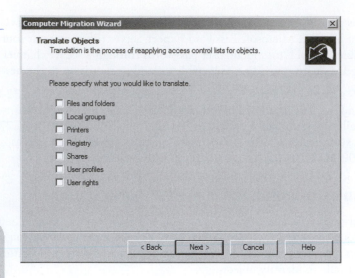

Because you are actually changing the domain membership of the computers you migrate, they must execute a restart before they can function as members of the target domain. ADMT therefore installs an agent on each system you select for migration that automatically restarts the computer after an interval you specify on the wizard's Computer Options page.

DECOMMISSIONING THE SOURCE DOMAIN

Once you have migrated all of the security principals from the source to the target domain, there should be nothing left in the source directory except for domain controllers and any objects you have deliberately chosen not to migrate. You can now demote these computers from their domain controller status and join them to the new domain as member servers or install Windows Server 2008 R2 on them first.

Finally, you must also remove the trusts between the source and target domains that you created earlier to facilitate the migration.

PERFORMING AN INTRAFOREST MIGRATION

ADMT is capable of migrating objects between domains in the same forest, just as it can migrate objects from domains in different forests. However, if your source domains are located in a Windows Server 2003 or Windows 2000 Server Active Directory environment, you cannot create a new Windows Server 2008 R2 domain in the same forest unless you first upgrade the existing directory to Windows Server 2008 R2.

Therefore, an intraforest migration consists of both the domain upgrade and domain restructuring procedures described in this lesson. After upgrading your forest to Windows Server 2008 R2, you can restructure it by creating new domains and using ADMT to migrate your objects from source to target within the same forest.

■ Planning for Interoperability

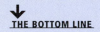

THE BOTTOM LINE

Enterprise administrators are often faced with circumstances that call for outside users to access the organization's resources, and achieving the interoperability necessary to make this possible can be difficult.

Interoperability issues typically occur in two ways: either users outside the organization have to access the enterprise network or there are non-Windows computers inside the enterprise that have to access Windows resources. Windows Server 2008 R2 includes a variety of tools that address these issues, as discussed in the following sections.

Using Active Directory Federation Services

Many organizations would like to deploy applications or services to business partners over the Internet, but this can be difficult to do while maintaining a sufficient level of security. *Active Directory Federation Services (AD FS)* is a service that can extend the boundaries of an AD DS environment to users in a partner enterprise.

Web-based applications can provide all sorts of services to users inside an enterprise, but there are many applications that can benefit outside users, such as vendors, partners, and clients, as well. The biggest problem inherent in this type of application deployment is providing secured network access to users external to the enterprise.

UNDERSTANDING ENTERPRISE INTEROPERABILITY OPTIONS

One way of providing outside users with access to your network's Internet-deployed resources is to create accounts for them in your AD DS database. This can enable users from other organizations to access your Web-based applications, log on to your Microsoft Exchange installation, or complete a full remote access authentication to your network. The problem with this solution is that it can quickly become an administrative nightmare, requiring your administrators to create and manage dozens or hundreds of user accounts.

Another possible solution—when a partner organization is also running AD DS —is to create a forest trust between your network and your partner's network. However, this type of trust requires domain controllers from the two forests to communicate, which raises security issues when the only link between the two enterprises is an Internet connection.

Active Directory Federation Services is an improvement on both of these solutions. AD FS is an *identity federation* solution that is essentially a different type of trust relationship between two entities. A federation trust relationship enables one AD DS network to trust the user accounts in another AD DS network. This provides cross-forest authentication capabilities for the two enterprises. When the administrators for one company want to provide users in a partner company with access to the Web applications hosted on their perimeter network, they can simply add user objects from the partner's network to the appropriate groups on their own network.

From the administrator's perspective, AD FS enables each organization to maintain autonomy over its own user accounts and its own resources. From a user's perspective, AD FS is invisible; a single sign-on provides access both to local network resources and those of the partner network.

UNDERSTANDING THE AD FS ARCHITECTURE

AD FS is a Windows Server 2008 R2 role that functions together with Active Directory Domain Services or Active Directory Lightweight Directory Services (AD LDS). To establish a federation partnership between two organizations, each must have an AD FS server with the Federation Service role service installed. Administrators then join these two servers together in a federation trust, which enables users in one enterprise to send authentication requests to resource servers in the other enterprise.

Unlike most Windows Server 2008 R2 roles, AD FS has role services that you must deploy on the various servers involved in a federation architecture. Each of these role services requires

TAKE NOTE*

A federation relationship represents a trust between two organizations in more than just name. Administrators grant their federation partners special access to their accounts and resources and, if abused or neglected, that access can result in a serious security breach. It is therefore important that potential partners reach a clear understanding of their roles in the federation before they actually implement the trust relationship.

TAKE NOTE*

Active Directory Federation Services is included only with the Enterprise and Datacenter versions of Windows Server 2008 R2.

that the server be a member of an AD DS domain and have Internet Information Services (IIS) installed.

The role services for the AD FS role, shown in Figure 4-14, are as follows:

- Federation Service—The primary AD FS service that authenticates users and issues them security tokens
- Federation Service Proxy—An intermediate service, located on a perimeter network, that provides secured Internet access to the Federation Service on an internal server
- AD FS Web Agents—Runs on web servers hosting various types of applications, processing the security tokens generated by the Federation Service

Figure 4-14

The *Select Role Services* page for the Active Directory Federation Services role

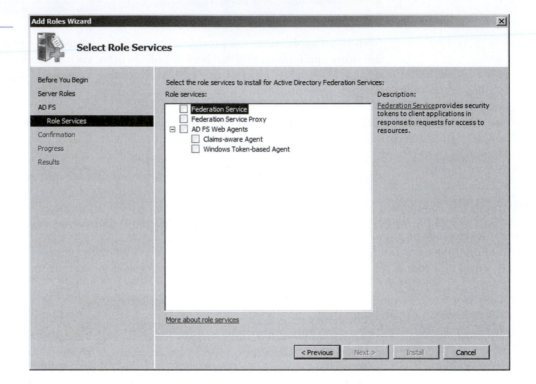

THE ACCOUNT PARTNER

The AD FS architecture designates one side of the federation as the account partner and the other side as the resource partner. The administrators on the account partner side designate an AD DS or AD LDS directory as the account store and maintain the user accounts that require access to the resources hosted by the resource partner.

The account partner requires a server running the Federation Service role service, which in turn requires access to the AD DS or AD LDS directory. Because administrators do not want to endanger their Active Directory installations by exposing them to the Internet, they typically place the server running Federation Services on the internal network.

They then deploy another server on a perimeter network, which runs the Federation Service Proxy role service, as shown in Figure 4-15. This network is exposed to the Internet, so the server can relay traffic between the resource partner side of the federation and the Federation Service server on the account partner side.

Figure 4-15

The Account Partner side of an
AD FS federation

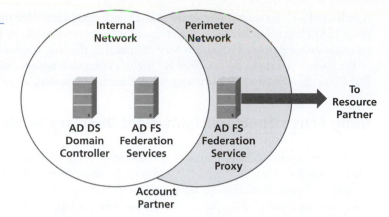

Because the account partner side is where the users are located, the Federation Service on that side is responsible for authenticating the users against the AD DS or AD LDS database. The service also gathers *federation claims*—which are certain agreed-upon attributes from the user accounts, such as group memberships—and packages them in a security token, which it sends to the resource partner.

THE RESOURCE PARTNER

The resource partner side of the federation contains the same basic components—an internal server running the Federation Service role service and a perimeter server running the Federation Service Proxy role service—but the tasks they perform are slightly different. When the Federation Service receives the security token from the account partner, it first confirms that the partner is trusted. Part of the configuration process on both sides of the federation consists of identifying the other partner and the account store or resource involved in the trust.

After confirming the account partner's identity, the Federation Service on the resource partner's server translates the account claims in the account partner's security token into equivalent resource claims. For example, membership in a specific group might entitle the user to additional access to a web application. The server then packages the resource claims into another security token, which it forwards to the web server hosting the application the user wants to access, as shown in Figure 4-16.

Figure 4-16

The resource partner side of an
AD FS federation

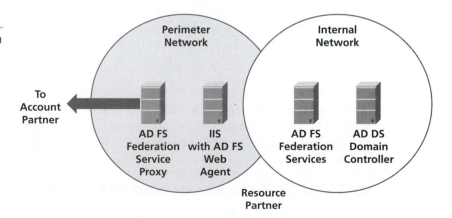

A federated web server has one of the AD FS web agents installed on it that takes the form of an ISAPI extension in IIS. The web agent is the consumer of the security tokens generated by the resource partner Federation Service, granting the user the access specified by the claims in the token. Windows Server 2008 R2 includes two web agents: one for current applications that know how to handle claims and one for applications that are not claims-aware.

Using Active Directory Lightweight Directory Services

There are situations in which none of the enterprise interoperability options discussed so far in this lesson are viable solutions. You might want to extend application services to users in organizations that do not have any AD DS infrastructure at all, or with whom you are not comfortable entering into a trust relationship. One alternative provided by Windows Server 2008 R2 is *Active Directory Lightweight Directory Services (AD LDS)*.

AD LDS is essentially a subset of Active Directory Domain Services that provides basic services for directory-enabled applications that do not require a full domain and forest infrastructure. For example, you can use AD LDS to provide authentication services to users external to the enterprise without having to expose AD DS domain controllers to an insecure environment.

AD LDS functions in much in the way that AD DS does, but on a much smaller scale. After you install the Active Directory Lightweight Directory Services role on a computer running Windows Server 2008 R2, you can create multiple AD LDS instances on that single computer. Each instance has a unique service name and port, to distinguish it from other instances, as well as its own data store and schema, so you can support applications with different requirements using one server. AD LDS also supports replication of individual instances to other servers, for high availability purposes or access from remote locations.

When using AD LDS as an extranet authentication solution, enterprise administrators typically place the server on a perimeter network, where it is accessible from the Internet. The user accounts that you create in the directory are not Windows security principals, and have no connection to any AD DS implementation that may or may not be running on the internal network.

Planning UNIX Interoperability

Interoperability is not limited to extending enterprise resources to external users. When those resources are primarily based on Windows, interoperability can also mean extending them to computers running other operating systems. The other operating systems that enterprise administrators are most likely to find on their networks are various flavors of UNIX.

Windows Server 2008 R2 includes a number of roles and features that enable computers running UNIX operating systems to interact with Windows services, and enable computers running Windows to access UNIX services. These roles and features are described in the following sections.

USING SERVICES FOR THE NETWORK FILE SYSTEM

Windows operating systems rely on a protocol called *Server Message Blocks (SMB)* for their file sharing, but in the UNIX world, the standard is the *Network File System (NFS)*. Unlike SMB, which is proprietary, NFS is based on an open standard published by the Internet Engineering Task Force (IETF) as RFC 1813, "NFS Version 3 Protocol Specification" in 1995.

As defined in RFC 1813, NFS is a "machine, operating system, network architecture, and transport protocol independent" service designed to "[provide] transparent remote access to shared file systems across networks." As a result of this open standard, virtually all UNIX distributions available today include both NFS client and server support.

To accommodate organizations that have heterogeneous networks containing both Windows and UNIX computers, Windows Server 2008 R2 includes the ***Services for Network File System*** role service, which provides NFS Server and NFS Client capabilities. Simply stated, an NFS server exports part of its file system, and the NFS client integrates the exported information, a process called "mounting," into its own file system. The result is that the client can access the server's files just as if they were a local resource.

In NFS, the bulk of the file-sharing process rests on the client. If a server crash or a network service interruption should occur, the client just continues to resend its requests until it receives a response from the server. If the client computer fails, there is no deleterious effect on the server and no need for a complex reconnection sequence.

NFS clients, on the other hand, are said to be smart because they are responsible for integrating the files they receive from the server into their local file systems.

TAKE NOTE*

The Services for NFS implementations in Windows Server 2008 and Windows Server 2008 R2 are substantially simpler than their predecessors in Windows Server 2003. Gone are the Gateway for NFS and Server for PCNFS modules, as well as the PCNFS elements of Client for NFS and the server functionality from User Name Mapping.

CREATING NFS SHARES

When you install the Services for Network File System role service in the File Services role, the system adds an NFS Sharing tab to every volume and folder on the computer's drives, as shown in Figure 4-17. To make a volume or folder accessible to NFS clients, you must explicitly share it, just as you would for Windows network users.

Figure 4-17

The NFS Sharing tab of a folder's Properties sheet

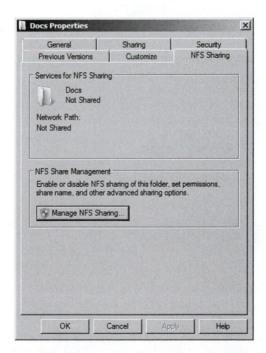

OBTAINING USER AND GROUP INFORMATION

UNIX operating systems have their own user accounts, separate from those in Windows and AD DS. To prevent NFS clients running on UNIX systems from having to perform a separate logon when accessing NFS shares, the Windows Server 2008 R2 NFS Server implementation can look up the user information sent by the client and associate the UNIX account with a particular Windows account.

In UNIX, when a user successfully authenticates with an account name and password, the operating system assigns him or her a user identifier (UID) value and a group identifier (GID) value. The NFS client includes the UID and GID in the file access request messages it sends to the NFS server. For the Windows Server 2008 R2 NFS server to grant the UNIX user access to the requested file, it must associate the UID and GID with a Windows or AD DS account and use that account to authenticate the client.

NFS Server supports two mechanisms for obtaining user and group information, as follows:

- Active Directory lookup—The NFS Server searches the AD DS database for the UID and GID values in an NFS file access request and uses the accounts associated with those values to authenticate the client. To use this mechanism, you must install the Identity Management for UNIX and Server for Network Information Services role services in the Active Directory Domain Services role on your domain controllers. This role service extends the Active Directory schema by adding a UNIX Attributes tab containing UID and GID fields to the Properties sheet for every user and group object, as shown in Figure 4-18. You must populate these fields with the appropriate values for the UNIX clients that need access to Windows NFS shares.

Figure 4-18

The UNIX Attributes tab of a user object's Properties sheet

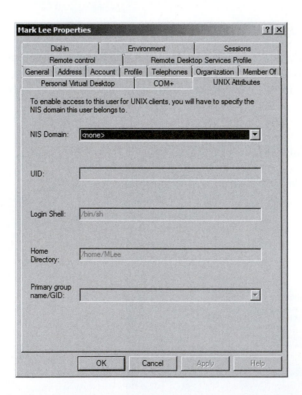

- User Name Mapping—The User Name Mapping service was the primary authentication mechanism in previous versions of Windows Services for NFS. It is essentially a lookup service that maintains a list of UNIX accounts, using their UID and GID values, and their equivalent Windows or AD DS accounts. The server component of User Name Mapping is not included in Windows Server 2008, but NFS Server still retains the client

component, which enables it to access an existing User Name Mapping server and perform account lookups.

USING IDENTITY MANAGEMENT FOR UNIX

While Services for NFS is designed to provide UNIX clients with access to Windows resources, *Identity Management for UNIX* is a role service of the Active Directory Domain Services role that is intended to integrate computers running Windows into a UNIX infrastructure.

The role service consists of two components: Server for Network Information Services and Password Synchronization, plus tools to manage the two, as discussed in the following sections.

SERVER FOR NETWORK INFORMATION SERVICES

Network Information Service (NIS) is directory service that many UNIX distributions use as a repository for user and group information. Unlike AD DS, NIS is a simple directory that is neither hierarchical nor object-oriented. It is more akin to a "yellow pages" directory, which in fact used to be the service's name.

The Server for Network Information Services role service enables an AD DS domain controller running Windows Server 2008 R2 to assume the role of the master NIS server for your network, presumably replacing a UNIX server. After installing the role service on a domain controller, administrators can use the NIS Data Migration Wizard, as shown in Figure 4-19, to migrate NIS domain maps from UNIX systems to the domain controller, which stores the information in the AD DS database.

Figure 4-19

The NIS Data Migration Wizard

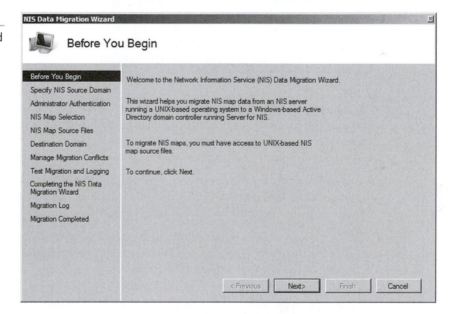

Once the AD DS domain controller is functioning as the NIS master server for the network, administrators can manage accounts for both AD DS and UNIX at the same time, using one set of tools. By installing the Server for Network Information Services role service on additional domain controllers, they can function as NIS subordinate (or slave) servers.

> **TAKE NOTE***
>
> The Server for NIS role service cannot function as a subordinate for an NIS master server running on a UNIX system. When you migrate NIS data to the AD DS domain controller running Server for NIS, that computer replaces the UNIX server as the NIS master. It is only when you install the role service on additional domain controllers that they function as NIS subordinates.

PASSWORD SYNCHRONIZATION

UNIX systems maintain their own user accounts, separate from those in AD DS and on stand-alone Windows servers. For enterprises with users that must access both Windows and UNIX resources, maintaining these accounts in synchrony can require a great deal of administrative effort.

The **_Password Synchronization_** role service automates this task by detecting password changes in AD DS or Windows and sending those changes to selected UNIX systems using encrypted messages. After adding the role service, you can add UNIX computers in the Microsoft Identity Management for UNIX console, using the Add Computer dialog box, as shown in Figure 4-20.

Figure 4-20

The _Add Computer_ dialog box for Password Synchronization

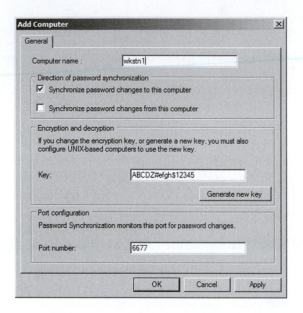

The Password Synchronization role server provides the Windows side of the service, but you must also install the correct components on your UNIX systems before synchronization can occur. To synchronize passwords on UNIX computers with changes to Windows user accounts, you must install the Password Synchronization daemon on the UNIX systems.

It is also possible to synchronize passwords in the other direction, from UNIX to Windows. To synchronize changes to UNIX accounts with Windows, you must install the Password Synchronization pluggable authentication module.

These UNIX modules are available for download from the Microsoft Download Center at http://www.microsoft.com/downloads/en/details.aspx?FamilyID=31518c70-1673-4be7-9e53-1c8a7d0d2643&displayLang=en. The download includes support for the following UNIX and Linux distributions:

- HP UX 11i
- IBM AIX 5L 5.2
- IBM AIX 5L 5.3
- Red Hat Enterprise Linux 4
- Red Hat Linux 8.0
- Red Hat Linux 9.0
- Novell SUSE Linux Enterprise Server 10
- Sun Microsystems Solaris 8
- Sun Microsystems Solaris 9
- Sun Microsystems Solaris 10

SKILL SUMMARY

IN THIS LESSON YOU LEARNED:

- In-place upgrades to Windows Server 2008 R2 are permissible from Windows Server 2003 SP2, Windows Server 2003 R2, or Windows Server 2008, as long as the platform, architecture, edition, and language are the same.

- In a domain-upgrade migration, you either upgrade one of the existing domain controllers in your source domain to Windows Server 2008 R2 or install a new domain controller running Windows Server 2008 R2 into the domain.

- An upgrade-then-restructure migration is a two-phase process in which you first upgrade your existing forest and domains to Windows Server 2008 R2 and then restructure the AD DS database by migrating objects into other domains within the same forest.

- In an interforest migration, you create a new Windows Server 2008 R2 forest—called a pristine forest because it is in no way an upgrade from your existing directory—and copy or move objects from your source domain into it.

- In an intraforest migration, you create a new domain in the same forest as your source domain and copy or move objects between the two.

- Active Directory Migration Tool is a wizard-based utility that enables you to perform both interforest and intraforest migrations.

- Interoperability issues typically occur in two ways: either users outside the organization have to access the enterprise network or there are non-Windows computers inside the enterprise that have to access Windows resources.

- Active Directory Federation Services is an identity federation solution that enables one AD DS network to trust the user accounts in another AD DS network.

- The administrators on the account partner side designate an AD DS or AD LDS directory as the account store and maintain the user accounts that require access to the resources hosted by the resource partner.

- The resource partner side of the federation contains the same basic components as the account partner, but the Federation Service receives the security token from the account partner, confirms that the partner is trusted, and creates another token for the web server hosting the application.

- AD LDS is essentially a subset of Active Directory Domain Services that provides basic services for directory-enabled applications that do not require a full domain and forest infrastructure.

- To accommodate organizations that have heterogeneous networks containing both Windows and UNIX computers, Windows Server 2008 R2 includes the *Services for Network File System* role service, which provides NFS Server and NFS Client capabilities.

- The Services for Network File System role service provides NFS Server and NFS Client capabilities. An NFS server exports part of its file system, and the NFS client integrates the exported information, a process called "mounting," into its own file system.

- Identity Management for UNIX is a role service of the Active Directory Domain Services role that is intended to integrate computers running Windows into a UNIX infrastructure.

- Network Information Service (NIS) is directory service that many UNIX distributions use as a repository for user and group information. Unlike AD DS, NIS is a simple directory that is neither hierarchical nor object-oriented.

Knowledge Assessment

Fill in the Blank

Complete the following sentences by writing the correct word or words in the blanks provided.

1. The yellow pages directory service used by many UNIX operating systems is called _____.

2. In the NFS client server application, the _____ side is relatively simple and dumb, while the _____ side contains most of the required intelligence.

3. Servers running the AD FS Federation Service Proxy are typically located on _____ networks.

4. During an interforest migration, you must create a _____ forest.

5. During a domain-restructure migration, it is the _____ attribute that enables you to migrate objects to another domain.

6. The correct order for migrating objects in the Active Directory Migration Tool is _____, _____, and _____.

7. To migrate passwords with the Active Directory Migration Tool, you must also install the _____ tool.

8. The account partner side of an Active Directory Federation Services installation can use _____ or _____ as its directory.

9. Before you can install the Active Directory Migration Tool, you must install _____.

10. Before you can upgrade a domain, you must modify the schema using the _____ tool.

True / False

Circle T if the statement is true or F if the statement is false.

T | F 1. You cannot perform an in-place upgrade of any 32-bit version of Windows Server to Windows Server 2008 R2.

T | F 2. Active Directory Lightweight Directory Services is only included with the Enterprise and Datacenter editions of Windows Server 2008 R2.

T | F 3. An interforest migration requires you to upgrade your down-level domains to Windows Server 2008 R2.

T | F 4. To maintain memberships during a domain-restructure migration, you must migrate user objects first and then groups.

T | F 5. To synchronize passwords on UNIX computers with changes to Windows user accounts, you must install the Password Synchronization pluggable authentication module on the UNIX systems.

T | F 6. Windows Server 2008 R2 can host multiple AD LDS directories on a single server.

T | F 7. When preparing the forest for a domain upgrade, you must work on the computer that is functioning as the infrastructure operations master.

T | F 8. In an AD FS partnership, both the Account Partner and the Resource Partner side must have a server running the Federation Service role service.

T | F 9. Upgrading a domain controller in a Windows Server 2003 domain to Windows Server 2003 R2 automatically raises the domain functional level to Windows Server 2008 R2.

T | F 10. You cannot upgrade a Windows NT 4.0 server to Windows Server 2008 R2.

Review Questions

1. List the steps involved in an interforest migration.

2. List three advantages of the domain-upgrade migration process and three advantages of the domain-restructure migration process.

■ Case Scenario

Scenario 4-1: Creating a Federation

Your company, Contoso, Ltd., is developing a web-based application that will enable select client firms to examine Contoso's stock on hand. To provide these clients with secure access to the application, you have been instructed to set up Active Directory Federation Services partnerships with them.

Most of the client firms have Windows servers and the expertise to deploy AD FS themselves. However, one client partner runs UNIX systems and no one on their IT staff has Windows experience. What is the minimum number of Windows servers the client will need to function as an AD FS account partner, and what roles and role services will they have to install?

5 LESSON

Planning a Branch Office Deployment

OBJECTIVE DOMAIN MATRIX

TECHNOLOGY SKILL	OBJECTIVE DOMAIN	OBJECTIVE NUMBER
Designing a Branch Office Strategy	Design the branch office deployment.	3.2

KEY TERMS

Administrative Role Separation
BranchCache
distributed-cache mode

Dsmgmt.exe
hosted-cache mode
Password Replication Policy

**Read-Only Domain Controller
(RODC)**

■ Designing a Branch Office Strategy

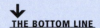
THE BOTTOM LINE

Recent Windows releases, including Windows Server 2008 R2 and Windows 7, have devoted a great deal of attention to branch office computing and the complications that distance and isolation present to IT administrators. However, before the administrators at the branch offices can take charge, enterprise administrators must create the policies that the branch offices will follow.

CERTIFICATION READY
How do you design a branch office deployment?
3.2

What constitutes a branch office? This is a question that can have various answers, even within a single enterprise. For a large organization, a branch office can be a headquarters on another continent with hundreds or thousands of users. Smaller organizations might have branch offices with only a handful of users. Obviously, these offices have vastly different requirements, and enterprise administrators must distinguish between them in their branch office strategies.

For the purposes of this lesson, imagine an organization with branches of three sizes: a large office with 1,000 users, a medium-sized office with 100 users, and a small office with 10 users. Each of these offices has users that must access resources hosted by the corporate headquarters, but they have varying amounts of money, equipment, and administrative expertise with which to do that. Table 5-1 lists the basic resources allotted to each branch size. You will learn about the additional resources needed by each as the lesson progresses.

Table 5-1

Basic Branch Offices Resources

Branch Office Size	Large	Medium	Small
Number of users	1,000	100	10
Connection to HQ	44.736 Mbps (T-3)	1.544 Mbps (T-1)	512 Mbps (VPN)
IT support	Full staff	1 administrator	Branch manager

Long before the branch offices open, enterprise administrators at the corporate headquarters must devise strategies for the design, deployment, and ongoing maintenance of the three branch office types.

Using AD DS in the Branch Office

In Lesson 2, "Designing an Active Directory Hierarchy," and Lesson 3, "Building an Active Directory Topology," a great deal of the discussion concerning Active Directory Domain Services (AD DS) design involved remote locations such as branch offices. Creating AD DS design policies for three different sizes of branch office requires enterprise administrators to evaluate the physical and organizational resources available in each branch and integrate them into a company-wide AD DS strategy.

As discussed in Lesson 2, the forest and domain structure is the first step in designing the AD DS strategy for the enterprise. For a large remote location, such as a 1,000-user branch office, creating a separate forest or domain is a logical choice. The main reason for this is that the office has a full staff of IT technicians, which means that they are capable of administering an autonomous domain or forest by themselves.

A separate domain is the more likely solution for the large office, but a separate forest is a possibility if the office meets any of the standard requirements, such as specialized schema requirements or the need for administrative isolation.

In a medium-sized location, such as a 100-user branch office, there is less likely to be a full IT staff capable of maintaining an entire separate domain. However, an office of this size is likely to have one or two dedicated IT staffers to maintain the network. Therefore, a separate organizational unit (OU) is preferable. You can grant the IT staffers at the branch office the permissions needed to administer the OU, without giving them complete autonomy.

TAKE NOTE*

One of the Windows Server 2008 R2 features that makes a dedicated branch office OU a practical solution in more situations is the ability to assign fine-grained password policies. In earlier versions of Windows Server, if a branch office required password policies different from those at the main office, the only solution was to create a dedicated domain. Today, administrators can create fine-grained password policies and apply them to a single OU. For more information, see "Using Fine-Grained Password Policies" in Lesson 3, "Building an Active Directory Topology."

In a small office of 10 users or less, there is typically no dedicated IT staff at all. There might be a branch manager or other employee able to perform basic tasks, such as supervising backups and creating user accounts, but even a delegated OU might be too much technical responsibility.

Designing a Branch Office Topology

While it is possible to run a branch office with no Active Directory Domain Services presence at all, this can cause more problems than it resolves in an enterprise that is reliant on AD DS for authentication and administration. Therefore, you should expect to need AD DS in all of your branch offices, but how you deploy it depends on the size of the office and its business requirements.

In a large branch office running its own domain, there must be at least two AD DS domain controllers, for fault-tolerance purposes, with one or both functioning as Domain Name Service (DNS) servers as well. There must also be a Global Catalog server, to provide the branch office users with the ability to search the other domains in the forest.

For a medium-sized office with 100 users, there should be at least one domain controller, to provide the users with local authentication capabilities, as well as a DNS server and a Global Catalog server. An office of this size should be equipped with a server closet, to physically secure the domain controller and other vital components.

Although a small branch office might have its own servers for local data storage, it should generally not have a domain controller, mainly because there is no one at the location who is qualified to maintain it. Small offices also typically lack the physical security needed to protect a domain controller from unauthorized access or theft. Therefore, the users will have to access a domain controller at another location to authenticate.

TAKE NOTE*

In designing a branch office strategy, there is always the possibility that circumstances could force modifications that counter general design guidelines. For example, a small branch office, despite having only a few users, might house a senior official of the company who demands a certain level of performance. The only way to achieve this performance might be to install a domain controller at the site, despite conditions that would generally rule against it.

The other AD DS-related services and elements you might consider having in a branch office include the following:

- DNS server—Despite the lack of a domain controller, a small branch office can benefit from its own DNS server providing local name resolution services. A DNS server does not require a dedicated computer, consumes few resources, and presents a minimum security risk when configured properly.

- Operations masters—Operations masters do not belong in branch offices except in cases where the branch office has its own domain or forest, as in the large office described here. For medium and small offices that are only part of a larger domain, the operations masters should be located in the headquarters site, where IT staffers perform most of the domain administration tasks.

- Sites—The large and medium-sized offices must both be represented in AD DS by their own site objects, because they are connected to the headquarters office by relatively slow wide-area network (WAN) links. The links all run at different speeds, so the faster site links must have lower costs that reflect these differences.

In addition to the basic resources, Table 5-2 adds the additional topology specifications for the three branch office sizes considered in this lesson.

Table 5-2

Branch Office Topology Specifications

Branch Office Size	Large	Medium	Small
Number of users	1,000	100	10
Connection to HQ	44.736 Mbps (T-3)	1.544 Mbps (T-1)	512 Mbps (VPN)
IT support	Full staff	1 administrator	Branch manager
Domain controllers	2	1	0
DNS servers	2	1	1
Global Catalog server	1	1	0
Separate site object	Yes	Yes	No

Evaluating Domain Controller Options

Of all the services and components listed in the previous section, the decision of whether to include a domain controller in a branch office is the most critical and provides the most options.

In addition to the standard full-domain controller, Windows Server 2008 and Windows Server 2008 R2 both include two new types of domain controller: server core and read-only, as discussed in the following sections.

USING A FULL-DOMAIN CONTROLLER

A full-domain controller, which is the result of performing a full installation of Windows Server 2008 or Windows Server 2008 R2 and promoting the server to a domain controller with the default options, provides all of the standard domain controller capabilities. The domain controller replicates the AD DS bidirectionally with the other domain controllers in the domain and includes all of the standard AD DS management tools.

A full-domain controller also provides the largest attack surface, which is one of the main reasons why you might hesitate to deploy it in a branch office environment. An attacker can access the AD DS database and modify its contents inappropriately. The domain controller will then replicate the content to the other domain controllers, potentially contaminating the entire enterprise.

Full-domain controllers also have a potential for accidental misuse that can be no less damaging than a deliberate attack. For these reasons, you should only deploy full-domain controllers in a branch office when there are appropriate personnel available to maintain them and when the facility has a sufficiently secure location for the servers to prevent unauthorized access.

USING A SERVER CORE DOMAIN CONTROLLER

Server Core is an installation option included with all versions of Windows Server 2008 and Windows Server 2008 R2 that reduces the footprint of the operating system by eliminating many of its applications and services, along with the Explorer interface and most of the graphical tools.

To install Server Core, you must choose it from the *Select the operating system you want to install* page of the Install Windows wizard, as shown in Figure 5-1. Once you have installed Server Core, you cannot change the operating system to a full installation, nor can you convert an existing full installation to Server Core.

Figure 5-1

The *Select the operating system you want to install* page of the Install Windows wizard

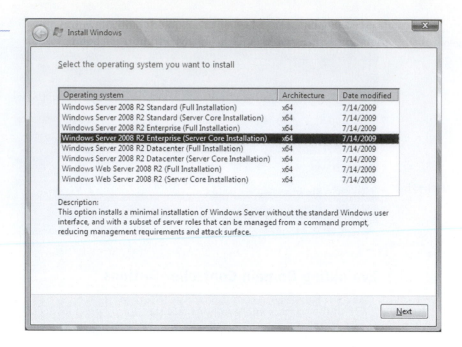

The result of the Server Core installation is a server that boots to the command prompt shown in Figure 5-2, but is much more secure than a full installation.

Figure 5-2

The Windows Server Core interface

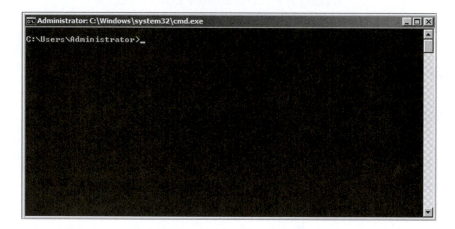

Because a Server Core installation only runs a fraction of the operating system code, it has fewer avenues of attack and fewer applications and services through which an attacker might try to obtain elevated privileges. This limited attack surface can be a valuable feature in a branch office that does not have the same physical security as a large headquarters.

Although Server Core does not include all of the roles found in a full installation, it does include Active Directory Domain Services, and therefore is capable of functioning as a

domain controller. A Server Core domain controller is inherently more secure than one on a fully installed system, but there is also a trade-off.

Server Core lacks most of the graphical administration tools found in a full installation, forcing the administrator to do more work from the command prompt. A Server Core domain controller can therefore require a greater level of administrative expertise than might be found in some branch offices.

Some graphical administration is possible by using Microsoft Management Console (MMC) snap-ins from a remote system, but for the most part, administrators must be familiar with the command line tools supplied with Windows Server 2008 R2 or the Windows PowerShell interface.

USING A READ-ONLY DOMAIN CONTROLLER

TAKE NOTE*

Because RODCs cannot write to the AD DS database, they cannot function in any of the operations master roles, nor can they function as bridgehead servers.

Placing a *Read-Only Domain Controller (RODC)* in a branch office increases security by limiting the AD DS replication to incoming traffic only. As a result, the domain controller remains updated with changes administrators make to the read/write replicas on the network, as well as to the schema, configuration partitions, and Global Catalog, but no outgoing replication traffic leaves the RODC. If attackers manage to gain access to the domain controller—whether by remote or physical means—they can damage the local copy of the AD DS database, but those damages cannot contaminate the rest of the domain.

INSTALLING AN RODC

To install an RODC, your branch office network must meet the following prerequisites:

- The RODC server must be running Windows Server 2008 or Windows Server 2008 R2.
- The RODC server must have access to a read/write domain controller running Windows Server 2008 or Windows Server 2008 R2 that functions as the Primary Domain Controller (PDC) emulator operations master. This server must be the nearest domain controller to the RODC in terms of site cost.
- The AD DS forest must be running at least at the Windows Server 2003 forest functional level.
- Unless you are running a new Windows Server 2008 or Windows Server 2008 R2 forest, you must modify the forest schema by running Adprep.exe with the /RODCPrep parameter on the domain controller functioning as the schema operations master.

One of the primary reasons for installing an RODC in a branch office is that there are no administrators at the site who have the training to manage the AD DS database. However, if no one in the branch office has administrative credentials for the domain, how do you promote a server to a domain controller, a task that requires Domain Admins privileges?

To address this problem, Microsoft has incorporated the ability to stage an RODC installation into Windows Server 2008 and Windows Server 2008 R2. Staging an installation enables a domain administrator to create the necessary AD DS account for the RODC before the server is actually deployed.

To install an RODC in two stages, use the following procedure to perform the first stage.

STAGE AN RODC INSTALLATION

GET READY. Log on to a member server running Windows Server 2008 R2, using an account with domain administrator privileges.

1. Click Start > Administrative Tools > Active Directory Users and Computers. The Active Directory Users and Computers console appears.

2. Expand the domain node, right-click the Domain Controllers container, and, from the context menu, select Pre-create Read-only Domain Controller Account. The Active Directory Domain Services Installation Wizard appears.

3. Click Next to bypass the *Welcome* page. The *Operating System Compatibility* page appears.

4. Click Next to continue. The *Network Credentials* page appears, as shown in Figure 5-3.

Figure 5-3

The *Network Credentials* page of the Active Directory Domain Services Installation Wizard

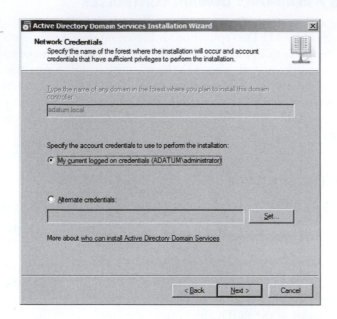

5. Click Next to use the credentials with which you logged on to the computer. The *Specify the Computer Name* page appears, as shown in Figure 5-4.

Figure 5-4

The *Specify the Computer Name* page of the Active Directory Domain Services Installation Wizard

6. In the Computer Name text box, type the name of the computer that will be the RODC and click Next. The *Select a Site* page appears, as shown in Figure 5-5.

Figure 5-5

The *Select a Site* page of the Active Directory Domain Services Installation Wizard

7. Choose the site where you will be installing the RODC and click Next. The *Additional Domain Controller Options* page appears.

8. Click Next. The *Delegation of RODC Installation and Administration* page appears, as shown in Figure 5-6.

Figure 5-6

The *Delegation of RODC Installation and Administration* page of the Active Directory Domain Services Installation Wizard

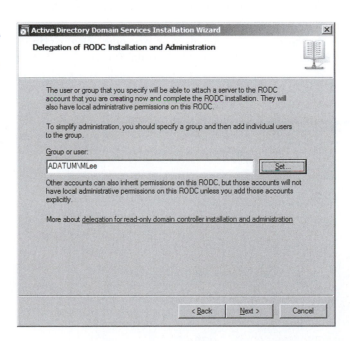

9. Click Set. The Select User or Group dialog box appears, as shown in Figure 5-7.

Figure 5-7

The Select User or Group
dialog box

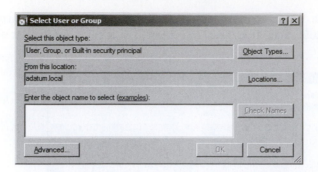

10. In the *Enter the object name to select* box, type the name of the user or group that you want to designate as the local administrator of the RODC and click OK. The user or group you specified appears in the wizard in the *Group or user* text box.

11. Click Next. The *Summary* page appears.

12. Click Next. The *Completing the Active Directory Domain Services Installation Wizard* page appears.

13. Click Finish. The wizard creates the account for the domain controller in the AD DS database.

At this point, the AD DS account is ready to be joined to the RODC in its final location, using only the account you specified in the wizard.

To complete the RODC installation, use the following procedure.

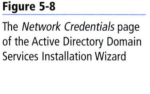 **COMPLETE AN RODC INSTALLATION**

GET READY. Log on to a member server running Windows Server 2008 R2, using an account with domain administrator privileges.

1. Click Start > All Programs > Accessories > Command Prompt. A Command Prompt window appears.

2. At the command prompt, type **dcpromo /UseExistingAccount:Attach** and press Enter. The Active Directory Domain Services Installation Wizard appears.

3. Click Next to bypass the *Welcome* page. The *Network Credentials* page appears, as shown in Figure 5-8.

Figure 5-8

The *Network Credentials* page
of the Active Directory Domain
Services Installation Wizard

4. In the *Type the name of any domain in the forest where you plan to install this domain controller* text box, type the name of your domain.

5. Click Set. A Network Credentials dialog box appears.

6. In the User Name text box, type the name of the user you designated as the local administrator of the RODC, or a member of the group you designated. Type the password associated with the user and click OK.

7. Click Next. The *Select Domain Controller Account* page appears, as shown in Figure 5-9.

Figure 5-9

The *Select Domain Controller Account* page of the Active Directory Domain Services Installation Wizard

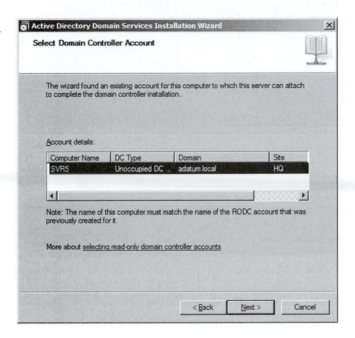

8. Select the RODC account you created earlier and click Next. The *Location for Database, Log Files, and SYSVOL* page appears.

9. Click Next to accept the default values. The *Directory Services Restore Mode Administrator Password* page appears.

10. Type an appropriate password in the Password and Confirm Password text boxes and click Next. The *Summary* page appears.

11. Click Next. The wizard installs AD DS and the *Completing the Active Directory Domain Services Installation Wizard* page appears.

12. Click Finish. The wizard closes and offers to restart the computer.

13. Restart the computer.

Once the computer restarts, it functions as a read-only domain controller for AD DS.

USING THE PASSWORD REPLICATION POLICY

As another measure of security, an RODC does not store user credentials as read/write domain controllers do. RODCs are designed for locations—such as branch offices—that have reduced physical security, and are therefore more liable to be stolen or accessed by unauthorized persons. By not caching credentials, an RODC reduces the information compromised if someone steals the computer.

Because it does not cache credentials by default, an RODC requires access to a read/write domain controller to authenticate users. The RODC forwards all authentication requests to the read/write domain controller, which in the case of a branch office installation, generates WAN traffic and requires a functioning WAN connection for authentication to take place.

However, it is possible to modify the default *Password Replication Policy* so that the RODC caches password for selected users. Administrators can therefore cache passwords for the branch office users on the RODC, eliminating the need to forward authentication requests for those users while still protecting the passwords for the other user accounts in the AD DS database from theft.

To modify the Password Replication Policy, you must open the Properties sheet for the server in the Active Directory Users and Computers console and select the Password Replication Policy tab, as shown in Figure 5-10.

Figure 5-10

The Password Replication Policy tab of an RODC's Properties sheet

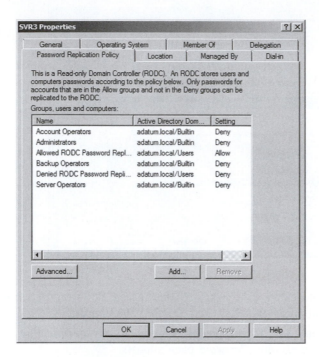

RDOCs are capable of functioning as Global Catalog servers and as read-only DNS servers as well, providing the same protection to your DNS information as to the AD DS database. Finally, the RODC option is compatible with the Server Core installation option, providing the securest possible combination for a branch office domain controller.

DELEGATING ADMINISTRATION

Using security precautions such as Server Core and read-only domain controllers in your branch offices can help to protect your domains from attack, but equally important to their safety are the privileges you grant to the administrators at the branch office sites.

For medium-sized or large branch offices that have dedicated IT personnel, you can assume that these people have the training and the experience to use administrative credentials responsibly. However, you will in most cases want to restrict their access to the AD DS objects they are responsible for managing.

In smaller branch offices that rely on nontechnical people to perform basic administrative tasks, the problem can be even more acute. You might want to grant these people little or no access to the AD DS database, but they may still be responsible for maintaining the servers in the office—including those functioning as domain controllers.

USING THE DELEGATION OF CONTROL WIZARD

One of the main reasons for dedicating an entire organizational unit to a branch office is so that you can grant the branch office administrators access to the AD DS objects they are responsible for managing without granting them access to anything else. The Delegation of Control Wizard enables you to select security principals—users or groups—and grant them access to the contents of an OU in a variety of ways.

The *Tasks to Delegate* page, shown in Figure 5-11, provides the security principals with the ability to perform tasks common for branch office administrators, such as creating and managing user accounts, groups, and passwords.

Figure 5-11

The *Tasks to Delegate* page of the Delegation of Control Wizard

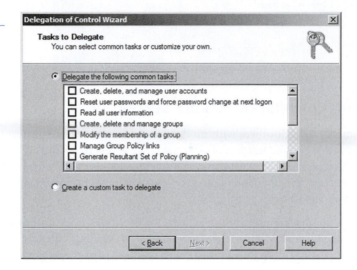

On the *Active Directory Object Type* page, shown in Figure 5-12, you can create customized tasks for selected object types by assigning them specific Active Directory permissions.

Figure 5-12

The *Active Directory Object Type* page of the Delegation of Control Wizard

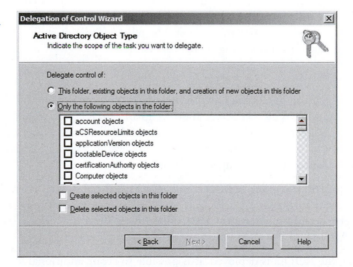

As shown in Figure 5-13, the *Permissions* page enables you to select permissions for the entire object or for specific object properties. This provides enterprise administrators with a highly granular degree of access control.

Figure 5-13

The *Permissions* page of the Delegation of Control Wizard

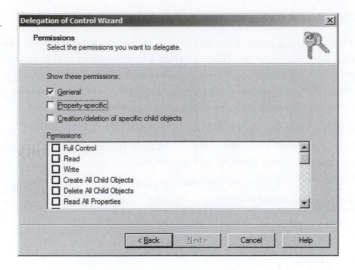

USING ADMINISTRATOR ROLE SEPARATION

In smaller branch offices with no dedicated IT staff, you might want to grant local users or managers a certain amount of administrative access to an RODC without giving them any privileges in the AD DS domain. This is possible using a feature called *Administrative Role Separation*, which enables you to designate a local administrator for an RODC without granting any domain permissions.

RODC local administrators are able to log on to the server and perform system maintenance tasks that require administrative access, such as installing software and device drivers, but they cannot perform domain administration tasks, nor can they log on to other domain controllers.

TAKE NOTE *

While RODC local administrators do not have permissions to access the domain directly, they do have access to the RODC drives on which a replica of the AD DS database is stored. Access to the drives could therefore enable an individual with these permissions to access the information in the AD DS database. For this reason, administrators to whom you grant these permissions must still be reliable individuals and must take steps to protect their credentials from being shared or stolen.

When you use the Active Directory Domain Services Installation Wizard to promote a computer running Windows Server 2008 R2 to an RODC, you create the first local administrator on the *Delegation of RODC Installation and Administration* page. As with all privilege assignments, the best practice is to assign the privilege to a group instead of an individual user, and then add users to the group as needed.

The individuals that receive this privilege have the ability to attach the RODC server to the account that the wizard will create in AD DS, even though they lack the Domain Admins or Enterprise Admins that this task would otherwise require. These individuals can also remove the Active Directory Domain Services role from the server.

Once the RODC is deployed, it is possible to create additional local administrators by using the Dsmgmt.exe program from the server's command prompt. *Dsmgmt.exe* is an interactive command-line program that administrators can use to manage AD DS partitions and their behavior. The sequence of commands to designate local administrators is as follows:

```
local roles
list roles
```

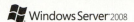

```
add domain\username administrators

quit

quit
```

A successful procedure generates the `Successfully updated local role` message, as shown in Figure 5-14. Issuing the `Show role administrators` command from the `local roles:` prompt displays a list of the users and groups that are designated as local administrators.

Figure 5-14

Adding local administrators with Dsmgmt.exe

■ Choosing Branch Office Services

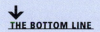
THE BOTTOM LINE

As noted earlier in this lesson, branch offices have fewer users than a main office or headquarters, but those users still have needs that administrators must meet in addition to from Active Directory Domain Services.

In addition to client workstations, and depending on the size of the office, you might want to deploy a variety of other infrastructure and application servers at a branch office. Business and security requirements can compel enterprise administrators to equip a branch office with all of the services found in a main office, but in most cases, a branch office provides users with a subset of the services they need locally.

Some of the services you might find at a branch office are as follows:

- DHCP server—All but the smallest branch offices can benefit from Dynamic Host Configuration Protocol (DHCP) servers, to prevent IT staff from having to manually configure workstation TCP/IP settings. DHCP is a service that consumes relatively few resources and is simple to set up, so virtually any branch office with a server can support it.

- Routing and Remote Access Services (RRAS)—RRAS can provide a branch office with a variety of services, including remote dial-up and virtual private network (VPN) access, DHCP relay, and network address translation (NAT). Generally speaking, only a large branch office would benefit from remote access, as the users could just as easily connect to remote access servers at the headquarters, and having a domain controller at the site is recommended, to provide local authentication. DHCP relay enables clients to access DHCP servers on other networks, which could conceivably enable branch office workstations to obtain TCP/IP settings from DHCP servers at another site. NAT is built into most of the routers that branch offices use to access the Internet, but an extremely small branch could avoid even that expense by sharing a server's Internet connection using NAT.

For more information on creating an enterprise WSUS hierarchy, see Lesson 11, "Deploying Software Updates."

- Windows Server Update Services (WSUS)—Computers in branch offices require the same maintenance as those in main offices or headquarters and it is a relatively simple matter to extend company-wide software update policies to branch offices using WSUS servers. To eliminate the need for WSUS administration at the branch office sites, it is possible to configure WSUS servers to obtain updates from the organization's other WSUS servers at the main office.

- Distributed File System (DFS) Replication—DFS replication can automatically maintain copies of key files at branch offices, providing remote users with continuous access to essential data. When planning for DFS and similar services at branch offices, enterprise administrators must consider the amount of WAN bandwidth they might consume.

- Microsoft Cluster Services—When business requirements call for network applications to be highly available, administrators can deploy cluster nodes in branch offices, to provide users with uninterrupted local access to applications, even if the WAN connection should fail.

- File servers—Whenever possible, enterprise administrators should implement main-office policies in branch offices as well. If main office users store their data files on servers, then branch office users should as well. Even small branches can benefit from a server for local file storage, without the need for a large expenditure or frequent maintenance.

As branch offices get smaller, requirements often diminish, as do budgets, so users are more likely to access network resources from servers at another location using WAN connections. This increases WAN traffic and decreases performance, costs that might eventually be offset by purchasing additional equipment for the branch office.

■ Using BranchCache

THE BOTTOM LINE

BranchCache is a new feature in Windows Server 2008 R2 and Windows 7 that enables networks with computers at remote locations to conserve bandwidth by storing frequently accessed files on local drives.

Caching is a process in which computers copy frequently used data to an intermediate storage medium so they can satisfy subsequent requests for the same data more quickly or less expensively. For example, virtually all computers have an area of high-speed memory between the system processor and the main system memory that functions as a cache. Repeated requests for the same data can be satisfied more quickly from the cache memory than the slower main memory. BranchCache works in much the same way, except that it is a disk storage cache that reduces the traffic between branch office computers and a server at another site.

WAN connections between offices are slower and more expensive than the local-area network (LAN) connections within an office. When a computer in a branch office requires a file stored on a server at the main office, the server must transmit the file over a WAN connection. If 20 computers at the branch office require that same file, the server must transmit it 20 times, using 20 times the WAN bandwidth.

BranchCache is a feature that can store a copy of the file on a computer at the branch office site, so that the server only has to transmit the files over the WAN connection once. All of the subsequent requests access the file from the cache on the local network.

Understanding Network Infrastructure Requirements

> To use BranchCache, you must have a server running Windows Server 2008 R2 at the home office and computers running Windows Server 2008 R2 or Windows 7 at the branch office.

BranchCache is a new feature introduced in Windows Server 2008 R2 and Windows 7; only computers running these operating systems can use it. The content server that stores the data initially must be running Windows Server 2008 R2. The workstations at the branch office that access the data must be running Windows 7.

BranchCache is a client/server application that supports two operational modes, as follows:

- *Distributed-cache mode*—Each Windows 7 workstation on the branch office network caches data from the content server on its local drive and shares that cached data with other local workstations.

- *Hosted-cache mode*—Windows 7 workstations on the branch office network cache data from the content server on a branch office server, enabling other workstations to access the cached data from there.

The major difference between the two modes is the need for a second branch-office server in hosted-cache mode, which makes the caching process more efficient, but adds to the expense of the implementation. In distributed-cache mode, each workstation is responsible for maintaining its own cache and processing cache requests from the other workstations on the local network.

Understanding BranchCache Communications

> BranchCache clients and servers exchange relatively small messages among themselves to coordinate their caching activities.

BranchCache supports file requests using Server Message Blocks (SMB), the standard Windows file-sharing protocol, Hypertext Transfer Protocol (HTTP), the standard protocol for web communications, and the Background Intelligent Transfer Service (BITS). The BranchCache communications process is as follows:

1. Client request (BranchCache)—A branch office workstation requests a file from the content server, and identifies itself as a BranchCache client.

2. Server reply (metadata)—The server replies to the client, not with the requested file, but with a message containing metadata that describes the file. The metadata is much smaller than the requested file itself, reducing the amount of WAN bandwidth consumed.

3. Client cache check—Using the metadata supplied by the server, the client sends messages to the local caching computers, asking if the requested file is available locally.

4. Caching computer reply—In hosted cache mode, the local caching server replies to the client, indicating whether the requested file is available in its cache. In distributed cache mode, caching workstations only reply in the positive. If the client workstation receives no replies, it assumes that the requested file is not cached locally.

5. Client request (non-BranchCache)—The client issues another file request, this time without the BranchCache identifier, and sends it either to a local caching computer or the content server.

6. Server reply (data)—The computer receiving the request replies by sending the requested file to the client.

7. Client data cache—On receiving the requested file, the client caches it for use by other branch office workstations. In hosted-cache mode, the client caches the file on the branch office server. In distributed-cache mode, the client caches the file on its own local disk.

As a result of this process, the traffic transmitted over the WAN consists primarily of small messages containing client requests and metadata replies, as well as one single copy of every requested file.

It is critical to understand that BranchCache is a read-only caching application. The metadata messages described here occur only when branch office clients are requesting files from the content server, not when they are writing modified files back to the server. BranchCache does not support write caching, which is a far more complicated process, because the systems must take into account the possibility of conflicts among multiple versions of the same file.

Configuring BranchCache Settings

To implement BranchCache on your network, you must install the appropriate modules on your server(s) and configure Group Policy settings on both servers and clients.

BranchCache requires a minimum of one content server and one or more branch office workstations. You can install additional content servers at any location that serves files to branch offices.

At the branch office, BranchCache in distributed-cache mode can typically support up to 50 workstations. To use hosted-cache mode, you must have a branch office server at each location where there are branch office workstations.

CONFIGURING A CONTENT SERVER

To use BranchCache on your network, your files must be stored on a content server running Windows Server 2008 R2. To support SMB requests, the server must have the BranchCache for Network Files role service installed in the File Services role. To support HTTP and BITS requests, you must install the BranchCache feature.

Once you have installed the required BranchCache modules, you must configure a Group Policy setting called Hash Publication for BranchCache. This setting is located in the Computer Configuration\Policies\Administrative Templates\Network\Lanman Server node of a Group Policy object (GPO) or in Local Computer Policy.

The Hash Publication for BranchCache setting, shown in Figure 5-15, enables the server to respond to file requests from BranchCache clients with metadata instead of the files themselves. In this setting, you can stipulate that the server publish hash metadata for all of its shared files or for only the shares you select.

Figure 5-15

The Hash Publication for BranchCache setting in Group Policy

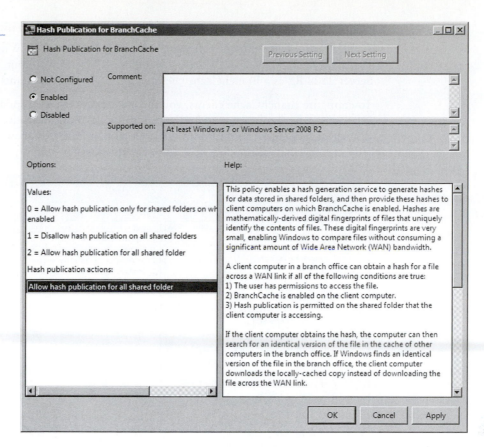

If you select the *Allow hash publication only for shared folders on which BranchCache is enabled* option, you must configure each share for which you want to enable BranchCache by opening the share's Properties sheet in the Share and Storage Management console, clicking Advanced, and selecting an appropriate option on the Caching tab of the Advanced dialog box, as shown in Figure 5-16.

Figure 5-16

The Caching tab of the Advanced dialog box

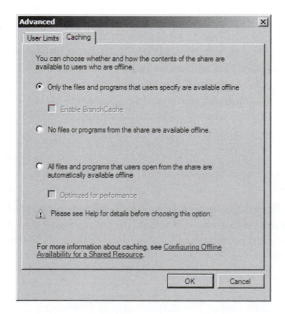

CONFIGURING BRANCHCACHE CLIENTS

BranchCache clients must be computers running Windows 7 or Windows Server 2008 R2. BranchCache is enabled by default in Windows 7. To use a computer running Windows Server 2008 R2 as a BranchCache client, you must install the BranchCache feature.

To configure BranchCache clients, you must configure the appropriate Group Policy settings, found in the Computer Configuration\Policies\Administrative Templates\Network\ BranchCache node of a GPO or in Local Computer Policy, as shown in Figure 5-17.

Figure 5-17

The BranchCache settings in Group Policy

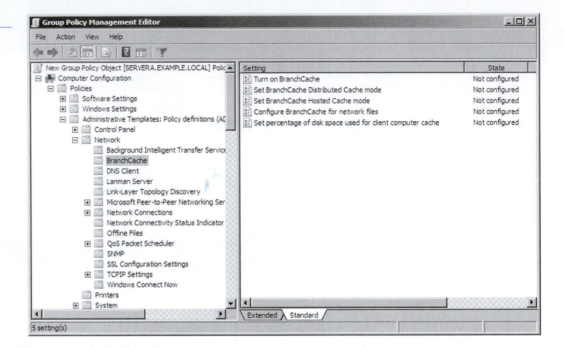

The BranchCache Group Policy settings are as follows:

- Turn on BranchCache—Enables BranchCache on the client computer. Enabling this setting along with either *Set BranchCache Distributed Cache mode* or *Set BranchCache Hosted Cache mode* configures the client to use one of those operational modes. Enabling this setting without either one of the mode settings configures the client to cache server data on its local drive only, without accessing caches on other computers.

- Set BranchCache Distributed Cache mode—When enabled along with the *Turn on BranchCache* setting, configures the client to function in distributed-cache mode.

- Set BranchCache Hosted Cache mode—When enabled along with the *Turn on BranchCache* setting, configures the client to function in hosted-cache mode. In the *Enter the location of the hosted cache* field, you must specify the address of the computer that will function as the hosted cache server on the branch office network.

- Configure BranchCache for network files—When enabled, this setting controls the round-trip network latency value that BranchCache uses to differentiate local from remote servers. The default setting is 80 ms. When you decrease the value, the client caches more files; increasing the value causes it to cache fewer files.

- Set percentage of disk space used for client computer cache—When enabled, this setting specifies the maximum amount of total disk space that the computer should devote to the BranchCache cache. The default value is 5 percent.

CONFIGURING A HOSTED-CACHE-MODE SERVER

To use hosted-cache mode on your branch office network, you must have a server running Windows Server 2008 R2 with the BranchCache feature installed. You must also configure the *Turn on BranchCache* and *Set BranchCache Hosted Cache mode* Group Policy settings.

The hosted-cache-mode server must also have a digital certificate issued by a certification authority (CA) that the BranchCache clients trust. You can install an internal CA on the network and use it to issue the certificate, or obtain a certificate from a commercial third-party CA.

Once you have obtained the certificate, you must use the Certificates snap-in on the hosted-cache server to import it. Finally, you must link the certificate to the BranchCache service by opening an elevated command prompt and typing the following command, replacing the thumbprint variable with the thumbprint value from the certificate you imported:

```
netsh http add sslcert ipport=0.0.0.0:443
certhash=thumbprint appid={d673f5ee-a714-454d-8de2-492e4c1bd8f8}
```

SKILL SUMMARY

IN THIS LESSON YOU LEARNED:

- For the purposes of this lesson, imagine an organization with branches of three sizes: a large office with 1,000 users, a medium-sized office with 100 users, and a small office with 10 users. Each of these offices has users that must access resources hosted by the corporate headquarters, but they have varying amounts of money, equipment, and administrative expertise with which to do that.

- A 100-user branch office is likely to have one or two dedicated IT staffers to maintain the network. Therefore, creating a separate organizational unit (OU) for the office is a viable solution. You can grant the IT staffers at the branch office the permissions needed to administer the OU, without giving them complete autonomy.

- While it is possible to run a branch office with no Active Directory Domain Services presence at all, this can cause more problems than it resolves in an enterprise that is reliant on AD DS for authentication and administration.

- A full-domain controller provides all of the standard domain controller capabilities, replicating the AD DS bidirectionally with the other domain controllers in the domain and including all of the standard AD DS management tools.

- Server Core is an installation option included with all versions of Windows Server 2008 and Windows Server 2008 R2 that reduces the footprint of the operating system by eliminating many of its applications and services, along with the Explorer interface and most of the graphical tools.

- A read-only domain controller (RODC) increases security in a branch office by limiting the AD DS replication to incoming traffic only. If attackers manage to gain access to the domain controller, they can damage the local copy of the AD DS database, but those damages cannot contaminate the rest of the domain.

- An RODC does not store user credentials as a read/write domain controllers do. RODCs are designed for locations that have reduced physical security, and are therefore more liable to be stolen or accessed by unauthorized persons. By not caching credentials, an RODC reduces the information compromised if someone steals the computer.

- It is possible to modify the default Password Replication Policy so that the RODC caches passwords for selected users.

- The Delegation of Control Wizard enables you to select security principals—users or groups—and grant them access to the contents of a branch office OU in a variety of ways.

- In smaller branch offices with no dedicated IT staff, you might want to use Administrative Role Separation to grant local users or managers a certain amount of administrative access to an RODC without giving them any privileges in the AD DS domain.

- BranchCache is a new feature in Windows Server 2008 R2 and Windows 7 that enables networks with computers at remote locations to conserve bandwidth by storing frequently accessed files on local drives.

■ Knowledge Assessment

Fill in the Blank

Complete the following sentences by writing the correct word or words in the blanks provided.

1. The Windows Server 2008 R2 installation option that suppresses the Explorer interface and most of the graphical administration utilities is called _____.

2. The BranchCache operational mode in which each branch office workstation caches data on its local drive is called _____.

3. By default, RODCs do not store user credentials as read/write domain controllers do. To modify the defaults so that an RODC caches passwords for selected users, you must modify the _____.

4. The feature that enables you to designate a local administrator for an RODC without granting any domain permissions is called _____.

5. To designate a user as an RODC local administrator, you use a tool called _____.

6. Administrators launch the Delegation of Control Wizard using the _____ console.

7. The ability to create fine-grained password policies has made it more practical to dedicate an entire _____ to a branch office.

8. If you are running a Windows Server 2003 forest, you must prepare the forest schema by running Adprep.exe with the _____ parameter on the schema operations master.

9. Content servers reply to requests from BranchCache clients with _____ instead of the requested files.

10. A branch office must have its own _____ if it is connected to other offices using links that are slower than the internal network.

True / False

Circle T if the statement is true or F if the statement is false.

T | F 1. To use BranchCache, servers must be running Windows Server 2008 or Windows Server 2008 R2.

T | F 2. A BranchCache installation in hosted cache mode requires a server in the branch office.

T | F 3. To install a read-only domain controller, the AD DS forest must be running at the Windows Server 2008 forest functional level or higher.

T|F 4. Operations masters do not belong in branch offices except in cases where the branch office has its own domain or forest.

T|F 5. It is possible to create a domain controller using a server core installation of Windows Server 2008 R2, or you can create a read-only domain controller, but you cannot create an RODC on a computer running server core.

T|F 6. To install a read-only domain controller, you must already have a read/write domain controller in the domain running Windows Server 2008 or Windows Server 2008 R2.

T|F 7. Windows Server Update Services servers in branch offices can obtain updates from other WSUS servers in the main office.

T|F 8. RDOCs are not capable of functioning as Global Catalog servers.

T|F 9. Using the Delegation of Control Wizard, administrators can provide users with access to specific AD DS object types or specific object properties.

T|F 10. A small branch office without qualified IT administrators to maintain it should generally not have a domain controller on the premises.

Review Questions

1. The following steps of a successful BranchCache file negotiation in hosted cache mode are in the wrong order. Specify the proper order in which the steps actually occur.

   a. Server sends requested file to client.

   b. Client sends request to content server.

   c. Client checks cache with metadata.

   d. Client sends request to caching server.

   e. Caching server confirms file availability.

   f. Content server replies with metadata.

2. Explain why it might be necessary to deploy a read-only domain controller for a branch office in two stages.

■ Case Scenario

Scenario 5-1: Designing a Branch Office

Contoso, Ltd. has recently opened a branch office in Brussels, its first in Europe. Although expansion is expected, the office is currently very small, with five sales associates and a vice president in charge of the European division, none of whom have IT training or experience. The initial plan calls for the office to have seven computers: six workstations and a file server. A 1.5 Mbps WAN connection provides them with access to Active Directory Domain Services domain controllers, email servers, and corporate databases located in the company headquarters in Montreal.

However, two problems have arisen, and the IT director has assigned you to handle them. First, due to trademarking issues, it was recently decided that the European operation must run under another name. It will therefore be necessary to create a new Active Directory Domain Services domain for the Brussels office and any future branches in Europe. Second, the VP in the Brussels office is not satisfied with the performance of the network. She is complaining that it takes too long to log on to the domain, and there are delays when establishing access to the North American servers.

How can you redesign the branch office network to address both of these problems without adding any computers or personnel to the Brussels office?

6 LESSON

Deploying Applications

OBJECTIVE DOMAIN MATRIX

TECHNOLOGY SKILL	OBJECTIVE DOMAIN	OBJECTIVE NUMBER
Selecting an Application Deployment Strategy	Plan for application delivery.	1.3
Using Remote Desktop Services	Plan for Remote Desktop Services.	1.4

KEY TERMS

application pool
assign
client access licenses (CALs)
fat client
presentation virtualization
publish
RemoteApp
Remote Desktop Connection Broker

Remote Desktop Connection Client
Remote Desktop Gateway
Remote Desktop Licensing Server
Remote Desktop Protocol (RDP)
Remote Desktop Services (RDS)
Remote Desktop Session Host
Remote Desktop Virtualization Host
Remote Desktop Web Access

System Center Configuration
  Manager (SCCM) 2007
thin client
worker process
worker process isolation
  mode

■ Selecting an Application Deployment Strategy

THE BOTTOM LINE

Enterprise administrators are responsible for the high-level infrastructure services, such as Active Directory Domain Services (AD DS)—the invisible foundation for the network—but they must also see to it that users are provided with their most basic tools: the applications they use every day.

Depending on a variety of factors, including the size of the organization, the number and type of applications involved, the licensing model in use, and the IT staff available, there are a number of ways that administrators can choose to deploy applications to end-user workstations. The following sections examine some of the application deployment solutions supported by servers running Windows Server 2008 R2 and workstations running Windows 7.

Planning an Application Deployment

CERTIFICATION READY
How do you plan for application delivery?
1.3

As always, the first step in any large-scale deployment project is planning. You must decide which applications your users will need and how you intend to deploy them.

Application deployment is not a process that can wait until your network infrastructure, your servers, and your workstations are already in place. Planning for your applications should be a part of the workstation deployment process from the very beginning.

IDENTIFYING USER REQUIREMENTS

For enterprise administrators to provide users with workstations, they must determine what tasks the users have to accomplish. A large organization will typically have users with widely varying task requirements. Order entry operators might spend all of their time running a single order-taking application, while administrative assistants might require many different applications to complete their required tasks. Meanwhile, graphic designers and research scientists might require highly specialized software products to do their jobs.

This phase of the planning process typically involves creating a list of user types and the tasks that each one regularly performs. With these lists, administrators can select applications to perform each task and devise a series of workstation configurations to suit particular types of users.

IDENTIFYING APPLICATION REQUIREMENTS

To create workstation configurations, administrators must know the hardware and software requirements for each application a user workstation must run. Typically, the hardware requirements for an application add to the memory requirement for the computer. However, some applications might have other specialized hardware or software prerequisites.

Administrators can conceivably create a separate workstation configuration for each type of user, but this would complicate the process of configuring, deploying, and maintaining the computers enormously. It is also possible to create a single workstation configuration to suit all users, but in most cases, the requirements of the organization's high-end users would drive the price of the workstation up too high. In most cases, the ideal solution for the average enterprise falls somewhere between these two extremes.

USING FAT CLIENTS VS. THIN CLIENTS

One of the most critical factors in the planning of an application deployment—one that can affect the configuration of the workstations and the initial outlay for their purchase—is where the applications will actually be running. Most enterprises use fat clients to support applications on their workstations. A *fat client*, as shown in Figure 6-1, is a computer with a lot of memory and a large hard disk: sufficient resources to run the applications the user needs locally.

Figure 6-1

Fat clients

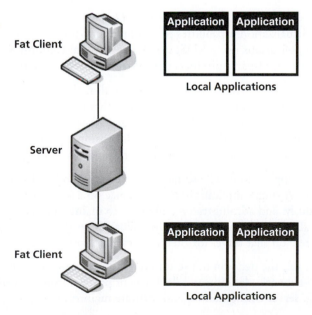

When using fat clients, administrators must select a method for deploying the applications on each workstation, and they must maintain those applications on each workstation individually. Because the applications on a fat client run locally, they are not dependent on the network for their performance.

A *thin client*, by contrast, is a computer that functions as a terminal for applications running on servers, as shown in Figure 6-2. Thin clients require only a minimum of hardware because their primary function is to display the applications running on another computer and carry the user's mouse and keyboard input from the workstation to the applications. This is called *presentation virtualization*.

Figure 6-2

Thin clients

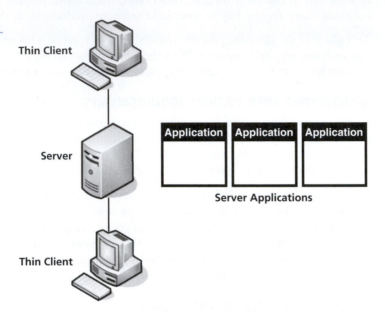

Unlike application virtualization or operating system virtualization, in which a software component is actually running in a virtualized environment, presentation virtualization moves only the input to and the output from an application to another place. The application itself runs on the same server, no matter which client workstation is operating it.

Windows Server 2008 R2 includes *Remote Desktop Services (RDS)*, which provides presentation virtualization capabilities in a number of permutations. For more information on deploying applications using RDS, see "Using Remote Desktop Services" later in this lesson. There are also third-party products that provide similar capabilities.

Because they require fewer hardware resources, thin clients are naturally less expensive than fat clients. However, some or all of the money that the organization saves on workstation computers must be applied to the servers that actually run the applications. Administrators must also consider the additional bandwidth consumed by the communication between the servers running the applications and the workstations accessing them.

Server-based applications are also far easier to deploy and maintain than local workstation applications. A single application, installed once on a server, can support dozens of users simultaneously, and administrators only have to maintain the one copy. On the other hand, the server also becomes a single point of failure. If an RDS server goes down, then all of the users that rely on that server for their applications cannot work.

As you can see, the decision to use thin or fat clients can have far-reaching effects on every part of the network planning and deployment process, from network bandwidth, to computer purchasing, server configuration, and software maintenance.

It is not necessary to commit to a fat-client or thin-client strategy exclusively on your entire network, or even on a single workstation. You can mix fat and thin clients on your network, and you can even mix local and server-based applications on a single workstation. For example, you might want to use RDS to deploy Microsoft Office to all of your users throughout the enterprise, but install other, more specialized applications to individual workstations locally.

Choosing a Deployment Method

Once an enterprise administrator has determined what applications a workstation requires, the next step is to decide how the IT staff should deploy those applications.

In most enterprise environments, the object is to create a series of uniform workstation configurations, to facilitate maintenance and troubleshooting later. Whichever method you choose to deploy applications, the result should be an identical operating environment on each workstation of the same type.

INSTALLING APPLICATIONS MANUALLY

The simplest type of application deployment is the same one that individuals use for their home systems: manual installation to the computer's local hard disk. Most commercial applications include a wizard-based installation program that is easy to use and provides customizing options.

The problem with this type of deployment is the time and effort it requires for each computer. A process that takes 20 to 30 minutes of interaction on a single computer, when multiplied by hundreds of computers, can take days or weeks to accomplish, and that is just for one application. If each workstation requires several applications, the job can quickly overwhelm virtually any IT staff.

Thus, the tradeoff in application deployment, as in operating system deployment, is between manual and automatic processes. When installing applications manually becomes impractical, there are a variety of automated methods that enable administrators to deploy applications without an interactive installation process on each computer.

Planning and configuring an automated deployment can be a complicated process in itself, however. For a small deployment, as in a branch office or for a situation in which you need only a few workstations of a certain configuration, manual application installations can actually be more efficient than a complex, automated procedure.

Eventually, though, you reach a deployment size at which the time and effort spent automating the procedure is less than the time it would take to install the applications manually. At this point, you might consider some of the following alternative deployment options.

DEPLOYING APPLICATIONS USING GROUP POLICY

One method of automating application deployment using only the infrastructure supplied by AD DS is to use the Group Policy Software Installation settings. Group Policy enables you to deploy software in the form of Windows Installer packages. In this context, a package is a database file that contains the software components, registry settings, and installation instructions needed to install an application.

These packages have an MSI extension, which all Windows versions associate with the built-in Windows Installer installation engine. Windows Installer reads the instructions in the package file and executes the installation procedure. Depending on the configuration of the package file, the installation may be fully automated, or there may be interactive components.

While it is possible to install packages manually by executing the file—Microsoft distributes many components and utilities in MSI package format—administrators can automate package distribution by creating Group Policy settings in the Software Installation node of a Group Policy object (GPO), as shown in Figure 6-3. This enables you to deploy applications to specific computers or users in such a way that they are available through the Start menu or the Get Programs control panel.

Figure 6-3

The Software Installation node of a Group Policy object

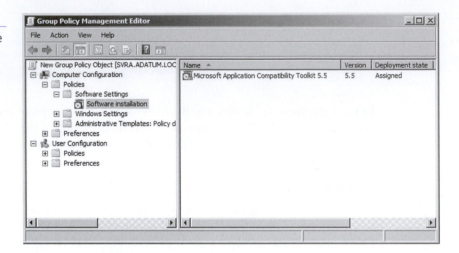

CREATING PACKAGES

The primary drawback of Group Policy application deployment is that Windows does not include any means of creating Windows Installer package files. Some application developers include MSI packages with their products, but for those that don't, you must use a third-party package creation tool, of which there are many.

CREATING A SOFTWARE DISTRIBUTION POINT

Creating a Software Installation package in a GPO does not store the MSI file in the AD DS database. You must create a software distribution point that is accessible to the Group Policy Management Editor console and from which the target computers can download the package files deployed to them.

A software distribution point is simply a network share that contains a separate folder for each application, configured with the permissions needed to provide administrators with read/write access and users with read-only access.

ASSIGNING AND PUBLISHING PACKAGES

Group Policy objects have two Software Installation nodes, one under Computer Configuration and one under User Configuration. Adding a package to either one of these nodes causes AD DS to advertise the software in the package to the computers or users receiving the GPO. Depending on the settings you select when you add the package, as shown in Figure 6-4, the target computers can deploy the software in one of three ways, as follows:

- *Assign* (to computer)—When you assign a package to a computer, an automated software installation occurs as soon as the system starts and downloads the GPO.
- *Assign* (to user)—When you assign a package to a user, the policy adds the application to the computer's Start menu, and can associate certain file-name extensions with the

application's executable. The installation occurs when the user launches the application from the Start menu for the first time or opens a file associated with the application.

- *Publish*—When you publish a package to a user (you cannot publish to a computer), the policy adds the application to the Get Programs control panel in Windows 7 or Windows Server 2008 R2 (or the Add or Remove Programs control panel in earlier versions), enabling the user to install the application on demand at any time.

Figure 6-4

Deployment options in the Software Installation node of a Group Policy object

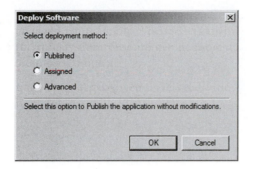

Selecting the Advanced option opens the Properties sheet for the new package, enabling you to further configure the behavior of the policy during the deployment.

DEPLOYING APPLICATIONS USING SYSTEM CENTER CONFIGURATION MANAGER

System Center Configuration Manager (SCCM) 2007 is a Microsoft network management product that provides administrators with a variety of valuable functions, not the least of which is software deployment. SCCM is not included with Windows Server 2008 R2; you must purchase the software separately.

The price of the SCCM 2007 product is considerable, and you must purchase a separate client access license for each workstation you intend to manage with it. SCCM also requires access to a Microsoft SQL Server database to store its information and an agent on each workstation.

For administrators, the SCCM product represents a significant commitment in time and money, and is not typically something you purchase and install for just one task. It is, rather, an investment in the entire lifecycle of your workstations, from deployment to maintenance and updates to retirement.

SCCM uses packages to deploy software, just as Group Policy does, but the packages themselves are of a completely different format than the Windows Installer packages Group Policy uses. In addition, SCCM includes the Configuration Manager console, which is the tool you use to create your own packages.

As with Group Policy, you must create one or more distribution points to deploy software with SCCM. Because SCCM is designed to be almost infinitely scalable, you can create multiple distributions throughout the enterprise.

SCCM is essentially a delivery service that sends packages to particular destinations at specified times. When you create a package using the Configuration Manager's New Package Wizard, shown in Figure 6-5, you specify the files you want to deliver—such as the installation files for an application.

Figure 6-5

The New Package Wizard in
SCCM's Configuration Manager

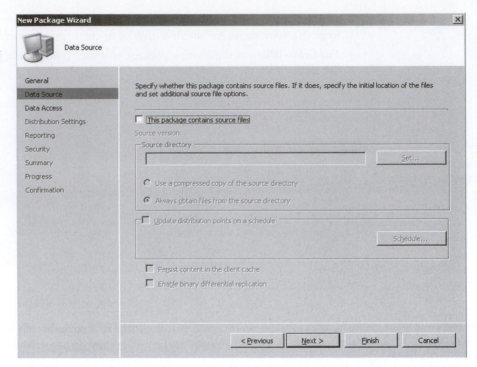

Then, you create a program you want to run on the destination computer, using the New
Program Wizard, as shown in Figure 6-6. To deploy an application, the program would
usually be a Setup.exe file, along with the command line parameters necessary to initiate
the installation process.

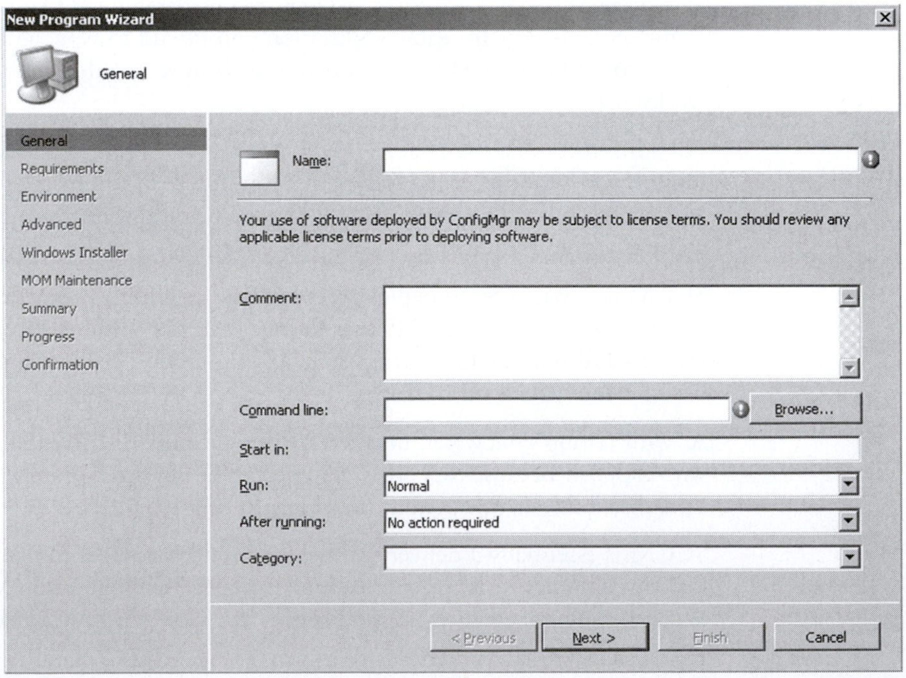

Figure 6-6

The New Program Wizard in
SCCM's Configuration Manager

Then, you create a collection, which is a list of the computers to which you want to deploy the package. Finally, you advertise the package to the collection. The agents on the destination computers download the packages from a distribution point, execute the program, and install the application.

USING WEB-BASED APPLICATIONS

An increasingly popular alternative to locally installed applications is the use of web servers and web browsers as the components of a client/server application. web servers were originally designed as relatively simple applications that supplied clients with static content, in response to their requests.

However, as the web grew in popularity, it also grew in complexity. web site owners soon wanted to use their servers to provide more than just static content files. They wanted to take the information in their company databases and provide it to web clients on demand. They wanted clients to be able to select products from a catalog and pay for them with a credit card. As a result, developers began to create web servers with application capabilities.

As time passed, developers created various methods of implementing applications in a web environment. Some web-based applications execute scripts or compiled code on the server, while in others, the server supplies script code to the client. Many web development solutions combine the two. The primary advantage of web applications over traditional client/server applications is that there is no need to develop, install, configure, or maintain complicated application packages on every client computer. Developers can update their applications on the server, instead of having to distribute new files to hundreds or thousands of clients.

In most cases, web applications use a three-part architecture. The first part is a client browser application, such as Internet Explorer, running on the end-user's computer. The second part is a web server with some type of dynamic content generation capability, such as Internet Information Services (IIS), and the third part is a database server that stores the information the web server uses to dynamically generate web pages.

Internet Information Services (IIS) version 7, included with Windows Server 2008 R2, has role services that support a variety of application development environments, some venerable and others quite recent, including the following:

- ASP.NET
- Active Server Pages (ASP)
- Common Gateway Interface (CGI)
- Internet Server Application Programming Interface (ISAPI)
- Server Side Includes (SSI)

IIS is designed to support multiple Web sites and multiple applications, and it does so by isolating application functions in separate address spaces called application pools.

An *application pool* is an operational division within IIS that consists of a request queue and one or more worker processes. A *worker process* is a host for user-developed application code that is responsible for processing requests it receives from protocol listeners—modules that wait for incoming client requests—and returning the results to the client. Because each application pool occupies its own protected address space, a crashed application cannot affect any process running outside of that pool. This is known as *worker process isolation mode*.

TAKE NOTE*

Another form of web-based application deployment is provided by Remote Desktop Services in the form of Remote Desktop web Access, which enables clients to launch server-based applications from a web browser. For more information, see "Using Remote Desktop Web Access" later in this lesson.

■ Using Remote Desktop Services

THE BOTTOM LINE

Remote Desktop Services (RDS) is a role that enables a server running Windows Server 2008 R2 to host applications and entire desktops for multiple clients all over the network. In this arrangement, the server does all of the actual application computing; the clients function only as terminals. Because the only application running on the client computer is a small communications program, RDS is an implementation of the thin-client computing concept described earlier in this lesson.

TAKE NOTE *

Prior to Windows Server 2008 R2, RDS was known as Terminal Services. The basic architecture of the service has not changed; only the module names have been modified.

CERTIFICATION READY
How do you plan for Remote Desktop Services?
1.4

At its most basic level, RDS works by executing applications on a server running Windows Server 2008 R2, and enabling workstation computers to control those applications from a remote location. A client program running on the workstation establishes a connection to an RDS server, and the server creates ah session for that client. The session can provide the client with a full-featured Windows desktop, a desktop containing one application, or a single application in its own window, appearing exactly as if the application was running on the client computer.

A single RDS server can support many clients simultaneously, depending on the hardware resources in the server and the clients' requirements. You can deploy an application or desktop to dozens or hundreds of clients using a single RDS server. Because every client has its own session, each instance of the application runs in its own memory space, independent of the others. It is also possible to run many applications on a single RDS server, and deploy an instance of each one to every client.

To make an application or desktop appear on a client workstation, the RDS server transmits graphical data and instructions that enable the client to render the application interface on its own display. In return, the client program transmits the user's keystrokes and mouse movements back to the server to operate the applications running there.

As a result, no actual application data is passed between the client and the server, just the client user's input and the application's output in graphical form. The application runs wholly on the RDS server, using its processor, memory, and other resources. The only thing running on the workstation is the client program, which has minimal resource requirements.

Evaluating Remote Desktop Advantages

RDS represents a fundamental shift in PC networking philosophy. As discussed earlier in this lesson, a commitment to server-based applications can alter a network's entire computer deployment lifecycle. Some administrators think of RDS as a return to the good old mainframe days, while others consider it a step backward.

There are various ways that you can use RDS on your network, and as a result, it can provide distinct advantages, including the following:

- Reduced client hardware requirements—Client computers only have to run a single application: the RDC program. The hardware requirements for the client computer are therefore minimal. This enables administrators to purchase inexpensive workstation computers and avoid constantly upgrading hardware to support the latest versions of desktop operating systems and applications.

- Simplified application deployment—Deploying applications on a large fleet of computers can be a long and difficult undertaking, even with distribution tools such as Group

Policy and SCCM 2007. RDS enables administrators to deploy applications to as many clients as needed by installing them only on servers.

- Easy configuration and updates—RDS Services eliminates the need to install, configure, and update applications on individual workstations. When an administrator configures or updates a single copy of an application on an RDS server, all of the clients reap the benefits.

- Low network bandwidth consumption—RDS connections use relatively little network bandwidth, because most of the data exchanged by the clients and servers over the network consists of keystroke, mouse, and display instructions, instead of large application and data files. For remote users accessing RDS servers over the Internet, the bandwidth required is much less than that for a virtual private network (VPN) or direct dial-up connection.

- Conservation of licenses—Instead of purchasing application licenses for individual workstations, which might or might not be in use at any given time, you can maintain a pool of licenses on the RDS server that the system allocates to users as they log on. For example, an office with 100 workstations would require 100 licenses for an application installed on each computer, even if there were never more than 50 users running the application at any one time. Using RDS, 50 application licenses would be sufficient, because only the users actually connected to the server need a license.

- Power savings—The total power consumption of a network consisting of standard workstations and servers is substantially greater than that of a typical RDS installation, which can use client computers with slower processors and less memory.

- No client backups—In a typical RDS installation, users access all of their applications and data files from servers. As a result, there is usually no need to back up the client computers, which yields savings in time and backup media.

- Remote control help and training—RDS enables administrators to tap into a client session (with the client's permission), to observe what the user is doing or to interact with the user in real time. Administrators can therefore demonstrate procedures to a user, for help and training purposes, without having to travel to the user's location.

You can use the technology to solve specific problems or use it to completely change the way your network operates.

Designing a Remote Desktop Infrastructure

> At its heart, RDS is a relatively simple mechanism. Any administrator can install the RDS role on a server and configure a client to access the service in minutes. However, for the enterprise administrator, implementing a fully functional production environment using RDS can be considerably more complicated.

All client/server applications, by definition, require three basic elements: a server program, a client program, and a protocol that enables the two programs to communicate. RDS implements these elements with the following three components:

- *Remote Desktop Session Host*—A role service that runs on a computer running Windows Server 2008 R2, which enables multiple clients to connect to the server and run individual desktop or application sessions.

- *Remote Desktop Connection client*—A program running on a workstation computer, as shown in Figure 6-7, which establishes a connection to an RDS server using RDP and displays a session window containing a desktop or application. All Windows versions include the Remote Desktop Connection client program.

Figure 6-7

The Remote Desktop
Connection client

- ***Remote Desktop Protocol (RDP)***—A networking protocol that enables communication between the RDS server and the client.

In addition to Remote Desktop Session Host, the Remote Desktop Services role also includes the following additional role services, as shown in Figure 6-8:

Figure 6-8

The Remote Desktop Services
role services

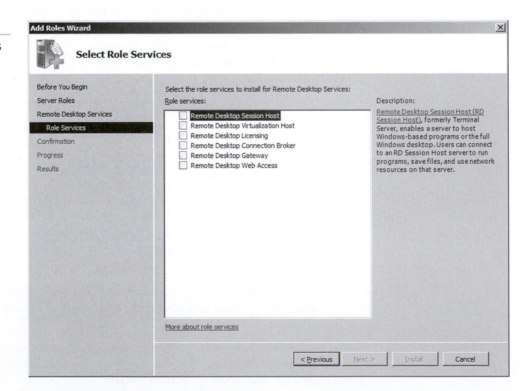

- ***Remote Desktop Virtualization Host***—Integrates RDS with Hyper-V, enabling clients to establish connections to individual virtual machines rather than individual sessions on the host machine.

- *Remote Desktop Licensing*—Enables administrators to manage the client access licenses (CALs) required for workstations to access RDS servers.
- *Remote Desktop Connection Broker*—Enables clients to reconnect to the same session when RDS is running on a server farm or to the same virtual machine when using Remote Desktop Virtualization Host.
- *Remote Desktop Gateway*—Enables remote users on the Internet to access RDS servers on an internal network using HTTPS connections to a Web server as a gateway.
- *Remote Desktop Web Access*—Publishes RDS applications and desktops as icons in a Web browser window, enabling clients to access them without having to run the Remote Desktop Connection client program.

USING RDS DESKTOPS

Enterprise administrators can make use of the capabilities that RDS provides in various ways. Some administrators adopt RDS as a complete client solution. Instead of deploying any applications at all on each workstation, they run an RDC client, connect to RDS servers, and access a remote desktop that contains all of the applications they need. When you configure RDS properly, many users cannot even tell that their applications are not running on the local computer.

Whether this is a practical solution for your network depends largely on the hardware in the computers involved. If you have already purchased high-end workstations for your users, it makes no sense to use that powerful hardware just to run the RDC program. However, if you are building a new network, or if your workstations are low-powered or outdated, RDS can be an economical alternative to purchasing new desktops or upgrading the old ones.

TAKE NOTE*

> RDS might save you money on workstation hardware, but consider the fact that you might have to upgrade your servers (or purchase additional new ones) to support the RDS traffic, and you will certainly have to purchase Remote Desktop *client access licenses (CALs)* for your users.

Even if you decide that it is not practical to use RDS for your clients' entire desktops, you might still use it for individual applications. You can use RDS to deploy some of your applications, automatically deploy a desktop containing only a single application, or use RemoteApp to deploy applications directly to client windows without a desktop.

USING REMOTEAPP

RemoteApp is a relatively new RDS feature that enables workstations to run RDS applications within individual windows. The windows are resizable, they have standard taskbar buttons, and they are not constrained by an RDS desktop. In fact, a RemoteApp window is, in most cases, indistinguishable from a window containing a local application.

By eliminating the RDS desktop, RemoteApp does away with much of the confusion that frequently affects both users and support staff. Users no longer have to switch back and forth between local and remote desktops; they can combine local applications and RemoteApp applications in the same workspace, just as if all the applications were local.

RemoteApp is part of the Remote Desktop Session Host role service and includes a separate configuration tool, the RemoteApp Manager snap-in for Microsoft Management Console (MMC), as shown in Figure 6-9.

Figure 6-9

The RemoteApp Manager
snap-in

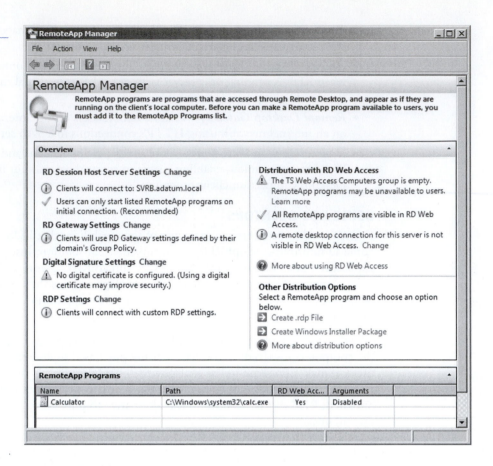

To use RemoteApp, you must complete the following steps:

- Configure the RDS server by specifying what applications you want to provide to your clients.
- Package the applications by creating Remote Desktop Protocol (RDP) files or Microsoft Installer (MSI) packages.
- Deploy the application packages using shared drives or Group Policy.

Once you have configured the RDS server to run the selected applications using RemoteApp, you must deploy them to your clients. The RDC client can only provide a full desktop; it cannot host RemoteApp applications. Instead, you use the RemoteApp Manager console to create either Remote Desktop Protocol or Microsoft Installer packages.

A Remote Desktop Protocol package is a file with an RDP extension, which users can execute to launch the RemoteApp application on the RDS server. You can deploy Remote Desktop Protocol packages by placing them on shared drives accessible to your users, copying them to the clients' local drives, sending them as email attachments, or using any other standard file distribution method.

Microsoft Installer (MSI) packages are another means of distributing Remote Desktop Protocol packages. When a client computer executes a Microsoft Installer package, the installation program copies the RDP file contained within it to a local drive and creates a shortcut that enables the user to launch the RemoteApp program from the Start menu.

You can distribute Microsoft Installer packages to clients as files, just as you would Remote Desktop Protocol packages, but the real advantage in this method is to use Group Policy to automatically distribute and install the packages to large groups of clients, as discussed earlier in this lesson.

Clients can also access RemoteApp programs through a Remote Desktop Web Access site.

USING REMOTE DESKTOP WEB ACCESS

In addition to using the RDC client, it is also possible for users to access Remote Desktop sessions using a standard web browser, such as Internet Explorer. The Remote Desktop Web Access role service configures an RDS server to use Internet Information Services (IIS) to publish a web page that provides access to desktop sessions or individual RemoteApp applications, as shown in Figure 6-10. When a user double-clicks an icon for a RemoteApp application on the web page, the application launches in a separate window, just as with the RDC client, not in the browser window.

Figure 6-10

A Remote Desktop Web Access web page

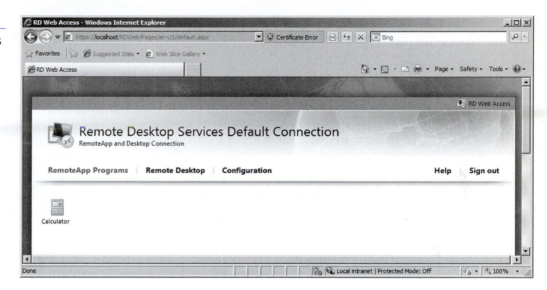

For relatively unsophisticated users, Remote Desktop Web Access greatly simplifies the process of connecting to Remote Desktop desktops and applications. Instead of instructing users how to connect to a particular RDS server and access applications using RDC, you can simply supply them with a URL, in any of the usual ways, including shortcuts, favorites, and hyperlinks, and tell them to click an icon.

To install Remote Desktop Web Access on a computer running Windows Server 2008 R2, you must add the Remote Desktop Web Access role service. You can choose to install Remote Desktop Web Access on the same computer as the other Remote Desktop role services, or on another server by itself. When you install Remote Desktop Web Access on a computer that is not an RDS server itself, you will have to configure it later to access the resources of a Windows Server 2008 R2 computer that is an RDS server.

Remote Desktop Web Access requires Internet Information Services 7.0 to run, and IIS 7 in turn requires the Windows Process Activation Service. If these components are not already installed on your computer, the Add Roles Wizard prompts you to add the Web Server (IIS) role and the Windows Process Activation Service feature.

USING REMOTE DESKTOP GATEWAY

To clients accessing application through Remote Desktop Web Access, it might appear as though the computer is using a standard Hypertext Transfer Protocol (HTTP) connection to run RemoteApp programs and remote desktops. This would mean that any client could connect to the RDS server, whether it is located on the same intranet or on the Internet. Actually, this is not the case.

A client's initial connection to the Remote Desktop Web Access Web page does involve a standard HTTP connection, using port TCP 80, but once the user clicks a RemoteApp icon or establishes a Remote Desktop connection, HTTP is no longer involved. Remote Desktop Web Access is actually an application running on the IIS 7 Web server, which provides the same functionality as the Remote Desktop Connection client. This means that the connection between the client and the RDS server is using the same RDP traffic as a Remote Desktop Connection session.

Remote Desktop Gateway is a RDS role service that enables Internet users to access RDS servers on private networks, despite the presence of intervening firewalls and network access translation (NAT) servers.

UNDERSTANDING REMOTE DESKTOP GATEWAY COMMUNICATIONS

The switch from the HTTP protocol to RDP during the Remote Desktop Web Access connection establishment process is transparent to the client, but it is actually critical to the security of the RDS server. The ability to access a server running Windows Server 2008 R2 from another location on the network is a tremendous convenience to administrators and end users alike, but it can also be an alarming security hazard. Remote Desktop connections can provide clients with full control over an RDS server, potentially compromising its internal resources.

Protecting RDS servers from potential intruders within the organization (accidental or not) is a matter of controlling the RDS authentication and authorization processes. In other words, administrators use account security to control who can access an RDS server and permissions to specify exactly what each user can do.

Fortunately, protecting RDS servers from Internet intrusion is not a special consideration, because the port number that the RDP protocol uses (TCP port 3389) is blocked by default on most firewalls. This means that while Internet users might conceivably be able to connect to the Web Access web page using port 80 (assuming the web server is accessible from the Internet), they are not able to connect to port 3389 to launch an RDS application.

The connection establishment process by which the client on the Internet uses the Remote Desktop Gateway server to access an RDS server on a private network is as follows:

1. The Internet client initiates the RDS connection process by executing an RDP file, clicking a RemoteApp icon, or accessing a Remote Desktop Web Access site.

2. The client initiates an SSL connection to the Remote Desktop Gateway server, using port 443, as shown in Figure 6-11.

Figure 6-11

A client connects to the Remote Desktop Gateway server using SSL on port 443

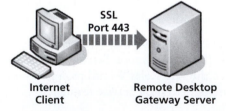

SSL
Port 443

**Internet
Client**

**Remote Desktop
Gateway Server**

RDS Server

3. The Remote Desktop Gateway authenticates and authorizes the client, using connection authorization policies (CAPs).

4. If the authentication and authorization processes succeed, the client requests a connection from the Remote Desktop Gateway server to an RDS server on the private network.

5. The Remote Desktop Gateway server authorizes the request using resource authorization policies (RAPs) to confirm the availability of the RDS server and the client's permission to access that server.

6. If the authorization succeeds, the SSL connection between the client and the Remote Desktop Gateway server is established, forming the tunnel, as shown in Figure 6-12.

Figure 6-12

An authenticated and authorized client connected to the Remote Desktop Gateway server

7. The Remote Desktop Gateway server establishes an RDP connection with the RDS server requested by the client, using port 3389.

8. The client initiates a session with the RDS server by encapsulating its RDP traffic within SSL packets and sending them to port 443 on the Remote Desktop Gateway server.

9. The Remote Desktop Gateway server strips off the SSL header and relays the client's RDP traffic to the Remote Desktop server, using port 3389, as shown in Figure 6-13.

Figure 6-13

The Remote Desktop Gateway server establishes an RDP connection to the RDS server, using port 3389

10. At this point, the client and the RDS server are exchanging standard RDP messages, just as they would if both were located on the same local network. The Remote Desktop Gateway server continues to function as an intermediary throughout the duration of the RDS session, communicating with the client using SSL and the RDS server using RDP, as shown in Figure 6-14.

Figure 6-14

The Remote Desktop Gateway server connects to clients using SSL and RDS servers using RDP

COMPARING REMOTE DESKTOP GATEWAY WITH VPNs

But what about administrators who want to provide Internet users with access to RDS servers? This could be an extremely useful capability. Generally speaking, the technology of choice for remote network access has, in recent years, been virtual private networking (VPN). In a VPN connection, computers use a technique called tunneling, which encapsulates an entire client/

server session within another protocol. Because the internal or payload protocol is carried by another protocol, it is protected from most standard forms of attack.

One of the inherent problems with VPN connections is the amount of bandwidth they require. A VPN connection between an Internet user and a host network requires slightly more bandwidth than a standard LAN connection. The client and server typically must exchange application and/or document files, which in some cases can be extremely large. However, Internet connections are nearly always much slower than LAN connections. A broadband Internet connection will typically provide satisfactory performance for most network applications, but VPN over a dial-up connection can be an extremely slow and frustrating experience.

Because Remote Desktop clients and servers only exchange a minimal amount of data, however, an RDS server connection can function perfectly well over a low-bandwidth connection, such as a dial-up. This is what makes RDS a good solution for Internet client connections. The biggest problem, of course, is security. Opening up port 3389 in your Internet firewall would enable remote clients to access your RDS servers, but this would also be an invitation for abuse.

The Remote Desktop Gateway role service enables RDS to support Internet clients securely, using the same tunneling concept as a VPN connection, except in this case, the computers encapsulate RDP traffic within Secure Sockets Layer (SSL) packets. SSL uses TCP port number 443, which most organizations with an Internet presence leave open in their firewalls, so that Internet clients can establish secure connections to their web servers.

DEPLOYING A REMOTE DESKTOP GATEWAY SERVER

The Remote Desktop Gateway role service is essentially a tunnel through your network's defenses that enables specific users on the Internet to pass through your firewalls, proxy servers, NAT routers, and other protective devices to reach the RDS servers on your private internal network. Therefore, Remote Desktop Gateway must run on a computer that is accessible both to the Internet and to your internal network, such as a perimeter network, as shown in Figure 6-15.

Figure 6-15

A Remote Desktop Gateway server on a perimeter network

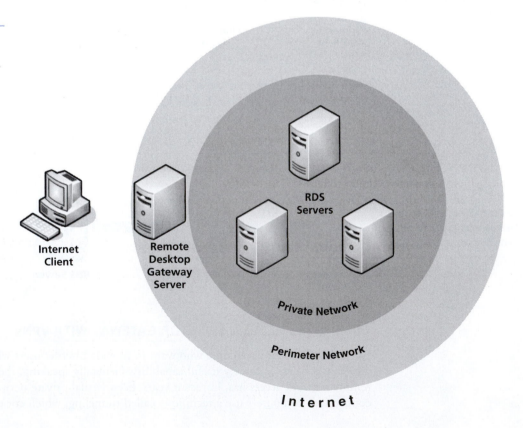

Internet Client

Remote Desktop Gateway Server

RDS Servers

Private Network

Perimeter Network

Internet

A typical Remote Desktop Gateway deployment consists of three basic elements: Internet clients, a Remote Desktop Gateway server, and RDS servers.

To deploy a Remote Desktop Gateway server, you must perform the following tasks:

- Install the Remote Desktop Gateway role service.
- Obtain and install a certificate for the Remote Desktop Gateway server.
- Create connection authorization policies.
- Create resource authorization policies.
- Configure the client to use the Remote Desktop Gateway.

Understanding Remote Desktop Licensing

Windows Server 2008 R2 includes a limited form of Remote Desktop that you can use for remote administration, whether you install the Remote Desktop Services role or not. This feature enables up to two users to connect to the server using the Remote Desktop Connection client, with no licenses or restrictions.

To use the Remote Desktop Services role for multiple user connections, you must purchase the appropriate number of Remote Desktop Services client access licenses (CALs) and install a *Remote Desktop Licensing server* to deploy them.

To facilitate the deployment of your RDS servers and clients, Windows Server 2008 R2 provides a grace period during which clients can connect to an RDS server without a license. This grace period begins when the first client connects to the RDS server and lasts a maximum of 120 days. Once the grace period has expired, all clients must have a CAL to connect to the server. When a client without a CAL attempts to connect, the RDS server directs it to the Remote Desktop Licensing server, which issues a permanent license. If no Remote Desktop Licensing server is available, or if the Remote Desktop Licensing server has no available CALs, the connection attempt fails.

PLANNING A REMOTE DESKTOP LICENSING DEPLOYMENT

The process of installing a Remote Desktop Licensing server and preparing it for use consists of the following basic steps:

1. Install the Remote Desktop Licensing role service.
2. Activate the Remote Desktop Licensing server.
3. Install the CALs on the Remote Desktop Licensing server.
4. Configure the licensing settings on the RDS servers.

An RDS deployment needs only one Remote Desktop Licensing server for the entire installation, no matter how many RDS servers you have on your network. The resource requirements for the Remote Desktop Licensing role service are minimal. Remote Desktop Licensing is not involved in the process of checking whether a client possesses a license; the RDS Services service performs that task. The Remote Desktop Licensing service requires only about 10 megabytes of memory and the license database requires one megabyte of storage space for every 1,200 licenses. The processor requirements are negligible because the service issues a license to each client only once.

+ MORE INFORMATION

The Remote Desktop Licensing role service included with Windows Server 2008 R2 and Windows Server 2008 can provide licensing services for terminal servers running on Windows Server 2003 and Windows 2000 Server computers. However, a down-level server cannot provide licensing services for Windows Server 2008 R2 or Windows Server 2008 RDS servers. If you are running even one Windows Server 2008 R2 or Windows Server 2008 RDS server, you must install a Windows Server 2008 R2 or Windows Server 2008 Remote Desktop Licensing server.

When planning a Remote Desktop Licensing server deployment, you must consider how your RDS servers are going to locate the licensing server. While it is possible to manually configure each RDS server with the name or IP address of a specific Remote Desktop Licensing server, automatic licensing server detection is a more convenient alternative.

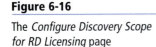

TAKE NOTE*

To issue licenses to clients in other domains, the computer running the license server must be a member of the Terminal Server License Servers group in each domain.

When clients attempting to connect to an RDS server require licenses, the server attempts to discover a Remote Desktop Licensing server in the following order:

1. A licensing server specified in the RDS server configuration or a Group Policy setting
2. A licensing server installed on the same computer as the RDS server
3. A licensing server that is published in the Active Directory database
4. A licensing server running on a domain controller in the RDS server's domain

For a small RDS deployment, you can run the Remote Desktop Licensing role service on the same computer as the other RDS role services. An RDS server can always locate a Remote Desktop Licensing server running on the same computer. For larger deployments with multiple RDS servers, you can install Remote Desktop Licensing on one of the RDS servers, or on any other server.

Another important part of the RDS planning process is deciding whether you want the Remote Desktop Licensing server to issue Per Device or Per User CALs. The license types are the same as those used for Windows Server 2008 R2 clients. You can issue Per Device licenses, which enable any user working at a licensed computer to access RDS servers, or Per User licenses, which enable specific users to access RDS servers with any computer. Once you decide which type of licenses to use, you must be sure to purchase licenses of the appropriate type and configure your RDS servers to accept that type of license.

DEPLOYING A REMOTE DESKTOP LICENSING SERVER

To deploy a Remote Desktop Licensing server, you must complete the following tasks:

- Install the Remote Desktop Licensing role service—When you install the Remote Desktop Licensing role service, you must specify the server's discovery scope by selecting the Workgroup, Domain, or forest option on the *Configure Discovery Scope for RD Licensing* page, shown in Figure 6-16.

Figure 6-16

The *Configure Discovery Scope for RD Licensing* page

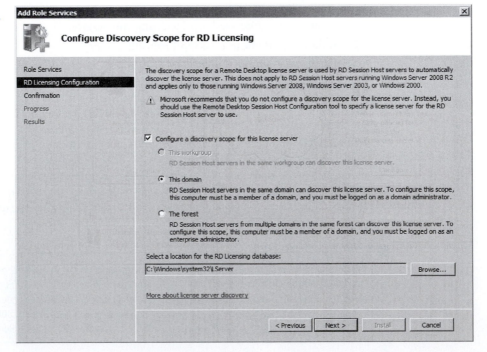

- Activate the Remote Desktop Licensing server—An unactivated Remote Desktop Licensing server can only issue temporary, 90-day per device or per user CALs. When you activate the server, Microsoft issues it a digital certificate that certifies the identity of the server and its owner.

- Install client access licenses—CALs are available from Microsoft through a number of channels, including retail License Packs and various volume licensing programs. When you purchase CALs, you must select either per device or per user licenses and configure your RDS servers accordingly. Once you have purchased the CALs, you must install them on the Remote Desktop Licensing server, so that the server can distribute them to your clients.

- Configure Remote Desktop Licensing settings—Once you have an operational Remote Desktop Licensing server on your network, you must configure the Remote Desktop Licensing Mode, as shown in Figure 6-17, which specifies whether the server should issue per device or per user licenses to clients, and the Licensing Server Discovery Mode, which specifies how the RDS server will locate a Remote Desktop Licensing server.

Figure 6-17

The Remote Desktop Session Host Configuration console

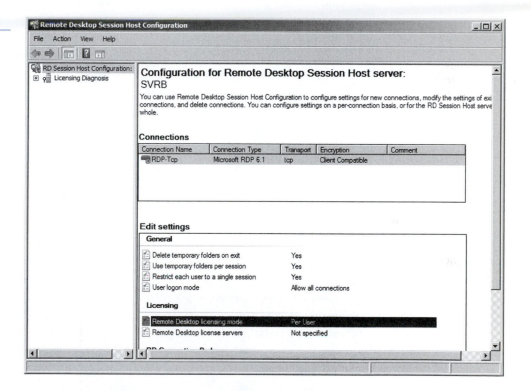

SKILL SUMMARY

IN THIS LESSON YOU LEARNED:

- For enterprise administrators to provide users with workstations, they must determine what tasks the users have to accomplish. To create workstation configurations, administrators must know the hardware and software requirements for each application a user workstation must run.

- A fat client is a computer with a lot of memory and a large hard disk: sufficient resources to run the applications the user needs locally. A thin client, by contrast, is a computer that functions as a terminal for applications running on servers.

- Thin clients require only a minimum of hardware because their primary function is to display the applications running on another computer and carry the user's mouse and keyboard input from the workstation to the applications. This is called presentation virtualization.

- The simplest type of application deployment is the same one that individuals use for their home systems: manual installation to the computer's local hard disk.

- One method of automating application deployment using only the infrastructure supplied by AD DS is to use the Group Policy Software Installation settings. Group Policy enables you to deploy software in the form of Windows Installer packages that contain the software components, registry settings, and installation instructions needed to install an application.

- System Center Configuration Manager (SCCM) 2007 is a Microsoft network management product that provides administrators with a variety of valuable functions, not the least of which is software deployment.

- An increasingly popular alternative to locally installed applications is the use of web servers and web browsers as the components of a client/server application. Web servers were originally designed as relatively simple applications that supplied clients with static content, in response to their requests.

- At its most basic level, Remote Desktop Services works by executing applications on a server running Windows Server 2008 R2 and enabling workstation computers to control those applications from a remote location.

- All client/server applications, by definition, require three basic elements: a server program, a client program, and a protocol that enables the two programs to communicate. RDS implements these elements with the Remote Desktop Session Host, the Remote Desktop Connection client, and the Remote Desktop Protocol (RDP).

- RemoteApp is a relatively new RDS feature that enables workstations to run RDS applications within individual windows.

- In addition to using the RDC client, it is also possible for users to access Remote Desktop sessions using a standard Web browser, such as Internet Explorer. The Remote Desktop Web Access role service configures an RDS server to use Internet Information Services (IIS) to publish a web page that provides access to desktop sessions or individual RemoteApp applications.

- Remote Desktop Gateway is a RDS role service that enables Internet users to access RDS servers on private networks, despite the presence of intervening firewalls and network access translation (NAT) servers.

- To use the Remote Desktop Services role for multiple user connections, you must purchase the appropriate number of Remote Desktop Services client access licenses (CALs) and install a Remote Desktop Licensing server to deploy them.

■ Knowledge Assessment

Fill in the Blank

Complete the following sentences by writing the correct word or words in the blanks provided.

1. Clients can access a Remote Desktop Services server for _____ days before they require a client access license.

2. The _____ role service enables clients of a Remote Desktop server farm to resume working in the same session or virtual machine after a disconnection.

3. _____ is the name of the process in which a Remote Desktop Licensing server obtains a digital certificate from Microsoft.

4. The port number that the RDP protocol uses for Remote Desktop applications is _____.

5. An application pool is an operational division within IIS that consists of a _____ and one or more worker processes.

6. The Remote Desktop _____ role service publishes RDS applications and desktops as icons in a Web browser window, enabling clients to access them without having to run the Remote Desktop Connection client program.

7. A Remote Desktop Gateway server must run on a _____ network.

8. To use the Remote Desktop Web Access role service, you must also have a computer running the _____ role.

9. To deploy complete desktops to Remote Desktop Connection client, the only RDS role service you have to install is _____.

10. For clients to be able to download the Windows Installer packages you publish using Group Policy, you must create a _____.

True / False

Circle T if the statement is true or F if the statement is false.

T | F 1. SCCM 2007 includes a tool that enables you to create your own package files.

T | F 2. To deploy Remote Desktop Services applications using RemoteApp, you must first install the Remote Desktop Connection Broker role service.

T | F 3. Clients access the Remote Desktop Gateway server using the HTTP protocol.

T | F 4. You can publish a Windows Installer package to a user with Group Policy, but not to a computer.

T | F 5. An RDS deployment needs only one Remote Desktop Licensing server for the entire installation, no matter how many RDS servers you have on your network.

T | F 6. Presentation virtualization requires a server capable of running Hyper-V.

T | F 7. Application pools are designed to prevent crashed applications from affecting any process running outside of the pool.

T | F 8. An RDS connection through a Remote Desktop Gateway requires slightly more bandwidth than a virtual private network connection.

T | F 9. An unactivated Remote Desktop Licensing server can only issue temporary, 120-day per device or per user CALs.

T | F 10. Applications deployed using RemoteApp are, in most cases, indistinguishable from locally installed applications.

Review Questions

1. Place the following steps of the Remote Desktop Gateway connection establishment process in the proper order.

   a. A tunnel is established between the client and the Remote Desktop Gateway server.

   b. The Remote Desktop Gateway authenticates and authorizes the client.

    c. The Remote Desktop Gateway server establishes an RDP connection with the RDS server.

    d. The client initiates a session with the RDS server.

    e. The client initiates an SSL connection to the Remote Desktop Gateway server.

    f. The client requests a connection to an RDS server on the private network.

    g. The Remote Desktop Gateway server strips off the SSL header and relays the client's RDP traffic to the RDS server.

    h. The Remote Desktop Gateway server authorizes the client's request.

    i. The Internet client clicks a RemoteApp icon.

2. List the four primary steps involved in deploying a Remote Desktop Licensing server.

■ Case Scenarios

Scenario 6-1: Configuring RemoteApp Applications

Howard has just set up a Remote Desktop Services server on his network by installing Windows Server 2008 R2, adding the Remote Desktop Services role, and installing Microsoft Office on the server. He has also added the individual Office applications to the RemoteApp Programs list in the RemoteApp Manager console. However, when clients connect to the server using the Remote Desktop Connection client, they see an entire RDS desktop, instead of the individual RemoteApp applications in separate windows. What must Howard do to resolve this problem?

Scenario 6-2: Deploying Remote Desktop Services

Some months ago, Kathleen installed the Remote Desktop Services role on one of her Windows Server 2008 R2 servers, and she has been using it to provide clients with access to a custom-designed credit reporting application. This morning, she began receiving calls from users complaining that they could no longer access their Remote Desktop Services desktops. What is the most likely cause of the problem, and what must Kathleen do to resolve it?

Deploying Software Updates

OBJECTIVE DOMAIN MATRIX

TECHNOLOGY SKILL	OBJECTIVE DOMAIN	OBJECTIVE NUMBER
Using Microsoft Update	Design for software updates and compliance management.	4.2

KEY TERMS

autonomous WSUS server
compliance management
configuration baseline
Desired Configuration
  Management

disconnected WSUS server
downstream server
Microsoft Update
replica WSUS server
synchronization

upstream server
Windows Server Update
  Services (WSUS)
Windows Update

Designing a Software Update Strategy

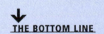

Enterprise administrators rarely have to install software updates themselves. In fact, they often do not participate in the day-to-day operations of the update infrastructure, either. However, enterprise administrators are ultimately responsible for seeing to it that all the computers on the network receive the necessary operating system and application updates on a timely basis.

As with all network services, the size and scope of the update infrastructure vary with those of the network itself. The more computers there are to update and the more the network is complicated by the presence of branch offices, traveling clients, and wide-area network (WAN) connections, the more complicated the task of updating them becomes.

Using Microsoft Update

All versions of Windows are equipped with a *Windows Update* client that, when activated, automatically downloads operating system updates from Microsoft's Web servers and installs them. An optional service called *Microsoft Update* expands the capability of the client by enabling it to download and install updates for other Microsoft software products, including Microsoft Office.

The simplest software update strategy you can implement on a network is merely to activate this client and let each computer manage its own updates. However, in an enterprise environment, this practice can result in a number of problems, including the following:

- **Bandwidth utilization**—Each computer running the Windows Update client downloads its own copy of each update from the Microsoft servers on the Internet. A large network can therefore consume a huge amount of Internet bandwidth in downloading hundreds of copies of the same files.

- **Update approval**—The default settings of the Windows Update client do not give administrators an opportunity to evaluate the updates before it installs them. It is possible to configure the client to download the updates automatically and install them manually, but this would require administrators to manage each computer individually.

- **Compliance**—The default Windows Update configuration provides no means for administrators to confirm that the client has installed all of the required updates successfully on each computer.

On all but the smallest networks, the Windows Update client with its default settings is not a reliable update solution. Although Windows 7 displays messages to end-users recommending that they activate the client, Windows Update is disabled on a new workstation installation, as shown in Figure 7-1. There is no way for administrators to confirm that the users have activated the client or to determine whether the users have modified the client settings.

CERTIFICATION READY
How do you design for software updates and compliance management?
4.2

Figure 7-1

The default Windows Update control panel settings

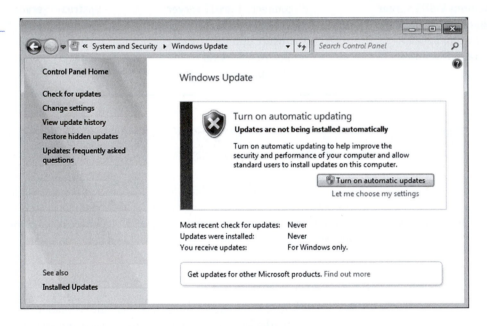

To address these problems, there are a number of alternative solutions you can use to design an update deployment strategy for your network, including the following:

- Modify the Windows Update client defaults.
- Install a Windows Server Update Services (WSUS) server.

For more information on these alternatives, see the following sections.

Configuring the Windows Update Client

Despite the drawbacks listed earlier, there are situations in which the Windows Update client is the best solution for updating software.

Some of these situations are as follows:

- Small offices—For any automated administrative effort, there is a point of no return: the point at which the time spent automating a task is greater than it would take to perform the task manually. For branch offices with just a handful of computers, it can be easier to activate the Windows Update client manually than deploy a complex automation tool.

- Mobile workstations—Automated update solutions typically involve deploying a server on the enterprise network, which clients access instead of the Microsoft servers to obtain their updates. For traveling users with laptops or other mobile computers, who rarely or never connect to the corporate network, this is clearly not a viable solution.

For these situations, it might be practical to configure the Windows Update client in each computer manually, using the *Change Settings* page of the Windows Update control panel, as shown in Figure 7-2.

Figure 7-2

The *Change Settings* page of the Windows Update control panel

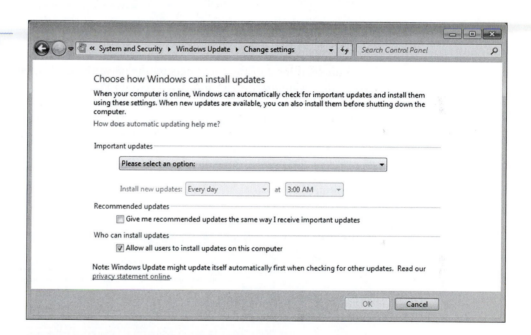

Configuring Windows Update Group Policy Settings

In an enterprise environment, the computers using the Windows Update client by itself are typically a small part of a much larger operation. It is therefore still desirable to maintain an administrative policy for these computers and implement it by configuring the client using Group Policy settings supplied through Active Directory Domain Services (AD DS).

The Group Policy settings that control the behavior of the Windows Update client are found in the Computer Configuration\Policies\Administrative Templates\Windows Components\ Windows Update folder in every Group Policy object, as shown in Figure 7-3.

In a situation where only a few of an enterprise network's computers use the Windows Update client by itself, it will probably be necessary for an administrator to create a GPO that implements Windows Update settings different from those applied to the rest of the network.

Figure 7-3

The Windows Update Group
Policy settings

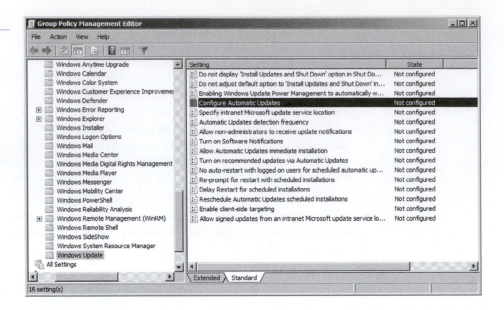

For example, if most of the computers on the network obtain their updates from WSUS
servers, they will need their own different Group Policy settings. To apply these exceptional
settings to the few computers that need them, the administrator will have to use one of the
standard techniques for isolating those few computers within the AD DS hierarchy, such as
creating a separate organizational unit (OU) for them or adding them to a group and using
Security Filtering to limit the dissemination of the GPO to that group.

The key Group Policy setting for the Windows Update client is Configure Automatic Updates,
as shown in Figure 7-4.

Figure 7-4

The *Configure Automatic
Updates* setting dialog box

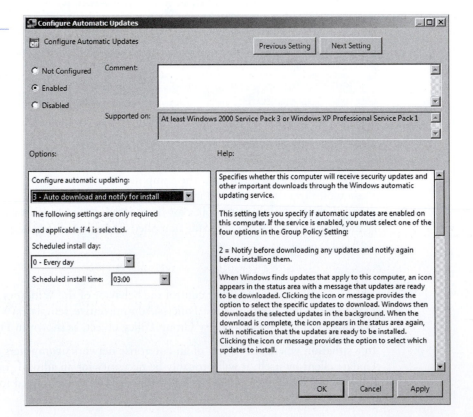

This setting, when enabled, activates the client, specifies the degree of user interactivity in the update process, and schedules the time and day when automated update installations should occur. In an enterprise environment, it is typical for administrators to completely automate the update process, leaving the user no choice on whether the computer should download and install updates.

There are two main issues that can complicate an automated update process of this type. The first is the fact that some updates must replace files that are in use while the operating system is running. The client therefore requires the system to restart to replace these files. A involuntary restart can cause problems for the user working at the workstation, so there are Group Policy settings that can modify the default behavior of the client in this respect, for example:

- Delay restart for scheduled installations—When enabled, this setting specifies the time interval (in minutes) that the client waits after completing an update installation before it restarts the system. When disabled or not configured, the default time interval is 15 minutes.

- Re-prompt for restart with scheduled installations—When a user postpones a restart requested by the client, this setting, when enabled, specifies the time interval (in minutes) before the client prompts the user again.

- No auto-restart with logged on users for scheduled automatic updates installations— When enabled, this setting prevents the client from automatically restarting the computer when a user is logged on. Instead, the client notifies the user to restart the system to complete the update installation.

The second issue is the behavior of the Windows Update client when the computer is shut off during the time of a scheduled update. Obviously, when the computer is not running, an update cannot occur. The next time that the computer starts, the client performs all scheduled tasks that it has missed.

However, the following Group Policy settings can control the behavior of the client when this occurs:

- Enabling Windows Update Power Management to automatically wake up the system to install scheduled updates—When enabled, causes the computer to wake from a hibernation state when there are updates to be installed. If the computer is running on battery power, the client aborts the update installation and returns the computer to the hibernation state after two minutes.

- Reschedule automatic updates scheduled installations—When enabled, specifies the time interval (in minutes) that the client should wait after system startup before it performs a missed, scheduled update installation. When not configured, the client waits a default time interval of one minute before initiating a missed, scheduled installation. When disabled, the client defers the update until the next scheduled installation.

Using Windows Server Update Services

↓ **THE BOTTOM LINE**

Windows Server Update Services (WSUS) is a service included in Windows Server 2008 R2 that enables a local server on your network to function as the back end for the Windows Update client, just as the Microsoft Update servers do on the Internet.

By installing a WSUS server on your network, you can use it to supply updates to all of the other servers and workstations on your network. The WSUS server downloads all new updates from the Microsoft Update servers on the Internet, and your other computers download the updates from the WSUS server. This way, you are only paying for the bandwidth needed to download one copy of every update.

In addition to conserving bandwidth, WSUS enables administrators to screen the available updates, test them in a lab environment, and approve them for deployment to the clients. This enables administrators to retain ultimate authority over which updates get installed on the network clients and when the installations occur.

A single WSUS server can support many Windows Update clients, which means that one server is theoretically enough for all but the largest networks. However, WSUS also supports a number of architectural variations, to accommodate topologies that include remote users and branch offices with limited communication capabilities.

Understanding WSUS Architectures

There are several architectural configurations you can use when deploying WSUS on an enterprise network, depending on its size and the number of remote locations involved.

There are five basic WSUS architecture configurations, as follows:

- Single WSUS server
- Replica WSUS servers
- Autonomous WSUS servers
- Low-bandwidth WSUS servers
- Disconnected WSUS servers

USING A SINGLE WSUS SERVER

In the simplest configuration, a single WSUS server downloads updates from the Microsoft Update Web site and all of the other computers on the network download the updates from that WSUS server, as shown in Figure 7-5. A single WSUS server can support as many as 25,000 clients, so this configuration is suitable for most enterprise networks.

Figure 7-5

The WSUS single-server architecture

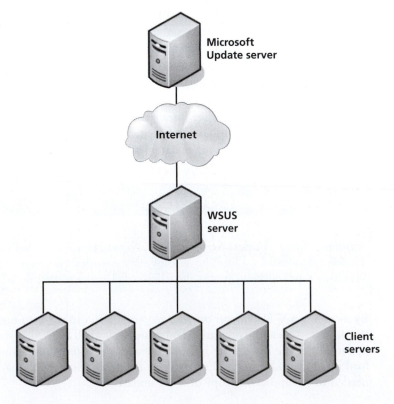

Microsoft Update server

Internet

WSUS server

Client servers

USING REPLICA WSUS SERVERS

For enterprise networks with remote locations, such as well-connected branch offices, it might be preferable to run a separate WSUS server at each site. This enables clients to access their updates from a local source, rather than burden the WAN connection to a home office server with multiple downloads of the same files.

In a ***replica WSUS server*** configuration, one central WSUS server downloads updates from the Microsoft Update site on the Internet. Administrators at that central site evaluate and approve the downloaded updates, and the WSUS servers at other sites—called ***downstream servers***—obtain the approved updates from that first server, as shown in Figure 7-6.

This minimizes the amount of Internet bandwidth expended and enables the administrators of the central server to manage the updates for the entire enterprise.

Figure 7-6

A replica WSUS server architecture

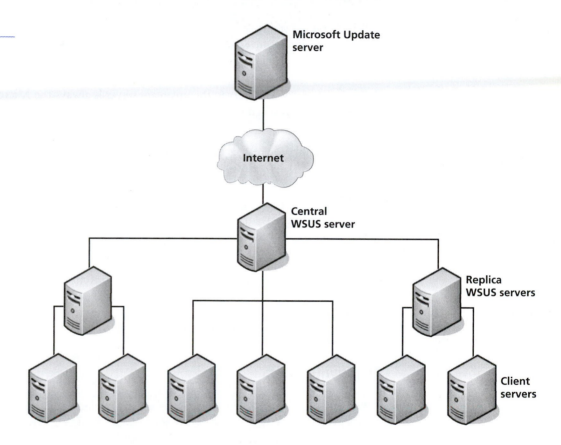

USING AUTONOMOUS WSUS SERVERS

Autonomous WSUS servers function in much the same way as replica WSUS servers, except that the remote servers download all available updates from the central server, and administrators at each site are responsible for evaluating and approving updates for their own users.

USING LOW-BANDWIDTH WSUS SERVERS

Both of the multiple-server WSUS architectures described here assume that all of the remote sites are well connected, with WAN connections that can readily support the transmission of update files—possible in multiple languages—on a regular basis. This is not always the case, however. Some remote sites might have relatively low-bandwidth connections to the home office, and faster connections to the Internet.

In cases like these, it is possible to configure a WSUS server at a remote site to download only the list of approved updates from the central WSUS server, using the WAN connection, without downloading the updates themselves. The remote server then downloads the approved updates from the Microsoft Update servers on the Internet, using its relatively fast connection to do so.

USING DISCONNECTED WSUS SERVERS

The *disconnected WSUS server* architecture is the same as a replica or autonomous server architecture, except that instead of the central WSUS server transmitting updates directly to the downstream servers, administrators save the updates to an offline medium, such as DVD-ROMs, and ship them to the remote sites, where other administrators import them for deployment.

Designing a WSUS Architecture

When you use multiple WSUS servers on your enterprise network, you create an architecture by specifying the *upstream server* from which each server should obtain its updates.

For your central WSUS server, the upstream server is always the Microsoft Update servers on the Internet. You can then configure second-level servers to use the central server as their upstream server.

It is also possible to create a three-level architecture by configuring WSUS to use a second-level server as its upstream server. While Microsoft has tested WSUS architectures up to five levels deep, they recommend using no more than three levels.

The usual reason for creating a WSUS architecture with multiple levels is to provide users at a remote site with a local server from which they can download updates. However, branch offices and other remote sites don't always have high-speed connections to the headquarters where the main WSUS server is located.

If, for example, a branch office has a low-speed connection to the headquarters but a high-speed connection to the Internet, you can configure the branch office WSUS server to download only the metadata for the approved updates from the headquarters WSUS server and download the updates themselves from the Internet.

Deploying WSUS

WSUS 3.0 SP2 is the first WSUS release to be included with the Windows Server operating system. Windows Server 2008 R2 includes WSUS as a role you can install using the Server Manager console, just as you would any other role.

Prior to Windows Server 2008 R2, WSUS was a separate (although free) program that you had to download and install manually. The WSUS download in still available from the Microsoft Download Center at http://www.microsoft.com/downloads/en/details. aspx?FamilyId=a206ae20-2695-436c-9578-3403a7d46e40&displaylang=en for installation on downlevel servers.

You must also obtain the downloadable version of WSUS to install the administration interface on a separate server. You cannot install the administration tool by itself using the role in Windows Server 2008 R2.

The setup procedure for WSUS, whether you install the role or use the stand-alone installation, consists of the basic steps described in the following sections.

UNDERSTANDING HARDWARE PREREQUISITES

The hardware prerequisites for a WSUS server are basically the same as those for the Windows Server 2008 R2 operating system itself, with the following exceptions:

- Memory—1 GB of memory is required and 2 GB is recommended. If you are running the database on the same server as WSUS, performance is likely to be sluggish with 1 GB. If you are using the full version of Microsoft SQL Server instead of the Windows Internal Database, be sure to consider the system requirements for the SQL Server product you are using as well.

- Storage—The system partition and the partition on which you install WSUS must be formatted using the NTFS file system. The database requires a minimum of 2 GB of storage space and the content files a minimum of 20 GB.

PROVIDING HIGH AVAILABILITY

There are techniques you can use to enhance the performance of your WSUS servers and ensure that they remain available to clients at all times. You can install multiple WSUS servers and join them together into a Network Load Balancing Cluster, using a shared failover cluster running SQL Server as the back end. In an arrangement like this, you must use a full SQL Server installation, because multiple WSUS servers cannot share the single database instance created by Windows Internal Database server.

INSTALLING INTERNET INFORMATION SERVICES

Windows Update clients connect to a WSUS server by accessing a Web site, just as they do when connecting to the Microsoft Update site directly. Therefore, when you install the Windows Server Update Services role, the Add Roles Wizard prompts you to install the Web Server (IIS) role as well, as shown in Figure 7-7, with a variety of role services, including the following:

- Static Content
- Default Document
- ASP.NET
- ISAPI Filters
- ISAPI Extensions
- .NET Extensibility
- Windows Authentication
- Request Filtering
- Dynamic Content Compression
- IIS 6 Metabase Compatibility

Figure 7-7

The *Add role services required for Windows Server Update Services* dialog box

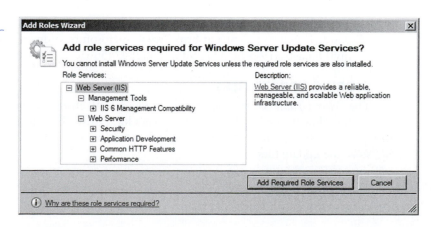

If the Web Server (IIS) role is already installed on the server, then the wizard installs any additional role services that WSUS requires. The Add Roles Wizard proceeds to install the two roles, and then launches the Windows Server Update Services 3.0 SP2 Setup Wizard.

INSTALLING THE ADMINISTRATION CONSOLE

If you install WSUS using the stand-alone installation file, the Windows Server Update Services 3.0 SP2 Setup Wizard displays an *Installation Mode Selection* page, as shown in Figure 7-8. This enables you to install the administration console on a server other than the one running WSUS.

Figure 7-8

The *Installation Mode Selection* page in the Windows Server Update Services 3.0 SP2 Setup Wizard

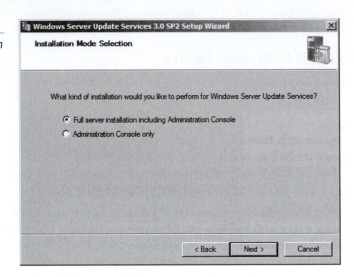

This page does not appear when you install the Windows Server Update Services role in Windows Server 2008 R2. You can only perform a full installation. However, you can use the stand-alone file to install the administration console on another computer and use it to manage WSUS on your server running Windows Server 2008 R2.

CHECKING FOR SOFTWARE PREREQUISITES

To use the administrative user interface provided with WSUS, you must install Microsoft Report Viewer Redistributable 2008 or later. After you agree to the terms of the End User License Agreement, the wizard detects whether you have this component and prompts you to install it, if necessary. However, the wizard does not abort the WSUS installation if this component is not present on the server. You can install Microsoft Report Viewer before or after the WSUS installation.

Microsoft Report Viewer Redistributable 2008 is available as a free download from the Microsoft Download Center at http://www.microsoft.com/downloads/en/details.aspx?FamilyID=6ae0aa19-3e6c-474c-9d57-05b2347456b1.

STORING UPDATE FILES

The *Select Update Source* page, shown in Figure 7-9, enables you to specify whether you want to store downloaded updates on the server's local drive. The Store updates locally check box is selected by default, and you can specify the drive and folder where you want the server to store the update files.

Figure 7-9

The *Select Update Source* page in the Windows Server Update Services 3.0 SP2 Setup Wizard

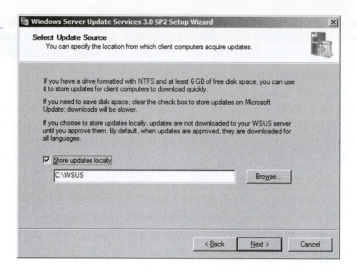

If you clear the Store updates locally check box, the WSUS server will only download metadata regarding the available updates, not the updates themselves. This conserves disk space on the server and essentially configures WSUS to function as a clearing house for the updates available on the Microsoft Update web servers. Administrators can select the updates they want to deploy, and the Windows Update clients on the network download the actual update files from the Microsoft update servers on the Internet.

This is the configuration to use in the situation described earlier in which a branch office has a relatively slow connection to the main WSUS server and a fast connection to the Internet. By configuring the branch office WSUS server not to store updates locally, the amount of data it must download from the main WSUS server is minimized, and yet the administrator maintains control over the updates that are deployed to clients

SELECTING A DATABASE

WSUS requires a SQL Server database to store configuration settings for the WSUS server, metadata for each available update, and information about client/server interaction. By default, WSUS installs the Windows Internal Database feature for this purpose on Windows Server 2008 R2, but you can also use a full version of Microsoft SQL Server 2005 SP2 or SQL Server 2008.

On the *Database Options* page, shown in Figure 7-10, you can select whether to install Windows Internal Database, use an existing SQL Server database on the local computer, or use a SQL Server instance hosted on another computer.

Figure 7-10

The *Database Options* page in the Windows Server Update Services 3.0 SP2 Setup Wizard

For a single WSUS server configuration, there is no performance advantage to using SQL Server over Windows Internal Database. SQL Server included database management tools, which Windows Internal Database does not, but WSUS is designed to function without direct administrative access to its database.

A full version of SQL Server does provide the ability to house the database on a back-end server, separate from WSUS. This enables administrators to provide shared database access to a cluster of WSUS servers using Network Load Balancing. A multiple server configuration consisting of two front-end WSUS servers and a single back-end SQL Server database server, as shown in Figure 7-11, can conceivably service as many as 100,000 clients.

Figure 7-11

A high-capacity multiple-server WSUS configuration

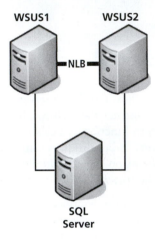

To use a full version of SQL Server with WSUS, you must configure the servers as follows:

- The SQL Server must be configured to use Windows authentication.
- The SQL Server must have the nested-triggers option activated.
- The computer running SQL Server cannot be a domain controller.
- The WSUS server cannot be configured to use Remote Desktop Server (Terminal Services).
- The servers running WSUS and SQL Server must be members of the same AD DS domain, or there must a cross-domain trust between the domains.

Every WSUS server must have its own database instance. The Windows Internal Database provides only a single instance. SQL Server can provide multiple instances, which enables administrators to use the server for other purposes.

While it is theoretically possible for multiple WSUS servers to use separate instances on the same SQL Server installation, there are no scenarios in which this would be a sensible practice, and performance would likely be poor.

SELECTING A WEB SITE

If you are installing the Web Server (IIS) role for the first time on the WSUS server, WSUS will offer to use the IIS Default Web site and the standard hypertext Transfer Protocol (HTTP) port 80 for client access to the server, as shown on the *Web Site Selection* page in Figure 7-12.

If the web server (IIS) role is already installed on the server, or if you want to reserve the Default Web site for another purpose, then WSUS will install any additional web server (IIS) role services it needs to operate and enable the installer to create a new Web site for WSUS on the same server using port number 8530.

TAKE NOTE*

Be sure to note the URL displayed on the *Web Site Selection* page after you have made your selection. This is the URL that you must configure your clients to use when connecting to the WSUS server.

Figure 7-12

The *Web Site Selection* page in the Windows Server Update Services 3.0 SP2 Setup Wizard

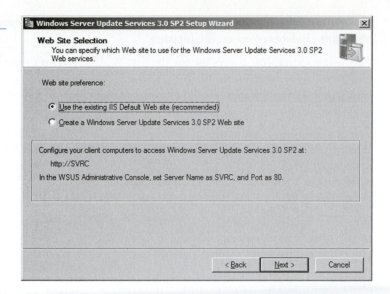

Configuring WSUS

When the Windows Server Update Services 3.0 SP2 Setup Wizard completes the WSUS installation, it automatically launches the Windows Server Update Services Configuration Wizard.

The following sections describe the parameters you can configure with the wizard, forming your WSUS architecture and preparing the server to download updates.

CHOOSING AN UPSTREAM SERVER

On the *Choose Upstream Server* page, shown in Figure 7-13, you specify the source for the server's updates. The process by which a WSUS downloads updates from an upstream server

Figure 7-13

The *Choose Upstream Server* page in the Windows Server Update Services Configuration Wizard

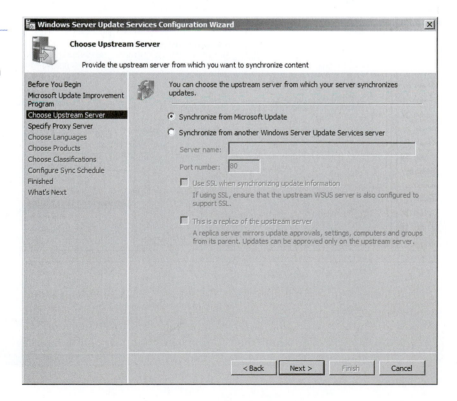

is called *synchronization*. The default setting is for the server to synchronize from the Microsoft Update servers on the Internet.

This is the setting you always use for the first WSUS server on your network, the one farthest upstream. If you have additional WSUS servers that you want to place downstream, you configure this page by selecting Synchronize from another Windows Server Update Services server and supplying the name and port number of the upstream server.

The port number of an upstream server is determined by the Web site you chose on the *Web Site Selection* page of the Windows Server Update Services 3.0 SP2 Setup Wizard. If the upstream server is using the IIS Default Web site, the port number is 80 (or 443 if you are using Secure Sockets Layer SSL). If you created a new site for WSUS, the port number will in most cases be 8530.

When you specify the name and port of another WSUS server, the default behavior is for WSUS simply to download all of the updates available on the upstream server. Administrators must then evaluate and approve updates, just as on the upstream server.

However, if you select the This is a replica of the upstream server check box, WSUS downloads only the approved updates from the upstream server along with all of its settings and groups. A WSUS server that is a replica of an upstream server requires no administration, and is therefore suitable for a branch office or remote site that has the same requirements as the rest of the network.

To encrypt the update information exchanged with the upstream server, select the Use SSL when synchronizing upstream information check box. You must configure the upstream server to use SSL also.

CONNECTING TO AN UPSTREAM SERVER

If your network configuration requires that the server use a proxy to access the upstream server you specified on the *Choose Upstream Server* page, you can configure the appropriate settings on the *Specify Proxy Server* page, as shown in Figure 7-14.

Figure 7-14

The *Specify Proxy Server* page in the Windows Server Update Services Configuration Wizard

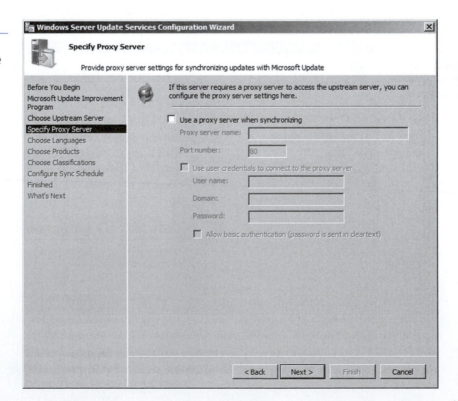

At this point, before you can proceed with the wizard, WSUS must connect to the upstream server. The *Connect to Upstream Server* page appears, as shown in Figure 7-15. Clicking Start Connecting begins the synchronization process.

Figure 7-15

The *Connect to Upstream Server* page in the Windows Server Update Services Configuration Wizard

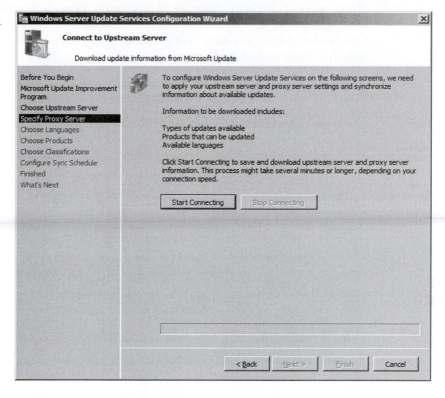

CHOOSING LANGUAGES

On the *Choose Languages* page, shown in Figure 7-16, you can configure a WSUS server to download updates only in the languages that its clients require. However, you must remember

Figure 7-16

The *Choose Languages* page in the Windows Server Update Services Configuration Wizard

that if you have a WSUS architecture with multiple levels, all of the servers upstream from a particular server must include support for that language as well.

For example, if your central WSUS server is in Chicago and supports only English-language clients, you can configure the server to download updates in English only. However, if you have second-level WSUS servers in Europe and Asia downloading their updates from the Chicago server, then you must configure the Chicago server to download updates in all of the languages those second-level servers will need as well.

CHOOSING PRODUCTS

The *Choose Products* page, shown in Figure 7-17, enables you to select the Microsoft software products installed on your Windows Update clients, including operating systems, Microsoft Office components, and other applications. You can select any and all of the products for which you want to download and deploy updates.

Figure 7-17

The *Choose Products* page in the Windows Server Update Services Configuration Wizard

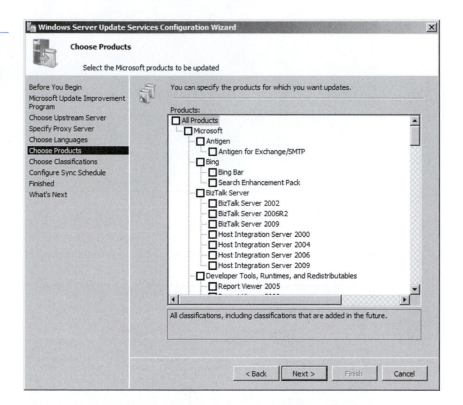

CHOOSING CLASSIFICATIONS

On the *Choose Classifications* page, shown in Figure 7-18, you select the types of updates you want to download and deploy. WSUS provides more classifications than Windows Update does for individual clients, enabling you to exercise more control over how much data the server downloads and stores.

Figure 7-18

The *Choose Classifications* page in the Windows Server Update Services Configuration Wizard

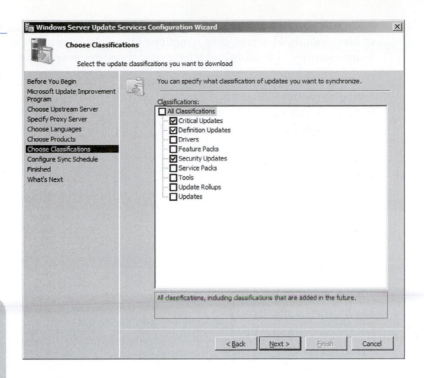

Do not neglect the fact that the more languages, products, and classifications you select on these pages, the more data your WSUS server will have to download, process, and store.

For example, selecting the Service Packs classification is sure to add a great deal of data to your update store, as service packs each can easily run to several hundred megabytes in size. Some administrators might prefer to download and deploy service packs independently of the WSUS system.

CREATING A SYNCHRONIZATION SCHEDULE

WSUS servers must synchronize with their upstream sources—whether on the Internet or other WSUS servers—on a regular basis to keep their update stores current. Administrators can choose to synchronize their servers manually, which is the default setting in WSUS, or they can use the *Set Sync Schedule* page, as shown in Figure 7-19.

Figure 7-19

The *Set Sync Schedule* page in the Windows Server Update Services Configuration Wizard

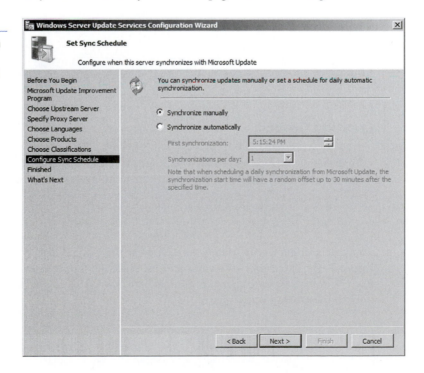

Microsoft generally releases new updates on a monthly schedule, usually around the twelfth of every month. However, they sometimes ignore the regular schedule when a particularly serious security issue arises and release special updates at any time.

For servers that synchronize from upstream WSUS servers, the synchronization frequency is left up to the administrators. There is no need to synchronize a downstream server unless the upstream server has synchronized first. In addition, a replica WSUS server need not synchronize until administrators have evaluated and approved updates on the upstream server that is its source.

FINISHING

The *Finished* page of the wizard enables you to launch the administrative console or perform your first synchronization, as shown in Figure 7-20.

Figure 7-20

The *Finished* page in the Windows Server Update Services Configuration Wizard

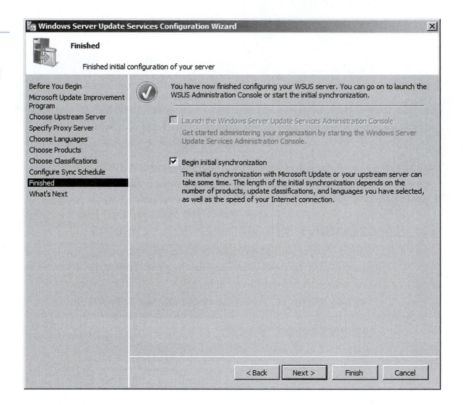

Creating Groups

To exercise control over which Windows Update clients on the network receive specific updates, WSUS uses a system of groups that are independent of the security groups in AD DS and the local groups created by Windows.

To create and manage WSUS groups, you use the Update Services console, as shown in Figure 7-21. There are two default groups, called All Computers and Unassigned Computers. Each Windows Update client computer that connects to the WSUS server is added automatically to these two groups.

Figure 7-21

Computer groups in the Update Services console

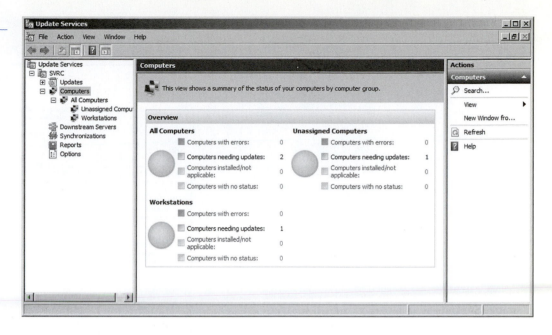

After creating your own groups in the console, you can then move computers from the Unassigned Computers group to the group of your choice in one of two ways:

- Server-side targeting—By manually selecting a computer in the Update Services console, you can change its membership to any existing group using the Set Computer Group Membership dialog box, shown in Figure 7-22.

Figure 7-22

The *Set Computer Group Membership* dialog box

- Client-side target—By enabling the *Enable client-side targeting* Group Policy setting, as shown in Figure 7-23, you can configure clients receiving the setting to automatically add themselves to the group you specify in the policy setting.

Figure 7-23

The *Enable client-side targeting* dialog box

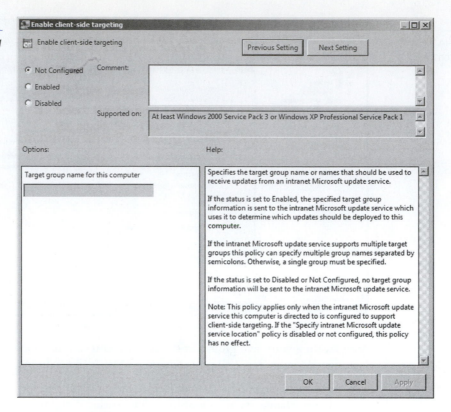

Evaluating Updates

One of the primary advantages of WSUS is that it provides administrators with an opportunity to evaluate and test updates before deploying them on production networks.

The process of evaluating and testing updates is one that must be developed by the enterprise administrator. Microsoft tests its updates carefully before releasing them to the public, but they cannot possibly test every combination of operating systems, device drivers, applications, and other software components. Conflicts and incompatibilities may occur, and it is up to the enterprise administrator to develop policies that screen updates for these types of issues before they deploy them.

Depending on the nature of the updates and the complexity of the workstation configurations, the update evaluation process might consist of any or all of the following:

- A waiting period, to determine whether other users experience problems
- A pilot deployment on a small subsection of the network
- An internal testing regimen conducted on a laboratory network

Once the evaluation process for a particular update is completed, an administrator can approve the update for deployment using the Update Services console on the WSUS server, as shown in Figure 7-24.

Figure 7-24

The WSUS Update Services
console

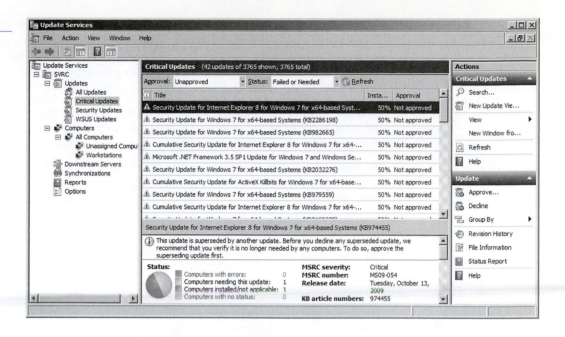

By right-clicking an update and selecting Approve from the context menu, you open the
Approve Updates dialog box, as shown in Figure 7-25, in which you specify which groups
you want to receive that update.

Figure 7-25

The *Approved Updates*
dialog box

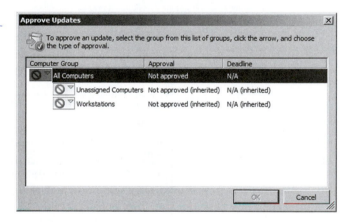

Configuring WSUS Clients

> Before the client computers on the network can download updates from the WSUS
> server, you must configure their Windows Update clients.

The Windows Update control panel in the Windows operating systems does not provide
any means of configuring the client to use an internal WSUS server instead of the Microsoft
Update servers, and even if it did, individual client configuration would not be a practical
solution for an enterprise network. Instead, you configure the Windows Update clients on
your network using additional Group Policy settings.

As usual, in an enterprise environment, the recommended practice is to create a new Group Policy object (GPO), configure the required Windows Update settings, and link the GPO to an appropriate domain, site, or organizational unit object. If you are using multiple WSUS servers, you can distribute the client load among them by creating a separate GPO for each server and linking them to different objects.

Like the Windows Update Group Policy settings discussed earlier in this lesson, the settings for WSUS clients are located in the Computer Configuration\Policies\Administrative Templates\Windows Components\Windows Update folder.

As with a client that downloads updates from the Microsoft Update servers on the Internet, you must enable the Configure Automatic Updates setting and configure the other settings to your preferences, just as described in "Configuring the Windows Update Client" section earlier in this lesson.

For WSUS clients, the key Group Policy setting is Specify intranet Microsoft update service location, as shown in Figure 7-26.

Figure 7-26

The *Specify intranet Microsoft update service location* setting dialog box

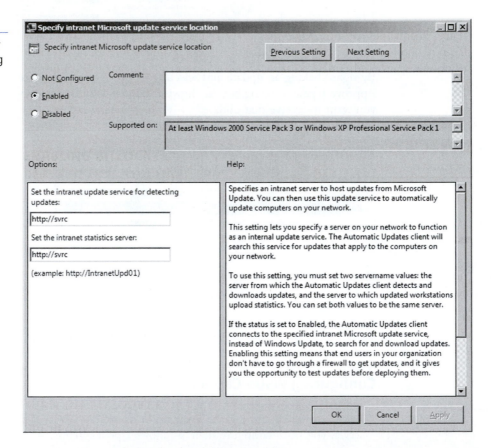

In the Set the intranet update device for detecting updates and Set the intranet statistics server text boxes, type the URL displayed earlier on the *Web Site Selection* page of the Windows Server Update Services 3.0 SP2 Setup Wizard. This causes the Windows Update client to connect to your WSUS server for updates, rather than the Microsoft Update servers.

If you have configured your WSUS server not to store updates locally, then the client will contact the WSUS server to determine which files it needs and then download those files from the Internet servers.

In addition, you can configure the following settings, which take effect only when you enable the Specify intranet Microsoft update service location setting:

- Automatic updates detection frequency—When enabled, specifies the interval (in hours) at which the client checks the server for new updates.
- Allow signed updates from an intranet Microsoft update service location—When enabled, allows clients to download and install updates not signed by Microsoft. However, updates must be signed with a certificate found in the computer's Trusted Publishers store. This enables administrators to deploy their own updates using WSUS.

Using System Center Configuration Manager

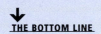

As discussed in Lesson 6, "Deploying Applications," System Center Configuration Manager 2007 is a network management product that, in addition to deploying applications, can also work together with WSUS to create a comprehensive software update solution that is suitable for even the largest enterprise.

Although WSUS servers can form a hierarchy by synchronizing with each other—at least in one direction—their ability to interact is limited. SCCM can incorporate your WSUS servers into its own network management infrastructure, enabling you to manage software update deployments for your entire enterprise from SCCM's Configuration Manager console.

When integrated into the SCCM infrastructure, WSUS servers function as software update points. Computers on the network still download updates from the WSUS servers, but they do so using the SCCM clients that you must install on every system.

WSUS by itself is an excellent software update solution for Microsoft products, but it is not designed to update other applications, leaving a big hole in the enterprise administrator's software update solution. Apart from centralized management, another big benefit that SCCM provides in the software update process is the ability to deploy updates for third-party products.

Ensuring Compliance

On an enterprise network, the update deployment process does not end when the updates are made available to the clients. Administrators must confirm that the updates have actually been deployed, a process called *compliance management*.

Compliance management is typically a feature of the technology used to deploy the system updates. WSUS and SCCM 2007 both have reporting capabilities that enable administrators to monitor client compliance enterprise update policies.

Monitoring Compliance with WSUS

WSUS includes reporting capabilities that enable administrators to review the communications between Windows Update clients and WSUS servers.

WSUS reports, like the one in Figure 7-27, specify the number of updates a particular client needs and can provide information about updates that have failed, as reported by the client.

Figure 7-27

A computer report generated
by WSUS

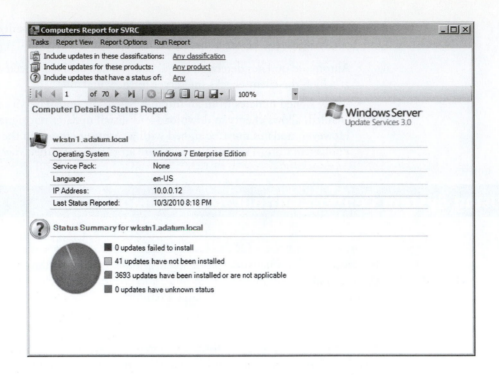

WSUS also provides reports on specific updates, as shown in Figure 7-28. Administrators
can generate both computer and update reports in summary, detailed, or tabular format, and
export them as Excel or PDF files.

Figure 7-28

An update report generated
by WSUS

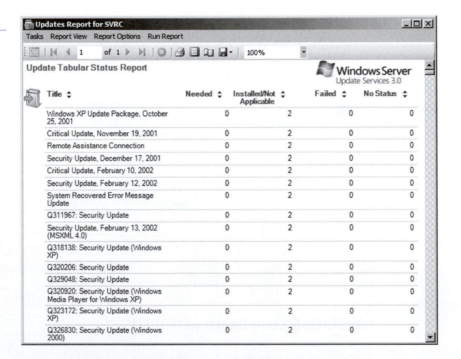

If your WSUS server is using a full version of SQL Server to store its database, you can use
the tools provided with the server—or third-party tools—to generate your own reports. In
addition, for multilevel WSUS installations, the top-level server can also generate reports that
incorporate all of the information gathered by the downstream servers on the network.

Despite all of the reporting capabilities provided by WSUS, it does have limitations as a compliance management tool. WSUS cannot actually probe client computers to determine that a specific update has been installed successfully. However, SCCM can.

Monitoring Compliance with SCCM 2007

> The compliance management capabilities of SCCM 2007 go well beyond monitoring the deployment of system updates.

SCCM 2007 uses an entirely different technique to evaluate a client computer's compliance with administrative standards. Software updating is just one of SCCM's capabilities: when it monitors client compliance, SCCM looks at the entire picture, including whether the operating system is installed correctly, the proper applications are installed, and the appropriate security settings are configured. SCCM can even detect applications that should not be installed on the client.

This feature in SCCM is called *Desired Configuration Management*, and it works by comparing a client computer to an established *configuration baseline*. Administrators can download preconfigured baselines that conform to Microsoft best practices or build their own using SCCM Configuration Manager.

As mentioned in Lesson 6, SCCM is essentially a delivery service, and Desired Configuration Management works by delivering a baseline to a selected collection of client computers. The SCCM agent running on each client downloads the baseline and compares it to the computer's actual configuration.

For example, the agent confirms that each application and update specified in the baseline has been properly installed on the computer, and it does so by scanning for the applications and updates themselves. When the comparison is completed, the client agent reports back to the SCCM server, which compiles the data and stores it in its SQL database.

SCCM enables you to monitor the progress of the Desired Configuration Management process, and also to generate reports on the compliance or lack of compliance for specific clients.

SKILL SUMMARY

IN THIS LESSON YOU LEARNED:

- Enterprise administrators are responsible for seeing to it that all of the computers on the network receive the necessary operating system and application updates on a timely basis.

- Windows Server Update Services (WSUS) is a service included in Windows Server 2008 R2 that enables a local server on your network to function as the back end for the Windows Update client, just as the Microsoft Update servers do on the Internet.

- In a replica WSUS server configuration, one central WSUS server downloads updates from the Microsoft Update site on the Internet, and the WSUS servers at other sites obtain the approved updates from that first server.

- Autonomous WSUS servers download all available updates from the central server, and administrators at each site are responsible for evaluating and approving updates for their own users.

- When you use multiple WSUS servers on your enterprise network, you create an architecture by specifying the upstream server from which each server should obtain its updates.

- The process by which a WSUS downloads updates from an upstream server is called synchronization.

- To exercise control over which Windows Update clients on the network receive specific updates, WSUS uses a system of groups.

- System Center Configuration Manager 2007 is a network management product that can work together with WSUS to create a comprehensive software update solution suitable for even the largest enterprise.

- Compliance management is typically a feature of the technology used to deploy the system updates. WSUS and SCCM 2007 both have reporting capabilities that enable administrators to monitor client compliance with enterprise update policies.

■ Knowledge Assessment

Matching

Complete the following exercise by matching the terms with their corresponding definitions.

_____ **1.** upstream server

_____ **2.** Windows Update

_____ **3.** Microsoft Update

_____ **4.** compliance management

_____ **5.** downstream server

_____ **6.** autonomous WSUS server

_____ **7.** replica WSUS server

_____ **8.** synchronization

_____ **9.** disconnected WSUS server

_____ **10.** Windows Server Update Services (WSUS)

A. The process by which a WSUS server downloads updates from an upstream server

B. An Internet Web site from which Windows Update clients and WSUS servers download updates for the Microsoft operating systems and other Microsoft software products

C. A WSUS server that downloads all available updates from an upstream server, so that administrators at each site can evaluate and approve updates for their own users

D. The specified server from which each WSUS server on your enterprise network obtains its updates

E. A service included in Windows Server 2008 R2 that enables a local server on your network to function as the back end for the Windows Update client

F. Any server that obtains updates from an upstream WSUS server

G. A downstream WSUS server that receives its updates on an offline medium, such as DVD-ROMs shipped to a remote site, rather than downloading them

H. A Windows client that, if activated on the workstation, automatically downloads operating system updates and installs them

I. A WSUS server that obtains approved updates from an upstream WSUS server

J. The process by which administrators confirm that updates have actually been deployed

Multiple Choice

Select one or more correct answers for each of the following questions.

1. Which of the following tasks must you complete on your Windows Update client computers before they can download updates from a WSUS server?
   a. Open the Windows Update control panel and reconfigure the client.
   b. Enable the *Specify intranet Microsoft update service location* Group Policy setting.
   c. Open Server Manager and install the WSUS Client feature.
   d. All of the above.

2. Which of the following does not have to be installed to run Windows Server Update Services 3.0 SP2?
   a. The Web Server (IIS) role
   b. SQL Server 2005 SP2 or later
   c. Windows Process Activation Service
   d. Microsoft Report Viewer 2008 or later

3. Which of the following is not one of the problems that can result when you activate the Windows Update client on your network computers using the default settings?
   a. Update installation without administrator approval
   b. Excessive bandwidth utilization
   c. Installation of incompatible updates
   d. No confirmation of client compliance

4. Which of the following is not one of the basic types of WSUS server?
   a. Disconnected WSUS server
   b. Autonomous WSUS server
   c. Replica WSUS server
   d. High-bandwidth WSUS server

5. To use a full version of Microsoft SQL Server with WSUS, which of the following is not one of the options you must configure on the SQL server?
   a. The SQL Server must have the nested-triggers option deactivated
   b. The SQL Server must be configured to use Windows authentication
   c. The computer running SQL Server cannot be a domain controller
   d. The WSUS server cannot be configured to use Remote Desktop Server (Terminal Services)

6. Which of the following is not a prerequisite when installing WSUS as a role?
   a. The WSUS server must have at least 1 GB of memory.
   b. The server must be running Windows Server 2008 R2 or later.
   c. The WSUS content files require a minimum of 2 GB of storage space.
   d. You must format the partition on which you install WSUS using the NTFS file system.

7. Which of the following Group Policy settings does not modify the default behavior of the client with regard to an involuntary restart that might cause problems for a user working at the workstation?
   a. Reschedule automatic updates scheduled installations
   b. Delay Restart for scheduled installations
   c. Re-prompt for restart with scheduled installations
   d. No auto-restart with logged on users for scheduled automatic updates installations

8. Which of the following is the feature that provides compliance monitoring in System Center Configuration Manager 2007?
   a. Configuration Baseline
   b. Software Update Management
   c. WSUS Compliance
   d. Desired Configuration Management

9. Which of the following tasks must you perform to install the WSUS administration console on a server other than the one running WSUS?
   a. Download the WSUS installation file from the Microsoft Download Center.
   b. Install the Windows Server Update Services role and deselect the Administration Console role service.
   c. Install the WSUS console feature.
   d. There are no additional tasks to perform. The WSUS administration console is installed on Windows Server 2008 R2 by default.

10. Which of the following best describes the function of the *Enable client-side targeting* Group Policy setting?
   a. Enables clients to download updates from a WSUS server instead of the Microsoft Update servers on the Internet
   b. Enables client computers to automatically add themselves to a WSUS group
   c. Enables administrators to manually add WSUS client computers to groups
   d. Automatically creates WSUS computer groups

Review Questions

1. List the Group Policy settings that you must enable for a Windows Update client to download updates from a WSUS server.

2. Name the three ways you can narrow down the types of updates that a WSUS server downloads from its upstream server.

■ Case Scenario

Scenario 7-1: Designing a WSUS Architecture

Oscar, an administrator at Contoso, Ltd., has been assigned the task of rolling out new servers throughout the enterprise. The servers will be running Windows Server 2008 R2, and Oscar is in the process of creating a long-term plan to replace the servers at each of the company's five offices. He wants to install Windows Server Update Services on one of the servers at each office, so that clients can download updates from a local source, but is running into some administrative problems in the process.

The one Canadian office, in Vancouver, operates under another name and has its own IT administrative staff. However, their Internet connection is considerably more expensive than those of the U.S. offices and is priced based on the bandwidth they use. The Portland and Seattle offices have high-speed connections to the company headquarters in San Francisco, but they do not maintain their own IT administrators. The newly created branch office in Austin is tiny, only two sales associates. They have a high-speed Internet connection, but use a VPN connection to connect to the headquarters network.

How should Oscar configure the WSUS architecture for the home office and the four branches?

Planning for Network Access

OBJECTIVE DOMAIN MATRIX

TECHNOLOGY SKILL	OBJECTIVE DOMAIN	OBJECTIVE NUMBER
Planning for Remote Network Access	Design for network access.	1.2

KEY TERMS

back-end firewall
Challenge Handshake
    Authentication Protocol (CHAP)
demilitarized zone (DMZ)
Direct Access
Extensible Authentication
    Protocol (EAP)
front-end firewall
internal network
Internet Key Exchange, Version 2
    (IKEv2)
IP security extensions (IPsec)
Layer 2 Tunneling Protocol (L2TP)
Microsoft Challenge Handshake
    Authentication Protocol
    version 2 (MS-CHAP v2)
NAP Administration Server

NAP Agent
NAP Enforcement Client
    (NAP EC)
NAP Enforcement Server
    (NAP ES)
NAP Health Policy Server
Network Access Protection
    (NAP)
Password Authentication
    Protocol (PAP)
perimeter network
Point-to-Point protocol (PPP)
Point-to-Point Tunneling
    Protocol (PPTP)
Protected Extensible
    Authentication Protocol
    (PEAP)

remediation network
Remote Authentication Dial
    In User Service (RADIUS)
Routing and Remote Access
    Services (RRAS)
Secure Socket Tunneling
    Protocol (SSTP)
Secured Password (EAP-
    MSCHAPv2)
Statement of Health (SoH)
System Health Agents (SHAs)
System Health Validator
    (SHV)
System SoH
tunneling
Virtual Private Network
    (VPN)

■ Creating a Perimeter Network

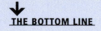
THE BOTTOM LINE   A perimeter network is a buffer zone between an enterprise's internal network and the Internet.

Most of the components of an enterprise network—infrastructure as well as clients and servers—must be protected from potential intruders on the Internet. This ***internal network*** is surrounded by firewalls, providing the maximum possible protection. However, there are also elements of the network that need to be accessible from the Internet or that provide internal users with access to the Internet. These elements are located in a semi-protected area called a perimeter network.

A ***perimeter network***—sometimes called a ***demilitarized zone*** or ***DMZ***—is a subnet located between an internal network and an external or public network, usually the Internet. It was originally designed as a place where an organization could host its own Internet services, such as web and email servers. Today, however, enterprise perimeter networks typically host a variety of additional services, such as application servers and remote access technologies.

Erecting Perimeter Firewalls

To protect an enterprise network, administrators erect a system of firewalls that examine the traffic coming in from and going out to the public network. Traffic that does not confirm to rules set down by the administrators is blocked.

In a typical perimeter network configuration, there are two firewalls, one between the internal network and the perimeter network, called the ***back-end firewall***, and another between the perimeter network and an Internet service provider (ISP) on the public network, called the ***front-end firewall***, as shown in Figure 8-1.

Figure 8-1

A perimeter network protected by two firewalls

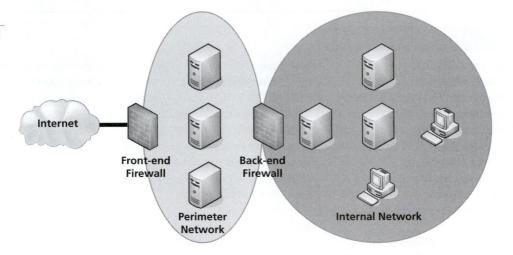

Some networks use a single firewall with three network interfaces to create the perimeter network. One interface connects to the internal network, one to the ISP on the public network, and the third to the perimeter network.

The problem inherent to the single-firewall arrangement is that the one device forms a single point of failure. Two separate firewalls form two distinct layers of protection, both of which an attacker must penetrate to reach the internal network. In fact, some experts recommend the use of firewalls from two different manufacturers, so that attackers must penetrate two completely different systems.

The firewalls guarding the perimeter network and many of the services deployed there must work together to provide protection for the internal network by regulating access in three ways:

• Authentication—The process of confirming a user's identity by comparing presented credentials with the information stored in an existing account or directory service.

• Authorization—The process by which a user is granted access to a specific network resource on the basis of existing permissions and security settings.

• Auditing—The logging and documentation of all authentication and authorization activities, including requests for access and the outcome of the requests.

Windows Server 2008 includes a variety of tools and services that enable administrators to ensure that only the correct users can access the network and that they meet established security standards for the enterprise.

Understanding Perimeter Network Services

> The original function of a perimeter network was to host the organization's presence on the Internet. Web servers had to be directly accessible from the Internet, while the other computers on the network were better off protected by a firewall. It only made sense to place the Internet servers on a separate subnet.

Today, perimeter networks adhere to the same basic principles, but their requirements have changed considerably. The services that require exposure to the Internet are more numerous, the threats from the Internet are more dangerous, and the firewalls that protect the perimeter are more complex.

For example, early web servers did little but provide home pages and image files to Internet browsers. To support the server, the front-end firewall had only to admit traffic on Hypertext Transfer Protocol (HTTP) port 80.

Today, web servers are far more complex. They might need access to database servers on the internal network, requiring careful configuration of the back-end firewall, and provide elaborate applications to clients on the Internet. This increases the attack surface exposed to the Internet, calling for more careful configuration of the front-end firewall as well.

It is also common for perimeter servers today to host many services other than web servers. Some of the other devices commonly found on perimeter networks are as follows:

- File Transfer Protocol (FTP)—Now obsolescing rapidly, FTP is a simple service that enables Internet clients to download and upload files and perform simple file-management tasks.

- Simple Mail Transfer Protocol (SMTP)—SMTP is the main server-to-server email protocol used on the Internet. SMTP servers establish an email domain presence for incoming messages and enable internal clients to send outgoing messages to addresses on the Internet. The SMTP service is sometimes incorporated into a comprehensive email product, such as Microsoft Exchange, but it can also be a separate server that communicates with other email servers on the internal network.

- Network address translation (NAT)—A routing technique that enables computers with private IP addresses to access Internet resources. A NAT router accepts traffic from the private network, substitutes a registered IP address for the private one, and forwards the traffic to the destination server on the Internet. When the router receives a response from the Internet server, it performs the same process in reverse and forwards the response to the computer in the internal network.

- Proxy server—An application that functions as an intermediary between clients and specific types of servers. Proxy servers receive requests from clients on the internal network and forward them to servers on the Internet, then receive responses from the servers and forward them to the clients. As they do this, proxy servers typically provide additional services, such as data caching and content filtering.

- Virtual private network (VPN)—A remote access technique in which clients use the Internet to establish a secure connection to a VPN server, which in turn provides access to resources in an internal network. The VPN client and server use a technique called tunneling to encapsulate data in a secure channel.

- Remote Authentication Dial In User Service (RADIUS)—A client/server application that provides authentication, authorization, and accounting for network access services.

- Remote Desktop Gateway—A web-based application that enables clients on the Internet to access Remote Desktop servers on an internal network.

■ Planning for Remote Network Access

THE BOTTOM LINE

Traveling users, telecommuters, and extranet clients are an ever-increasing part of the typical company network, and enterprise administrators are responsible for providing these people with a satisfactory user experience. However, giving external users access to the network is also one of the most potentially hazardous practices in networking. Protecting that access is also the administrator's responsibility.

CERTIFICATION READY
How do you design for
network access?
1.2

Remote network users do not have permanent connections, so they cannot log on to the network in the usual manner. However, the remote access solutions in Windows Server 2008 R2 and the Windows client operating systems enable users to access network resources from any location with a telephone line or an Internet connection.

For the enterprise administrator, providing remote users with this type of access requires a good deal more than just creating accounts and setting permissions. Users expect the ability to access the data they need from any location, but they also expect that data to remain secure at all times.

This security is especially difficult when you consider that the remote client systems are sometimes not under the direct control of the network administrators. Users might be working with home computers, mobile computers that are rarely supervised, or workstations on a partner company's network.

This is why Windows Server 2008 R2 includes tools such as RADIUS, to provide centralized authentication, authorization, and auditing services, and Network Access Protection (NAP), which enforces company standards or the security of remote computers.

Windows Server 2008 R2 supports three types of remote client connections:

- Dial-up networking—Remote users connect to a server using standard asynchronous modems and telephone lines.
- Virtual private networking—Remote users connect to a server using a tunneled connection through the Internet.
- DirectAccess—A new IPv6-based remote access technology that enables users to access the network without manually establishing a connection.

Remote network access is a client/server application, so enterprise administrators must design a server infrastructure at the network site before Windows clients can connect to it. The first step in planning a remote access networking solution for an enterprise network is to decide which connection type you plan to use.

Dial-up networking connections require the server to be equipped with at least one modem and telephone line. For a single-user connection, enabling an administrator to dial in from home, for example, a standard off-the-shelf modem is suitable. For multiple connections, there are modular rack-mounted modems available that enable you to connect dozens of users at once, if necessary.

In today's networking world, however, hardware and telephone costs and the near-ubiquity of high-speed Internet connections have caused dial-up remote connections to be almost entirely replaced by virtual private network (VPN) connections. VPN connections require no special hardware, because they use the same Internet connection as any of the other perimeter network services.

DirectAccess is a new technology that is designed to provide the user with a more streamlined remote access experience. Rather than having to establish a connection to a server manually, as with dial-up and VPN connections, DirectAccess automatically and transparently connects the client computer to the remote network.

Whichever types of connection you plan to use, the server must be accessible from outside of the network, so the computer naturally belongs on the perimeter network. In each case, administrators must always be conscious of the types of communication that reach the server from the Internet, and that pass from the perimeter network to the internal network.

Using Virtual Private Networking

Virtual private network connections violate standard networking concepts to provide security for private connections transmitted over the public Internet.

A dial-up connection is a dedicated link between the two modems that remains in place during the entire session, as shown in Figure 8-2. The client and the server establish a connection using the ***Point-to-Point Protocol (PPP)***, during which the remote access server authenticates the client and the computers negotiate a set of communication parameters they have in common. PPP takes the place of the Ethernet protocol at the data-link layer, by encapsulating the datagrams created by Internet Protocol (IP) at the network layer, to prepare them for their transmission. PPP is much simpler than Ethernet because the two computers are using a dedicated connection, and there is no need to address each packet to a particular destination, as they must on a local-area network (LAN).

Figure 8-2

A dial-up remote access connection

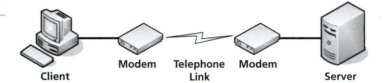

In a ***virtual private network (VPN)*** connection, the remote client and the remote access server are both connected to the Internet using local service providers, as shown in Figure 8-3. This eliminates long-distance telephone charges common in dial-up connections, as well as the additional hardware expense, since both computers most likely have Internet connections already. The client establishes a connection to the VPN server using the Internet as a network medium and, after authentication, the server grants the client access to the network.

Figure 8-3

A VPN remote access connection

To configure a server running Windows Server 2008 R2 to function as a dial-up or VPN server, you must install the Network Policy and Access Services role and select the ***Routing and Remote Access Services (RRAS)*** role service. To create a VPN server, the computer must have two network interfaces, one of which connects to the Internet and the other to the internal network. VPN clients connect to the server through the Internet connection, and if the authentication and authorization processes succeed, the server allows traffic to pass through the server and out the internal network connection.

SECURING VPN COMMUNICATIONS

While it is theoretically possible for someone to tap into the telephone line used by a dial-up connection, intercept the analog signals exchanged by the two modems, convert them into digital data packets, and access the data, it is not likely to occur and remote networking connections are almost never compromised in this manner. Therefore, the data transmitted during a dial-up connection is considered to be relatively secure.

A VPN is another matter, however, because the client and the server transmit their data over the Internet, which makes the data packets accessible to anyone with the equipment needed to capture them. For this reason, VPN clients and servers use a specialized protocol when establishing a connection that encapsulates their data packets inside another packet, a process called *tunneling*. The VPN protocol establishes a virtual connection, or tunnel, between the client and the server, which encrypts data encapsulated inside.

In the tunneling process, the two computers establish a PPP connection, just as they would in a dial-up connection, but instead of transmitting the PPP packets over the Internet as they are, they encapsulate the packets again using one of the VPN protocols supported by the Windows operating systems. As shown in Figure 8-4, the original PPP data packet generated by the computer consists of a network layer IP datagram, encapsulated within a data-link layer PPP frame. The system then encapsulates the entire frame in another IP datagram, which the VPN protocol encrypts and encapsulates one more time, for transmission over the network.

Figure 8-4

VPN protocol encapsulation

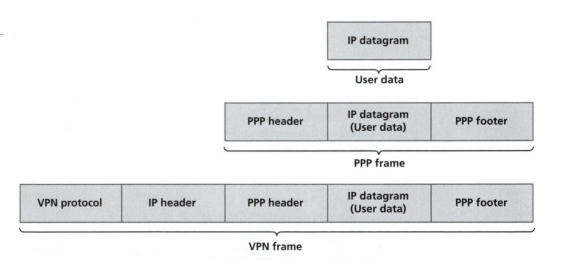

Having a data-link layer frame inside a network layer datagram is a violation of the Open System Interconnection (OSI) reference model's most basic principles, but this is what makes tunneling an effective carrier mechanism for private data transmitted over a public network. Intruders can intercept the transmitted packets, but they cannot decrypt the inner PPP frame, which prevents them from obtaining any of the information inside.

Windows Server 2008 R2 supports a number of VPN protocols that create tunnels in different ways, including the following:

- *Point-to-Point Tunneling Protocol (PPTP)*—The oldest and least secure of the VPN protocols, PPTP takes advantage of the authentication, compression, and encryption mechanisms of PPP, tunneling the PPP frame within a Generic Routing Encapsulation

(GRE) header and encrypting it with Microsoft Point-to-Point Encryption (MPPE), using encryption keys generated during the authentication process. PPTP therefore can provide data protection, but not other services, such as packet origin identification or data integrity checking. For authentication, PPTP supports the Microsoft Challenge Handshake Authentication Protocol version 1 (MS-CHAP v1), *Microsoft Challenge Handshake Authentication Protocol version 2 (MS-CHAP v2)*, Extensible Authentication Protocol (EAP), or Protected Extensible Authentication Protocol (PEAP). Although it can use them (with EAP), one of the advantages of PPTP is that it does not require the use of a public key infrastructure (PKI) to generate certificates. Because of PPTP's long history, many operating systems support it, including Windows Server 2008 R2, Windows Server 2008, Windows Server 2003, Windows 7, Windows Vista, and Windows XP.

- *Layer 2 Tunneling Protocol (L2TP)*—L2TP relies on the *IP security extensions (IPsec)* for encryption, and as a result performs a double encapsulation. The system adds an L2DP header to the PPP frame and packages it with the User Datagram Protocol (UDP). Then it encapsulates the UDP datagram with the IPsec Encapsulating Security Payload (ESP) protocol, encrypting the contents using the Data Encryption Standard (DES) or Triple DES (3DES) algorithm, with encryption keys generated during IPSec's Internet Key Exchange (IKE) negotiation process. L2TP/IPsec can use certificates or preshared keys for authentication, although administrators typically use the latter only for testing. The end result is that the L2TP/IPsec combination provides a more complete set of services than PPTP, including packet origin identification, data integrity checking, and replay protection. The Windows Server 2008 R2, Windows Server 2008, Windows Server 2003, Windows 7, Windows Vista, and Windows XP operating systems all support L2TP.

- *Secure Socket Tunneling Protocol (SSTP)*—First introduced in Windows Server 2008 and supported only by clients running Windows Vista SP1 or later, SSTP encapsulates PPP traffic using the Secure Sockets Layer (SSL) protocol supported by virtually all Web servers. The advantage of this is that administrators do not have to open an additional external firewall port in the server, as SSTP uses the same TCP port 443 as Secure Sockets Layer (SSL). SSTP uses certificates for authentication, with the EAP-TLS authentication protocol, and in addition to data encryption, provides integrity checking and enhanced key negotiation services.

- *Internet Key Exchange, version 2 (IKEv2)*—New in Windows Server 2008 R2 and Windows 7, IKEv2 uses TCP port 500 and provides data confidentiality, data integrity, and data authentication services, with support for IPv6 and the new VPN Reconnect feature (using the MOBIKE protocol) as well as authentication by EAP, using PEAP, EAP-MSCHAPv2, or smart cards. IKEv2 does not support older authentication mechanisms such as POP and CHAP, however. By default, Windows 7 computers use IKEv2 when attempting to connect to remote access servers, only falling back on the other protocols when the server does not support it as well.

Authenticating VPN Users

Windows remote access connections use an authentication system that is entirely separate from the Kerberos authentication system used by clients on the local network. However, authentication is even more important for remote access clients than for local ones, because of the increased likelihood of intrusion.

All remote access connections, whether dial-up or VPN, use PPP to package their data, and the PPP connection establishment process includes a sequence in which the client and the server negotiate the use of a specific authentication protocol. In this sequence, each computer sends a list of the authentication protocols it supports to the other, and the two then agree to use the strongest protocol they have in common.

RRAS in Windows Server 2008 R2 includes support for a number of authentication protocols, as shown in Figure 8-5, including the following:

Figure 8-5

The *RRAS Authentication Methods* dialog box

- ***Extensible Authentication Protocol (EAP)***—EAP is a shell protocol that provides a framework for the use of various types of authentication mechanisms. The primary advantage of EAP is that it enables a computer to use mechanisms other than passwords for authentication, including public key certificates and smart cards, as well as providing an extensible environment for third-party authentication mechanisms. RRAS supports several types of EAP-based authentication: Smart Card or other certificates, **Protected EAP (PEAP)** and **Secured Password (EAP-MSCHAPv2)**. EAP-MSCHAPv2 is the strongest password-based mechanism in RRAS, requiring a certificate only at the server.

- Microsoft Challenge Handshake Authentication Protocol version 2 (MS-CHAPv2)—Version 2 of MS-CHAP improves on version 1 by adding two-way authentication and increasing the strength of the encryption. Version 2 uses a new encryption key for each connection and for each direction in which data is transmitted. This makes the encryption far more difficult to crack.

- ***Challenge Handshake Authentication Protocol (CHAP)***—CHAP is a challenge-response authentication protocol that uses the MD5 hashing scheme to encrypt passwords. CHAP provides relatively weak protection compared to some of the other authentication protocols. It does not support encryption of the connection data, and the passwords it uses must be stored in a reversibly encrypted format. This means that if users are establishing connections with their standard Windows user accounts, the network administrator must weaken the encryption of those passwords to accommodate CHAP.

- ***Password Authentication Protocol (PAP)***—PAP is the least secure of the RRAS authentication protocols because it uses simple passwords for authentication that it transmits in clear text over the link between the computers.

- IKEv2—RRAS permits Windows 7 clients to authenticate with the machine certificates they use for the IKEv2 protocol.

TAKE NOTE *

Windows Server 2008 R2 no longer includes support for MS-CHAPv1, EAP-Message Digest, or the Shiva Password Authentication Protocol (SPAP).

TAKE NOTE *

In the Windows Server 2008 R2 RRAS implementation, CHAP and PAP are included only for backwards compatibility and, because of their inferior security, the service disables them by default.

DESIGNING A VPN SERVER STRATEGY

To design an enterprise VPN strategy, an administrator must decide which of the protocol options the servers should use. This decision depends primarily on the capabilities of the client computers that will be connecting to the VPN servers.

If all of the client computers are running Windows 7, then you can safely disable all but the latest and most secure VPN and authentication protocols. The older the operating system versions running on the clients, the more likely it is that you will have to maintain support for older and less secure protocols on your VPN servers.

SELECTING VPN PROTOCOLS

By default, RRAS allows remote users to connect using any one of the available protocols. However, enterprise administrators might want to disable some of these protocols to enhance the security of the network.

PPTP is the oldest of the VPN protocols, and therefore has the greatest client compatibility. All Windows operating systems going back to Windows NT 4.0 and Windows 95 include VPN client support for PPTP, and because the protocol does not require a certificate infrastructure, it is easy to administer. However, PPTP uses weaker cryptography than the other protocols and performs only a user-level authentication through PPP.

The L2TP/IPsec combination is less popular than PPTP, but it is more secure in several ways. IPsec provides more services than PPTP, including packet data authentication, data integrity, replay protection, and data confidentiality. PPTP only provides packet data authentication. L2TP/IPsec also requires both user-level and computer-level authentication, and only performs the authentication after IPsec secures the connection.

L2TP/IPsec can use certificates for both VPN server and clients, and is not supported by as many Windows versions as PPTP. A VPN client must be running at least Windows 2000 Server or Windows XP to use L2TP.

SSTP provides excellent security, and uses SSL ports that are already open on most firewalls, but it is even more restricted in the operating systems that support it. VPN clients must be running Windows Server 2008 or later, Windows XP SP3 or later, Windows Vista SP2 or later, or Windows 7.

Newest and quite strong, but most restricting of all the VPN protocols, is IKEv2, which supports VPN Reconnect, a new feature that enables client computers to automatically reestablish a broken connection to a VPN server.

SELECTING AUTHENTICATION PROTOCOLS

The other main design issue for a VPN strategy is whether you intend the clients to authenticate using passwords or certificates. Passwords are always easier to administer, but inherently less secure. However, you can maintain a secure network with passwords if you are careful to impose policies that force users to select complex passwords and change them frequently.

If you must use passwords, then MS-CHAPv2 is the authentication protocol you should select. Virtually all Windows operating systems going back to Windows NT 4.0 and Windows 95 include client support for MS-CHAPv2, making it one of the most compatible authentication protocols as well.

Certificates are more secure than passwords, but you must select a method for getting them to your client computers. Some of the possibilities are as follows:

- Smart cards—Distributing certificates on smart cards is easy for users and administrators, but it also adds considerable expense to the equation, in terms of both the cards themselves and the card readers required on every client computer. An organization distributing laptops to its sales force can provide the necessary hardware with reasonable economy, but this is not so for VPN clients using their home computers, their own laptops, or workstations at a partner's office.

- User enrollment—Remote clients can manually request, receive, and install certificates through the Active Directory Certificate Services Web enrollment interface. This requires administrators to deploy the interface on an Internet-facing Web server and supply the remote users with explicit instructions for the procedure. There are inevitably problems requiring technical support, and administrators must be extremely careful in maintaining the security of the Web server.

- Administrator enrollment—In situations where administrators have access to the remote client computers, they can perform the enrollment and install the resulting certificate on the computer. This eliminates the need to explain the process to the end-user, but it is only a viable solution for portable computers, not for computers in user's homes or the offices of client partners.

- Group policy distribution—Administrators can use Group Policy to deploy certificates to users, but this solution is also viable only for computers that are members of an Active Directory Domain Services domain and have access to a domain controller.

For clients that will use certificates, EAP is the authentication protocol of choice, although its VPN client support is limited to servers running Windows 2000 Server or newer and workstations running Windows XP or newer.

Using RADIUS

All remote access services must authenticate users before they permit them to access the network. On a large enterprise network, there can be multiple servers providing dial-up, VPN, and other remote access services, and this can complicate the authentication process. RADIUS is a client/server application that provides centralized authentication, authorization, and accounting for the remote access services on a network.

When users connect to a remote access server, they can authenticate using an AD DS account, but it is not always practical to add all remote users to the AD DS database. You can also create individual accounts for remote users on the remote access server's local security accounts manager (SAM). The problem with this arrangement is that if you have redundant remote access servers, you must duplicate the local accounts on each one.

The *Remote Authentication Dial In User Service (RADIUS)* is designed to address this problem by providing centralized authentication, authorization, and accounting (AAA) service for dial-up and VPN servers, as well as other network access devices.

To use RADIUS, an administrator configures a remote access server to send all incoming authentication requests to a designated RADIUS server, which checks the users' credentials and informs the server of the results. Many Internet service providers use RADIUS to authenticate their users, because it enables them to maintain all of their user account information in one place, despite having users connecting to many different remote access servers.

UNDERSTANDING THE RADIUS COMPONENTS

RADIUS is an open standard, published by the Internet Engineering Task Force (IETF), defining a protocol for carrying authentication, authorization, and configuration information between a server desiring to authenticate users and a shared authentication server. There are many RADIUS implementations, most of which are interoperable.

Prior to Windows Server 2008, Microsoft's implementation of RADIUS was called Internet Authentication Service (IAS). Starting in Windows Server 2008 and Windows Server 2008 R2, Microsoft integrated RADIUS into the Network Policy Server (NPS) role.

In addition to its RADIUS capabilities, NPS can also function as a RRAS server and a Network Access Protection (NAP) health policy server. These components can run independently or interact to provide a comprehensive and secure remote access solution.

TAKE NOTE*

The Windows Server 2008 R2 Enterprise and Datacenter versions of NPS support an unlimited number of RADIUS clients and remote RADIUS server groups. The Standard version of NPS supports only 50 RADIUS clients and two remote RADIUS server groups. Windows Server 2008 R2 Web Edition does not include NPS.

NPS includes the following RADIUS components:

IMPORTANT*

When discussing RADIUS components, it is important to understand that a RADIUS client is not the end user on a remote access client computer, requesting access to the network. The RADIUS client is actually the remote access server that is requesting authentication services from the RADIUS server.

- RADIUS client—A network device that provides users with access to protected resources and that sends authentication requests and accounting messages to a RADIUS server. RADIUS clients are registered with specific RADIUS servers, enabling them to authenticate users. RADIUS clients can be RRAS servers, wireless access points, infrastructure switches, RADIUS proxies, or other network access devices.

- RADIUS server—A network device that provides centralized authentication, authorization, and accounting services for multiple RADIUS clients. The RADIUS server exchanges messages with RADIUS clients, the authentication database, and the RADIUS accounting data store.

- RADIUS proxy—A network server that routes traffic between RADIUS clients and RADIUS servers on different networks. By installing a RADIUS proxy on the perimeter network with the RADIUS clients, you can place the RADIUS servers and other components on the protected internal network.

- RADIUS accounting—RADIUS can save detailed information about the requests generated by RADIUS clients and the responses they receive from RADIUS servers to log files or to a SQL Server database.

UNDERSTANDING RADIUS COMMUNICATIONS

In a typical RADIUS transaction, a remote user, such as a VPN client, attempts to establish a connection with a remote access server using PPP. On reaching the authentication stage of the PPP connection establishment process, the remote access server, which at this time is functioning as a RADIUS client, generates an Access-Request message and sends it to its assigned RADIUS server.

For the message to reach the RADIUS server, it might use a RADIUS proxy as an intermediary.

The Access-Request message contains credentials supplied by the user, in the form of an account name and password or a digital certificate. The RADIUS server uses these credentials to authenticate the user against a local account database or an external authentication database, such as a SQL, Lightweight Directory Access Protocol (LDAP), or Active Directory server.

After evaluating the user's credentials, the RADIUS server generates one of the following three responses:

- Access-Reject—Indicates that the user has not met the conditions required for a successful authentication.

- Access-Challenge—Indicates that the user's credentials have met the conditions required, but that an additional response is required to complete a successful authentication.

On receiving the Access-Challenge message, the RADIUS client returns a message to the user, requesting additional information, such as a PIN. When the user submits a response, the RADIUS client generates a new Access-Request message and sends it to the RADIUS server.

- Access-Accept—Indicates that the user has met all the conditions required for a successful authentication.

Using DirectAccess

DirectAccess is a new feature in Windows Server 2008 R2 and Windows 7 that enables remote users to automatically connect to the company network whenever they have Internet access.

To use a VPN connection, a user on the client computer must connect to the Internet, and then manually establish a connection to the VPN server. Although a simple matter to an enterprise administrator, these are for many users complex and irritating procedures, often performed by rote and without understanding what is occurring.

These procedures can be particularly vexing for users who are traveling or working from home, and don't have access to technical support. A VPN connection can provide them with access to the company network, but they have to remember to initiate the connection first. If the connection should fail while they are working, they have to re-establish it, a process that can take several minutes each time.

Windows Server 2008 R2 and Windows 7 include a new remote access solution called *DirectAccess* that addresses these problems by enabling clients to remain connected to the company network whenever they have access to the Internet, reestablishing the connection automatically whenever it is broken.

UNDERSTANDING DIRECTACCESS BENEFITS

Designed as a replacement for VPNs, DirectAccess eliminates the need for clients to manually establish connections to their office networks. As soon as the client computer accesses the Internet, the system automatically initiates the connection to the office network. If the client becomes disconnected from the Internet, as when the user wanders out of range of a Wi-Fi hot spot, DirectAccess re-establishes the network connection as soon as the computer regains access to the Internet.

DirectAccess provides other benefits to users and administrators, including the following:

- Bidirectional—Network administrators can initiate connections to client computers in order to install updates and perform maintenance tasks.
- Encrypted—All traffic between DirectAccess clients and servers is encrypted using the IPsec protocols.
- Authenticated—DirectAccess clients perform both a computer authentication and a user authentication, and support the use of smart cards or biometric devices.
- Authorized—Administrators can grant DirectAccess clients full intranet access or limit them to specific resources.
- Verified—Administrators can use Network Access Protection (NAP) and Network Policy Server (NPS) to screen clients for the latest updates before allowing them access to the network.

UNDERSTANDING THE DIRECTACCESS INFRASTRUCTURE

Microsoft designed DirectAccess to be all but invisible to the client, but the cost of this invisibility is a complicated communications process and a long list of back-end infrastructure

requirements. Chief among these requirements is that DirectAccess is only supported by Windows 7, in its Enterprise and Ultimate editions, and by Windows Server 2008 R2 in the Standard, Enterprise, and Datacenter editions.

For this reason, the adoption of this new technology is likely to be relatively slow. Many organizations are deploying Windows 7 workstations, but upgrading servers is typically a slower and more careful process, and it might be some time before many organizations have all of the necessary components in place.

DIRECTACCESS AND IPv6

DirectAccess is also heavily reliant on IPv6, the new version of the Internet Protocol (IP) that expands the IP address space from 32 bits to 128 bits. Because IPv6 addresses are globally routable, a DirectAccess client can use the same address wherever it happens to be in the world.

Although Windows Server 2008 R2 and Windows 7 include support for IPv4 and IPv6 and load stacks for both protocols by default, IPv6 is not yet deployed universally. Many networks, and most notably the Internet, still use IPv4. Therefore, DirectAccess also relies on a variety of transition technologies that enable IPv4 networks to carry IPv6 traffic. These technologies are as follows:

X REF

For more information on IPv4/IPv6 transition technologies, see Lesson 1, "Naming and Addressing."

- 6to4—Provides IPv6 connectivity over IPv4 networks for hosts with public IP addresses.
- Teredo—Provides IPv6 connectivity over IPv4 networks for hosts with private IP addresses behind a Network Address Translation (NAT) router.
- IP-HTTPS—Provides Secure Sockets Layer (SSL) tunneling as a backup for systems that cannot use 6to4 or Teredo.
- Intra-Site Automatic Tunnel Addressing Protocol (ISATAP)—Provides IPv6 connectivity for IPv4 intranets.
- Network Address Translation—Protocol Translation (NAT-PT)—A hardware device that enables DirectAccess clients to access IPv4 applications.

DIRECTACCESS AND IPSEC

IPsec is a collection of IP extensions that provide additional security for network communications. DirectAccess relies on IPsec for authentication of users and computers and for encryption of the data exchanged by clients and servers.

IPsec uses tunneling to protect communications between computers connecting over a private network. During the DirectAccess connection process, the client uses one IPsec tunnel to access the DNS server and AD DS domain controller on the host network. Then the systems negotiate the creation of a second tunnel that provides the client with access to the other resources on the network.

IPsec consists of two protocols, Authenticated Header (AH) and Encapsulating Security Payload (ESP), and two operational modes, transport mode and tunnel mode. Windows 7 and Windows Server 2008 R2 both include full support for IPsec, but if other servers on your network do not, DirectAccess has ways to work around that limitation.

The way in which the host network uses IPsec is dependent on the access model you elect to use. If all of the servers on your network support IPv6, then DirectAccess clients can establish connections that go through the DirectAccess server and all the way to their application servers, using IPsec in transport mode. This is called the end-to-end access model, as shown in Figure 8-6.

Figure 8-6

The end-to-end access model

To keep IPsec traffic off of the company intranet, you can use the end-to-edge access model, as shown in Figure 8-7. In this model, DirectAccess clients establish tunnel-mode connections to an IPsec gateway server (which may or may not be the same computer functioning as the DirectAccess server). The gateway server then forwards the traffic to the applications servers in the intranet.

Figure 8-7

The end-to-edge access model

A third model, called modified end-to-edge, adds an additional IPsec tunnel that goes all the way to the application server, as shown in Figure 8-8, enabling clients to perform another authentication directly with the application server.

Figure 8-8

The modified end-to-edge access model

DIRECTACCESS SERVER REQUIREMENTS

The primary access point for DirectAccess clients is a server running Windows Server 2008 R2 on the perimeter network, which you create by installing the DirectAccess Management Console feature using Server Manager. The DirectAccess server must also have the following:

- Membership in an AD DS domain
- Two network interface adapters installed
- Two IPv4 addresses that are consecutive, static, public, and resolvable by the Internet DNS, for Teredo support
- A direct connection to the Internet (that does not use NAT or a similar technology)
- A direct connection to the company intranet
- The Group Policy Management feature installed

In addition to the DirectAccess server, the host network must also have the following:

- An AD DS domain with at least one domain controller running Windows Server 2008 R2

- A Windows server functioning as an enterprise root or enterprise subordinate certification authority
- An AD DS security group containing the computer objects for all of the DirectAccess clients as members, so that they can receive Group Policy settings
- A network detection server that hosts a Web site on the company intranet, which clients use to confirm their connections
- Transition technologies that enable clients to use IPv6 to access the DirectAccess server, the AD DS domain controller, and the application servers they need
- Firewall exceptions that enable the clients to access all of the servers they need, using the appropriate protocols

DIRECTACCESS CLIENT REQUIREMENTS

DirectAccess clients must be running Windows 7 Enterprise, Windows 7 Ultimate, or Windows Server 2008 R2, and they must be joined to the same domain as the DirectAccess server. You must deploy the client computers on the company network first, so they can join the domain and receive certificates and Group Policy settings, before you send them out into the field.

UNDERSTANDING THE DIRECTACCESS CONNECTION PROCESS

The DirectAccess connection establishment process is invisible to the user on the client computer, but there is a great deal going on behind the scenes. The individual steps of the connection process are as follows:

1. The client attempts to connect to a designated network detection server on the intranet. A successful connection indicates that the client is connected to the host network locally. If the client fails to connect to the server, then the DirectAccess connection establishment process begins.

2. The client connects to the DirectAccess server on the host network using IPv6. If a native connection using IPv6 is not possible, the system falls back on using 6to4, Teredo, or, if necessary, IP-HTTPS.

3. The client and the DirectAccess server authenticate each other using their computer certificates. This occurs before user logon and provides the client with access to the domain controller and the DNS server on the intranet.

4. The client establishes a second connection through the DirectAccess server to the domain controller and performs a standard AD DS user authentication, using NTLMv2 credentials and the Kerberos V5 authentication protocol.

5. The DirectAccess server uses AD DS group memberships to authorize the client computer and user to access the intranet.

6. If required, the client submits a health certificate to a Network Policy Server (NPS) on the host network, to verify its compliance with existing policies.

7. The client begins to access application servers and other resources in the intranet, using the DirectAccess server as a gateway.

CONFIGURING DIRECTACCESS

The process of installing and configuring DirectAccess is relatively simple, and again favors the simplicity of the client side. In Windows Server 2008 R2, you install DirectAccess by adding the DirectAccess Management Console feature and running the setup procedure in that console. This configures the server and also creates the Group Policy settings needed to configure the DirectAccess clients. There is no separate installation procedure for the clients; you simply have to ensure that they receive the Group Policy settings.

When you initiate the DirectAccess Setup process, the console performs a prerequisite check and displays any errors that you must resolve before the procedure can continue, as shown in Figure 8-9.

Figure 8-9

The DirectAccess prerequisite check on Windows Server 2008 R2

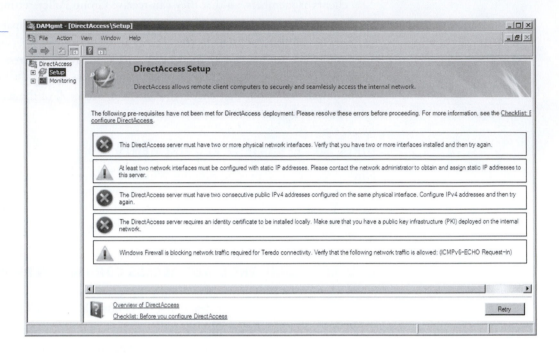

When you have met all the prerequisites, a diagram appears, as shown in Figure 8-10, that takes you through the four steps of the setup.

Figure 8-10

The DirectAccess setup diagram on Windows Server 2008 R2

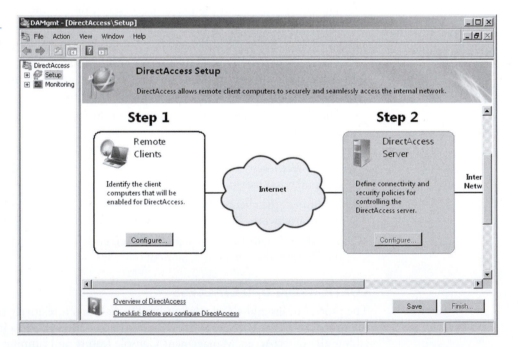

The four steps are as follows:

1. The *DirectAccess Client Setup* page appears, as shown in Figure 8-11, in which you specify the security group to which you've added the client computers as members.

Figure 8-11

The *DirectAccess Client Setup* page on Windows Server 2008 R2

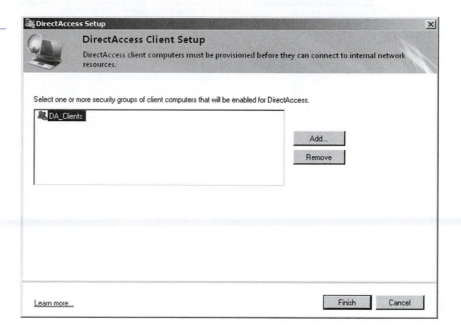

2. The *DirectAccess Server Setup* page appears, as shown in Figure 8-12, in which you specify which of the server's network interfaces provides access to the Internet and which to the intranet.

Figure 8-12

The *DirectAccess Server Setup* page on Windows Server 2008 R2

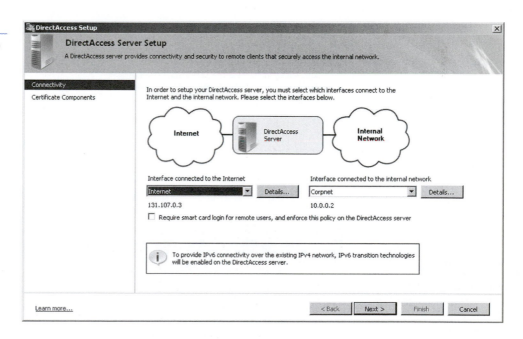

3. The *Infrastructure Server Setup* page appears, as shown in Figure 8-13, in which you specify the URL of the network location server.

Figure 8-13

The *Infrastructure Server Setup* page on Windows Server 2008 R2

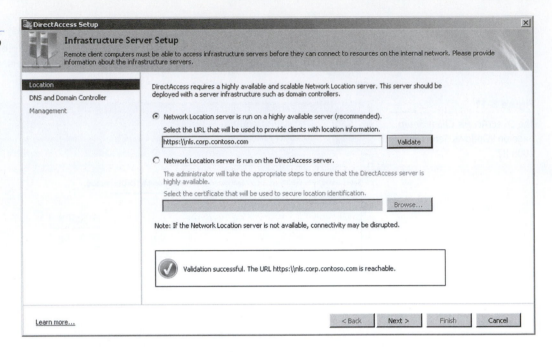

4. The *DirectAccess Application Server Setup* page appears, as shown in Figure 8-14, in which you identify the application servers that require authentication and specify the groups that can access specific applications.

Figure 8-14

The *DirectAccess Application Server Setup* page on Windows Server 2008 R2

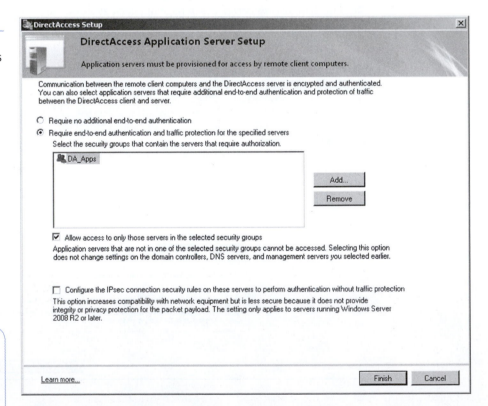

+ **MORE INFORMATION**

For a comprehensive enterprise DirectAccess solution, consider adding the Microsoft Forefront Unified Access Gateway (UAG) product. See http://www .microsoft.com/forefront/ unified-access-gateway/en/us for more information.

While the clients do not have to be connected to the intranet as you perform the server setup, you must connect them at some time afterwards, so they can receive the Group Policy settings that the setup process creates.

■ Using Network Access Protection

Authentication is an important element of remote access security, but it is not the only element. Even a user whose identity has been confirmed unquestionably can potentially be a danger to the network, and Network Access Protection is a tool that can prevent authorized users from causing damage.

In addition to its RRAS and RADIUS capabilities, NPS also includes a *Network Access Protection (NAP)* server. NAP is a tool that enables administrators to create and enforce health policies that specify what operating system updates, configuration settings, and software components a client must have before it is permitted to access the network.

For example, administrators can create policies that require clients to have all of the latest software updates installed, an up-to-date anti-virus product, an operational firewall, and a specified set of Group Policy settings, as shown in Figure 8-15. If a client fails to meet the requirements specified in the policies, NAP shunts the client to a *remediation network*, which contains services, such as Windows Server Update Services, that can bring it into compliance. Once the client meets all of the requirements specified in the policies, NAP enables it to access the internal network.

Figure 8-15

NAP policy settings

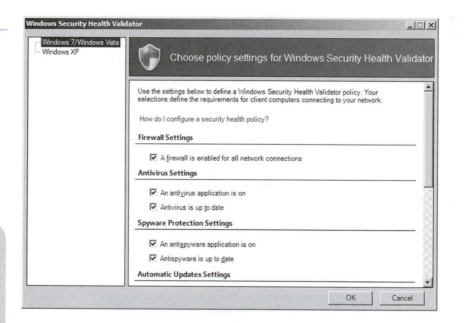

TAKE NOTE*

It is important to understand that NAP is not designed to protect networks against deliberate attacks. A client can meet all of the necessary requirements to gain access to the network and still launch an attack once inside. It is also conceivable that attackers could devise some form of masquerade that would make clients appear to comply with the NAP requirements when they really do not.

Understanding the NAP Infrastructure

NAP is a client/server application that enterprise administrators can use to protect VPN connections and also other services as well, including IPsec, IEEE 802.1X wireless connections, and Dynamic Host Configuration Protocol (DHCP) address assignments.

These various services, in combination with NAP, provide differing levels of security. The primary combinations, in descending order of strength, are as follows:

- NAP and IPsec—Because it can function with any existing infrastructure, NAP enforcement with IPsec provides the strongest solution, with the varying combinations of IPsec protocols providing a great deal of flexibility.

- NAP and 802.1X—When you use NAP in combination with an 802.1X switch or wireless access point, noncompliant wireless clients are shunted to a restricted network.
- NAP and VPN—Implementing NAP with a VPN server is a relatively simple process, and a combination that is difficult for clients to bypass.
- NAP and DHCP—In combination with DHCP, NAP enforces its protection before the client is able to obtain an IP address from the DHCP server. Obviously, this applies only to DHCP clients, however. Computers with static IP addresses bypass the NAP enforcement loop.

To validate VPN clients, the NAP transaction is integrated into the PPP connection establishment process, during the authentication phase. Once the client completes the authentication transaction with the VPN server, the NAP client begins the process of reporting the system's health to the NAP server.

The process begins with the ***System Health Agents (SHAs)*** on the client computers, which are individual modules that monitor specific services. Each separate SHA generates a ***Statement of Health (SoH)*** for the service it monitors and forwards it to the NAP Agent on the client computer.

The ***NAP Agent*** compiles the statements from the SHAs into a ***System SoH***, and forwards it to the ***NAP Enforcement Client (NAP EC)*** for VPN connections, as shown in Figure 8-16. The client computer can have multiple ECs, one for each service NAP protects.

Figure 8-16

The NAP client infrastructure

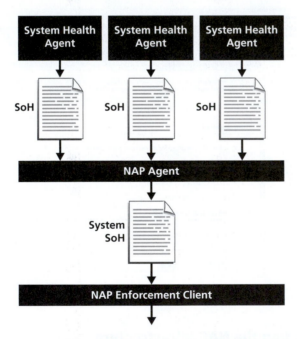

The NAP EC is the last stop on the client computer; it is responsible for transmitting the System SoH to the ***NAP Health Policy Server***. The NAP Health Policy Server, part of the Network Policy Server role in Windows Server 2008 R2, evaluates the System SoH it receives from the client.

The server side of the NAP infrastructure is in some ways a mirror image of the client. For every NAP Enforcement Client there is a ***NAP Enforcement Server (NAP ES)***, and for every System Heath Agent there is a ***System Health Validator (SHV)***. There is also a ***NAP Administration Server*** that facilitates communication with the NPS service.

Administrators can deploy the various servers in their own ways, but one typical arrangement uses a separate VPN server on the perimeter network, deployed using RRAS, as shown in Figure 8-17. The VPN server functions as the NAP ES and communicates with the NAP Health Policy Server using RADIUS messages. The NAP Health Policy Server can be located on the internal network, and provides the NPS service and all of the other NAP functions, including the NAP Administration Server and the SHVs.

Figure 8-17

The NAP server infrastructure

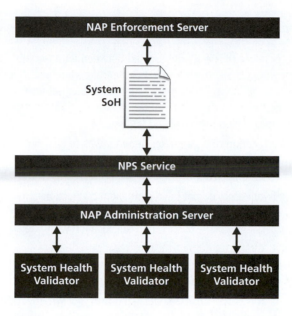

Understanding NAP Communications

> NAP communication involves multiple modules running on both client and server computers, and often requires a series of complex transactions.

If the NAP Policy Server determines that the client meets all of the requirements defined in the health policies created by the administrator, it sends a positive response to the client and the VPN server. The VPN server then proceeds with the rest of the PPP connection establishment process and grants the client access to the internal network.

If the client does not meet the requirements in the health policies, the NAP Policy Server sends a reply to the VPN server that contains a set of packet filters and a reply to the client containing health remediation instructions that explain what the client must do before it can be granted full access to the internal network.

The VPN uses the packet filters to grant the client limited access to the network. The client can communicate only with selected remediation servers. Some administrators create a physical remediation network, placing the servers on a subnet separate from the perimeter and the internal networks. However, the remediation network can also be a logical separation, implemented solely by the packet filters.

The client uses its access to communicate directly with the remediation servers, requesting the updates it needs to comply with the required health policies. Once the client has installed the updates, the SHAs generate new SoHes and the client must begin the whole VPN authentication process over again.

SKILL SUMMARY

IN THIS LESSON YOU LEARNED:

- A perimeter network is a subnet located between an internal network and an external or public network, usually the Internet. In a typical perimeter network, there are two firewalls, one between the internal network and the perimeter network, called the back-end firewall, and another between the perimeter network and an Internet service provider (ISP) on the public network, called the front-end firewall.

- The original function of a perimeter network was to host the organization's presence on the Internet. Web servers had to be directly accessible from the Internet, while the other computers on the network were better off protected by a firewall.

- Remote network users do not have permanent connections. However, the remote access solutions in Windows Server 2008 R2 and the Windows client operating systems enable users to access network resources from any location with a telephone line or an Internet connection.

- In a virtual private network (VPN) connection, the remote client and the remote access server are both connected to the Internet using local service providers.

- VPN clients and servers use a specialized protocol when establishing a connection that encapsulates their data packets inside another packet, a process called tunneling.

- All remote access connections, whether dial-up or VPN, use PPP to package their data, and the PPP connection establishment process includes a sequence in which the client and the server negotiate the use of a specific authentication protocol.

- RADIUS is a client/server application that provides centralized authentication, authorization, and accounting for the remote access services on a network.

- Windows Server 2008 R2 and Windows 7 include a new remote access solution called DirectAccess, which enables clients to remain connected to the company network whenever they have access to the Internet, reestablishing the connection automatically whenever it is broken.

- Network Access Protection (NAP) is a tool that enables administrators to create and enforce health policies that specify what operating system updates, configuration settings, and software components a client must have before it is permitted to access the network.

■ Knowledge Assessment

Matching

Complete the following exercise by matching the terms with their corresponding definitions.

_____ **1.** Layer 2 Tunneling Protocol (L2TP)

_____ **2.** EAP-MSCHAPv2

_____ **3.** MOBIKE

_____ **4.** System Health Agents

_____ **5.** Remediation network

_____ **6.** IPsec

_____ **7.** RADIUS

_____ **8.** System Health Validators

_____ **9.** Internet Key Exchange, Version 2 (IKEv2)

_____ **10.** tunneling

    A. Implemented as VPN Reconnect
    B. Found on NAP servers
    C. Provides AAA services
    D. Default VPN protocol in Windows 7
    E. Destination for NAP failures
    F. Default VPN authentication protocol in Windows 7
    G. PPP frames carried inside datagrams
    H. Provides encryption and authentication services
    I. VPN protocol
    J. Found on NAP clients

Multiple Choice

Select one or more correct answers for each of the following questions.

1. Which of the following cannot be a RADIUS client?
    a. A RRAS server
    b. A RADIUS proxy
    c. A wireless access point
    d. A RADIUS accounting

2. In Windows Server 2008 R2, Network Access Protection is implemented as part of which role?
    a. Routing and Remote Access Services
    b. Network Policy Server
    c. RADIUS
    d. Active Directory Domain Services

3. Which of the following is the most secure password-based authentication protocol supported by RRAS in Windows Server 2008 R2?
    a. EAP (PEAP)
    b. EAP-MSCHAPv2
    c. CHAP
    d. POP

4. Which of the following servers is likely to be found on a NAP remediation network?
   a. Windows Server Update Services
   b. Active Directory Domain Services domain controller
   c. Routing and Remote Access Services
   d. Network Policy Server

5. Which of the following IPv6/IPv4 transition technologies takes the form of a hardware device?
   a. ISATAP
   b. 6to4
   c. NAT-PT
   d. Teredo

6. What is the main advantage of using DirectAccess over VPN connections?
   a. Users don't have to manually connect to the remote network.
   b. DirectAccess uses IPv4 rather than IPv6.
   c. DirectAccess supports more operating systems than VPNs.
   d. DirectAccess connections are unidirectional.

7. Which of the following is not a prerequisite for a DirectAccess server?
   a. Membership in an AD DS domain
   b. Two network interface adapters
   c. Two consecutive public IPv4 addresses
   d. A NAT connection to the Internet

8. Which of the following components separates a perimeter network from the Internet?
   a. back-end firewall
   b. front-end firewall
   c. demilitarized zone
   d. internal network

9. Which of the following protocols does a dial-up client use to connect to a remote access server?
   a. PPTP
   b. L2TP
   c. PPP
   d. IPsec

10. Which of the following steps in the DirectAccess connection establishment process occurs first?
    a. The client and the DirectAccess server authenticate each other using their computer certificates.
    b. The client attempts to connect to a designated network detection server on the intranet.
    c. The client establishes a connection to the domain controller and performs a standard AD DS user authentication.
    d. The client submits a health certificate to a Network Policy Server (NPS) on the host network.

Review Questions

1. Place the following steps of the DirectAccess connection establishment process in the correct order:
   a. Client and DirectAccess server authenticate each other.
   b. Client fails to connect to network detection server.
   c. Client establishes a connection through the DirectAccess server to a domain controller.

    d. Client begins to access application servers and other resources on the intranet.

    e. DirectAccess server authorizes the client using AD DS group memberships.

    f. Client performs Active Directory Domain Services authentication.

    g. Client connects to DirectAccess server.

 2. List five servers that are likely to be found on a perimeter network.

■ Case Scenario

Scenario 8-1: Deploying a Remote Access Solution

Contoso, Ltd. has recently created a new division that, for the first time, is pursuing contracts in the private sector, rather than the government. A new team of 20 outside salespeople are traveling throughout the country, demonstrating the company's new software products to potential clients. The salespeople have been equipped with laptop computers, but to demonstrate the products, they must access a demonstration server at the company headquarters in Dallas, TX.

Because the salespeople are meeting potential clients at sites with various facilities, they must be able to access the demo server using a wireless Internet connection, a wired network, or a dial-up telephone line. Your job is to design a server configuration for the Dallas office that will accommodate all the needs of the sales staff, who might all be connecting to the demo server simultaneously.

Your procedure for deploying the server consists of the following steps:

- Place a server with two network interfaces on the perimeter network.
- Install Windows Server 2008 R2 on the server.
- Install the Network Policy and Access Services role with the Routing and Remote Access Services role service.
- Run the Routing and Remote Access Server Setup Wizard and select the Remote Access option with the VPN and Dial-up options.

What essential step or steps are missing from this procedure?

9 **LESSON**

Selecting Data Management Solutions

OBJECTIVE DOMAIN MATRIX

TECHNOLOGY SKILL	OBJECTIVE DOMAIN DESCRIPTION	OBJECTIVE DOMAIN NUMBER
Ensuring Data Availability	Design for data management and data access.	4.4
Planning Data Collaboration	Design for data management and data access.	4.4
Securing Data	Design for data management and data access.	4.4

KEY TERMS

access-based enumeration
Active Directory Rights
  Management Services
  (AD RMS)
BitLocker
BitLocker To Go
data recovery agent (DRA)
DFS namespace
DFS replication
Distributed File System (DFS)
Encrypting File System (EFS)

encryption
File Server Resource Manager
  (FSRM)
hot spares
Logical Unit Number (LUN)
Network-Attached storage
  (NAS)
RAID 0
RAID 0+1
RAID 1
RAID 1+0

RAID 5
redundant array of
  inexpensive disks (RAID)
rights policy templates
Server Message Block (SMB)
SharePoint
storage area network (SAN)
universal naming convention
  (UNC)
WAN acceleration

■ Ensuring Data Availability

THE BOTTOM LINE

Data is the most important thing on the computer. Without data, most of your local and network applications will not function. In addition, when data is not available, users are hampered and possibly cannot do their job. Therefore, as a network administrator, you need to take steps to make sure that data is available when needed.

One of the basic and most critical network services provided by a Windows Server 2008 network is file services. If you think about it, just about everything you do for a corporation deals with data. A user accesses his or her files stored on his or her Desktop, My Documents, or his or her home folder on a network server. A group may access data files on a shared folder on a server. Microsoft Exchange, which provides email, and SQL databases are stored as files on disk. Therefore, you need to make sure your disks are always available.

The question is, are you going to have 100 percent availability for your data? As much as you strive for 100 percent availability, it will never happen. First, data is normally stored on hard drives, and today most disks are mechanical devices. Mechanical devices are high-failure items, which mean that they fail more than electronic-only devices. In addition, servers and disk enclosures fail, which can cause your data to become unavailable.

Before we discuss different technologies to make your data more available, you should always keep in mind that technology costs money. While you may have paid thousands of dollars to make your data available, what you bought may not always be the best choice. You have to look how at how important the data is and what would happen if the data were not available. Databases stored on an Exchange server or SQL server is usually extremely important to a company. Therefore, it is worth some money to ensure that the data is always available.

Using Redundant Arrays of Inexpensive Disks

Since most drives are half-electronic and half-mechanical devices, you can connect multiple drives to provide data production, system reliability, and better performance. *Redundant arrays of inexpensive disks (RAID)* uses two or more drives in combination to create a fault-tolerance system to protect against physical hard-drive failure and to increase hard-drive performance. For the RAID levels, see Table 9-1. A RAID can be accomplished in either hardware or software and is usually used with network servers.

There are several levels of RAID. *RAID 0* stripes data across all drives. When data is striped, block 1 is written on the first disk, block 2 is written on the second disk and it continues until it gets to the last disk. Then the next data block is written to the next available space on the first disk. With striping, all available hard drives are combined into a single large virtual file system, with the file system's blocks arrayed so they are spread evenly across all the drives. For example, if you have three 500 GB hard drives, RAID 0 provides a 1.5 TB virtual hard drive. When you store files, the files are written across all three drives. When a large file is written, part of it is written to the first drive, the next chunk to the second drive, more to the third drive, and perhaps more wrapping back to the first drive to start the sequence again. Unfortunately, with RAID 0, there is no parity control or fault tolerance; therefore, it really is not a true form of RAID. If one drive fails, you lose all data on the array. However, RAID 0 does have several advantages because it has increased performance through load balancing.

Table 9-1

RAID Levels

RAID Level	RAID Functionality	Number of Disks Required	Description
RAID 0	Stripe set without parity	2, minimum	Implemented in Windows Server 2008 as a striped volume, RAID 0 provides no fault tolerance, but it does enhance performance, due to the parallel read and write operations that occur simultaneously on all the drives. RAID 0 has no error-detection mechanism, so the failure of one disk causes the loss of all data on the volume.
RAID 1	Mirror set without parity	2, minimum	Implemented in Windows Server 2008 as a mirrored volume, a RAID 1 array provides increased read performance, as well as fault tolerance. The array can continue to serve files as long as one of the disks remains operational.
RAID 3	Byte-level strip set with dedicated parity	3, minimum	Not implemented in Windows Server 2008, RAID 3 array stripes data at the byte level across the disks, reserving one disk for parity information. A RAID 3 array can survive the loss of any one disk, but because every write to one of the data disks requires a write to the parity disk, the parity disk becomes a performance bottleneck.
RAID 4	Block-level stripe set with dedicated parity	3, minimum	Not implemented in Windows Server 2008, RAID 4 is identical in structure to RAID 3, except that a RAID 4 array uses larger, block-level strips, which improves performance on the data disks. The parity disk can still be a performance bottleneck, however.
RAID 5	Stripe set with distributed parity	3, minimum	Implemented in Windows Server 2008 as a RAID 5 volume, RAID 5 stripes data and parity blocks across all of the disks, making sure that a block and its parity information are never stored on the same disk. Distributing the parity eliminates the performance bottleneck of the dedicated parity drive in RAID 3 and RAID 4, but the need to calculate the parity information still adds overhead to the system. A RAID 5 array can tolerate the loss of any one of its drives and can rebuild the missing data when the drive is repaired or replaced.
RAID 6	Stripe set with dual distributed parity	4, minimum	Not implemented in Windows Server 2008, RAID 6 uses the same structure as RAID 5, except that it stripes two copies of the parity information with the data. This enables the array to survive the failure of two drives. When a RAID 5 array suffers a drive failure, the array is vulnerable to data loss until the failed drive is replaced and the missing data rebuilt, which in the case of a large volume can take a long time. A RAID 6 array remains protected against data loss, even while one failed drive is rebuilding.

A common RAID configuration used in networked PCs and servers is **RAID 1**, known as disk mirroring. Disk mirroring copies a disk or partition onto a second hard drive. As information is written, it is written to both hard drives simultaneously. If one of the hard drives fails, the PC will still function because it can access the other hard drive. You can then replace the failed drive and data will be copied from the remaining good drive to the replaced drive.

Another common RAID is **RAID 5**, which is similar to striping, except one of the hard drives is used for parity (error correction) to provide fault tolerance. To increase performance, the error correction is spread across all hard drives in the array to prevent one drive from doing all the work of calculating the parity bits. If one drive fails, you still keep working since the missing data can be filled in by doing parity calculations with the remaining drives. When the failed drive is replaced, the missing information will be rebuilt from the remaining drives. However, if two drives fail, you do lose all data on the array. RAID 5 has better performance than RAID 1. RAID 5 usually requires at least three drives, with more preferable. If you have 3×500 GB drives, you will have 2×500 GB = 1000 GB of disk space, since one of the drives must be used for parity. If you have 6×500 GB drives, you will have 5×500 GB = 2500 GB of disk space.

There are two other forms of RAID worth mentioning that are considered hybrid RAID or nested RAID:

- **RAID 1+0** is a mirrored dataset (RAID 1), which is then striped (RAID 0). A RAID 1+0 array requires a minimum of four drives: two mirrored drives to hold half the striped data, plus another two mirrored drives for the other half of the data. The array continues to operate if one or more drives fail in the same mirror set, but if drives fail on both sides of the mirror, all the data on the RAID system will be lost.

- **RAID 0+1** is a striped dataset (RAID 0), which is then mirrored (RAID 1). Similarly to RAID 1+0, RAID 0+1 requires a minimum of four drives: two to hold the striped data plus another two to mirror the first pair. The array continues to operate if one or more drives fail within the striped set. If your drives fail on both striped sets, all the data on the RAID system will be lost.

For the best redundancy and performance, you should use RAID 1+0.

RAID can be implemented with hardware using a special controller that is built into the motherboard or is an expansion card. The more expensive servers would typically use hardware RAID, since software RAID requires some processing by the computer whereas hardware RAID is handled by the controller. One disadvantage of hardware RAID is that hardware usually requires a longer boot time.

Windows clients such as Windows XP, Windows Vista and Windows 7 can support RAID 0 and RAID 1, whereas Windows Servers, including Windows Server 2003 and Windows Server 2008, support RAID 0, RAID 1, and RAID 5.

A third form, which can be difficult to distinguish from hardware RAID, is firmware/driver-based RAID (sometimes referred to as FakeRAID); Adaptec calls it "HostRAID." Since the operating-system-based RAID doesn't always protect the boot process and is impractical on some desktop version of Windows, and since hardware RAID controllers are expensive and proprietary, a firmware/driver-based RAID is used in which the RAID is implemented by firmware; when the operating system loads the appropriate drivers, the operating system takes over.

Using Hot Spares

Hot spares are much like they sound. When drives need to be fault tolerant, you can include hot spare drives in your RAID array. When a drive fails, the system automatically grabs the hot spare drive, replaces the failed drive, and rebuilds or restores the missing data.

Remember that most hard drives are half-electronic, half-mechanical devices. Mechanical devices are considered high-failure items because they fail more often than non-mechanical electronic devices. This is one of reasons servers use some form of RAID to provide fault tolerance.

Taking RAID a step further, a hot spare drive is an extra drive installed within a RAID set that is inactive until an active drive fails. When a drive fails, the system automatically replaces the failed drive with the spare and starts rebuilding the array with the spare. Of course, rebuilding an array can take several hours, especially on busy systems. A hot spare can be shared by multiple RAID sets.

Using Network-Attached Storage and Storage-Area Networks

For larger corporations, servers may connect to centralized devices that contain large amounts of storage. These devices offer better performance and better fault tolerance and provide quick recovery.

Network-attached storage (NAS) is a file-level data storage device that is connected to a computer network to provide shared drives or folders, usually using SMB. NAS devices usually contain multiple drives in a form of RAID for fault tolerance and are usually managed via a Web interface.

A *storage-area network (SAN)* is an architecture used to make disk arrays, tape libraries, and optical jukeboxes appear as locally attached drives on a server. SANs always use some form of RAID and other technology to make the system redundant against drive failure and to offer high performance. They also usually contain spare drives. To provide a high level of data throughput, SANs use the SCSI protocol and either the iSCSI or Fibre Channel interface.

While SANs offer performance and redundancy, there are also other benefits to consider. Since you designate storage areas within the SAN and assign them to servers, if you have problems with that server, you can quickly and easily move the storage areas to another server.

SANs also offer snapshotting and volume cloning. When you need to install or upgrade a component within a server, you can first take a snapshot, which is a temporary image at the time of the snapshot. You can then make changes or upgrades to the server. If you have a problem, you can roll back to the snapshot and continue on before you do the upgrade. The rolling back can take minutes.

Volume cloning allows you to copy a storage area to another storage area within a SAN or to another SAN. This allows you quickly to create a test environment or to duplicate an environment. You can also establish storage replication between SAN units even if they are in different locations.

A host adapter, sometimes referred to as host bus adapter (HBA), connects a host system such as a computer to a network or storage devices. The term is primarily used for connecting SCSI, Fibre Channel and eSATA devices, but devices for connecting to IDE, Ethernet, FireWire, USB, and other systems may also be called host adapters. Today, the term host bus adapter (HBA) most often refers to a Fibre Channel interface card.

Logical Unit Numbers (usually called *LUNs*) allow SANs to break their storage down into manageable pieces, which are then assigned to one or more servers in the SAN. A LUN is a logical reference that can comprise a disk, a section of a disk, a whole disk array, or a section of a disk array. LUNs serve as logical identifiers through which you can assign access and control privileges. If a LUN is not mapped to a given server, that server cannot see or access the LUN. You only need to identify the server or cluster that will access the LUN, and then select which HBA ports on that server or cluster will be used for LUN traffic.

■ Planning Data Collaboration

THE BOTTOM LINE

Usually when you think of file services on a Windows network, you think of file sharing. As explained in Lesson 4, Windows servers support file sharing using **Server Message Block (SMB)** and Network File System (NFS). When multiple people need to access the same data files or multiple people need to collaborate on a report or a project, you need more than just a simple shared folder.

CERTIFICATION READY
What technology can you use to make a shared folder fault tolerant?
4.4

When you share a folder in Windows, you are usually using SMB, also known as Common Internet File System (CIFS). SMB has been around for years to provide shared access to files and printers. While SMB is usually associated with computers running Windows, it is also accessible by most other operating systems including Linux, UNIX, and Macintosh. To access a shared Windows folder, you use the **universal naming convention (UNC)** based on the *servername**sharedname* format.

When you share a folder, you must always plan for security of those folders. You need to ensure that those users who need access to the folder to do their job have access to it and those users who do not need access do not have access to i. To control who can access a shared folder, you combine share permissions with NTFS permissions.

By now, you should understand that you should always choose NTFS over FAT or FAT32. NTFS is superior in every way: it accommodates much larger volumes, provides better security using NTFS permissions and encryption, and is more resistant to corruption. The only reason to use FAT and FAT32 on a Windows system is to provide backward compatibility or for a removable storage device that does not accommodate NTFS.

When assigning permissions to a shared folder, you need to look at the users and groups that will be accessing the shared folder. Remember that it is always better to assign rights and permissions to groups than to individual users.

To calculate the final access permissions on a shared folder, you need to:

1. Calculate the effective rights for the NTFS permissions for the user and all the groups of which the user is a member. Explicit permissions overwrite inherited permissions. Generally, it is the least restrictive permission that is valid, with the exception that permissions that are denied always win out.

2. Calculate the effective rights for the Share permissions for the user and for all groups of which the user is a member. Generally, it is the least restrictive permission that is valid, with the exception that permissions that are denied always win out.

3. Combine the share permissions and the NTFS permissions. The more restrictive permissions are then applied.

Of course, if a user accesses the files directly on the computer without going through the file share (examples are logging onto the server or through a terminal session), the shared permissions do not apply to the user.

Since shared permissions do not apply to users who access a folder directly and calculating the final access permissions can be complicated, it is usually recommend to set share permissions to Full Control for the Everyone group and to rely entirely on NTFS permissions to restrict access.

Granting a user Full Control NTFS permission on a folder enables that user to take ownership of the folder unless the user is restricted in some other way. Therefore, you should be cautious in granting Full Control. Last, by default, the Everyone group does not include the Anonymous group, so permissions applied to the Everyone group do not affect the Anonymous group.

Designing a Share Strategy

Once an enterprise administrator has determined what applications a workstation requires, the next step is to decide how the IT staff should deploy those applications.

When planning file services, you need to look at the following business requirements:

- High availability—Since users need to access data files to do their job, you need to plan for and anticipate failures that may make the files unavailable. Besides using technology to make a server fault tolerant, there are several methods for managing redundant shared folders.

- Geographic distribution—Many companies have multiple sites that are linked with slower WAN links or links with higher latency. Since files accessed locally are much faster than files accessed across a WAN link, you need to synchronize files between servers in different physical locations. Synchronizing files allows users to access a local copy of files, which is much faster than accessing centralized data over a WAN link.

- File storage management—As an enterprise administrator, you need to develop plans for managing file storage, including who will have access to it, who will administer it, and how to control its size.

While the shared folder is the most basic component of a file service design, several technologies can be used to enhance file sharing, including the following:

- Server Message Block (SMB) Version 2.0—A new version of the file- sharing protocol in Windows Vista, Windows 7, and Windows Server 2008 that increases file-sharing performance by reducing the number of packets transmitted on the network.

- *Access-based enumeration*—Limits the files and folders that the user has permission to access.

- Failover clustering—Provides high availability but requires shared storage between the cluster nodes. It also requires Windows Server 2008 Enterprise or Data Center Edition. Failover clustering is discussed in Lesson 12.

- DFS—Provides a method to organize multiple shared folders and to provide high availability and file synchronization between servers.

- FSRM—Provides file-storage management by controlling how storage can be used and reporting on current usage.

- *WAN acceleration*—Not a feature of Windows Server 2008, though BranchCache acts as a WAN accelerator. WAN acceleration is implemented by dedicated hardware devices on the network to enhance communication over WAN links, particularly with shared folders and some types of HTTP traffic. BranchCache was discussed in Lesson 5.

UNDERSTANDING SMB2

Microsoft introduced SMB 2.0 with Windows Vista in 2006. SMB2 was designed to increase performance by compounding multiple actions into a single request, significantly reducing the number of round trips that client traffic needs to make. In addition, SMB2 supports larger buffer sizes, which can provide better performance with large file transfers and make better use of faster networks. Last, SMB2 introduces "durable file handles" that allow a connection to an SMB server to survive brief outages, such as may occur in a wireless network, without having to negotiate a new session.

UNDERSTANDING ACCESS-BASED ENUMERATION

Access-based enumeration was introduced with Windows Server 2003 Service Pack 1. When you access a shared folder, Windows will only list those files for which you have the List Folder Contents permission. Not showing those files that you do not have access helps

eliminate confusion by reducing the number of files and folders that you normally see.

UNDERSTANDING WAN ACCELERATION

WAN Acceleration products try to accelerate a broad range of applications accessed by using a local cache to eliminating redundant transmissions. To maximize the use of the local cache, it is designed to compress and prioritize data, and streamline chatty protocols such as SMB. While WAN acceleration is not a feature of Windows Server 2008, Windows Server 2008 R2 does offer BranchCache, which acts as a WAN accelerator.

Using Distributed File System

> ***Distributed File System (DFS)*** is a set of client and server services that allow a company using Microsoft Windows server to organize SMB file shares into a distribute file system. It can also provide replication among file servers.

DFS has two major logical components:

- DFS namespace
- DFS replication

DFS NAMESPACE

DFS namespace allows you to take multiple file shares based on SMB and combine them into a single logical network path. In other words, it allows you to create a shared folder that contains other shared folders. When accessing the shared folders within a DFS namespace, users do not have to worry about where each shared folder is stored. See Figure 9-1.

Figure 9-1

DFS namespace

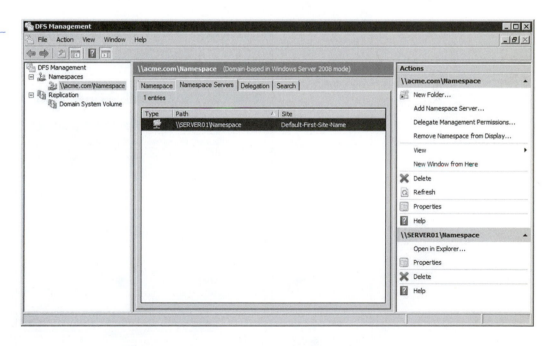

DFS namespace can be divided into stand-alone DFS root and domain-based DFS roots. Stand-alone DFS roots allow a DFS root that exists only on the local computer and does not use Active Directory. A stand-alone DFS can only be accessed on the computer on which it is created. It does not offer any fault tolerance and cannot be linked to any other DFS. For this reason, you can imagine that stand-alone DFS root is not used often.

Domain-based DFS roots exist within Active Directory, which distributes their information to other domain controllers within the domain. Of course, since this information is replicated on domain controllers, a domain-based DFS root must be hosted on a domain controller.

Slightly different from the UNC path that uses *servername**sharednamed*, domain-based DFS files use the domain name instead of the server name. Therefore, DFS namespace use *domainname**dfsroot**path*. If a server fails, the client can select a different server transparently to the user. Unfortunately, if a user has an open file, there may well be problems with the file since open files cannot be failed over.

Windows Server 2008 has made some improvements to the DFS namespace. DFS namespaces have been enhanced with access-based enumeration and cluster support for stand-alone namespaces. To enable these features, DFS must be changed to Windows Server 2008 mode.

Of course, there are some limits in using DFS namespace. Each folder in a namespace can have one or more targets. Use multiple targets for each folder to increase availability. You can then use replication to synchronize data between folder targets.

When domain-based namespaces have more than 5000 folders, performance issues can appear. Use stand-alone namespaces when there are more than 5000 folders in a namespace.

DFS REPLICATION

DFS replication was introduced in Windows Server 2003 R2, which improved on the File Replication Server (FRS). DFS replication improved on FRS by only copying those parts of files that have changed (remote differential compression). DFS replication also uses data compression and allows the administrator to schedule when the replication occurs. See Figure 9-2.

Figure 9-2

DFS replication

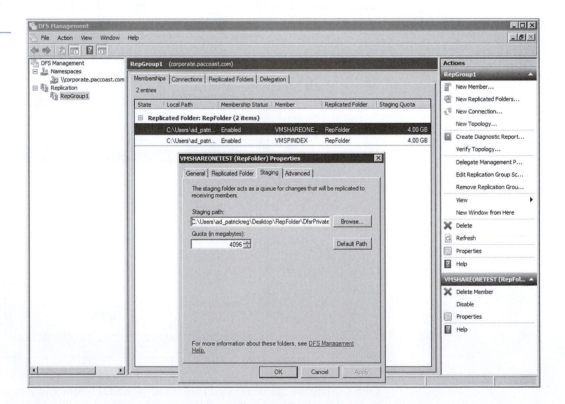

While you could use a failover cluster to provide redundancy, a failover cluster can provide redundancy only between servers in the same physical area. DFS can also provide redundancy

and DFS servers can be geographically dispersed. As a result, DFS can benefit the following scenarios:

- If you have DFS servers dispersed geographically, users can access those files that are local rather always accessing files over a slower WAN link.
- For companies with multiple sites, you can use DFS replication to copy files to centralized servers so as to perform backups more efficiently.

Of course, the disadvantage of DFS replication is that two users could access the same file at the same time from two different locations and make changes to that file. As a result, a replication conflict could occur.

With Windows Server 2008, DFS replication has the following improvements:

- A new content-freshness check to prevent servers that have been offline for a long time from overwriting current data.
- Faster recovery from unexpected shutdowns of DFS replication or the computer and volumes that host DFS.
- Increased performance that provides faster replication of files, better utilizes available bandwidth, and accommodates high-latency networks.
- A propagation report that is generated based on propagation of a test file as a diagnostic test.
- The replicate-now option, which lets you initiate replication of a folder immediately despite the replication schedule.

DESIGNING DFS

If you decide to implement DFS, you first need to plan your DFS design. This should include the following steps:

1. Identify data to replicate.
2. Make initial namespace decisions.
3. Design the replication topology.
4. Plan for high availability and business continuity, including regularly backing up namespace, data, and Active Directory.
5. Plan for delegation.
6. Design for namespace hierarchy and functionality.
7. Design replication schedules and bandwidth throttling.
8. Review performance and optimization guidelines.
9. Plan for DFS Replication deployment.

Last, after DFS is implemented, you also need to monitor it make sure it is performing as planned.

DEPLOYING DFS

Of course, DFS namespace has some limits. Each folder in a namespace can have one or more targets. Use multiple targets for each folder to increase availability. Replication is then used to synchronize data between folder targets.

The best practices for deploying DFS namespaces include:

- Use DFS namespaces to create a unified folder hierarchy. This makes it easier for users to locate files because they do not need to browse multiple servers.
- Use multiple folder targets to increase availability of individual folders.

- Use the lowest-cost method for ordering target referrals. In most cases, you prefer users to access files from a target that is within the local Active Directory site.
- Use scalability mode for more than 16 namespace servers. Scalability mode reduces the namespace polling performed by the namespace servers and reduces the load on Active Directory.
- Specify a primary server by using target priority to reduce replication conflicts.
- When a primary server is specified, then all users access files on a single server.

The best practices for deploying DFS Replication include:

- To reduce replication complexity and improve DFS performance, use a mesh replication topology only with fewer than 10 members. If you need a topology with more than 10 active nodes, consider a hub-and-spoke replication topology in which a centralized server acts as a distribution point to the other DFS servers. For more information about the various DFS topologies, visit http://technet.microsoft.com/en-us/library/cc784885(WS.10).aspx.
- Use bandwidth throttling to ensure that replication does not overwhelm WAN links, particularly WAN links with low bandwidth.
- Use cross-file remote differential compression (RDC) to reduce replication traffic. Cross-file RDC recognizes patterns in multiple files and uses those patterns to reduce replication.
- Use replication filters to prevent replication of unwanted file types. Replication filters can restrict replication based on the file extension.
- Size Staging folders and Conflict and Deleted folders appropriately. The Staging folder (4 GB default size) should be at least twice the size of the largest replicated file. If the Conflict and Deleted folder (660 MB default size) is too small, then conflicts can be purged before they are addressed. Both folders are purged to 60% usage when they reach 90% usage.

DFS AND SYSVOL

SYSVOL is a collection of folders that contain a copy of the domain's public files, including system policies, logon scripts, and important Group Policy objects (GPOs). Shared subdirectories in the SYSVOL tree are replicated to every domain controller in the domain.

In Windows Server 2008, DFS Replication is the default file replication service for domains that are initially created on domain controllers running Windows Server 2008. However, in a domain that is upgraded from another operating system to Windows Server 2008, File Replication Service is the default replication service for SYSVOL replication.

Windows Server 2008 ships a command line tool called dfsrmig.exe that administrators can use to initiate migration of SYSVOL replication from FRS to the DFS Replication service.

Using File Server Resource Manager

File Server Resource Manager (FSRM) was introduced with Windows Server 2003 R2. FRSM is a suite of tools that enable administrators to place storage limits on volumes and folders, prevent users from saving specific file types to the server, and generate comprehensive storage reports. While FRSM helps administrators control and monitor existing storage resources from a central location, it also aids in planning and implementing future changes to the storage infrastructure.

The File Server Resource Manager Microsoft Management Console (MMC) snap-in allows you to do the following:

- Quota management—Set soft or hard space limits on a volume or folder tree.
- File screening management—Define filtering rules that monitor or block attempts by users to save certain file types on a volume or folder tree.
- Storage reports management—Generate built-in reports to track quota usage, file screening activity, and patterns of storage use.

See Figure 9-3.

Figure 9-3

File Server Resource Manager

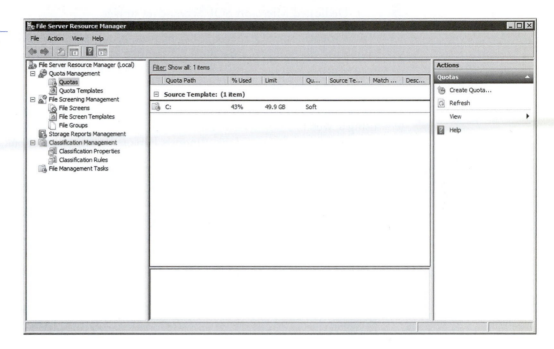

To help simplify administering multiple servers, you can:

- Reuse resource management rules across an organization by applying standard storage limits or file screens to new volumes or folders.
- Use or modify built-in templates or create new ones to capture your system policies.
- Manage updates to quotas or file screens from a central location by updating the properties of templates.

■ Using Sharepoint

THE BOTTOM LINE

Microsoft **SharePoint** is a family of software products for collaboration, file sharing, and Web publishing. SharePoint server farms can host Web sites, portals, intranets, extranets, Internets, Web content management systems, search engines, wikis, blogs, and social networking, as well as provide a framework for Web application development. While SharePoint is not intended to replace file sharing, it can be valuable to any company.

Windows SharePoint Services (WSS) 3.0 and Microsoft SharePoint Foundation are free add-ons for Microsoft Windows Server 2003 and 2008; the corresponding fee-based products are Microsoft Office SharePoint Server 2007 (MOSS) and Microsoft SharePoint Server 2010.

Microsoft SharePoint Server is built on the ASP.NET framework and interfaces with Active Directory. Microsoft SharePoint Server has three major components:

- Windows Server Web Front End role (Internet Information Server – IIS), which processes HTTP requests to the Server
- An application layer that provides such features as Search and Excel Services
- Dedicated Microsoft SQL Server data storage

While you can use SQL Server 2008 Express, it is limited to a 4 GB database. Even a modest company will easily outgrow the 4 GB limit as it starts to use this server. SharePoint 2007 recommends keeping databases under 100 GB and SharePoint 2010 recommends keeping databases under 200 GB.

Since SharePoint works on top of Microsoft's Web server, IIS, SharePoint is usually accessed using a Web browser. SharePoint can also be used through Windows 7 Federated Search, DAV "Internet folders" accessed via Windows Explorer, Microsoft Outlook, and Microsoft Office.

After you install SharePoint, you must run the configuration wizard and create a collection. You are then ready to start creating sites from a site template such as a blank site, team site, document workspace, or basic meeting workspace.

Collaboration sites are designed and configured based on team type, size, complexity, and objective. Collaboration sites often include sections for sharing information and data, sharing documents, sharing calendar or event information, generating and discussing ideas, and adding, assigning, and tracking tasks. See Figure 9-4.

Figure 9-4

SharePoint

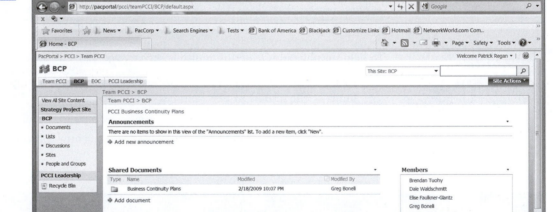

As SharePoint is embraced by a company, you will need to develop a SharePoint farm to accommodate a heavier load and to provide redundancy. A farm is a group of SharePoint Servers. For example, one or more servers can be dedicated as front ends for the users to access, while another server is used to crawl content to create the search index. A SQL Server installation is typically used for a back-end server. To provide redundancy for SQL, you typically use a failover cluster.

Since SharePoint is basically a Web site, it can be protected by using a digital certificate to provide SSL. If SharePoint needs to be used over the Internet, you can further protect SharePoint by using the Microsoft Internet Security and Acceleration (ISA) Server 2006 or Microsoft ForeFront Threat Management Gateway (ForeFront TMG) by protecting the server from direct external access via a HTTP publishing rule.

What makes SharePoint extremely powerful is its business intelligence and workflows. For example, say that you decide to create a list of servers deployed on your network. You can create workflows that start when someone requests a server. When the request is made, emails can be automatically generated and sent to management to approve the server. You can also add more workflows to ensure proper planning and deployment of the server, including making sure that the correct steps are taken before the server goes into production. Examples may include:

- Did you add a DNS entry for the server?
- Did you enable backups for the server?
- Did you enable monitoring of the server if it goes down?

Since all servers are placed in this list, it gives you a quick method to see what your company has running at any one time and can also be used for inventory.

SharePoint also offers file versioning and you can use workflows to publish a document within SharePoint for all to see. For example, a support person creates a report. A workflow can be created to for his or her manager to approve the document. This allows updates or tweaks to be completed before the documents are published.

■ Securing Data

THE BOTTOM LINE

Besides making sure that your data is always available, you also need to make sure that your data is secure.

CERTIFICATION READY
What technology makes data unreadable by unauthorized users?
4.4

Earlier in the lesson, we discussed NTFS and share permissions. However, using NTFS and share permissions are not the only way to protect your files. *Encryption* is the process of converting data into a format that cannot be read by another user. Decryption is the process of converting data from encrypted format back to its original format.

Using Encrypting File System

> *Encrypting File System (EFS)* is a core file encryption technology used to store encrypted files on NTFS file system volumes. Encrypted files cannot be used unless the user has access to the keys required to decrypt the information. After a file has been encrypted, you do not have to manually decrypt it before you can use it. Once you encrypt a file or folder, you work with the encrypted file or folder just as with any other file or folder.

TAKE NOTE★

Encryption can also be used to protect data on laptops, which are much more likely to be stolen because they are mobile devices. On Windows 7, EFS can be used to encrypt individual folders or files and BitLocker can be used to encrypt entire volumes.

If a hard drive is stolen from a system, it could be installed on a Windows system in which the thief is an administrator; as an administrator, the thief could take ownership, if necessary, and access every file and folder on the disk. This is one of the reasons your servers must have physical security: to make sure that an authorized person cannot get to the servers to steal hard drives or other essential components. To help protect your data in these situations, you can use encryption.

ENCRYPT A FOLDER OR FILE USING EFS

GET READY. To encrypt a folder or file:

1. Right-click the folder or file you want to encrypt, and then click **Properties**.
2. Click the **General** tab, and then click **Advanced**.
3. Select the **Encrypt Contents to secure data** check box, click **OK**, and then click **OK** again. See Figure 9-5.

Figure 9-5

Encrypt Content using EFS

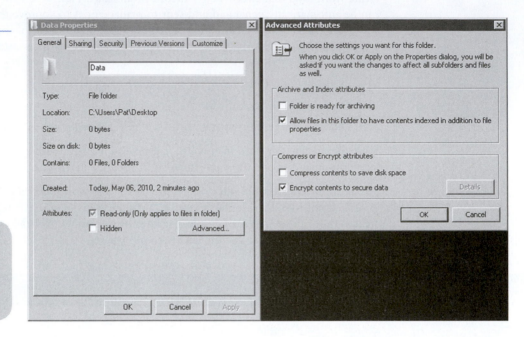

TAKE NOTE*

You cannot encrypt a file with EFS while compressing a file with NTFS. You can only do one or the other.

 DECRYPT A FOLDER OR FILE

GET READY. To decrypt a folder or file

1. Right-click the folder or file you want to decrypt, and then click **Properties**.
2. Click the **General** tab, and then click **Advanced**.
3. Clear the **Encrypt Contents to secure data** check box, click **OK**, and then click **OK** again.

The first time you encrypt a folder or file, an encryption certificate is automatically created. If your certificate and key are lost or damaged and you don't have a backup, you won't be able to use the files that you have encrypted. Therefore, you should always back up your encryption certificates.

BACK UP EFS CERTIFICATE

GET READY. To back up your EFS certificate:

1. Execute the certmgr.msc. If you are prompted for an administrator password or confirmation, type the password or provide confirmation.
2. In the left pane, double-click **Personal**.
3. Click **Certificates**.
4. In the main pane, click the certificate that lists Encrypting File System under Intended Purposes. If there is more than one EFS certificate, you should back up all of them.

5. Click the **Action** menu, point to All Tasks, and then click Export.

6. In the Certificate Export wizard, click **Next**, click **Yes**, export the private key, and then click **Next**.

7. Click **Personal Information Exchange**, and then click **Next**.

8. Type the password you want to use, confirm it, and then click **Next**. The export process will create a file to store the certificate.

9. Type a name for the file and the location (include the whole path) or click **Browse**, navigate to a location, type a file name, and then click **Save**.

10. Click **Next**, and then click **Finish**.

You should then store the certificate in a safe place.

Using BitLocker

> Unlike EFS, *BitLocker* allows you to encrypt entire disks. Therefore, if a drive or laptop is stolen, the data remains encrypted if the drive is installed into another system.

TAKE NOTE *

BitLocker is a feature of Windows 7 Enterprise and Windows 7 Ultimate. It is not supported on other editions of Windows 7.

BitLocker Drive Encryption is the feature in Windows 7 Ultimate and Enterprise edition that makes use of a computer's TPM hardware. A Trusted Platform Module (TPM) is a microchip is built into a computer that is used to store cryptographic information, such as encryption keys. Information stored on the TPM can be more secure from external software attacks and physical theft. BitLocker Drive Encryption can use a TPM to validate the integrity of a computer's boot manager and boot files at startup, and to guarantee that a computer's hard disk has not been tampered with while the operating system was offline. BitLocker Drive Encryption also stores measurements of core operating system files in the TPM.

The system requirements of BitLocker are:

- Because BitLocker stores its own encryption and decryption key in a hardware device that is separate from your hard disk, you must have one of the following:
  - A computer with Trusted Platform Module (TPM). If your computer was manufactured with TPM version 1.2 or higher, BitLocker will store its key in the TPM.
  - A removable USB memory device, such as a USB flash drive. If your computer doesn't have TPM version 1.2 or higher, BitLocker will store its key on the flash drive.
- Your computer must have at least two partitions: a system partition (which contains the files needed to start your computer and must be at least 200 MB) and an operating-system partition (which contains Windows). The operating-system partition will be encrypted and the system partition will remain unencrypted so your computer can start. If your computer doesn't have two partitions, BitLocker will create them for you. Both partitions must be formatted with the NTFS file system.
- Your computer must have a BIOS that is compatible with TPM and supports USB devices during computer startup. If this is not the case, you will need to update the BIOS before using BitLocker.

BitLocker has five operational modes that define the steps involved in the system boot process. These modes, in descending order from most to least secure, are as follows:

- TPM + startup PIN + startup key—The system stores the BitLocker volume encryption key on the TPM chip, but an administrator must supply a personal identification number (PIN) and insert a USB flash drive containing a startup key before the system can unlock the BitLocker volume and complete the system boot sequence.

- TPM + startup key—The system stores the BitLocker volume encryption key on the TPM chip, but an administrator must insert a USB flash drive containing a startup key before the system can unlock the BitLocker volume and complete the system boot sequence.

- TPM + startup PIN—The system stores the BitLocker volume encryption key on the TPM chip, but an administrator must supply a PIN before the system can unlock the BitLocker volume and complete the system boot sequence.

- Startup key only—The BitLocker configuration process stores a startup key on a USB flash drive, which the administrator must insert each time the system boots. This mode does not require the server to have a TPM chip, but it must have a system BIOS that supports access to the USB flash drive before the operating system loads.

- TPM only—The system stores the BitLocker volume encryption key on the TPM chip, and accesses it automatically when the chip has determined that the boot environment is unmodified. This unlocks the protected volume and the computer continues to boot. No administrative interaction is required during the system boot sequence.

When you enable BitLocker using the BitLocker Drive Encryption control panel, you can select the TPM + startup key, TPM + startup PIN, or TPM only option. To use the TPM + startup PIN + startup key option, you must first configure the *Require additional authentication at startup* Group Policy setting, found in the Computer Configuration\Policies\Administrative Templates\Windows Components\BitLocker Drive Encryption\Operating System Drives container.

ENABLING BITLOCKER

 DETERMINE IF YOU HAVE TPM

GET READY. To find out if your computer has Trusted Platform Module (TPM) security hardware:

1. Open the Control Panel, click **System and Security**, and click **BitLocker Drive Encryption**.

2. In the left pane, click **TPM Administration**. If you are prompted for an administrator password or confirmation, type the password or provide confirmation.

The TPM Management on Local Computer snap-in tells you if your computer has the TPM security hardware. If your computer doesn't have it, you'll need a removable USB memory device to turn on BitLocker and store the BitLocker startup key that you'll need whenever you start your computer.

 TURN ON BITLOCKER

GET READY. Log on to Windows 7 using an account with administrative privileges.

1. Click **Start**, then click **Control Panel** > **System and Security** > **BitLocker Drive Encryption**. The BitLocker Drive Encryption control panel appears.

2. Click **Turn on BitLocker** for your hard disk drives. The *Set BitLocker startup preferences* page appears. See Figure 9-6.

Figure 9-6

Turning on BitLocker

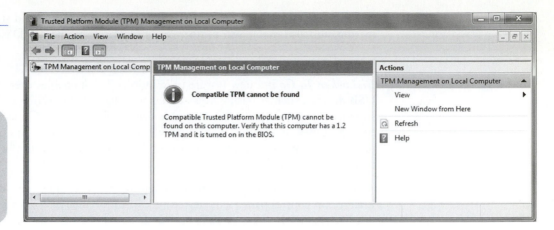

BitLocker is a feature of Windows 7 Enterprise and Windows 7 Ultimate. It is not supported on other editions of Windows 7.

3. Click **Require a Startup key at every startup**. A *Save your Startup key* page appears.

4. Insert a USB flash drive into a USB port and click **Save**. The *How do you want to store your recovery key?* page appears.

5. Select one of the options to save your recovery key and click **Next**. The *Are you ready to encrypt this drive?* page appears.

6. Click **Continue**. The wizard performs a system check and then restarts the computer.

7. **Log on** to the computer. Windows 7 proceeds to encrypt the disk.

Once the encryption process is completed, you can open the BitLocker Drive Encryption control panel to ensure that the volume is encrypted, or to turn off BitLocker, as when performing a BIOS upgrade or other system maintenance.

The BitLocker control panel applet enables you to recover the encryption key and recovery password at will. You should consider carefully how to store this information, because it will allow access to the encrypted data. It is also possible to escrow this information into Active Directory.

DATA RECOVERY AGENTS AND BITLOCKER

If for some reason the user loses the startup key and/or startup PIN needed to boot a system with BitLocker, the user can supply the recovery key created during the BitLocker configuration process and gain access to the system. If the user loses the recovery key, you can use a data recovery agent designated with active Directory to to recover the data on the drive.

A *data recovery agent (DRA)* is a user account that an administrator has authorized to recover BitLocker drives for an entire organization with a digital certificate on a smart card. In most cases, administrators of Active Directory Domain Services (AD DS) networks use DRAs to ensure access to their BitLocker-protected systems, to avoid having to maintain large numbers of individual keys and PINs.

To create a DRA, you must first add the user account you want to designate to the Computer Configuration\Policies\Windows Settings\Security Settings\Public Key Policies\BitLocker Drive Encryption container in a GPO or to the system's Local Security Policy. Then, you must configure the Provide The Unique Identifiers For Your Organization policy setting in the Computer Configuration\Policies\Administrative Templates\Windows Components\BitLocker Drive Encryption container with unique identification fields for your BitLocker drives.

Finally, you must enable DRA recovery for each type of BitLocker resource you want to recover, by configuring the following policies:

- Choose How BitLocker-Protected Operating System Drives Can Be Recovered
- Choose How BitLocker-Protected Fixed Drives Can Be Recovered
- Choose How BitLocker-Protected Removable Drives Can Be Recovered

These policies enable you to specify how BitLocker systems should store their recovery information, and also enable you to store this information in the AD DS database.

USING BITLOCKER TO GO

BitLocker To Go is a new feature in Windows 7 that enables users to encrypt removable USB devices, such as flash drives and external hard disks. While BitLocker has always supported the encryption of removable drives, BitLocker To Go enables you to use the encrypted device on other computers without having to perform an involved recovery process. Because the system is not using the removable drive as a boot device, a TPM chip is not required.

To use BitLocker To Go, you insert the removable drive and open the BitLocker Drive Encryption control panel. The device appears in the interface, with a *Turn on BitLocker* link just like that of the computer's hard disk drive.

Using AD Rights Management Services

By using *Active Directory Rights Management Services (AD RMS)* and the AD RMS client, you can protect information through a usage policy that remains with the information, no matter where it is moved. You can use AD RMS to help prevent sensitive information from intentionally or accidentally getting into the wrong hands. You can even specify when a document or email expires.

When using AD RMS, data files and emails can be encrypted. The Active Directory Rights Management Services server role handles certificates and licensing. Users can define who can open, modify, print, forward, or take other actions on the information. Organizations can create custom usage policy templates such as "confidential-read only" that can be applied directly to the information. See Figure 9-7.

Figure 9-7

AD Rights Management
Services

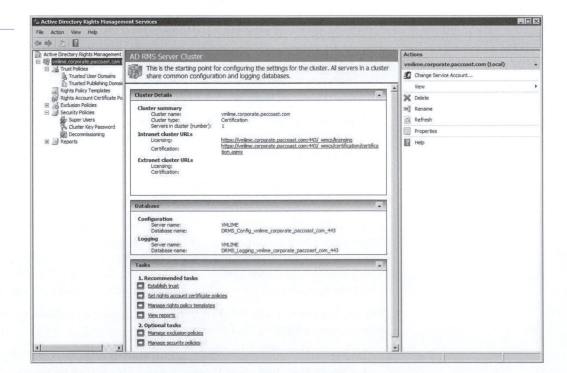

AD RMS support is included with Windows Vista, Windows 7, and Windows Server 2008. It is also supported by Internet Explorer 7 and 8, Microsoft Office 2007 and 2010, and SharePoint 2007 and 2010. For Windows XP clients to support AD RMS, you must download and install the RMS client. It can be used with Windows Servers, Microsoft Exchange, and Microsoft SharePoint.

To install the AD RMS Server Role, do the following:

1. Log on to the server on which you want to install AD RMS.

2. Open Server Manager. Click Start, point to Administrative Tools, and then click Server Manager.

3. In the Roles Summary box, click Add Roles.

4. Read the Before You Begin section, and then click Next.

5. On the Select Server Roles page, select the Active Directory Rights Management Services box.

6. The Role Services page appears, informing you of the AD RMS-dependent role services and features. Make sure that Web Server (IIS), Windows Process Activation Service (WPAS), and Message Queuing are listed, and then click Add Required Role Services. Click Next.

7. Read the AD RMS introduction page, and then click Next.

8. On the Select Role Services page, verify that the Active Directory Rights Management Server check box is selected, and then click Next.

9. Select the Create a new AD RMS cluster option, and then click Next.

10. Select the Use a different database server option, and then click Select.

11. If you choose to use the Windows Internal database to host the AD RMS databases for a single-server installation, steps 11 and 12 are not required. Type the name of the computer that will be hosting AD RMS databases, and then click OK.

12. In Database Instance, choose the appropriate instance, click Validate, and then click Next.

13. On the Specify Service Account page, click Specify, type the domain user account and password that should be used as the AD RMS service account, click OK, and then click Next.

14. Ensure that the Use AD RMS centrally managed key-storage option is selected, and then click Next.

15. If you choose to protect the AD RMS cluster key by using a cryptographic storage provider, step 15 is not required. Type a strong password in the Password box and in the Confirm password box, and then click Next.

16. Choose the Web site where the AD RMS Web services will be installed, and then click Next. In a default installation, the name of the Web site should be Default Web Site.

17. As a best security practice, the AD RMS cluster should be provisioned by using an SSL-encrypted connection. Select the Use an SSL-encrypted connection (https://) option.

18. Type the fully qualified domain name of the AD RMS cluster in the Internal Address box, and then click Validate. If you want to change the default port on which AD RMS communicates, you can do that on this page of the wizard as well. If validation succeeds, the Next button will become active. Click Next.

19. Select the Choose an existing certificate for SSL encryption option, click the appropriate certificate or click Import to import the certificate, and then click Next. Self-signed certificates should only be used for test environments. In a production environment, we strongly recommend using an SSL certificate issued from a certification authority, such as Verisign.

20. Type a name that will help you identify the AD RMS cluster in the Friendly name box, and then click Next.

21. Ensure that the Register the AD RMS service connection point now option is selected, and then click Next to register the AD RMS service connection point (SCP) in Active Directory Domain Services (AD DS). In order to register the AD RMS SCP, you must be logged on to the AD RMS server with a user account with write access to the Services container in AD DS.

22. Read the Introduction to Web Server (IIS) page and then click Next.

23. Click Next again, leaving the Web server defaults.

24. Click Install to provision AD RMS on the computer. It can take up to 60 minutes to complete the installation.

25. Click Finish.

26. Log off from the server, and then log back on to update the permissions granted to the logged-on user account. The user account that is logged on when the AD RMS server role is provisioned is automatically made a member of the AD RMS Enterprise Administrators group. A user must be a member of that group to administer AD RMS.

Any user that has a system of rights account certificates can access and work with protected information from an AD RMS-enabled application, including assigning usage rights and conditions to any data files created with the rights-enabled application. When a user accesses the protected data file, a request is sent to the AD RMS licensing service. AD RMS then issues a usage license that provides access according to what was assigned by the creator of the file.

There are three types of administrative roles included with AD RMS. They are:

- AD RMS Enterprise Administrators—Members of this group can manage all AD RMS policies and settings. By default, the local Administrators group is added to this group.
- AD RMS Template Administrators—Members of this group can manage rights policy templates.
- AD RMS Auditors—Members of this group can manage audit logs and reports.

Use of these roles enables you to delegate management tasks without granting complete administrative control over the entire AD RMS cluster.

Rights policy templates are used to control the rights that a user or group has on a particular piece of rights-protected content. AD RMS stores rights policy templates in the configuration database. Optionally, it maintains a copy of all rights policy templates in a shared folder that you specify.

When publishing protected content, the author selects the rights policy template to apply from the templates that are available on the local computer. To make rights policy templates available to use for offline publishing, the administrator must deploy them to user computers from a shared folder.

The AD RMS rights include the following:

- Full control—If this right is granted, a user can exercise all rights in the license, whether or not the rights are specifically granted to that user.
- View—If this right is granted, the AD RMS client allows protected content to be decrypted. Typically, when this right is granted, the application will allow the user to view protected content.
- Edit—If this right is granted, the AD RMS client allows protected content to be decrypted and then re-encrypted using the same content key. Typically, when this right is granted, the application will allow the user to change protected content and then save it to the same file. This right is effectively identical to the Save right.

- Save—If this right is granted, the AD RMS client allows protected content to be decrypted and then re-encrypted using the same content key. Typically, when this right is granted, the application will allow the user to change protected content and then save it to the same file. This right is effectively identical to the Edit right.

- Export (Save As)—If this right is granted, the AD RMS client allows protected content to be decrypted and then re-encrypted using the same content key. Typically, when this right is granted, the application will allow the user to use the "Save As" feature to save protected content to a new file.

- Print—Typically, when this right is granted, the application will allow the user to print protected content.

- Forward—Typically, when this right is granted, the application will allow an e-mail recipient to forward a protected message.

- Reply—Typically, when this right is granted, the application will allow an e-mail recipient to reply to a protected message and include a copy of the original message.

- Reply All—Typically, when this right is granted, the application will allow an e-mail recipient to reply to all recipients of a protected message and include a copy of the original message.

- Extract—Typically, when this right is granted, the application will allow the user to copy and paste information from protected content.

- Allow Macros—Typically, when this right is granted, the application will allow the user to run macros in the document or use an editor to modify macros in the document.

- View Rights—If this right is granted, the AD RMS client allows a user to view the user rights that are assigned by the license.

- Edit Rights—If this right is granted, the AD RMS client allows a user to edit the user rights that are assigned by the license.

SKILL SUMMARY

IN THIS LESSON YOU LEARNED:

- Data is the most important thing on the computer. Without data, most of your local and network applications will not function. In addition, when data is not available, users are inconvenienced and might not be able to do their jobs.

- File services are among the most basic and most critical services that a Windows Server 2008 network delivers.

- Redundant arrays of inexpensive disks (RAID) use two or more drives in combination to create a fault-tolerance system to protect against physical hard-drive failure and to increase hard-drive performance.

- A common RAID configuration used in networked PCs and servers is RAID 1, known as disk mirroring. Disk mirroring copies a disk or partition onto a second hard drive. Information is written to both hard drives simultaneously.

- Another common RAID is RAID 5, which is similar to striping except that one of the hard drives is used for parity (error correction) to provide fault tolerance.

- RAID 1+0 is a mirrored data set (RAID 1) that is then striped (RAID 0). A RAID 1+0 array requires a minimum of four drives—two mirrored drives to hold half of the striped data, plus another two mirrored for the other half of the data.

(continued)

SKILL SUMMARY *(continued)*

- RAID 0+1 is a stripped data set (RAID 0) that is then mirrored (RAID 1). Similar to RAID 1+0, RAID 0+1 requires a minimum of four drives: two to hold the striped data, plus another two to mirror the first pair.

- Hot spares is a fault-tolerance technique that combines hot spare drives with RAID. When a drive fails, the system automatically grabs the hot spare drive, replaces the failed drive, and rebuilds or restores the missing data.

- Network-attached storage (NAS) is a file-level data storage device that is connected to a computer network to provide shared drives or folders, usually using SMB.

- A storage area network (SAN) is an architecture used for disk arrays, tape libraries, and optical jukeboxes to appear as locally attached drives on a server. SANs always use some form of RAID and other technology to make the system redundant against drive failure and to offer high performance.

- When you share a folder in Windows, you are usually using SMB, also known as Common Internet File System (CIFS).

- To access a shared folder, you use the universal naming convention (UNC) based on the \\servername\sharedname format.

- You should always choose NTFS over FAT or FAT32. NTFS is superior in every way: it accommodates much larger volumes, provides better security using NTFS permissions and encryption, and is more resistant to corruption.

- When planning file services, you need to look at the following business requirements: high availability, geographic distribution, and file-storage management.

- SMB2 was designed to increase performance by compounding multiple actions into a single request, significantly reducing the number of round trips the client needs to make. In addition, SMB2 supports larger buffer sizes, which can provide better performance with large file transfers and better use of faster networks.

- Access-based enumeration is the Windows technique by which, when you access a shared folder, only those files for which you have permissions are listed.

- Distributed File System (DFS) is a set of client and server services that allows a company using Microsoft Windows server to organize SMB file shares into a distributed file system. It can also provide replication between file servers.

- DFS namespace allows you to take multiple file shares based on SMB and combine them into one logical network path. In other words, it allows you to create a shared folder containing other shared folders.

- DFS replication copies files between shared folders. DFS replication improved on FRS by copying only those parts of files that have changed (remote differential compression). It also used data compression and allowed the administrator to schedule when replication occurs.

- Microsoft SharePoint is a family of software products for collaboration, file sharing, and web publishing. While it is not intended to replace file sharing, SharePoint can be valuable to any company. SharePoint server farms can host Web sites, portals, intranets, extranets, Internets, web content management systems, search engines, wikis, blogs, and social networking, as well as providing a framework for web application development.

- Encrypting File System (EFS) is a core file encryption technology used to store encrypted files on NTFS file system volumes.

- Unlike EFS, BitLocker allows you to encrypt entire disks. Therefore, if a drive or laptop is stolen, the data is still encrypted even if the thief installs it on another system on which he or she is an administrator.

- BitLocker To Go is a new feature in Windows 7 that enables users to encrypt removable USB devices, such as flash drives and external hard disks.

- By using Active Directory Rights Management Services (AD RMS) and the AD RMS client, you can protect information through a usage policy that remains with the information, no matter where it is moved.

- When using AD RMS, data files and emails can be encrypted. The Active Directory Rights Management Services server role handles certificates and licensing.

- Rights policy templates are used to control the rights that a user or group has on a particular piece of rights-protected content.

■ Knowledge Assessment

Fill in the Blank

Complete the following sentences by writing the correct word or words in the blanks provided.

1. To protect against disk failure, you should use _____.

2. _____ is also known as striping with parity.

3. For the best combination of fault tolerance and performance, you should use _____.

4. _____ provides file and print sharing in Windows.

5. Multiple servers can connect to SAN by assigning a _____ to each server.

6. To provide a copy of a shared folder to another server, you should use _____.

7. _____ allows you to take multiple file shared based on SMB and combine them into one logical network path.

8. To encrypt the entire C drive, you should use _____.

9. To encrypt a document within SharePoint, you should use _____.

10. For the best form of redundancy and performance, you should use _____.

True / False

Circle T if the statement is true or F if the statement is false.

T | F 1. For the most scalability, performance and redundancy, you should use a SAN to provide storage for your servers.

T | F 2. SMB2 will list only those files to which a user has permissions.

T | F 3. When you create a new domain based on Windows Server 2008, SYSVOL is replicated using FRS.

T | F 4. To quickly define disk quotas, you should use the DFS Manager.

T | F 5. To encrypt individual files and folders, you should use EFS.

T | F **6.** To control the rights that a user or group has on a document protected with AD RMS, you should use rights policy templates.

T | F **7.** SharePoint is accessed primarily with Windows Explorer.

T | F **8.** To encrypt traffic sent to and from a SharePoint site, you should use SSL.

T | F **9.** To protect against hard drive failure, you should use a form of RAID.

T | F **10.** RAID 0 offers redundancy if a drive fails.

Review Questions

1. If WSS 3.0 and SharePoint Foundation 2010 are free, why would you consider purchasing Microsoft Office SharePoint Server 2007 or SharePoint 2010? Hint: You may need to use a search engine to identify a more detailed answer.

2. You have a domain controller located at a remote site. You worry that someone will steal the hard drive, take it home, install it on a system, and decipher all of the passwords on the hard drive. What can you do to protect the hard drive?

■ Case Scenarios

Scenario 9-1: Accessing Files Overseas

You work for a corporation that has one large office in New York and another office in London. You created a shared folder on a New York Windows Server 2008 file server to hold project files that need to be used by members from both offices. However, the users in London sometimes have to wait a couple of minutes to open a larger file. What can you do to alleviate this problem?

Scenario 9-2: Protecting Documents

You have a shared folder in which the sales team keeps bid documents. It is important that these documents not get into the hands of a competitor. What can you do to ensure that they are protected?

Virtualizing Applications and Servers

OBJECTIVE DOMAIN MATRIX

TECHNOLOGY SKILL	OBJECTIVE DOMAIN MATRIX	OBJECTIVE DOMAIN NUMBER
Understanding Server Virtualization	Design the operating system virtualization strategy.	4.3
Virtualizing Applications Using App-V	Plan for application delivery.	1.3

KEY TERMS

Cluster-node connectivity fault tolerance
Cluster Shared Volumes (CSV)
Hyper-V
Hypervisor
integration services

Microsoft Application Virtualization (App-V)
partition
physical-to-virtual (P2V) conversion
snapshot

System Center Virtual Machine Manager (SCVMM)
virtual instance
virtualization
virtual machines (VMS)
Virtual Server 2005 R2

■ Understanding Server Virtualization

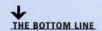

THE BOTTOM LINE

Server *virtualization* is the process of deploying and maintaining multiple instances of an operating system, called *virtual machines (VMs)*, on a single computer. Virtualization has become quite popular during the last few years. By using virtual machine technology, you can run multiple operating systems concurrently on a single machine, which allows separation of services while minimizing cost. It can also be used to create a Windows test environment in a safe, self-contained environment. Microsoft *Hyper-V* is a hypervisor-based virtualization system for x64 computers starting with Windows Server 2008. The *hypervisor* is installed between the hardware and the operating system and is the main component that manages the virtual computers.

CERTIFICATION READY
What are the advantages of Hyper-V over Virtual Server 2005 R2?
4.3

To run several virtual machines on a single computer, you need sufficient processing power and memory to handle the load. However, since most servers often sit idle, virtualization utilizes the server's hardware more efficiently. To keep each virtual server secure and reliable, each virtual server is placed in its own partition. A *partition* as it relates to virtual servers is a logical collection of isolated system resources in which an operating system executes. Each virtual machine accesses the hypervisor, which handles interrupts to the processor and redirects them to the respective partition.

Looking at Virtual Server 2005 R2

Over the last several years, Microsoft has introduced several software packages that allow a Windows system to host multiple virtual systems. *Virtual Server 2005 R2* SP1 is a product that you can download and install free from Microsoft's Web site.

You can install Windows Server 2005 R2 on Windows Server 2003 (Standard, Enterprise, and Datacenter editions), Windows XP, and Windows Vista. Host machines running under Virtual Server 2005 R2 include the following 32-bit operating systems:

- Microsoft Windows Server 2003 (Web, Standard, Enterprise, and Datacenter Edition)
- Microsoft Windows Server 2003 R2 (Web, Standard, Enterprise, and Datacenter Edition)
- Microsoft Windows Small Business Server 2003, Standard Edition
- Microsoft Windows Small Business Server 2003, Premium Edition
- Microsoft Windows 2000 Server and Advanced Server
- Microsoft Windows NT Server 4.0 with Service Pack 6a (SP6a)
- Microsoft Windows XP Professional Service Pack 2 (SP2)
- Red Hat Enterprise Linux 2.1 update 6, 3.0 update 6, and 4.0
- Red Hat Linux 7.3
- Red Hat Linux 9.0
- SUSE Linux Enterprise Server 9.0
- SUSE Linux 9.2, 9.3 and 10.0.
- Solaris 10

Virtual Server 2005 R2 SP1 has the following specifications:

- Supports up to 64 x86 hosts and 512 x64 hosts.
- You cannot host x64 virtual machines even if you are running on a 64-bit operating system.
- Supports up to 256 GB of memory and 32 processors.
- Each Guest VM can support up to 3.6 GB of RAM and a single virtual processor.
- Each Guest VM can support up to 4 virtual NICs.
- Each Guest VM can support up to 4 IDE or 28 SCSI virtual drives.
- Virtual Server 2005 R2 SP1 does not support symmetric multiprocessing (SMP) in the VM environment.

Virtual Server 2005 R2 provides a web-based management interface that allows configuration and management of a Virtual Server host and virtual machines.

While Hyper-V is a more robust virtual host server, there are some situations in which you may choose to use Virtual Server 2005 R2. Since Windows Server 2008 R2 and Hyper-V only run on 64-bit systems, you cannot use install Hyper-V on Windows Server 2003.

Looking at the Windows Server 2008 R2 Hyper-V Role

> While Microsoft designed Hyper-V to be a role included with the Windows Server 2008 operating system, Hyper-V was not included in the initial Windows Server 2008 release. Instead, Microsoft provides it as a separate download that adds the Hyper-V role to the operating system.

Windows Server 2008 R2 Hyper-V adds new features to the first version of Hyper-V, including:

- Live migration allows you to move a virtual machine between two virtualization host servers without any interruption of service.

- Increased hardware support for Hyper-V virtual machines including supporting up to 64 logical processors in the host processor pool. Also new, Hyper-V processor compatibility mode for live migration allows migration across different CPU versions within the same processor family (for example, "Intel Core 2-to-Intel Pentium 4" or "AMD Opteron-to-AMD Athlon"), enabling migration across a broader range of server host hardware.

- With Windows Server 2008 R2, Hyper-V uses Cluster Shared Volumes (CSV) storage to simplify and enhance shared storage usage. CSV enables multiple Windows Servers to access SAN storage using a single consistent namespace for all volumes on all hosts. Multiple hosts can access the same Logical Unit Number (LUN) on SAN storage.

- Improved ***cluster-node connectivity fault tolerance*** whereas another cluster node can replace a failed cluster node.

- Increased performance and reduced power consumption.

- Windows Server 2008 R2 has new networking features, including:
  - Support for Jumbo frames (up to 9014 bytes).
  - TCP Chimney, which allows offloading TCP/IP processing to the network hardware.
  - Virtual Machine Queue (VMQ) feature, which allows physical computer network interface cards (NICs) to use direct memory access (DMA) to place the contents of packets directly into VM memory, increasing I/O performance.

- Windows Server 2008 R2 Hyper-V supports hot plug-in and hot removal of storage.

- Broad support for simultaneously running different types of operating systems, including 32-bit and 64-bit systems across different server platforms, such as Windows, Linux, and others.

- Hyper-V includes new virtual switch capabilities. This means that virtual machines can be easily configured to run with Windows Network Load Balancing (NLB) Service to balance the load across virtual machines on different servers.

- With the new virtual service provider/virtual service client (VSP/VSC) architecture, Hyper-V provides improved access to and utilization of core resources, such as disk, networking, and video.

- Hyper-V provides the ability to take snapshots of a running virtual machine so you can easily revert to a previous state and thus improve the overall backup and recovery solution.

Hyper-V role supports the following operating systems:

- Windows Server 2008 R2 (VMs configured with 1,.2, or 4 virtual processors)
- Windows Server 2008 x64 Edition (VMs configured with 1,.2, or 4 virtual processors)
- Windows Server 2008 x86 (VMs configured with 1,.2, or 4 virtual processors)
- Windows Server 2003 x86 (VMs configured with 1,.2, or 4 virtual processors)
- Windows Server 2003 R2 x86 (VMs configured with 1 or 2 virtual processors)
- Windows Server 2003 R2 x64 with SP2 (VMs configured with 1 or 2 virtual processors)

- Windows Server 2003 x64 Edition with SP2 (VMs configured with 1 or 2 virtual processors)
- SUSE Linux Enterprise Server 10 with Service Pack 3 (x86 Edition or x64 Edition) (VMs configured with 1, 2, or 4 virtual processors)
- SUSE Linux Enterprise Server 11 (x86 Edition or x64 Edition) (VM configured with 1, 2, or 4 virtual processor)
- Red Hat Enterprise Linux (RHEL) 5.2, 5.3, 5.4 and 5.5 (x86 Edition or x64 Edition) (VMs configured with 1, 2, or 4 virtual processor)
- Windows 7 Professional, Enterprise, and Ultimate Edition x86 (VM configured with 1, 2, or 4 virtual processors)
- Windows 7 Professional, Enterprise, and Ultimate Edition x64 (VM configured with 1, 2, or 4 virtual processors)
- Windows Vista Business, Enterprise, and Ultimate x86 with SP1 (VM configured with 1 or 2 virtual processors)
- Windows Vista x64 Business, Enterprise, and Ultimate Edition with SP1 (VM configured with 1 or 2 virtual processors)

In addition to the specialized hardware requirements for Hyper-V, Microsoft has added a licensing requirement. For licensing purposes, Microsoft refers to each virtual machine that you create on a Hyper-V server as a ***virtual instance***. Each Windows Server 2008 version includes a set number of virtual instances; you must purchase licenses to create additional ones. Table 10-1 lists the Windows Server 2008 versions and the number of virtual instances included with each one.

Table 10-1

Windows Server 2008 Versions and Their Hyper-V Support.

OPERATING SYSTEM VERSION	NUMBER OF VIRTUAL INSTANCES INCLUDED
Windows Server 2008 Standard	1
Windows Server 2008 Enterprise	4
Windows Server 2008 Datacenter	Unlimited

Looking at Hyper-V Server 2008 R2

In addition to Hyper-V, which runs on top of Windows Server 2008 and Windows Server 2008 R2, Microsoft has also released Microsoft Hyper-V Server 2008 R2, which is a stand-alone product. To keep a small footprint and minimal overhead, Hyper-V Server contains only the Windows Hypervisor, Windows Server driver model, and virtualization components.

Hyper-V Server virtual machines provide:

- 32-bit (x86) and 64-bit (x64) virtual machines.
- Hyper-V Server 2008 R2 supports systems with up to 64 logical processors on the physical machine.
- Up to four virtual processors per virtual machine.
- Total memory of all running virtual machines supported up to 1 TB.
- Microsoft Hyper-V Server 2008 R2 can run up to 384 virtual machines or as many as will fit within 1 TB of memory, whichever comes first.

The key features in Microsoft Hyper-V Server 2008 R2 are:

- Live migration—Customers can dynamically move virtual machines from one physical machine to another with no downtime. Live migration is supported on up to 16 node failover clusters.
- Host clustering and Cluster Shared Volume (CSV) Support.
- Processor Compatibility Mode for live migration-allows live migration across different CPU versions within the same processor family, (e.g. "Intel Core 2-to-Intel Pentium 4" or "AMD Opteron-to-AMD Athlon") enabling migration across a broader range of Hyper-V host hardware.

You will usually manage Hyper-V Server remotely, using the Hyper-V Manager MMC or the System Center Virtual Machine Manager 2008 R2. However, Hyper-V Server includes a minimal, easy-to-use command-line-based UI for system configuration. This allows a user easily to configure system settings such as:

- Changing the computer name
- Joining the server to a domain
- Configuring DHCP/Static IP Address Settings
- Enabling Remote Desktop
- Enabling Failover Clustering
- Configuring Remote Administration settings

■ Using the Windows Server 2008 R2 Hyper-V Role

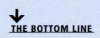
THE BOTTOM LINE

After you have the appropriate hardware and the required licenses, you can add the Hyper-V role using Server Manager. Microsoft recommends that you do not install other roles with Hyper-V. Adding the role installs the hypervisor software as well as the management interface, which takes the form of a Microsoft Management Console (MMC) snap-in called Hyper-V Manager. The Hyper-V Manager MMC snap-in provides administrators with a list of all virtual machines registered on a Windows Server 2008 system and enables them to perform actions on both the Hyper-V server and its virtual machines.

Installing Hyper-V

To install Hyper-V, you need the following:

TAKE NOTE*

In future versions of Windows, virtualization may not require hardware-assisted virtualization technology.

- An x64 (but not Itanium) version of Windows Server 2008 or Windows Server 2008 R2.
- 64-bit processors and BIOS that support hardware-assisted virtualization (Intel VT or AMD-V) technology.
- Hardware Data Execution Prevention (DEP), which Intel describes as eXecuted Disable (XD) and AMD describes as No eXecute (NS), is a technology used in CPUs to segregate areas of memory for storage of either processor instructions or data.

 INSTALL HYPER-V ROLE

GET READY. To use Hyper-V, you must first add the Hyper-V role by doing the following on a server running Windows Server 2008 R2:

1. Click Start, and then click Server Manager.
2. In the Roles Summary area of the Server Manager main window, click Add Roles.

3. On the Select Server Roles page, click Hyper-V.

4. On the Create Virtual Networks page, click one or more network adapters if you want to make their network connection available to virtual machines.

5. On the Confirm Installation Selections page, click Install.

6. The computer must be restarted to complete the installation. Click Close to finish the wizard, and then click Yes to restart the computer.

7. After you restart the computer, log on with the same account you used to install the role. After the Resume Configuration Wizard completes the installation, click Close to finish the wizard.

Creating Virtual Machines

After installing Hyper-V, you are ready to create some virtual machines and install the operating system on each virtual machine that you create.

Using Hyper-V, Manager, you can create new virtual machines and define the hardware resources that the system should allocate to them. In the settings for a particular virtual machine, depending on the physical hardware available in the computer and the limitations of the guest operating system, administrators can specify the number of processors and the amount of memory a virtual machine should use, install virtual network adapters, and create virtual disks using a variety of technologies, including storage-area networks (SANs).

By default, Hyper-V stores all the files that make up a virtual machine in one folder with the same name as the virtual server for simple management and portability. Renaming a virtual machine does not rename the virtual machine folder. By default, these folders are located in the Shared Virtual Machines folder, which is located in Documents and Settings\All Users\ Documents\Shared Virtual Machines.

Each virtual machine uses the following files:

- A virtual machine configuration (.vmc) file in XML format that contains the virtual machine configuration information, including all settings for the virtual machine.

- One or more virtual hard disk (.vhd) files to store the guest operating system, applications, and data for the virtual machine. So if you create a 12-GB partition for the virtual machine's hard drive, the virtual hard disk file will be 12 GB.

In addition, a virtual machine may also use a saved-state (.vsv) file, if the machine has been placed into a saved state.

 CREATE VIRTUAL MACHINES IN HYPER-V

GET READY. To create and set up a virtual machine:

1. Open Hyper-V Manager from the Administrative Tools. See Figure 10-1.

Figure 10-1

Hyper-V Manager

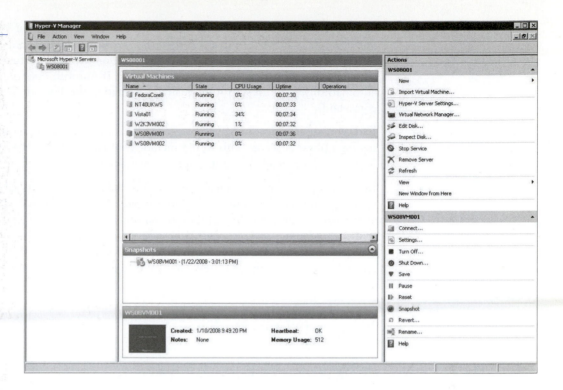

2. From the Action pane, click New, and then click Virtual Machine.

3. From the New Virtual Machine Wizard, click Next.

4. When it asks for the name and location, type the name of the virtual machine. Click the Next button.

5. When it asks how much memory to use, specify enough memory for the guest operating system to run efficiently. Click the Next button.

6. When it asks for the networking settings, select an existing virtual network if you want to establish network connectivity. Click the Next button.

7. When it asks to connect a virtual hard disk, specify the name, location, and size of a virtual hard disk. Click the Next button.

8. When the Installation Options page appears, choose one of the following options to install the operating system:

   - Install an operating system from a boot CD/DVD-ROM. You can use either a CD/DVD or an image file (.iso file).

   - Install an operating system from a boot floppy disk.

   - Install an operating system from a network-based installation server.

9. When the wizard is complete, click Finish.

 INSTALL THE OPERATING SYSTEM ON A VIRTUAL MACHINE

GET READY. To install the operating system:

1. From the Virtual Machines section of the results pane, right-click the name of the virtual machine you just created and click Connect. The Virtual Machine Connection tool will open.

2. From the Action menu in the Virtual Machine Connection window, click Start.

3. Proceed through the installation.

Some of the Windows built-in drivers do not run efficiently under a virtual environment For Hyper-V, you need to install *integration services*, which includes some basic drivers. To install the integration components, open the Action menu of Virtual Machine Connection and click Insert Integration Services Setup Disk. If Autorun does not start the installation automatically, you can start it manually by executing the %windir%\support\amd64\setup.exe command.

Last, you are then ready to configure and manage the virtual server just as if you were working on a physical server. This would include configuring the IP configuration, enabling remote desktop, loading the appropriate roles and features, installing software, and so on.

In many organizations, you may want to consolidate several physical servers to one machine running multiple virtual servers. Microsoft System Center Virtual Machine Manager (VMM) allows you to convert existing physical computers into virtual machines through a process known as *physical-to-virtual (P2V) conversion*. VMM simplifies P2V by providing a task-based wizard to automate much of the conversion process. Since the P2V process is completely scriptable, you can initiate large-scale P2V conversions through the Windows PowerShell command line.

Managing Virtual Machines

When you work with physical servers, there may be times where you have to add a network card, add or expand a hard drive, or move a network card cable from one switch to another. While virtual servers have the same needs, you now need to perform these tasks virtually.

MANAGING DISKS

When you create virtual hard drives, you can define the virtual hard disks as:

- Fixed-size virtual hard disk—Takes up the full amount of disk space when created, even if no data is using parts of the hard disk.
- Dynamically expanding hard disk—Expands as it needs space up to its full size.

One of the strengths of virtual servers is the ability to take snapshots. A *snapshot* is a point-in-time image of a virtual machine that you can return to. Say you are making a change to the system, such as loading a component or installing an update. If the change causes problems, you can quickly revert back to the snapshot before the change was made.

The snapshot files consist of the following:

- A copy of the VM configuration .xml file
- Any saved state files
- A differencing disk (.avhd) that is the new working disk for all writes and is the child of the working disk prior to the snapshot

With Hyper-V, you can create 10 levels of snapshot per virtual server.

To create a snapshot in Hyper-V, you select Snapshot from the Action menu or panel or click on the Snapshot button in the toolbar. When you create a snapshot, a dialog box will appear for you to enter a name for the snapshot. If you want, you can dismiss this dialog and have the snapshot use an auto-generated name. This auto-generated name will consist of the name of the virtual machine followed by the date and time when the snapshot was taken. See Figure 10-2.

Figure 10-2

Snapshots

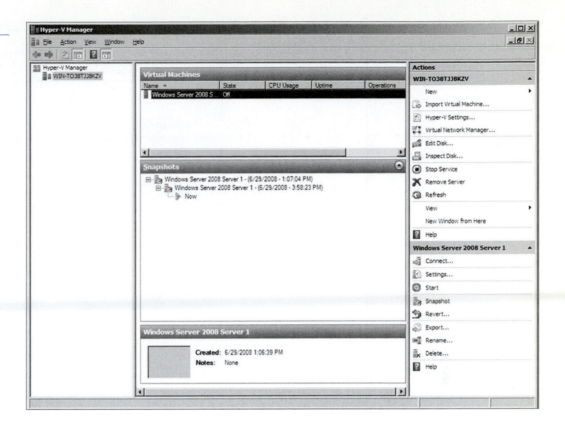

MANAGING VIRTUAL NETWORKS AND NETWORK CARDS

Virtual network consists of one or more virtual machines configured to either access internal network resources or external network resources. When the virtual network is configured to use external network resources, you would share the network adapter in the physical computer. If you decide not to configure the virtual machines to use the physical adapters, you can still configure the virtual machines to communicate with each other via the virtual network. Last, you can configure the virtual machines not to use a network adapter, which would cause the virtual machine to be completely isolated from other internal virtual machines.

 ADD A VIRTUAL NETWORK

GET READY. To add a virtual network:

1. Open Hyper-V Manager from the Administrative Tools.
2. Click Virtual Network Manager from the Actions menu. See Figure 10-3.

Figure 10-3

Virtual Network Manager

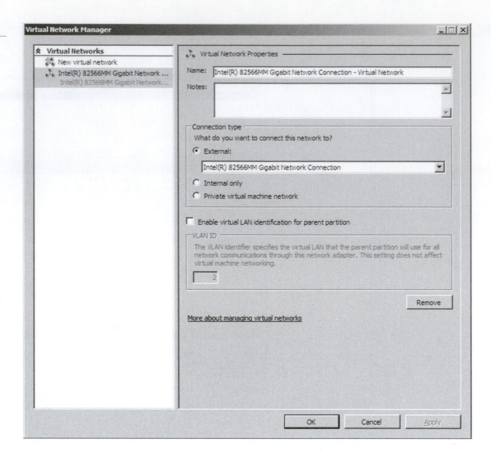

3. In the Create virtual network section, select the type of network you want to create.

4. Click Add to open the New Virtual Network page.

5. Type a name for the new network. Review the other properties and modify them if necessary.

6. Click OK to Apply to save the changes.

 MODIFY A VIRTUAL NETWORK

GET READY. To modify a virtual network:

1. Open Hyper-V Manager from Administrative Tools.

2. Click Virtual Network Manager from the Actions menu.

3. Click the name of the network you want to modify in the Virtual Networks section.

4. Edit the appropriate properties to modify the virtual network under the Virtual Network Properties section.

5. Click OK or Apply to save the changes.

REMOVE A VIRTUAL NETWORK

GET READY. To remove a virtual network:

1. Open Hyper-V Manager from the Administrative Tools.

2. Click Virtual Network Manager from the Action menu.

3. Click the name of the network you want to remove under Virtual Networks.

4. Click Remove from under Virtual Network Properties.

5. Click OK or Apply to save the changes.

 ADD A NETWORK ADAPTER

GET READY. To add a network adapter:

1. Open Hyper-V Manager from the Administrative Tools.

2. Under Virtual Machines, select the virtual machine that you want to configure.

3. Click Settings in the Action pane for the virtual machine name that you selected.

4. Click Add Hardware in the navigation pane.

5. Choose a network adapter or a legacy network adapter.

6. Click Add to open the adapter page.

7. Select the virtual network you want to connect to.

8. If desired, specify a static MAC address or virtual LAN identifier.

9. Click OK.

> ⊕ **MORE INFORMATION**
> For more information about Hyper-V, visit the following website: http://technet.microsoft.com/en-us/virtualization/default.aspx.

System Center Virtual Machine Manager

If you have a large number of VMs to manage, you should use *System Center Virtual Machine Manager (SCVMM)*. Virtual Machine Manager 2008 R2 helps enable centralized management of physical and virtual IT infrastructure, increased server utilization, and dynamic resource optimization across multiple virtualization platforms. It includes end-to-end capabilities such as planning, deploying, managing, and optimizing the virtual infrastructure.

System Center Virtual Machine Manager provides the following benefits:

- Centrally creates and manages virtual machines across the entire datacenter.
- Easily consolidates multiple physical servers onto virtual hosts.
- Rapidly provisions and optimizes new and existing virtual machines.
- Migrates servers from physical to virtual without any downtime.
- Its Performance and Resource Optimization (PRO) enables the dynamic management of virtual resources through management packs.
- When connected to a Fibre Channel SAN environment, moves virtualized servers from one Hyper-V host to another.
- Delegates permissions so that non-administrative users are able to create and manage their own VMs.

See Figure 10-4.

Figure 10-4

Virtual Machine Manager

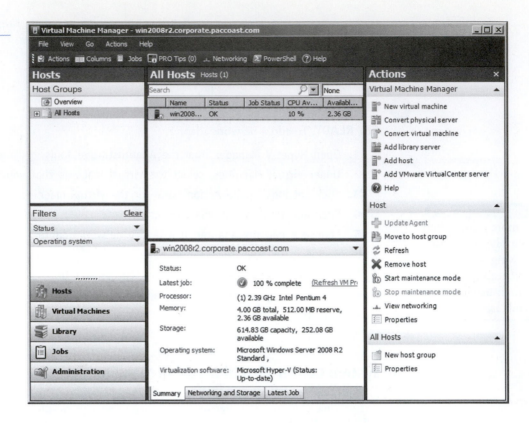

SCVMM can be installed on one server or several servers. SCVMM users the following components:

- SCVMM server—The server which the SCVMM software is installed.
- SCVMM agent—The software component that allows the server to manage the virtual hosts running Virtual Server 2005 R2 or Hyper-V. It is also used on the SCVMM library servers.
- SCVMM database—A SQL server to store VM configuration information.
- SCVMM Administrator console—The SCVMM administrator console installed on a server or administrator workstation to manage SVVMM remotely or directly.
- SCVMM self-service portal—A portal that allows non-administrators to manage VMs to which they have been delegated permission.
- SCVMM library server—A catalog of resources that are used to create VMs using SCM, including ISO images, scripts, hardware profiles, VM templates, virtual hard disks, and stored VMs.

Designing an Operating System Virtualization Strategy

After you have a bit of experience with virtual servers, it is easy to see all the advantages of using virtual machines. First, you can take many physical servers and shrink them to a handful of virtual hosting machines. As a result, you can use a smaller datacenter and the power and cooling requirements for the datacenter are significantly reduced. Since you can take snapshots and roll back if things don't go as planned, virtualization is great for testing changes to the system and rolling out patches. Virtualization is also great for creating a testing environment and for quickly creating temporary servers as needed.

When looking at costs, you need to look at the whole picture to determine if it is cost effective to virtualize your servers. For example, while the Windows Server 2008 Enterprise license is more expensive than a Windows Server 2008 Standard license, the Windows Server 2008 Enterprise license includes licenses for four hosted virtual instances. And don't forget that the Windows Server 2008 Datacenter, x64-bit version, has unlimited licenses for virtual hosts.

You should not virtualize all servers. For example, if servers that have high I/O requirements or high processor requirements require the same level of resources to perform as VMs, then there's no point in virtualizing them at all.

PLANNING FOR SERVER CONSOLIDATION

To help plan for server consolidation, you have the following tools:

- System Center Operations Manager
- Virtual Server Migration Toolkit
- System Center Virtual Machine Manager

To help you decide which servers you should virtualize, you can run the System Center Operations Manager (SCOM) to generate a virtualization candidate report listing the servers that should be virtualized, based on current usage levels.

The Virtual Server Migration Toolkit (VSMT) is useful in virtualizing a small number of servers. While this tool was made for Virtual Server 2005, it is compatible with Hyper-V. VSMT is a command-line-based kit that uses XML files to store configuration data used by the migration process. Unfortunately, using VSMT to migrate a virtual server requires downtime.

SVCMM includes capacity-planning technology that allows you to assign virtual machines to the virtual hosts in your environment with the appropriate available resources to support them, based on VM performance data. It also has tools designed to make the most efficient use of your VM and virtual host infrastructure.

PLANNING FOR SERVER FAULT TOLERANCE

A hosting server will run multiple virtual machines. So when a hosting server goes down, it can be more detrimental than a single server going down. Therefore, for many of these systems, you will need to provide the highest possible availability for systems and applications.

Hyper-V in Windows Server 2008 R2 includes a Live Migration feature that allows you to move a virtual machine between two virtualization host servers without any interruption of service. The users connected to the virtual machine might notice only a slight performance slowdown for a few moments. Otherwise, they will be unaware that you moved the virtual machine from one physical computer to another.

With Windows Server 2008 R2, Hyper-V uses *Cluster Shared Volumes (CSV)* storage as part of the Windows Failover Clustering feature. CSV enables multiple Windows Servers to access SAN storage using a single consistent namespace for all volumes on all hosts. Multiple hosts can access the same Logical Unit Number (LUN) on SAN storage. CSV enables faster live migration and easier storage management for Hyper-V when used in a cluster configuration. Taking it one step further, the CSV architecture implements a mechanism, known as dynamic I/O redirection, by which I/O can be rerouted within the failover cluster based on connection availability.

■ Virtualizing Applications Using App-V

 THE BOTTOM LINE

Hyper-V and Virtual Server both virtualize entire operating systems, but it is also possible to virtualize individual applications.

CERTIFICATION READY
How do you plan for
application delivery?
1.3

When you virtualize an operating system, you create a separate partitioned space with virtual resources that appear just like physical ones to users and applications. You can run as many applications as you need on a single virtual machine, depending on the resources available to it. Virtualizing an application is roughly the same thing, except that you are allocating a set of virtual resources to a single application.

In Lesson 6, we saw the RemoteApp Terminal Services feature, which enables clients to run terminal server applications within an individual window. While the window is resizable and has a standard system menu and title bar, it is an application that is running on another computer. If the client computer fails, the remote application will remain running, since it is on a remote host. If a terminal session fails on the remote host for another client, the other sessions continue to run because each session has its own memory and hardware resources.

Microsoft Application Virtualization (known as *App-V*, formerly Microsoft SoftGrid) creates a customized virtualized environment for an application that you can deploy to clients from a server, much as you do with RemoteApp applications using terminal servers. The main difference between the two is that the server actually transfers the virtual environment to the client, enabling the client to run the application using its own hardware, without needing to perform an application installation. With App-V, desktop and network users can reduce application installation time and eliminate potential conflicts between applications.

The App-V system architecture is composed of the following components:

- Virtual Application Server—Also known as Microsoft Systems Center Virtual Application Server or App-V Application Server. It hosts virtualized application packages and streams them to the client computers for local execution. It also authorizes requesting clients and logs their application usage. Applications are converted to virtualized packages using the App-V Sequencer.

- App-V Client—Also known as Microsoft Application Virtualization Client for Windows Desktops of Microsoft Desktop Optimization Pack (MDOP)) or Microsoft Application Virtualization Client for Remote Session Hosts (such as Terminal Services). It is the client-side runtime that requests the application server to stream an application, receives the streamed virtual application packages, sets up the runtime environment, and executes the application locally.

- App-V Management Console—The management console to set up, administer, and manage App-V servers. It can also be used to create, manage, update, and replicate virtualized application packages.

- App-V Sequencer—A tool for preparing applications for virtualization.

- App-V Datastore—Maintains application information in a SQL Server database.

When planning the deployment of App-V, since WAN links are generally too slow, you should ensure that each branch office has its own Virtual Application server.

SKILL SUMMARY

IN THIS LESSON YOU LEARNED:

- Virtualization is the process of deploying and maintaining multiple instances of an operating system, called virtual machines (VMs), on a single computer.

- Virtual Server 2005 R2 SP1 is a product that you can download and install free from Microsoft's Web site.

- You cannot install 64-bit operating systems on Virtual Server 2005 R2.

- A partition is a logical unit of isolation, in which operating systems execute.

- Microsoft Hyper-V is a hypervisor-based virtualization system for x64 computers starting with Windows Server 2008. The hypervisor is installed between the hardware and the operating system and is the main component that manages the virtual computers.

- For licensing purposes, Microsoft refers to each virtual machine that you create on a Hyper-V server as a virtual instance. Each Windows Server 2008 version includes a set number of virtual instances; you must purchase licenses to create additional ones.

- To keep a small footprint and minimal overhead, Hyper-V Server contains only the Windows Hypervisor, Windows Server driver model, and virtualization components.

- Live migration allows you to move a virtual machine between two virtualization host servers without any interruption of service.

- With Windows Server 2008 R2, Hyper-V uses Cluster Shared Volumes (CSV) storage to simplify and enhance shared storage usage.

- Hyper-V will only run on 64-bit machines. The system also needs to support hardware-assisted virtualization (Intel VT or AMD-V) technology and Hardware Data Execution Prevention (DEP).

- Some of the Windows built-in drivers do not run efficiently under a virtual environment. For Hyper-V, you need to install Integration Services, which includes some basic drivers.

- Microsoft System Center Virtual Machine Manager (VMM) allows you to convert existing physical computers into virtual machines through a process known as physical-to-virtual (P2V) conversion.

- A snapshot is a point-in-time image of a virtual machine that you can return to.

- A virtual network consists of one or more virtual machines configured to access local or external network resources.

- If you have a large number of VMs to manage, you should use System Center Virtual Machine Manager (SCVMM).

- Virtualization is great for server consolidation, testing changes to the system and rolling out patches, creating a testing environment, and quickly creating temporary servers as needed.

- SVCMM includes capacity-planning technology that allows you to assign virtual machines to the virtual hosts in your environment from the appropriate available resources to support them based on VM performance data.

- Microsoft Application Virtualization (known as App-V, formerly Microsoft SoftGrid) creates a customized virtualized environment for an application that you can deploy to clients from a server. App-V server actually transfers the virtual environment to the client, enabling the client to run the application using its own hardware, without the need to perform an application installation.

- When planning the deployment of App-V, since WAN links are generally too slow, you should ensure that each branch office has its own Virtual Application server.

Knowledge Assessment

Fill in the Blank

Complete the following sentences by writing the correct word or words in the blanks provided.

1. _____ is the process of deploying and maintaining multiple instances of an operating system on the same physical computer.

2. Microsoft's virtualization software that comes with Windows Server 2008 R2 is _____.

3. After you install Windows on a Hyper-V virtual machine, you should install _____ that include some basic drivers for Windows to perform better.

4. To convert a physical machine to a virtual machine, you will use the _____ wizard.

5. When you make a change to Windows running on a Hyper-V virtual machine, you should make a _____ in case you need to roll back.

6. To help you manage a large number of virtual machines, you should use _____.

7. To work with a cluster, Hyper-V uses _____.

8. _____ enables the client to run an application using its own hardware, without the need to perform an application installation.

9. In Hyper-V, hard drives used in virtual machines are stored in files with the _____ filename extension.

10. Hyper-V includes _____ that allow virtual machines to run with Windows Network Load Balancing (NLB) Service.

True / False

Circle T if the statement is true or F if the statement is false.

T F 1. Hyper-V will run on Windows Server 2003 R2 SP2, Windows Server 2008, and Windows Server 2008 R2.

T F 2. Live migration allows you to move a virtual machine between virtualization host servers without any interruption of service.

T F 3. Windows Server 2008 Enterprise includes licenses for four virtual instances.

T F 4. Hyper-V R2 Server requires Windows Server 2008 R2 Standard or Enterprise.edition.

T F 5. Hyper-V Server Role require x64 version of Windows, a 64-bit processor, and hardware-assisted virtualization.

T F 6. Microsoft Application Virtualization (App-V) was previously known as V-Remote.

T F 7. If you have a central office with a large data center and a large server with lots of RAM, you do not have to place Virtual Application Servers at each site.

T F 8. You can install Windows Server 2003 R2 x86 and x64 on Virtual Server 2005 R2 virtual machine.

T F 9. To manage Hyper-V, you would use the Hyper-V Manager or System Center Virtual machine Manager.

T F 10. You should not migrate machines that have high processor or I/O utilization.

Review Questions

1. Explain the difference between the virtualization used in products such as Microsoft Virtual Server 2005 and that used in Windows Server 2008's Hyper-V.

2. What are the differences between RemoteApp and App-V?

Case Scenario

Scenario 10-1: Isolating Server Applications

You have a network accounting application and a network sales application, neither of which is processor hungry. Both of these applications must be kept totally isolated. Both applications will access a centralized database server. What do you recommend?

LESSON 11

Securing Infrastructure Services

OBJECTIVE DOMAIN MATRIX

TECHNOLOGY SKILL	OBJECTIVE DOMAIN	OBJECTIVE DOMAIN NUMBER
Designing a Public Key Infrastructure	Design and implement public key infrastructure.	3.3

KEY TERMS

autoenrollment
Certificate Authority (CA)
certificate chain
certificate revocation list (CRL)
Certificates snap-in
certificate templates
Cryptographic Service
  Provider (CSP)
delta CRLs
digital certificate
digital signature

enrollment
enterprise CA
exit module
intermediate CA
issuing CA
Network Device Enrollment
  Service (NDES)
Online Certificate Status
  Protocol (OCSP)
policy module
Public Key Infrastructure (PKI)

registration authority (RA)
root CA
Secure Sockets Layer (SSL)
Simple Certificate Enrollment
  Protocol (SCEP)
smart card
standalone CA
subordinate CA
Transport Layer Security (TLS)
Web enrollment
X.509 version 3

■ Designing a Public Key Infrastructure

THE BOTTOM LINE

A *Public Key Infrastructure (PKI)* is a system consisting of hardware, software, policies, and procedures that create, manage, distribute, use, store, and revoke digital certificates. After you determine which PKI-enabled applications your organization plans to use, you must determine who needs a digital certificate and the type of digital certificate required.

CERTIFICATION READY
What are some of things that digital certificates are used for?
3.3

A *digital certificate*, which can be deployed to users, computers, network devices, and services, is an electronic document that contains a person's or organization's name, a serial number, expiration dates, a copy of the certificate holder's public key (used for encrypting messages and to create digital signatures), and the digital signature of the *Certificate Authority (CA)*. The Certificate Authority assigns the digital certificate so that a recipient can verify that the certificate is real.

The most common digital certificate is the ***X.509 version 3***. The X.509 version 3 standard specifies the format for the public key certificate, certificate revocation lists, attribute certificates, and a certificate path validation algorithm. See Figure 11-1.

Figure 11-1

X.509 Digital Certificate

Digital certificates carry information about their functions and capabilities in a variety of fields, including the following:

- Version—Identifies the version of the X.509 standard used to format the certificate.
- Serial number—Specifies a value assigned by the CA that uniquely identifies the certificate.
- Signature algorithm—Specifies the algorithm that the CA used to calculate the certificate's digital signature.
- Issuer—Specifies the name of the entity that issued the certificate.
- Valid from—Specifies the beginning of the period during which the certificate is valid.
- Valid to—Specifies the end of the period during which the certificate is valid.
- Subject—Specifies the name of the entity for which the certificate is issued.
- Public key—Specifies the type and length of the public key associated with the certificate.
- Enhanced key usage—Specifies the functions for which the certificate can be used.
- Key usage—Specifies additional functions for which the certificate can be used.
- Thumbprint algorithm—Specifies the algorithm used to generate a digest of the certificate data.
- Thumbprint—Contains a digest of the certificate data, used for digital signing.
- Friendly name—Specifies a common name for the entity listed in the Subject field.
- Certificate policies—Describes the policy that the CA followed to originally authenticate the subject.
- CRL distribution points—Specifies the location of the certificate revocation list (CRL), a document maintained and published by a CA that lists certificates that have been revoked.

TAKE NOTE*

Not every certificate has all of the fields listed here. The information within a given certificate is based on its origin and intended purpose.

Within the PKI, the certificate authority binds a public key with respective user identities and issues digital certificates containing the public key. For this system to work, the CA must be trusted. Typically, within an organization, you may install a CA on a Windows server, specifically on a domain controller, thus making it trusted within your organization. If you need to trust a CA outside of your organization, you would have to use a trusted third-party CA such as VeriSign or Entrust. It is the established commercial CAs responsibility to issue certificates that are trustworthy in most web browsers. See Figure 11-2.

Figure 11-2

Trusted CAs within Internet Explorer

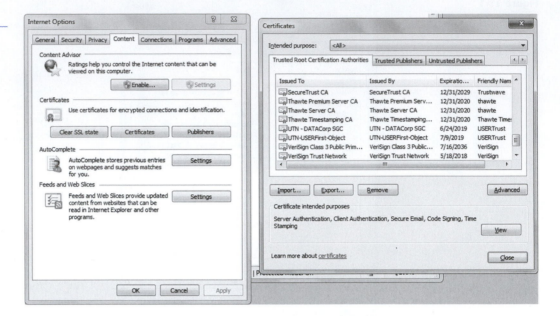

There are only so many root CA certificates that are assigned to commercial third-party organizations. Therefore, when you acquire a digital certificate from a third-party organization, you might need to use a certificate chain to obtain the root CA certificate. In addition, you may need to install an intermittent digital certificate that will link the assigned digital certificate to a trusted root CA certificate. The ***certificate chain***, also known as the certification path, is a list of certificates used to authenticate an entity. It begins with the certificate of the entity and ends with the root CA certificate. See Figure 11-3.

Figure 11-3

Certificate Chain

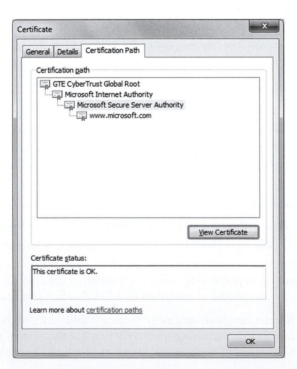

Understanding Certificates and Their Use

> Digital certificates are very common in today's computer world. They are used in encryption as the component that stores the public key, they are used to identify a person (authentication) or organization, and they are used to ensure that something has not been modified.

UNDERSTANDING THE SECURE SOCKETS LAYER

When you surf the Internet, there are times when you need to transmit private data over the Internet such as credit card numbers, social security numbers, and so on. During these times, you should be using SSL over http (https) to encrypt the data sent over the Internet. By convention, URLs that require an SSL connection start with https: instead of http.

Secure Sockets Layer (SSL) uses a cryptographic system that uses two keys to encrypt data, a public key known to everyone and a private or secret key known only to the recipient of the message. The public key is published in a digital certificate, which also confirms the identity of the web server.

When you connect to a site that is SSL-secured, a gold lock appears in the browser's address bar, along with the name of the organization to which the CA issued the certificate. Clicking the lock icon displays more information about the site, including the identity of the CA that issued the certificate. For even more information, you can click the View Certificate link to open the Certificate dialog box.

When visiting certain Web sites, Internet Explorer may find problems with the digital certificate such as that the certificate has expired, is corrupted, has been revoked, or does not match the name of the Web site. When this happens, IE will block access to the site and display a warning stating that there is a problem with the certificate. You then have a chance to close the browser window or ignore the warning and continue on to the site. Of course, if you chose to ignore the warning, make sure you trust the Web site and believe that you are communicating with the correct server.

Transport Layer Security (TLS) is an extension of SSL that is supported by Internet Engineering Task Force (IETF) so that it can be an open, community-supported standard that could then be expanded with other Internet standards. While TLS is often referred to as SSL 3.0, it does not interoperate with SSL. While TLS is usually the default for most browsers, it has a downgrade feature that allows SSL 3.0 to run when it's needed.

USING DIGITAL CERTIFICATES TO ENCRYPT DATA

Since email is sent over the Internet, you may be concerned with the data packets being captured and read. Therefore, there is a need to encrypt emails that contain confidential information. There are multiple protocols that can be used to encrypt emails. They include:

- Secure Multipurpose Internet Mail Extension (S/MIME)
- Pretty Good Privacy (PGP)

Secure Multipurpose Internet Mail Extension (S/MIME) is the secure version of MIME, used to embed objects within email messages. It is the most widely supported standard used to secure email communications and uses the PKCS #7 standard. S/MIME is included with popular web browsers and has also been endorsed by other vendors that make messaging products.

Pretty Good Privacy (PGP) is a freeware email encryption system that uses symmetrical and asymmetrical encryption. When an email is sent, the document is encrypted with the public key and also a session key. The session key is a one-use random number used to create the ciphertext. The session key is encrypted with the public key and sent with the ciphertext. When the message is received, the private key is used to extract the session key. The session key and the private key are used to decrypt the ciphertext.

For more information on EFS and BitLocker, see Lesson 9, "Selecting Data Management Solutions."

If someone steals a hard drive that is protected by NTFS permissions, they could take the hard drive, put it in a system in which they are an administrator and access all files and folders on the hard drive. Therefore, to truly protect a drive that could be stolen or accessed illegally, you can encrypt the files and folders on the drive.

Windows 7 offers two file-encrypting technologies, Encrypting File System (EFS) and BitLocker Drive Encryption. EFS protects individual files or folders while BitLocker protects entire drives.

Encrypting File System (EFS) can encrypt files on an NTFS volume that cannot be used unless the user has access to the keys required to decrypt the information. After a file has been encrypted, you do not have to manually decrypt it before you can use it. Once you encrypt a file or folder, you work with the encrypted file or folder just as you do with any other file or folder.

EFS is keyed to a specific user account, using the public and private keys that are the basis of the Windows public key infrastructure (PKI). The user who creates a file is the only person who can read it. As the user works, EFS encrypts the files he or she creates using a key generated from the user's public key. Data encrypted with this key can be decrypted only by the user's personal encryption certificate, which is generated using his or her private key.

Virtual Private Networks (VPNs) allow remote users to connect to a private network by using a tunneling protocol, such as Point-to-Point Tunneling Protocol (PPTP) and Layer 2 Tunneling Protocol (L2TP). Digital certificates are also used with IP Security (IPsec), which is often used to connect two computers or to have a remote computer connect to a corporate office over the Internet. The IP Security extensions enable you to encrypt and digitally sign communications to prevent intruders from compromising them as they are transmitted over a network. The Windows Server 2008 IPsec implementation does not have to use a PKI to obtain its encryption keys, but you can use the PKI for this purpose.

DIGITAL CERTIFICATES USED IN WIRELESS COMMUNICATIONS

Within a few months after Wired Equivalent Privacy (WEP) identified the security weaknesses, the IEEE created Wi-Fi Protected Access (WPA) as an interim standard prior to the ratification of 802.11i followed by WPA2. WPA provides strong data encryption via Temporal Key Integrity Protocol (TKIP), while Wi-Fi Protected Access 2 (WPA2) provides enhanced data encryption via Advanced Encryption Standard (AES), which meets the Federal Information Standard (FIPS) 140-2 requirement of some government agencies. To help prevent someone from hacking the key, WPA and WPA2 rotate the keys and change the way keys are derived.

Both WPA and WPA2 can run in both personal and enterprise mode. Personal mode, designed for home and small office networks, provides authentication via a preshared key or password.

Enterprise mode provides authentication using IEEE 802.1X and the Extensible Authentication Protocol (EAP). 802.1X provides an authentication framework for wireless LANs, allowing a central authority such as a RADIUS server (RADIUS is described in more depth later in this lesson) to authenticate a user. Because it uses EAP, the actual algorithm used to determine whether a user is authentic is left open so that multiple algorithms can be used and even added as new ones are developed. Enterprise mode uses two sets of keys: the session keys and group keys. The session keys are unique to each client associated between an access point and a wireless client for the duration of the active communications session. Group keys are shared among all clients connected to the same access point. Both sets of keys are generated dynamically and are rotated to help safeguard the integrity of keys over time. The encryption keys could be supplied through a certificate or smart card.

DIGITAL SIGNATURE

A *digital signature* is a mathematical scheme that is used to demonstrate the authenticity of a digital message or document. It is also used to ensure that the message or document has not been modified. The sender uses the receiver's public key to create a hash or mathematical calculation of the message, which is stored in the message digest. The message is then sent to the receiver. The receiver will then use his or her private key to decrypt the hash value, perform the same hash function on the message, and compare the two hash values. If the message has not been changed, the hash values will match.

To prove that a message comes from a particular person, you can perform the hashing function with your private key and attach the hash value to the document to be sent. When the document is sent and received by the receiving party, the same hash function is completed. You then use the sender's public key to decrypt the hash value included in the document. If the two hash values match, the user who sent the document must have known the sender's private key, proving who sent the document. It will also prove that the document has not been changed.

USING A SMART CARD

A *smart card* is a pocket-sized card with embedded integrated circuits consisting of non-volatile memory storage components, and perhaps dedicated security logic. Non-volatile memory is memory that does not lose its content when the power is turned off. Smart cards can contain digital certificates to prove the identity of someone carrying the card and may contain permissions and access information. Since a smart card can be stolen, some smart cards will not have any markings on it so that their purpose cannot be easily identified. In addition, many organizations will use a password or PIN in combination with the smart card.

Windows Server 2008 Enterprise edition allows you to define restricted enrollment agents that specify who can enroll smart card certificates on behalf of other users and which people the user can enroll. To configure enrollment agent restrictions, you use the Certification Authority snap-in.

USING SOFTWARE CODE SIGNING

Today, publishers can sign executable files, scripts, and drivers to prove where they came from and to determine whether a non-authorized person has modified the software. Microsoft's Authenticode is one technology that uses certificates to confirm that no one has modified the software a user downloads and installs and that the software actually comes from the specified publisher. In today's 64-bit versions of Windows, you cannot install a driver that a publisher has not signed.

Managing Certificates

> Larger organizations will have thousands of digital certificates to manage. Therefore, you will need to be familiar with the Windows tools that allow you to manage digital certificates.

To view the information in a certificate's fields in Windows Server 2008, you must open it in the *Certificates snap-in* for Microsoft Management Console (MMC). There is no short-cut to the Certificates snap-in in the Start menu. You must open a blank MMC console and add the Certificates snap-in to it. When you do this, you have to specify the focus of the snap-in as the current user's account, a computer account, or a service account. When you select the current user account option, the snap-in creates an interface like the one shown in Figure 11-4.

Figure 11-4

The Certificates snap-in

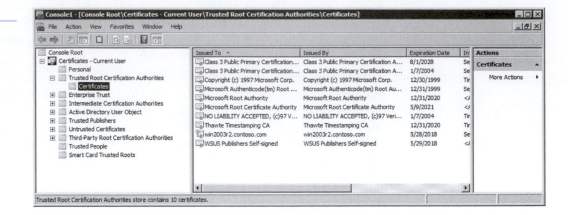

When you double-click one of the certificates listed in the console, a Certificate dialog box appears, containing the following tabs:

- General—Displays a list of the functions the certificate is capable of performing, plus the issuer, the recipient, and the dates of validity, as shown in Figure 11-5.

Figure 11-5

The General tab in a *Certificates* dialog box

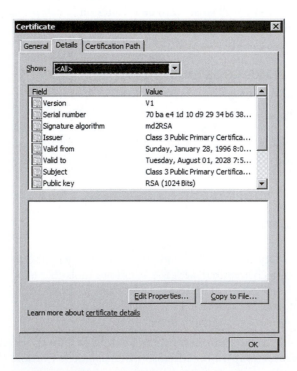

Figure 11-6

The Details tab in a *Certificates* dialog box

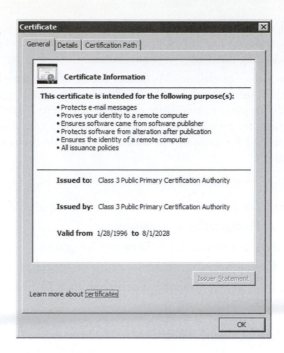

- Details—Displays the values for all of the certificate's fields, as shown in Figure 11-6.
- Certification Path—Contains a tree display of the certificate's issuing CA, and all of its trusted certification authorities leading back to the root.

Digital certificates can be imported and exported via an electronic file. Four common formats are:

- Personal Information Exchange (PKCS #12)—Supports secure storage of certificates, private keys, and all certificates in a certification path. The PKCS #12 format is the only file format that can be used to export a certificate and its private key. It will usually have a .p12 filename extension.
- Cryptographic Message Syntax Standard (PKCS #7)—Supports storage of certificates and all certificates in the certification path. It will usually have a .p7b or .p7c filename extension.
- Distinguished Encoding Rules (DER) encoded binary X.509—Supports supports storage of a single certificate. This format does not support storage of the private key or certification path. It will usually have a .cer, .crt or .der filename extension.
- Base64-encoded X.509—Supports storage of a single certificate. This format does not support storage of the private key or certification path.

Designing a CA Hierarchy

> After you decide that you have reason to install your own certification authorities, there are a number of decisions you must make to ensure that the CAs you install can perform the tasks you require from them.

Windows Server 2008 supports two basic types of CAs, as follows:

- ***Enterprise CA***—Enterprise CAs are integrated into the Windows Server 2008 Active Directory environment. They use certificate templates, publish their certificates and CRLs to Active Directory, and use the information in Active Directory to approve or deny certificate enrollment requests automatically. Because the clients of an enterprise CA must have access to Active Directory to receive certificates, enterprise CAs are not suitable for issuing certificates to clients outside the enterprise.

- **Standalone CA**—Standalone CAs do not use certificate templates or Active Directory; they store their information locally. In addition, by default, standalone CAs do not automatically respond to certificate enrollment requests, as enterprise CAs do. Requests wait in a queue for an administrator to manually approve or deny them. Standalone CAs are intended for situations in which users outside the enterprise submit requests for certificates.

You should deploy enterprise CA if:

- A large number of certificates must be enrolled and approved automatically.
- Availability and redundancy are mandatory.
- Clients need the benefits of Active Directory integration.
- Features such as autoenrollment or modifiable templates are required.
- Key archival and recovery is required to escrow encryption keys.

You should deploy a standalone CA if:

- Clients are heterogeneous and cannot benefit from Active Directory.
- You plan to issue certificates to routers through Network Device Enrollment Service (NDES)/ Simple Certificate Enrollment Protocol (SCEP).

You can configure each enterprise or standalone CA to function as either a root CA or a subordinate CA. The first CA you install in your organization must always be a root CA. A **root CA** is the parent that issues certificates to the **subordinate CAs** beneath it. If a client trusts the root CA, it must also trust all the subordinate CAs that have been issued certificates by the root CA.

As a result of these options, there are four different types of CAs that you can create on a Windows Server 2008 computer:

- Enterprise root
- Enterprise subordinate
- Standalone root
- Standalone subordinate

While subordinate CAs will have certificates assigned by the root CA, the root CA is the only CA that does not have a certificate issued to it by a higher authority. Instead, the root CA issues its own self-signed certificate, which functions as the top of the certificate chain for all the certificates issued by all the CAs subordinate to the root. When you install a subordinate CA, you must specify the name of a parent CA, which will issue a certificate to the subordinate. The parent does not have to be the root CA.

If the root CA is compromised, all of the certificates issued by it and its subordinates are also compromised. Therefore, you should use root CAs to issue certificates to subordinate CAs and then you should shut down the server and physically secure it.

Depending on the size and layout of the organization, you might decide to create many CAs, in multiple levels and in different locations. If your organization has multiple sites, you might decide to create a CA in each office, to give users local access to new certificates, just as you can do with domain controllers. You might also create separate CAs to perform different functions.

CREATING A CA HIERARCHY

While a CA hierarchy at a smaller company can have just two levels, larger organizations might have three or more levels. When this is the case, there are two distinct types of subordinate CAs, as follows:

- **Intermediate CAs**—Do not issue certificates to end users or computers; they issue certificates only to other subordinate CAs below them in the certification hierarchy. Intermediate CAs are not required, but using them enables you to take your root CA offline, which greatly increases its security.
- **Issuing CAs**—Provide certificates to end users and computers. Root and intermediate CAs are capable of issuing certificates to end users, but in a three-level arrangement, they typically do not.

When issuing certificates, the CA checks with a **registration authority (RA)** to verify information provided by the requester of a digital certificate. If the RA verifies the requester's information, the CA can then issue a certificate.

Installing Certification Authorities

When you install the Active Directory Certificate Services Role on a Windows Server 2008 computer, you can create any one of the four types of CA listed on page 268.

When you select the CA type, the Add Roles Wizard changes to include various additional configuration pages depending on the type you select. On most enterprise networks that use certificates for their internal applications, the first CA they install will be an enterprise root CA. The following sections describe the process of installing a CA and managing the templates you use to create certificates.

INSTALLING AN ENTERPRISE ROOT CA

To install the first CA on an enterprise network, the enterprise root CA, use the following procedure.

 INSTALL AN ENTERPRISE ROOT CA

GET READY. Log on to Windows Server 2008 using an account with administrative privileges. When the logon process is completed, close the Initial Configuration Tasks window and any other windows that appear.

1. Click Start, click Administrative Tools and then click Server Manager. The Server Manager console appears.
2. Select the Roles node and click Add Roles. The Add Roles Wizard appears.
3. Click Next.
4. Select the Active Directory Certificate Services checkbox and click Next. The *Introduction to Active Directory Certificate Services* page appears.

TAKE NOTE* Although the role is called Active Directory Certificate services, Active Directory is not required to install and run a CA. As noted earlier, standalone CAs need not use Active Directory in any way and can provide certificates to Internet and other clients outside the enterprise network.

5. Click Next. The *Select Role Services* page appears, as shown in Figure 11-7.

Figure 11-7

The *Select Role Services* page
of the Add Roles Wizard

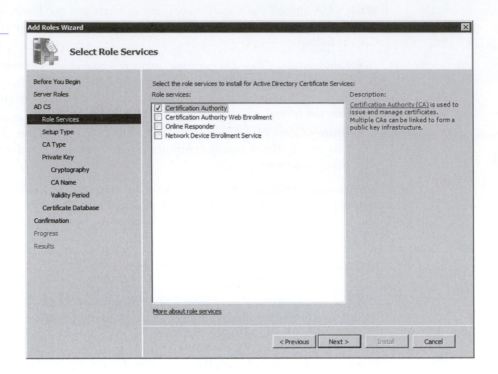

6. Leave the Certification Authority role service selected and click Next. The *Specify Setup Type* page appears, as shown in Figure 11-8.

Figure 11-8

The *Specify Setup Type* page of
the Add Roles Wizard

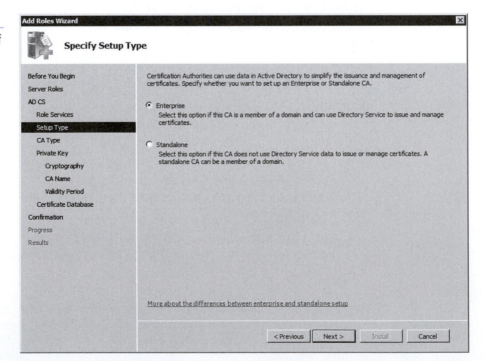

7. Select the Enterprise option and click Next. The *Specify CA Type* page appears, as shown in Figure 11-9.

Figure 11-9

The *Specify CA Type* page of the Add Roles Wizard

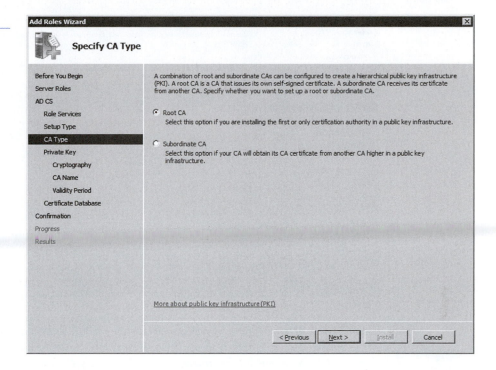

8. Select the Root CA option and click Next. The *Set Up Private Key* page appears, as shown in Figure 11-10.

Figure 11-10

The *Set Up Private Key* page of the Add Roles Wizard

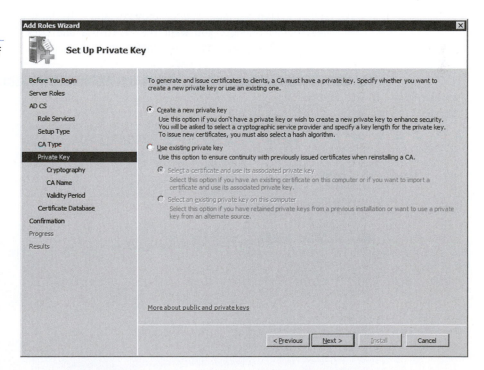

9. Select the Create a new private key option and click Next. The *Configure Cryptography for CA* page appears, as shown in Figure 11-23.

Figure 11-11

The *Configure Cryptography for CA* page of the Add Roles Wizard

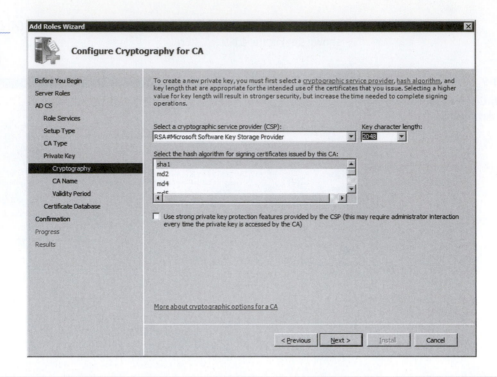

TAKE NOTE *

The Create a new private key option instructs the wizard to create a new private key for the CA. The Use existing private key option instructs the wizard to use the private key associated with an existing certificate or stored on the server, which you must import in the *Select Existing Certificate* page this option adds to the wizard. Select this option when you are reinstalling a CA.

10. Select a cryptographic service provider and a hashing algorithm. Then, type the *Key character length* you want the CA to use and click Next. The *Configure CA Name* page appears, as shown in Figure 11-12.

Figure 11-12

The *Configure CA Name* page of the Add Roles Wizard

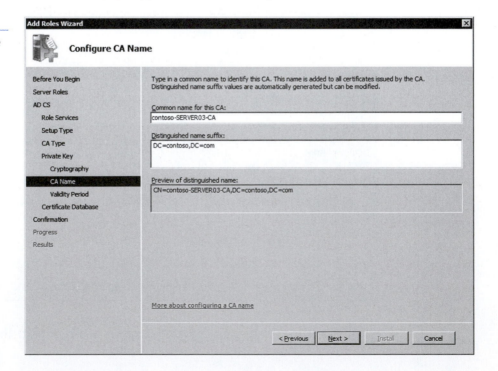

11. If you don't want to use the server's name to form the common name of the CA, specify a different name. Click Next. The *Set Validity Period* page appears, as shown in Figure 11-13.

Figure 11-13

The *Set Validity Period* page of the Add Roles Wizard

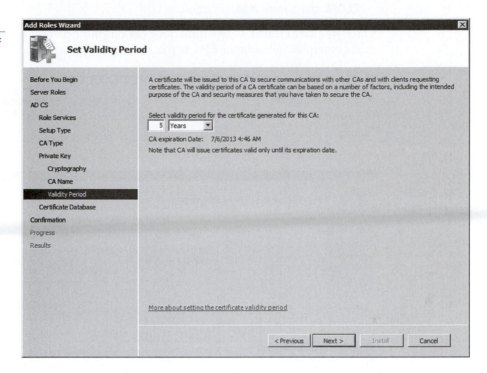

12. Specify a validity period for the certificate that will be self-generated by the CA and click Next. The *Configure Certificate Database* page appears, as shown in Figure 11-14.

Figure 11-14

The *Configure Certificate Database* page of the Add Roles Wizard

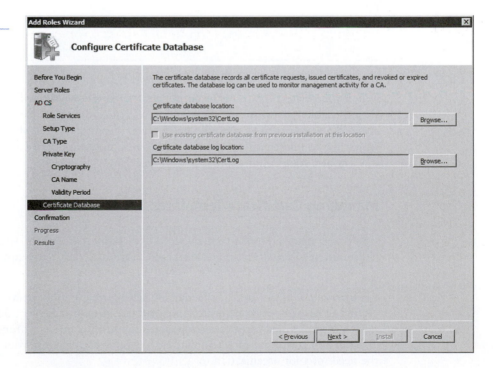

13. Click Next to accept the default database location settings.

14. Click Install

15. When the installation is complete, click Close.

CLOSE the Server Manager console.

Once you have created an enterprise root CA on your network, you can proceed to create as many enterprise subordinate CAs as you need.

INSTALLING AN ENTERPRISE SUBORDINATE CA

The only difference in the installation procedure for an enterprise subordinate CA is the inclusion of a *Request Certificate from a Parent CA* page in the Add Roles Wizard, as shown in Figure 11-15, in place of the Set *Validity Period* page.

Figure 11-15

The *Request Certificate from a Parent CA* page of the Add Roles Wizard

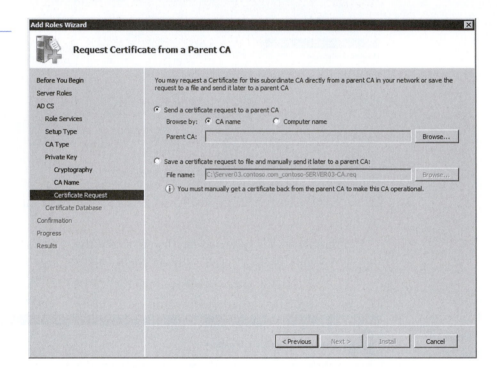

When you create a root CA, the computer generates its own certificate, so the Set Validity Period enables you to specify the life span of that certificate, and consequently the CA's life span. When you create a subordinate CA, you specify the name of a parent CA instead, from which the computer will obtain the certificate it needs to operate as a subordinate. The parent CA can be a root CA or another subordinate CA.

Managing Certificate Templates

In large organizations, if you have to assign certificates to users, you need a method to simplify certificate creation to keep each certificate consistent across an organization.

Certificate templates are sets of rules and settings that define the format and content of a certificate based on the certificate's intended use. Windows Server 2008 includes a large collection of predefined certificate templates, supporting a variety of functions and applications. You can also customize each template for a specific use or create your own templates to suit the needs of your organization.

Only enterprise CAs can issue certificates based on certificate templates; standalone CAs cannot. When an administrator defines a certificate template, the definition must be available to all CAs in the forest. To make the definition available, administrators publish the template in Active Directory and let the Active Directory replication engine propagate the template throughout the enterprise.

WORKING WITH CERTIFICATE TEMPLATES

To modify and publish certificate templates, you use the Certificate Templates snap-in for Microsoft Management Console (MMC), as shown in Figure 11-16, which is only available on a CA server or a server with the Certification Authority Tools feature installed. Using this snap-in, you can modify templates to suit your needs and deploy them on the network.

Figure 11-16

The Certificate Templates snap-in for MMC

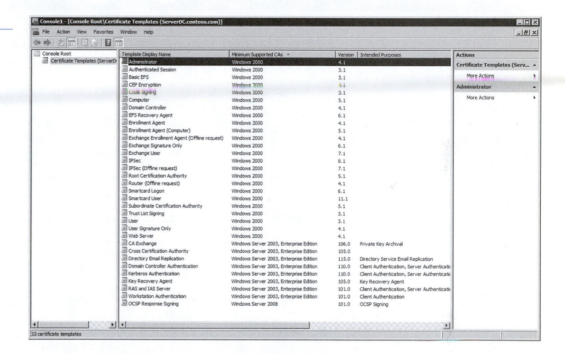

As with the Certificates snap-in mentioned earlier, Windows Server 2008 does not have a shortcut to a Certificate Templates console in the Start menu. You must add the Certificate Templates snap-in to an MMC console yourself to manage templates.

UNDERSTANDING CERTIFICATE TEMPLATE VERSIONS

Windows Server 2008's Active Directory Certificate Services role supports three types of certificate templates:

- Version 1 templates provide backward compatibility for CAs running Windows Server 2003, Standard Edition and Windows 2000 family operating systems. Version 1 templates have a major limitation. Because certificates are hard-coded, you cannot modify version 1 certificate template properties, such as certificate lifetime and key size.

- Version 2 certificate templates allow you to modify the certificate template properties. Some of the default templates supplied with Active Directory Certificate Services are version 2, however, and you can only use them to issue certificates with a CA running Windows Server 2003 or 2008 Enterprise Edition or Datacenter Edition.

- Version 3 can be issued only by CAs running Windows Server 2008 and can be issued only to clients running Windows Vista and Windows Server 2008.

You cannot modify or remove the default version 1 templates installed with Active Directory Certificate Services, but you can duplicate them. When you create a duplicate of a version 1 template, the result is a version 2 template, which you can modify as needed.

The certificate templates included with Windows Server 2008's Active Directory Certificate Services role are listed in Table 11-1.

Table 11-1

Windows Server 2008 Certificate Templates

Template Name	Template Version	Subject Type	Key Usage	Template Function
Administrator	1	User	Signature and Encryption	Allows user authentication, EFS encryption, secure email, and certificate trust list signing.
Authenticated Session	1	User	Signature	Authenticates a user to a Web server. Uses the private key to sign the authentication request.
Basic EFS	1	User	Encryption	Encrypts and decrypts data by using EFS. Uses the private key to decrypt the file encryption key (FEK) that encrypts and decrypts the EFS-protected data.
CA Exchange	2	Computer	Encryption	Used to store keys that are configured for private key archival.
CEP Encryption	1	Computer	Encryption	Enables the certificate holder to act as a registration authority (RA) for Simple Certificate Enrollment Protocol (SCEP) requests.
Code Signing	1	User	Signature	Used to digitally sign software.
Computer	1	Computer	Signature and Encryption	Provides both client and server authentication abilities to a computer account. The default permissions for this template allow enrollment only by computers running Windows 2000 and Windows Server 2008 family operating systems that are not domain controllers.
Cross-Certification Authority	2	Cross-certified CA	Signature	Used for cross-certification and qualified subordination.
Directory E-mail Replication	2	DirEmailRep	Signature and Encryption	Used to replicate email within Active Directory.
Domain Controller	2	DirEmailRep	Signature and Encryption	Provides both client and server authentication abilities to a computer account. Default permissions allow enrollment by only domain controllers.
Domain Controller Authentication	2	Computer	Signature and Encryption	Used to authenticate Active Directory computers and users.
EFS Recovery Agent	1	User	Encryption	Enables the subject to decrypt files previously encrypted with EFS.
Enrollment Agent	1	User	Signature	Used to request certificates on behalf of another subject.
Exchange Enrollment Agent (Offline request)	1	User	Signature	Used to request certificates on behalf of another subject and supply the subject name in the request.

Exchange Signature Only	1	User	Signature	Used by Exchange Key Management Service to issue certificates to Microsoft Exchange Server users for digitally signing email.
Exchange User	1	User	Encryption	Used by Exchange Key Management Service to issue certificates to Exchange users for encrypting email.
IPsec	1	Computer	Signature and Encryption	Provides certificate-based authentication for computers by using IP Security (IPsec) for network communications.
IPsec (Offline request)	1	Computer	Signature and Encryption	Used by IPsec to digitally sign, encrypt, and decrypt network communication when the subject name is supplied in the request.
Kerberos Authentication	2	Computer	Signature and Encryption	Used to authenticate Active Directory computers and users.
Key Recovery Agent	2	Key Recovery Agent	Encryption	Recovers private keys that are archived on the certification authority.
OCSP Response Signing	3	Computer	Signature	Used by an Online Responder to sign responses to certificate status requests.
RAS and IAS Server	2	Computer	Signature and Encryption	Enables Remote Access Services (RAS) and Internet Authentication Services (IAS) servers to authenticate their identities to other computers.
Root Certification Authority	2	CA	Signature	Used to prove the identity of the certification authorities
Router (Offline request)	1	Computer	Signature and Encryption	Used by a router when requested through SCEP from a certification authority that holds a Certificate Enrollment Protocol (CEP) Encryption certificate.
Smartcard Logon	1	User	Signature and Encryption	Authenticates a user with the network by using a smart card.
Smartcard User	1	User	Signature and Encryption	Identical to the Smartcard Logon template, except that it can also be used to sign and encrypt email.
Subordinate Certification Authority	2	CA	Signature	Used to prove the identity of the certification authorities.
Trust List Signing	1	User	Signature	Enables the holder to digitally sign a trust list.
User	1	User	Signature and Encryption	Used for email, EFS, and client authentication.
User Signature Only	1	User	Signature	Enables users to digitally sign data.
Web Server	1	Computer	Signature and Encryption	Authenticates the Web server to connecting clients. The connecting clients use the public key to encrypt the data that is sent to the Web server when using Secure Sockets Layer (SSL) encryption.
Workstation Authentication	2	Computer	Signature and Encryption	Enables client computers to authenticate their identities to servers.

In the Certificate Templates snap-in, you can tell the version of a template by looking at the value in the Minimum Supported CAs column. Templates with Windows 2000 in this column are version 1; templates with Windows Server 2003, Enterprise Edition are version 2; and templates with Windows Server 2008 are version 3.

MANAGING CERTIFICATE TEMPLATE PERMISSIONS

Every certificate template has an access control list (ACL) that you can use to allow or deny permission to Read, Write, Enroll, and Autoenroll the certificate template. To set permissions for a certificate template, you open a template's properties sheet with the Certificate Templates snap-in and click the Security tab, as shown in Figure 11-17.

Figure 11-17

The Security tab from a certificate template's properties sheet

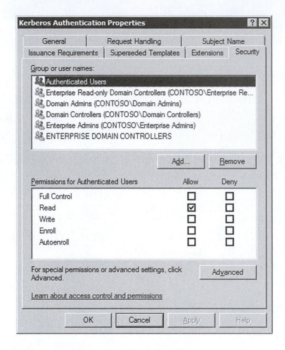

The permissions available are:

- Full Control—Allows a user or computer to modify all attributes of a certificate template and its permissions.
- Read—Allows a user or computer to find the certificate template in Active Directory.
- Write—Allows a user or computer to modify all the attributes of a certificate template.
- Enroll—Allows a user or computer to enroll for a certificate based on the certificate template. Note: To enroll a certificate, the user or computer must also have the Allow Read permission for the certificate template.
- Autoenroll—Allows a user or computer to automatically receive a certificate based on the template. Note: To recive a certificate through autoenrollment, the user or computer also needs both the Allow Read and Allow Enroll permissions.

To enable autoenrollment, you must configure the Allow Read, Allow Enroll, and Allow Autoenroll permissions to the same user/computer or group. If you assign Allow Read and Allow Enroll to one group and Allow Autoenroll to another group, users will not be allowed to autoenroll for certificates, even if they have membership in both groups. For best results, create a global or universal group for each certificate template. Then, grant the global or universal group all three permissions, and add the necessary user groups to this group.

Designing a Certificate Life Cycle

> Certificates do have a limited life. The longer a certificate remains in use, the more time intruders have to perform attacks to determine the certificate's key. Therefore, administrators will specify the length of the key and the length of time before a certificate expires. Additionally, administrators can revoke a certificate before it reaches its expiration date.

When designing a PKI solution and how it is it going to be used, you need to choose the length of a certificate's lifetime and the type of certificate to issue. In general, using longer encryption keys makes it possible to have longer certificate lifetimes and key lifetimes. While using longer certificate lifetimes reduces administrative overhead, which in turn reduces costs, keep in mind what technology is available to break the key. As computers get faster and faster, so does the number of attempts per second that a hacker can use to break a key.

Because a CA must have a certificate of its own to operate—either self-issued, in the case of a root CA, or issued by a parent—the expiration of the CA's certificate causes the CA itself to expire. A CA cannot issue certificates with expiration dates that are valid beyond the expiration date of its own certificate. Therefore, you should have a process in there to review the CA's digital certificate and renew it well before it expires.

Administrators can reduce the time required to administer a PKI by increasing the validity period of the root CA. As with any certificate, it is best to choose a validity period shorter than the time required for an attacker to break the root CA key's cryptography. Given the current state of computer technology, we can estimate that a 4096-bit private key would take decades to crack. While a determined attacker can eventually crack any private key, the end result is useless if the certificate expires before the attack is successful.

UNDERSTANDING CERTIFICATE REVOCATION

As mentioned earlier, digital certificates can be revoked at any time. You would want to revoke a certificate if the certificate has been compromised or if you want to ensure that the certificate cannot be used to grant access to a system or network. During signature verification and other activities that require certificate access, applications typically check the revocation list on the certificate's CA to determine whether the certificate and its key pair are still trustworthy.

Every CA publishes a *certificate revocation list (CRL)* that lists the serial numbers of certificates that it considers to be no longer valid. The specified lifetime of CRLs is typically much shorter than that of a certificate. For some CAs, a CRL may include the reason the certificate has been revoked and the date the certificate was revoked.

Active Directory Certificate Services enables clients to retrieve CRLs using a variety of different protocols, including the following:

- Shared folders
- Hypertext Transfer Protocol (HTTP)
- File Transfer Protocol (FTP)
- Lightweight Directory Access Protocol (LDAP)

By default, CRLs are published in four different locations.

- The *Servername*\CertEnroll share—Created automatically when you install Active Directory Certificate Services, clients on the network can access this share, as long as they have the required permissions.

- CN=CAName,CN=CAComputerName,CN=CDP,CN=Public Key Services,CN=Services, CN=Configuration,DC=ForestRootNameDN—Clients who need to retrieve the CRL by using LDAP can access it from this address.
- http://*servername*/certenroll—Web clients can retrieve the CRLs from this URL.
- file://*servername*/certenroll—Web clients can also retrieve the CRLs using the file prefix.

Enrolling and Revoking Certificates

Certificate *enrollment* is the process by which a client requests a certificate and a CA generates one.

The certificate enrollment process always follows the same high-level procedure, which is as follows:

1. Generating keys—When a client generates a request for a new certificate, the operating system passes the request information to a *Cryptographic Service Provider (CSP)* that is installed on the computer. The CSP generates the private key and the public key—referred to as a key pair—for the certificate request. If the CSP is software-based, it generates the key pair on the client computer. If the CSP is hardware-based, such as a smart card CSP, the CSP instructs the hardware device to generate the key pair. The client might also be assigned a key pair by some authority in the organization.

2. Collecting required information—The client collects the information the CA requires to issue a certificate.

3. Requesting the certificate—The client sends a certificate request, consisting of the public key and the additional required information, to the CA. The certificate request might be encrypted using the CA's own public key.

4. Verifying the information—The CA uses a policy module to process the applicant's certificate request. A *policy module* is a set of rules the CA uses to determine whether it should approve the request, deny it, or mark it as pending for later review by an administrator.

5. Creating the certificate—The CA creates a document containing the applicant's public key and other appropriate information and digitally signs it using its own private key. The signed document is the certificate. The digital signature of the CA authenticates the binding of the subject's name to the subject's public key. It enables anyone receiving the certificate to verify its source by obtaining the CA's public key.

6. Sending or posting the certificate—The CA uses an *exit module* to determine how it should make the new certificate available to the applicant.

UNDERSTANDING CERTIFICATE ENROLLMENT METHODS

When requesting certificates from an enterprise CA, a client can use the following methods:

- *Autoenrollment*—Applications automatically issue a certificate enrollment request and send it to the CA. The CA then evaluates the request and issues or denies a certificate. When everything works properly, the entire process is invisible to the end user. The autoenrollment operations on client computers and CAs are controlled by Group Policy settings and certificate template settings. Several default certificate templates are enabled for autoenrollment during CA installation. However, Group Policy settings must be enabled by an administrator before client computers can initiate autoenrollment.

- *Web enrollment*—When you install Active Directory Certificate Services with the Certification Authority Web Enrollment role service, the setup wizard creates a Web site that clients can use to request certificates from the CA. Although standalone CAs are more likely to use web enrollment, enterprise CAs support it as well. See Figure 11-18.

Figure 11-18

The Certification Authority Web Enrollment interface

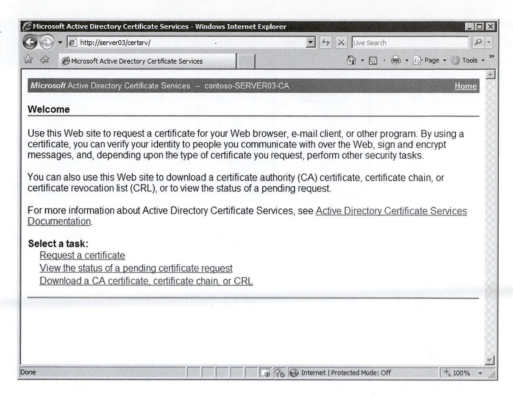

- Certificates snap-in—The Certificates snap-in for MMC enables users to manually request certificates, as well as view the certificates they already possess.

Additionally, a client computer that is not connected to the network cannot automatically enroll for a certificate because autoenrollment requires the client to communicate directly to the enterprise CA. In these circumstances, the client must submit all certificates requests to the CA manually.

ISSUING CERTIFICATES MANUALLY

When users send enrollment requests to an enterprise CA using the Certification Authority Web Enrollment interface, the response is usually immediate because enterprise CAs uses autoenrollment. With a standalone CA, however, the CA queues the requests until an administrator evaluates them and manually issues a certificate or denies the request, using the Certification Authority console.

To manually process an enrollment request, use the following procedure.

 ISSUE CERTIFICATES MANUALLY

GET READY. Log on to Windows Server 2008 using an account with administrative privileges. When the logon process is completed, close the Initial Configuration Tasks window and any other windows that appear.

1. Click Start, and then click Administrative Tools > Certification Authority. The Certification Authority console appears.

2. In the scope (left) pane, expand the node representing your server and click the Pending Requests folder, as shown in Figure 11-19.

Figure 11-19

The Pending Requests folder
of the Certification Authority
console

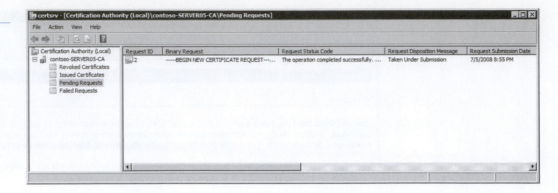

3. In the detail (right) pane, right-click a certificate request and, in the context menu, click All Tasks > Issue. The request moves to the Issued Certificates folder.

CLOSE the Certification Authority console.

Once the administrator has issued the certificate, the user can check the status of the request in the Certification Authority Web Enrollment site, as shown in Figure 11-20.

Figure 11-20

The *Certificate Issued* page in
the Certification Authority Web
Enrollment site

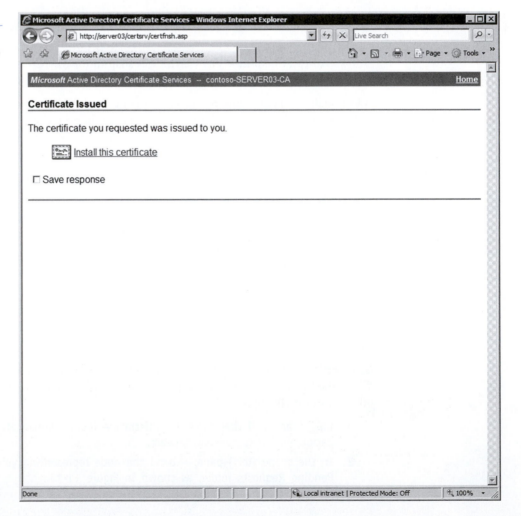

NETWORK DEVICE ENROLLMENT SERVICE

The *Network Device Enrollment Service (NDES)* is the Microsoft implementation of the *Simple Certificate Enrollment Protocol (SCEP)*, a communication protocol that makes it possible for software running on network devices such as routers and switches, which cannot otherwise be authenticated on the network, to enroll for X.509 certificates from a Certificate Authority (CA).

REVOKING CERTIFICATES

Administrators might occasionally need to revoke a certificate because a user has left the organization, a computer has been decommissioned, or a private key has been compromised. There are two ways to revoke certificates:

- The Certificates Authority snap-in
- The Certutil.exe command-line program

To revoke a certificate using the Certificates Authority snap-in, you select the Issued Certificates node; right-click the certificate you want to revoke; and, from the context menu, select All Tasks > Revoke Certificate to display the Certificate Revocation dialog box, as shown in Figure 11-21.

Figure 11-21

The Certificate Revocation dialog box

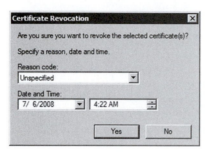

You must choose a reason for revoking the certificate, which will be included in the CRL. You can choose from the following reason codes, which are self-explanatory:

- Unspecified
- Key Compromise
- CA Compromise
- Change of Affiliation
- Superseded
- Cease of Operation
- Certificate Hold

TAKE NOTE✲

The CRLs that a CA publishes contain the reason codes administrators select when they revoke certificates. Before you select a reason code, think about whether you really want everyone who can access the CRL to know why you revoked it. If you have a key compromise or a CA compromise, do you want that to be public information? If not, just select Unspecified. In most cases, the reason you select for revoking a certificate has no bearing on the applications that use the certificate.

Applications discover that a certificate has been revoked by retrieving the certificate revocation list (CRL) from the CA. There are two kinds of CRLs: full CRLs, which contain a complete list of all the CA's revoked certificates, and delta CRLs. *Delta CRLs* are shorter lists of certificates that have been revoked since the last full CRL was published. After an application retrieves a full CRL, it can then download the shorter delta CRL to discover newly revoked certificates.

After you revoke a certificate, the CA must publish a new CRL before clients can discover that the certificate has been revoked. By default, Windows Server 2008 CAs publish delta CRLs daily and full CRLs weekly. You can change these settings using the Certificates Authority snap-in by right-clicking the Revoked Certificates node, opening its Properties sheet, and then clicking the CRL Publishing Parameters tab, as shown in Figure 11-22. This tab also shows you when the next scheduled updates will occur.

Figure 11-22

The Properties sheet for a CA's Revoked Certificates node

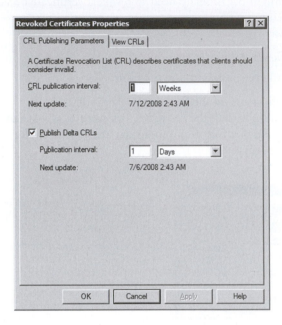

The **Online Certificate Status Protocol (OCSP)** is an Internet protocol used for obtaining the revocation status of an X.509 digital certificate. It was created as an alternative to certificate revocation lists (CRL), specifically addressing certain problems associated with using CRLs in a public key infrastructure (PKI).

SKILL SUMMARY

IN THIS LESSON YOU LEARNED:

- Public Key Infrastructure (PKI) is a system consisting of hardware, software, policies, and procedures that create, manage, distribute, use, store, and revoke digital certificates.

- A digital certificate, which can be deployed to users, computers, network devices and services, is an electronic document that contains a person's or organization's name, a serial number, expiration date, a copy of the certificate holder's public key (used for encrypting messages and to create digital signatures), and the digital signature of the Certificate Authority (CA).

- The Certificate Authority assigns the digital certificate so that a recipient can verify that the certificate is real.

- The most common digital certificate is the X.509 version 3.

- The certificate chain, also known as the certification path, is a list of certificates used to authenticate an entity. It begins with the certificate of the entity and ends with the root CA certificate.

- Secure Socket Layer (SSL) uses a cryptographic system that uses two keys to encrypt data, a public key known to everyone and a private or secret key known only to the recipient of the message.

- Transport Layer Security (TLS) is an extension of SSL.

- Any one of multiple protocols might be used to encrypt emails, including secure multipurpose Internet Mail Extension (S/MIME) and Pretty Good Privacy (PGP).

- Wireless Communications that use WPA or WPA2 Enterprise mode use digital certificates for authentication and encryption.

- A digital signature is a mathematical scheme that is used to demonstrate the authenticity of a digital message or document. It is also used to ensure that the message or document has not been modified.

- A smart card is a pocket-sized card with embedded integrated circuits consisting of non-volatile memory storage components, and perhaps dedicated security logic.

- To view the information in a certificate's fields in Windows Server 2008, you must open it in the Certificates snap-in for Microsoft Management Console (MMC).

- Enterprise CAs are integrated into the Windows Server 2008 Active Directory environment. They use certificate templates, publish their certificates and CRLs to Active Directory, and use the information in Active Directory to approve or deny certificate enrollment requests automatically.

- Standalone CAs do not use certificate templates or Active Directory; they store their information locally.

- A root CA is the parent that issues certificates to the subordinate CAs beneath it.

- While a CA hierarchy can have just two levels, larger organizations might have three or more levels. When this is the case, there are two distinct types of subordinate CAs, intermediate CAs and issuing CAs.

- When issuing certificates, the CA checks with a registration authority (RA) to verify information provided by the requester of a digital certificate. If the RA verifies the requester's information, the CA can then issue a certificate.

- Certificate templates are sets of rules and settings that define the format and content of a certificate based on the certificate's intended use.

- Windows Server 2008's Active Directory Certificate Services role supports three types of certificate templates: Version 1, Version 2, and Version 3.

- Version 1 templates provide backward compatibility for CAs running Windows Server 2003, Standard Edition and Windows 2000 family operating systems. Since certificates are hard-coded, you cannot modify version 1 certificate template properties.

- Version 2 certificate templates allow you to modify the certificate template properties. Some of the default templates supplied with Active Directory Certificate Services are version 2.

- Version 2 certificate templates can only be used by a CA running Windows Server 2003 or 2008 Enterprise Edition or Datacenter Edition.

- Version 3 can be issued only by CAs running Windows Server 2008, and can be issued only to clients running Windows 7, Windows Vista, and Windows Server 2008.

- Every certificate template has an access control list (ACL) that you can use to allow or deny permission to Read, Write, Enroll, and Autoenroll the certificate template.

SKILL SUMMARY (*continued*)

IN THIS LESSON YOU LEARNED:

- To enable autoenrollment, you must configure the Allow Read, Allow Enroll, and Allow Autoenroll permissions to the same user or group.

- Group Policy settings must be enabled by an administrator before client computers can initiate autoenrollment.

- Certificates have a limited life. The longer a certificate remains in use, the more time attackers have to figure out the key. Therefore, administrators will specify the length of the key and the length of time before a certificate expires. In addition, a certificate can be revoked before the certificate expires.

- Every CA publishes a certificate revocation list (CRL) that lists the serial numbers of certificates that it considers no longer valid.

- When requesting certificates from an enterprise CA, a client can use the autoenrollment, web enrollment, and certificates snap-in.

- The Network Device Enrollment Service (NDES) is the Microsoft implementation of the Simple Certificate Enrollment Protocol (SCEP), a communication protocol that makes it possible for software running on network devices such as routers and switches, which cannot otherwise be authenticated on the network, to enroll for X.509 certificates from a certification authority (CA).

- The Online Certificate Status Protocol (OCSP) is an Internet protocol used for obtaining the revocation status of an X.509 digital certificate.

■ Knowledge Assessment

Fill in the Blank

Complete the following exercise by filling in the blanks with the appropriate terms from this lesson.

1. A _____ is a system consisting of hardware, software, policies, and procedures to create, manage, and use digital certificates.

2. The most common digital certificate is _____.

3. A _____ begins with the certificate of the entity and ends with the root CA certificate.

4. A _____ is a mathematical scheme that is used to demonstrate the authenticity of a digital message or document.

5. To view the information in a certificate's fields in Windows Server 2008, you must open it in the _____ for Microsoft Management Console (MMC).

6. Enterprise CAs require _____.

7. A _____ is the parent that issues certificate to the subordinate CAs.

8. _____ are sets of rules and settings that define the format and content of a certificate based on the certificate's intended use.

9. Every CA publishes a _____ that lists the serial numbers of certificates that it considers to be no longer valid.

10. The _____ is the Microsoft implementation of the Simple Certificate Enrollment Protocol (SCEP).

True / False

Circle T if the statement is true or F if the statement is false.

T F 1. A digital certificate is an electronic document that contains a person's or organization's name, a serial number, expiration date, and the holder's public key.

T F 2. A digital certificate is issued by the RA.

T F 3. Digital certificates are not required for SSL but are recommended

T F 4. A smart card is a portable computer.

T F 5. Standalone CAs can issue certificates to users and computers that are part of an Active Directory Domain.

T F 6. Versions 2 and 3 certificates require Windows Server 2008 Enterprise or Datacenter edition.

T F 7. To control permissions to digital certificate templates, Windows uses NTFS permissions.

T F 8. The only methods to request a certificate are autoenrollment and Web enrollment.

T F 9. The Network Device Enrollment Service (NDES) is a communication protocol that makes it possible for software running on network devices such as routers and switches, which cannot otherwise be authenticated on the network, to enroll for X.509 certificates from a Certificate Authority (CA).

T F 10. Another alternative to obtain a revocation status of an X.509 digital certificate is RA status.

Review Questions

1. What are the six high-level procedures for certificate enrollment?

2. What are the permissions necessary to enable autoenrollment of digital certificates?

Case Scenario

Scenario 11-1: Installing a Certificate Authority

You are the IT administrator for Contoso, a large corporation with multiple sites. You want to deploy digital certificates to be used with L2TP with IPSec. The CA should be able to generate the certificates using a certificate template. Create a list of the tasks you must perform to install and configure the CA the director has requested, along with a reason for performing each task.

12 LESSON

Ensuring Business Continuity

OBJECTIVE DOMAIN MATRIX

TECHNOLOGY SKILL	OBJECTIVE DOMAIN	OBJECTIVE NUMBER
Ensuring Business Continuity	Plan for business continuity.	4.1
Backing Up and Restoring	Plan for business continuity.	4.1

KEY TERMS

active-passive cluster
authoritative restore
backup
backup site
cluster
cold site
differential backup
Directory Services Restore Mode
failover cluster

full backups
geographically dispersed
    clusters
grandfather-father-son (GFS)
high availability
hot site
incremental backups
load balancing/network load
    balancing (NLB)

Network Interface Card (NIC)
    teaming
non-authoritative restore
server-farm
service-level agreement (SLA)
shadow copies
uninterruptible power supply
    (UPS)
warm site

■ Ensuring Business Continuity

THE BOTTOM LINE

When a server goes down, it will probably cause your company to lose money. If the server is an external Web site or database that controls your sales, ordering, inventory, or production, its loss causes a stoppage in your sales, ordering, inventory, and production. If it is an internal server, its loss may not allow your users to perform their job. In either case, your company is losing money either through foregone revenue or lost productivity.

CERTIFICATION READY
What are the different areas you need to include when developing a business continuity plan?
4.1

As a server administrator, you need to minimize downtime by identifying potential failures and taking steps to avoid those failures and to reduce their effects if and when they do occur.

High availability is a system-design protocol and associated implementation that ensures a certain degree of operational continuity during a given measurement period. Generally, the term *downtime* is used to refer to periods when a system is unavailable. Availability is usually expressed as a percentage of uptime in a given year, as shown in Table 12-1.

Table 12-1

Availability Guidelines.

AVAILABILITY PERCENT	DOWNTIME PER YEAR	DOWNTIME PER MONTH
99%	3.65 days	7.20 hours
99.9% ("three nines")	8.76 hours	43.2 minutes
99.99% ("four nines")	52.6 minutes	4.32 minutes
99.999% ("five nines")	5.26 minutes	25.9 seconds
99.9999% ("six nines")	31.5 seconds	2.59 seconds

A high-availability design must include backup and recovery design. Backup design is essential because a properly designed backup is essential to recovering data. If data is not backed up, it cannot be recovered. Recovery design is essential to ensure that data can be recovered within the necessary timelines. Without a recovery design in place that has been tested to make sure that it works, and to establish how long the recovery process takes, valuable time will be lost in researching the appropriate process to follow for recovery.

A design to make services highly available attempts to avoid a situation where a recovery is required. Windows Server 2008 includes Network Load Balancing and Failover Clustering to make services highly available.

Understanding Service-Level Agreements

Often designers of servers and the services they provide are assigned *service-level agreements (SLAs)* stating how much a server or services must be available. Of course, a server design that can support five or six nines is going to be much more expensive than that supporting an availability of 99%.

As a server administrator, you need to minimize downtime by identifying potential failures and taking steps to avoid them and to reduce the effect of any such failures that might actually occur.

An SLA is an agreement, typically signed, between an IT group and an organization. It is important to define an SLA early because it documents the service expectations and requirements that an organization expects the IT service provider to deliver. An SLA might be written for the availability of a specific system component, a specific service, or an entire system.

It is important to define SLA agreements before designing and implementing an information system. You should design the system to meet the terms defined in the service-level agreement. A more highly available system typically has a higher cost than a less available system, and you should factor in the cost when negotiating the SLA.

An internal SLA between two departments within one organization rarely has legal consequences, but it does describe the relationship, expectations, and timescale for service deliveries. External SLA agreements are more formal, legally binding contracts than internal SLAs. An external SLA may have more structure because it usually includes cost and bonus clauses and sometimes penalty clauses. However, an external SLA always contains the service's specific cost and deliverables, which often include availability and security services.

Backup Sites

A *backup site* is the ultimate business-continuity and disaster-recovery mechanism. It is a location where a company or organization can relocate its services in case of a disaster such as fire, flood, earthquake, terrorism, or espionage.

The backup site can be a designated site owned by the company or organization or can be contracted with another company that specializes in disaster recovery services. These backup sites are of the following three kinds:

- *Cold Sites*—The least expensive of the three types of backup sites. A cold site is a site that is turned off and must be manually turn on and enabled to replace a primary site. A cold site may or may not have a backed-up copy of all applications and data and may or may not have the proper hardware and software already installed and configured. Of course, if a disaster does occur and the proper hardware and software already is not installed and configured, it will take longer to activate, especially if you have to ship and restore data.

- *Hot Sites*—The most expensive of the three types of backup sites. A hot site is a duplicate of the original site of the organization, including hardware, software, and data. For this to become a reality, you will need to have real-time synchronization between the primary site and the backup site using wide-area network links and specialized hardware and software. Some hot sites are automatically enabled to take over a primary site in the event of a failure, while others may require minimum action to enable.

- *Warm Sites*—A warm site is a compromise between hot and cold. It already has the hardware and software installed and configured, and connectivity is already established. Warm sites will have backups available but may take some time to restore. Warm sites usually need to be activated or enabled to take over the network services of a primary site.

When a company or organization needs to determine if they need a backup site or what type of backup site, they must first determine the risks to which they are vulnerable. Next, they need to determine the impact to the company or organization if their primary site or components within the primary site go down. Some companies lose substantial amounts of revenue when their network is down. Last, the company or organization will have to ask what it is worth to keep their network and network services running at all times, and how much outage the company can allow. Again, everyone will have to look at SLAs.

Using Fault-Tolerant Components

To make a server more fault tolerant, you should first look at what components are the most likely to fail and implement technology to make a system more fault tolerant.

The infrastructure used by an application must be highly available. This infrastructure includes both services and physical infrastructure. The methods used to create highly available infrastructure vary depending upon the components involved.

Some examples of infrastructure that require high availability are:

- Data-center cooling and power
- Server hardware, such as power supplies and disk systems
- Network hardware, such as network adapters and switches
- Active Directory Domain Services for authentication and configuration data
- DNS for resolving host names and locating domain controllers

Some of the components that can be made redundant within a system are:

- Disks—Use some form of RAID and hot spares.
- Power supplies—Use redundant power supplies.
- Network cards—Use redundant network cards.

RAID and hot spare disks were discussed in Lesson 9.

As mentioned earlier, mechanical devices fail more often than non-mechanical devices. A power supply is an electromechanical device that converts AC power into clean DC power and includes fans for cooling. Systems that cannot afford to be down should have redundant power supplies.

While you cannot install fault-tolerant processors and redundant memory, high-end servers have additional features to make the server more resistant to hardware failure and have additional monitoring of key components including processors, RAM, motherboard, and storage. For example, high-end servers use more expensive error-correcting code (ECC) memory that includes special circuitry for testing the accuracy of data as it passes in and out of memory. In addition, ECC memory corrects a single failed bit in a 64-bit block. Some of these servers, when combined with Windows Server 2008 Enterprise and Datacenter version, allow you to hot-add or hot-replace processors and memory without taking the server down.

TEAMING OF NETWORK CARDS

Network Interface Card (NIC) teaming is the process of grouping together two or more physical NICs into one single logical NIC, which can be used for network fault tolerance and increased bandwidth through load balancing. To make a system truly fault tolerant, you should also have redundant switches by which one network card of a team is connected to one switch and the other network card of the team is connected to another switch. This way, if the switch fails, you can still communicate over the network.

To support NIC teaming, the network card, network card driver, and switch must support the same teaming technology, such as 802.3ad link aggregation. You will then most likely have to install and configure specialized software to activate the team.

MANAGING POWER

Electricity can be thought of as the blood of the computer. Without electricity, the server will not run. Even redundant power supplies do not protect against a power outage or other forms of power fluctuations. For these situations, your company should look at uninterruptible power supplies and standby power generators to provide power when no power is available from the power company.

An *uninterruptible power supply* (UPS) is an electrical device consisting of one or more batteries to provide backup power when a power outage occurs. UPS units range in size from units designed to protect a single computer without a video monitor (around 200 VA rating) to large units powering entire data centers or buildings. For server rooms that contain many servers, you will most likely install one or more racks full of batteries or UPS devices. For smaller deployments, you may have a single UPS connected to an individual server or essential computer. You also need the UPS to protect other key systems and devices such as primary routers, switches, and telecommunication devices.

What most people new to IT do not realize is that UPSs are not usually designed to provide power for lengthy periods of time. Instead, they can provide power for momentary power outages, to perform a proper server shutdown, or to allow adequate time to switch over to a power generator.

A power generator or a standby power generator is a backup electrical system that operates automatically within seconds of a power outage. Automatic standby generator systems may also be required by building codes for critical safety systems such as elevators in high-rise buildings, fire protection systems, standby lighting, and medical and life-support equipment.

Of course, since power is such a critical component for your server and network, you will need to do periodic tests to make sure that the UPS can supply sufficient power for the necessary time and that the power generator can turn on as needed.

Understanding Clustering

A *server farm* or server *cluster* is a group of linked computers that work together as one computer. Depending on the technology used, clusters can provide fault tolerance (often referred to as availability), load balancing, or both. If system failure includes the processor, memory, or motherboard, a cluster that provides fault tolerance can still service requests.

The two most popular forms of clusters are failover clusters and load-balancing clusters. A common use of clusters would include:

- A failover cluster for the back-end servers such as a database (such as SQL server) or mail server (such as Exchange server).
- A load-balancing cluster for the front end that provides the web interface to the back-end servers.

USING FAILOVER CLUSTERS

A *failover cluster* is a set of independent computers that work together to increase availability of services and applications. The clustered servers (called nodes) are connected by physical cables and by software. If one of the nodes fails, another node begins to provide services (a process known as failover). Failover clusters can be used to provide a wide range of network services including database applications such as Exchange Server or SQL server, file servers, print services, or network services such as DHCP services.

The most common failover cluster is the *active-passive cluster*. In an active-passive cluster, both servers are configured to work as one, but only one at a time. The active node provides the network services while the passive node waits for the active node to become unavailable. If the active node goes down, the passive node becomes the active node and resumes providing network services.

Another type of failover cluster is the active-active node, which is designed to provide fault tolerance and load balancing. The network services are split into two groups. One cluster node runs one set of network services while the other cluster node runs the other set of network services. Both nodes are active. If one of the nodes fails, the remaining node will take over and provide all the network services.

To create a failover cluster using Windows Server 2008, you will need two servers that are compatible with Windows Server 2008 and have identical hardware components. In addition, the servers must run the same Windows Server 2008 Enterprise or Windows Server 2008 Datacenter version, including the same hardware platform (32-bit versus 64-bit). The servers should also have the same software updates and service packs installed. In addition, the servers must be part of the same domain.

As networking technology has matured and bandwidth has increased, many companies and organizations are using ***geographically dispersed clusters***, where the cluster nodes are located at two different sites. Geographically dispersed clusters provide automatic failover if the primary server is brought down. This reduces the total service downtime in the case of a loss of a business-critical server and requires a minimum number of servers.

Cluster nodes are kept aware of the status of the other nodes and services through *heartbeats* that can be sent through a dedicated network card. You can thus have at least two network adapters, one for the heartbeat and one to link normal network traffic. Since the servers provide access to the same files or databases, they often use the same central storage such as a SAN.

The recommended hardware for a failover cluster includes:

- Duplicate servers—The computers that will function as cluster nodes should be as similar as possible in terms of memory, processor type, and other hardware components.

- Shared storage—All the cluster servers should have exclusive access to shared storage, such as that provided by a Fibre Channel or iSCSI storage area network. The shared storage can also have a witness disk, which holds the cluster configuration database.

- Redundant network connections—Connect the cluster servers to the network in a way that avoids a single point of failure, including using redundant switches, routers, and network adapters.

You then validate your hardware configuration, and then create a cluster using the Failover Cluster Manager.

In addition to the hardware recommendations, your servers must also meet the following software requirements:

- Operating system—All the servers in a cluster must be running the same edition of the same operating system. In addition, the computers in a failover cluster must be running Windows Server 2008 Enterprise or Datacenter. The Standard and Web editions do not support failover clustering.

- Application—All of the cluster servers must run the same version of the redundant application.

- Updates—All of the cluster servers must have the same operating system and application updates installed.

- Active Directory—All of the cluster servers must be in the same Active Directory domain, and they must be either member servers or domain controllers. Microsoft recommends that all cluster servers be member servers, not domain controllers.

You can add as many as eight nodes to the cluster if the computers are running on the x86 or IA64 platform, or 16 nodes if the computers are using x64 hardware.

 VALIDATE A FAILOVER CLUSTER CONFIGURATION

GET READY. Log on to Windows Server 2008 using an account with administrative privileges. When the logon process is completed, close the Initial Configuration Tasks window and any other windows that appear.

   1. Click Start, and then click Administrative Tools > Failover Cluster Management. The Failover Cluster Management console appears, as shown in Figure 12-1.

Figure 12-1

Failover Cluster Management
console

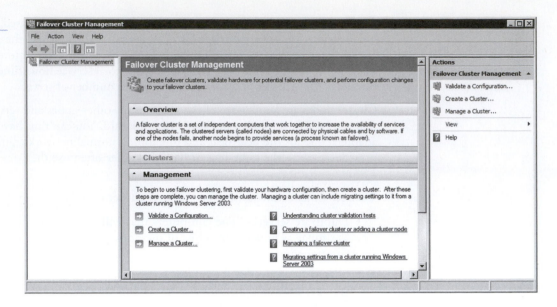

2. In the detail (middle) pane, in the Management box, click Validate a Configuration. The Validate a Configuration Wizard appears.

3. Click Next to bypass the *Before You Begin* page. The *Select Servers or a Cluster* page appears, as shown in Figure 12-2.

Figure 12-2

Selecting the servers to act as cluster nodes

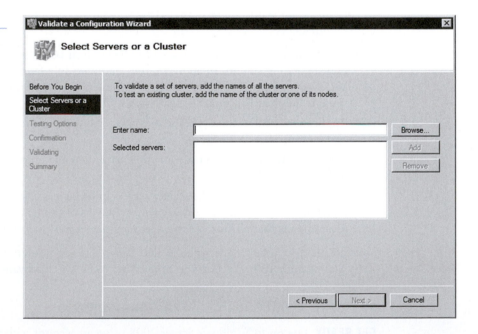

4. Key or browse to the name of the first server you want to add to the cluster and click Add. The server appears in the Selected servers list.

5. Repeat the process to add the rest of the cluster servers to the Selected servers list. Then, click Next. The *Testing Options* page appears.

6. Leave the Run all tests option selected and click Next. The *Confirmation* page appears.

7. Click Next. The *Validating* page appears as the wizard performs the testing process. When the testing process is completed, the *Summary* page appears.

8. Click View Report. An Internet Explorer window appears containing a detailed report of the validation tests.

9. Click Finish and close the Failover Cluster Management console.

 CREATE A FAILOVER CLUSTER

GET READY. Log on to Windows Server 2008 using an account with administrative privileges. When the logon process is completed, close the Initial Configuration Tasks window and any other windows that appear.

1. Click Start, and then click Administrative Tools > Failover Cluster Management. The Failover Cluster Management console appears.

2. In the detail (middle) pane, in the Management box, click Create a Cluster. The *Create Cluster Wizard* page appears.

3. If it appears, click Next to bypass the *Before You Begin* page. The *Select Servers* page appears, as shown in Figure 12-3.

Figure 12-3

Create Cluster Wizard page

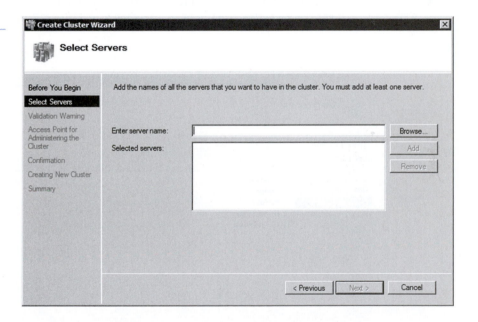

4. Key or browse to the name of the first server you want to add to the cluster and click Add. The server appears in the Selected servers list.

5. Repeat the process to add the rest of the cluster servers to the Selected servers list. Then, click Next. The *Access Point for Administering the Cluster* page appears, as shown in Figure 12-4.

Figure 12-4

The *Access Point for Administering the Cluster* page

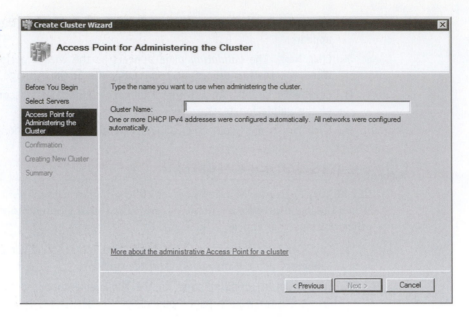

6. In the Cluster Name text box, key a name for the cluster and click Next. The wizard obtains an IP address for the cluster on each network using DHCP and the *Confirmation* page appears, as shown in Figure 12-5.

Figure 12-5

Confirmation page

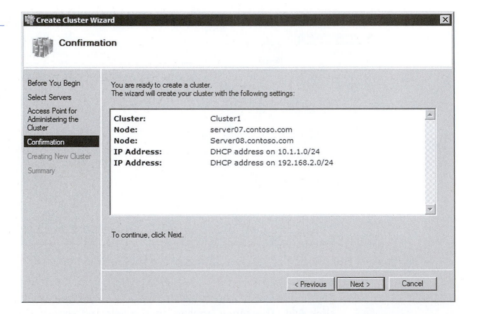

7. Click Next. The *Creating New Cluster* page appears.
8. When the cluster creation process is completed, the *Summary* page appears. Click Finish. The cluster appears in the console's scope (left) pane, as shown in Figure 12-6.

Figure 12-6

A created cluster

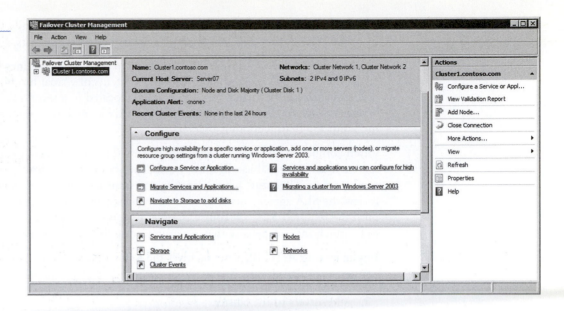

9. Close the Failover Cluster Management console.

USING LOAD-BALANCING CLUSTERS

Load balancing/network load balancing (NLB) is the configuration of multiple computers as one virtual server to share the workload among multiple computers. As far as the users are concerned, they are accessing the virtual machine and the requests are distributed among the nodes within the cluster. NLB enhances the availability and scalability of Internet server applications such as those used on web, FTP, firewall, proxy, virtual private network (VPN), and other mission-critical servers.

Each node in the NLB cluster is assigned a unique set of cluster IP addresses so that users can access the cluster. The requests are distributed among the various nodes. In addition, each node will have its own dedicated IP addresses for each host. For load-balanced applications, when a host fails or goes offline, the load is automatically redistributed among the computers that are still operating.

For each node to keep track of the status of one another, the NLB cluster exchanges heartbeat (or keep-alive) messages. By default, when a host does not send heartbeat messages within five seconds, it has failed. When a host has failed, the remaining hosts in the cluster converge to determine which hosts are still active members, elect the host with the highest priority as the new default host, and ensure that all new client requests are handled by the surviving hosts. Convergence generally takes only a few seconds, so interruption in client service by the cluster is minimal. During convergence, hosts that are still active continue handling client requests without affecting existing connections. All servers are in convergence when all hosts agree with the cluster membership for several heartbeat periods.

NLB is an effective way to provide availability and scalability for applications. The suitability of applications for NLB is determined by how they store data. Host priority and affinity can be used to control how requests are distributed to nodes in an NLB cluster. You can also select between unicast and multicast communication in an NLB cluster.

NLB is a software-based solution that is fully distributed. There is no central communication point that can act as a bottleneck of a single point of failure. It provides both scalability and availability.

To scale an application with NLB, additional nodes are needed. When a node is added, it can begin servicing application requests and reduce the load on existing servers. The availability of services in an NLB cluster is based on server failure. When one node in a cluster fails, the load is automatically distributed among the remaining nodes. However, NLB is not capable of detecting application failure. Consequently, if an application fails, the node is not removed from the NLB cluster and, as a result, clients will experience errors.

Hyper-V virtualization supports quick migration of virtual machines between servers. First, a virtual machine is paused, which writes the contents of virtual machine memory to disk. The disk storage with the virtual machine is then allocated to a second server. The virtual machine is then started on the second server. When a SAN is used, this process can be accomplished more quickly than rebooting a server.

Often companies have service-level agreements (SLAs) that specify how much a server or service must be available—in other words, specifying the maximum time a server or service can be down. Therefore, when planning and implementing servers and services, you need to review the SLA agreements so as to choose the appropriate hardware and software to accomplish the required SLA. Of course, a server design that can support five or six nines is going to be much more expensive than one supporting 99% availability.

Implementing an NLB cluster involves the following tasks:

1. Create the cluster.
2. Add servers to the cluster.
3. Specify a name and IP address for the cluster.
4. Create port rules that specify which traffic the cluster should balance among the cluster servers.

  CREATE AN NLB CLUSTER

GET READY. Log on to Windows Server 2008 using an account with administrative privileges. When the logon process is completed, close the Initial Configuration Tasks window and any other windows that appear.

1. Click Start, and then click Administrative Tools > Network Load Balancing Manager. The Network Load Balancing Manager console appears, as shown in Figure 12-7.

Figure 12-7

Network Load Balancing Manager console

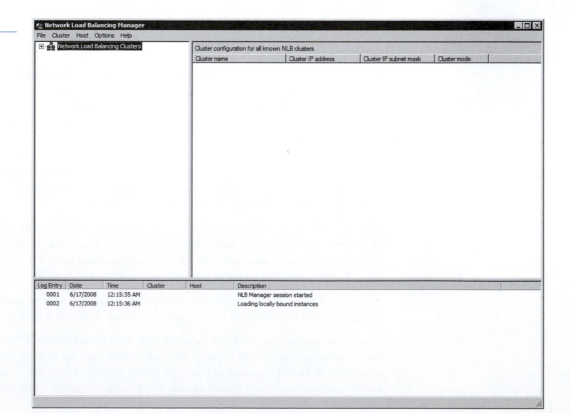

2. In the scope (left) pane, right-click Network Load Balancing Clusters and, from the context menu, select New Cluster. The *New Cluster: Connect* page appears, as shown in Figure 12-08.

Figure 12-8

New Cluster: Connect page

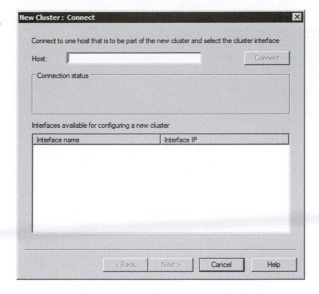

3. In the Host text box, key the name of the first server you want to add to the cluster and click Connect. The network interfaces in the computer appear.

4. Select the interface over which the server will receive traffic destined for the clustered application and click Next. The *New Cluster: Host Parameters* page appears, as shown in Figure 12-9.

Figure 12-9

New Clusters: Host Parameters page

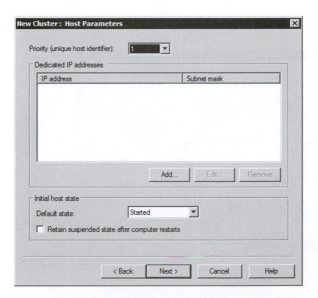

5. Configure the following parameters, if necessary:

- Priority—Specifies a unique identifier for each host in the cluster. The host with the lowest identifier handles all of the cluster traffic that is not forwarded by port rules.

- Dedicated IP addresses—Specifies the IP address and Subnet Mask that the host will use for noncluster traffic, that is, the original IP address of the server's network interface.

- Initial host state—Specifies whether the NLB service should start and add the host to the cluster each time Windows starts.

6. Click Next. The *New Cluster: Cluster IP Addresses* page appears, as shown in Figure 12-10.

Figure 12-10

New Cluster: Cluster IP Address page

7. Click Add. The Add IP Address dialog box appears.

8. In the IPv4 address and Subnet Mask text boxes, specify the IP address you want to use for the NLB cluster and its subnet mask value. This address must be different from the server's own host address and unique on the network. Then click OK. The address you specified appears in the *New Cluster: Cluster IP Addresses* page.

9. Click Next. The *New Cluster: Cluster Parameters* page appears, as shown in Figure 12-11.

Figure 12-11

New Cluster: Cluster Parameters page

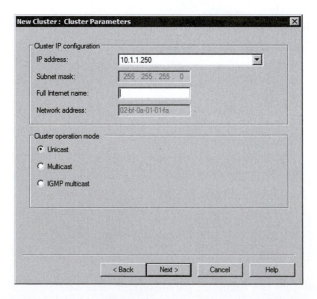

10. In the Full Internet name text box, key the name you want to assign to the cluster, such as cluster.contoso.com. In the Cluster operation mode box, specify whether you want the cluster's network address to be a unicast or multicast address.

11. Click Next. The *New Cluster: Port Rules* page appears, as shown in Figure 12-12.

Figure 12-12

New Cluster: Port Rules page

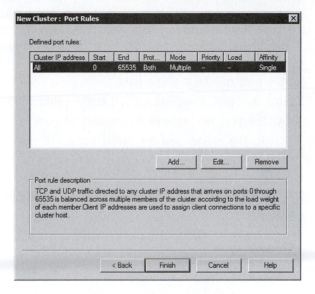

12. Click Add. The Add/Edit Port Rule dialog box appears, as shown in Figure 12-13.

Figure 12-13

Add/Edit Port Rule dialog box

13. Configure the following parameters:

- Cluster IP address—If the cluster has multiple IP addresses, use this drop-down list to select the one to which the rule should apply.
- Port range—Specifies the port numbers of the traffic you want to balance among the cluster servers. For example, to balance only standard incoming web traffic, you would use the values 80 and 80.
- Protocols—Specifies whether you want to balance TCP (Transmission Control Protocol) traffic, UDP (User Datagram Protocol) traffic, or both.
- Multiple host—When selected, causes the cluster to distribute incoming traffic among all of the servers in the cluster.

- Affinity—When the Multiple host option is selected, specifies that the cluster should forward incoming messages from the same IP address to a single host (the default). The None option specifies that the cluster can forward incoming messages from the same IP address to any host, and the Network option specifies that the cluster should forward incoming messages from the same network address to the same host.

- Single host—Specifies that the cluster should forward all of the incoming traffic for the port rule to a single host.

- Disable this port range—Blocks all traffic conforming to this port rule.

14. Click OK. The port rule appears in the Defined Port Rules list.

15. Click Finish. The cluster and the server appear in the scope pane, as shown in Figure 12-14.

Figure 12-14

The NLB cluster

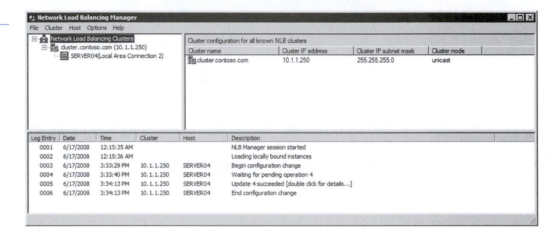

16. Close the Network Load Balancing Manager console.

Backing Up and Restoring

THE BOTTOM LINE

Data stored on a computer or on the network is vital to the users and probably the organization. It represents hours of work and its data is the sometime irreplaceable. One of the most essential components of any server design is the backup. No matter how much effort, hardware, and software you put into a system, you will eventually have failure. Sometimes when the downtime occurs, you may have data loss.

CERTIFICATION READY
What is the best method for data recovery?
4.1

A *backup* or the process of backing up involves making copies of data that can be used to restore the original after a data-loss event, system failure, or outage. These copies can be used to restore entire systems following a disaster or to restore a small set of files that were accidentally corrupted or deleted.

TAKE NOTE*

The best method for data recovery is backup, backup, backup.

When planning your backups, you also need to plan where backup files are going to be stored. If files are stored throughout your corporation, including on users' local computers, it is very difficult to back up all of these files. Therefore, you most likely will need to use some form of technology to keep your files in a limited number of locations. For example, you can use file redirection to store Desktop and My Documents on a file server by configuring the user profiles.

Multiple technologies are available to help centralize your data. Microsoft offers Distributed File System (DFS), which can be used to replicate shared folders to other servers. In addition, both Microsoft SQL Server and Microsoft Exchange Server have technology to replicate the databases to other servers, including servers in other locations.

Backup Media

With early networks and servers, a backup was done with floppy disks. Unfortunately, floppy disks were very limited in size, speed, and life span. Eventually, magnetic tapes were developed and become the standard mechanism for corporations to perform backups and storage. More recently, hard-disk storage has become a competing technology, and optical disks have become more common for backups.

Traditionally, magnetic tapes have been the most commonly used medium for bulk data storage, backup, and archiving. Tape is a sequential-access medium, so even though access times may be poor, the rate of continuously writing or reading data can actually be very large. For larger organizations, you will use multiple tape drives connected to a tape library that can automatically swap and manage tapes.

Recently, because of increased capacity at lower cost, hard drives have become a viable option for backups. Hard disks can be included in the SAN, NAS, internal hard drives, and external hard drives. Some disk-based backup systems, such as virtual tape libraries, support data deduplication, which can dramatically reduce the amount of disk storage capacity consumed by daily and weekly backup data.

Usually when hard disks are used for backups, they provide backup of recent data and the data will be copied to tape and taken offsite for longer term storage and archiving. If a failure occurs, you can quickly restore from the disks. If you need to recover or read data from the past, you will then have to retrieve the tapes from offsite and read them.

Another medium that is becoming more popular for backups is recordable optical disks such as CDs, DVDs and even Blu-ray. Unfortunately, the newer formats tend to cost more, which may prohibit their use for backups, and there is also some concern about the lifetime of selected optical disks.

Backup Items

When novices think of backups, they will most likely think of backing up data files such as Microsoft Word or Excel documents. However, more than just data files should be backed up. You have the program files that make the computer do what it needs to do. You also have mailboxes, email databases, SQL databases, and other data types that may need special software to read and back up. In addition, when determining what and how often to backup, you should look at the time it would take to reinstall, reconfigure, or recover the item. For example, it might take days to install and configure Microsoft Exchange, but only a relatively short time to restore it from backup.

When planning backups, you should separate your program files and your data files. Program files usually do not change and so they need not be backed up often. Data files change often, so they should be backed up more often. If you isolate them in different areas, you can create different backup policies for each area.

Databases usually consist of one or more database files and one or more log files. The primary data file is the starting point of the database and points to the other files in the database. Every database has one or more primary data file. The recommended file name extension for primary data files is .mdf.

Log files hold all the log information that is used to recover the database. For example, you can restore from backup the entire database as is or back up to a point in time if you have the complete log files. The recommended file name extension for log files is .ldf.

Another item that must be handled is the system state. The Windows system state is a collection of system components not contained in a simple file that can be backed up easily. It includes:

- The boot files
- The system registry settings
- The system protected files (SPF) Critical files needed to run Windows
- The Active Directory files
- The shared system volume (SYSVOL)
- The COM+ class registration database

Windows backup and most commercial backup software packages will back up the Windows system state. If you want to perform a complete restore of a system running Windows, you will need to back up all files on the drive and the system state.

Backup Methods

When planning and implementing backups, you will need to determine when and how often you are going to back up, what hardware and software you are going to use, where you will store the backups, and how long you will store them.

MEDIA MANAGEMENT METHODS

Your backup plan needs to balance accessibility, security, and cost. Larger organizations will often combine one of the following management methods:

- Online—The most accessible type of data storage, usually using hard disks or disk arrays. Restore can begin in milliseconds, but can be relatively expensive. In addition, online storage can be easily deleted or overwritten accidentally or intentionally.
- Near-line—Typically less accessible and less expensive than online storage, usually consisting of a tape library with the restore time beginning in seconds or minutes.
- Offline—Requires some direct human action to physically load tapes in a tape library or drive. Access time can vary from minutes to hours or even days if you have to order tapes from an offsite storage area.
- Backup site or Data Recovery (DR) site—In the event of a disaster, you can switch to the backup site/DR site while you fix or repair the primary site. Unfortunately, this method is the most expensive solution and the most difficult to implement properly.

BACKUP TYPES

Backup software should include different types of backups, each varying in the time needed to do a backup and restore. Traditional backups include:

- Full backup
- Full backup with incremental backups
- Full backup with differential backup

Full backups back up all files and data that have been designated. For files, it will shut off an archive attribute bit to indicate that the file has been backed up. For example, you do a full backup once a day, once a week, or once a month depending on the importance of the data and how often it changes. To perform a restore from a full backup, you just need to grab the last full backup. A full backup offers the fastest restore.

Full backups with *incremental backups* starts up with a full backup followed by several incremental backups. For example, once a week, you perform a full backup on Friday night, which shuts off the archive attribute indicating that the files were backed up. Then any new files or changed files have the archive attribute turned on. You then perform an incremental backup Monday, Tuesday, Wednesday, and Thursday night, which back up only new and changed files and shut off the archive attribute. When you do a restore, you restore the last full backup and then restore each incremental backup from oldest to newest. Full backups with incremental backups offer fastest backup.

Full backup with *differential backup* starts up with a full backup followed by several differential backups. For example, once a week, you perform a full backup on Friday night, which shuts off the archive attribute indicating that the files were backed up. Then any new files or changed files have the archive attribute turned on. You then perform a differential backup Monday, Tuesday, Wednesday, and Thursday night, which will only back up new and changed files since the last full backup but does not turn off the archive attribute. When you do a restore, you restore the last full backup and the last differential backup.

Another backup type that is available from backup software packages, including Microsoft Windows Backup software, is the *copy backup*. A copy backup backs up the designated files but does not shut off the archive attribute. This is used for impromptu backups such as you might do before you make a system or application change. Since copy backup does not modify the archive attribute, it will not interfere with your normal backup schedules.

BACKUP ROTATION SCHEMES

One of the questions you should ask yourself is how often you should do a backup. The answer will vary based on your needs. You must first look at how important your data is and how much effort would it require to recreate it if it is lost, assuming it can be recreated at all. You should also consider the effect on your company if the data is lost. Important or critical data should be backed up nightly. Data that does not change much can be backed up weekly, and data that does not change at all can be backed up monthly.

The next question should be how long should you keep backups? That question is not easy to answer because it is based on the needs of your organization, including legal requirements your organization must follow.

Another consideration you should keep in mind is that backups do fail from time to time. Therefore, you should periodically test your backups by doing a restore to make sure that a backup is working and that you are backing up the necessary files.

Second, you should have some type of rotation. One common backup rotation scheme is *grandfather-father-son (GFS)*. The son backup is done once a day and those backups are rotated on a daily basis. At the end of the week, the daily backup is promoted to a weekly backup. The weekly or father backups are rotated on a weekly basis, with one graduating to grandfather status each month. The monthly backups are traditionally stored offsite; of course, this is based on your assessment of what needs to be sent offsite.

Microsoft Windows Backup

Windows includes Microsoft Windows Backup, which will let you back up a system. When determining if you are going to use Microsoft Windows Backup, you should take into account that third-party backup software packages usually offer more features and options.

To access the backup and recovery tools for Windows Server 2008, you must install the Windows Server Backup Command-line Tools and Windows PowerShell items that are available in the Add Features Wizard in Server Manager. To run the Windows Server Backup, you must be a member of the Backup Operators or Administrators group. See Figure 12-15.

Figure 12-15

The Windows Server Backup console

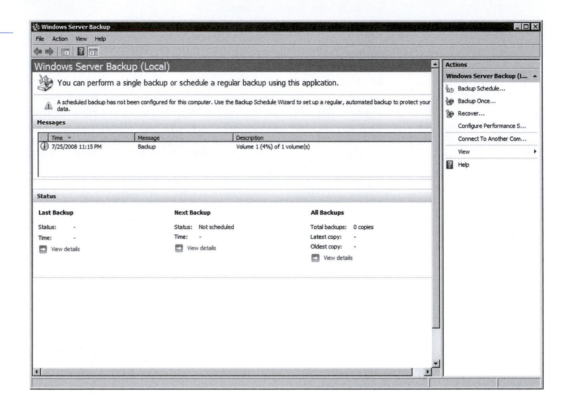

You can create a backup using the Backup Schedule Wizard or by using the Backup Once option. You can back up to any local drive or to a shared folder on another server.

When Windows Server Backup takes control of a backup disk, it creates separate new files for the backup job(s) it performs each day. The system retains the files for all the old jobs until the disk is filled or 512 jobs are stored, whichever comes first. Then the system begins deleting the oldest jobs as needed.

 CREATE A SINGLE BACKUP JOB

GET READY. Log on to Windows Server 2008. When the logon process is completed, close the Initial Configuration Tasks window and any other windows that appear.

1. Click Start. Then, click Administrative Tools > Windows Server Backup. The Windows Server Backup console appears.
2. In the actions pane, click Backup Once. The Backup Once Wizard appears, displaying the *Backup options* page, as shown in Figure 12-16.

Figure 12-16

The *Backup options* page of the Backup Once Wizard

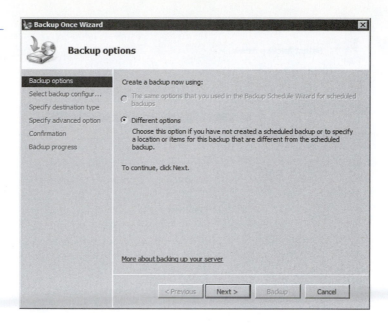

3. Click **Next** to accept the default Different options option. The *Select backup configuration* page appears, as shown in Figure 12-17.

Figure 12-17

The *Select backup configuration* page of the Backup Once Wizard

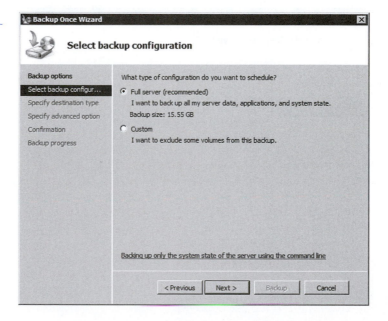

4. Select the **Custom** option and click **Next**. The *Select backup items* page appears, as shown in Figure 12-18.

Figure 12-18

The *Select backup items* page of the Backup Once Wizard

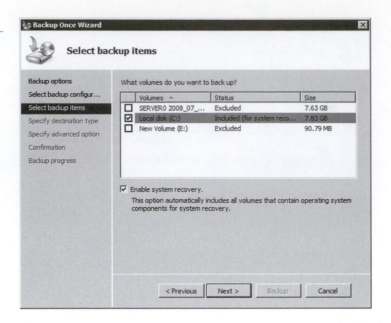

5. Select the volume(s) you want to back up. Leave the Enable system recovery check box selected and click Next. The *Specify destination type* page appears, as shown in Figure 12-19.

Figure 12-19

The *Specify destination type* page of the Backup Once Wizard

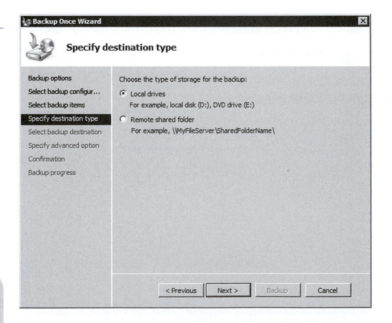

TAKE NOTE *

Selecting the Enable system recovery check box causes Windows Server Backup to back up the system state.

6. Leave the Local drives option selected and click Next. The *Select backup destination* page appears, as shown in Figure 12-20.

Figure 12-20

The *Select backup destination* page of the Backup Once Wizard

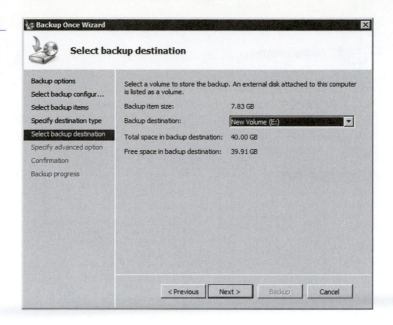

7. In the Backup destination dropdown list, select the volume that you will use for your backup drive and click Next. The *Specify advanced option* page appears, as shown in Figure 12-21.

Figure 12-21

The *Specify advanced option* page of the Backup Once Wizard

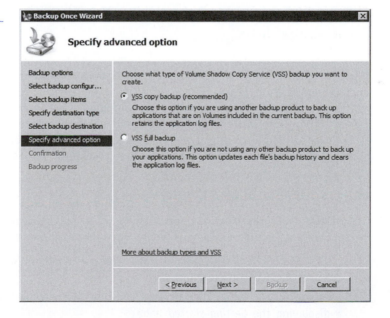

8. Leave the VSS copy backup option selected and click Next. The *Confirmation* page appears.

9. Click Backup. The *Backup progress* page appears, as shown in Figure 12-22, and the backup job begins.

Figure 12-22

The *Backup progress* page of
the Backup Once Wizard

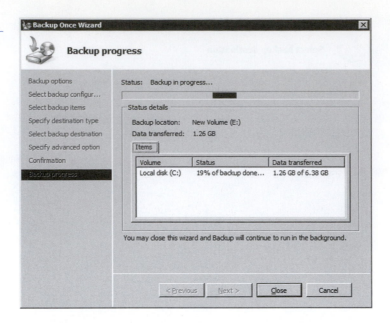

10. Click Close. The Backup Once Wizard closes. The backup job continues in the back-
    ground, even after you close the wizard and the console.

Performing a Scheduled Backup

> Windows Server Backup makes it possible to schedule a backup job to execute at the
> same time(s) each day.

When you create a scheduled backup job, the options are somewhat different from those for a
single, interactive job. First, you cannot use optical disks or network shares as backup drives;
you must use a hard disk connected to the computer, either internal or external. Second, you
cannot simply perform a backup to a file stored anywhere on the computer and manage it
using Windows Explorer, as you would any other file. Windows Server Backup reformats the
backup disk you select and uses it exclusively for backups.

 CREATE A SCHEDULED BACKUP

TAKE NOTE*

Note that the Enable
system recovery check
box does not appear on
the *Select backup items*
page because scheduled
jobs always back up
the system state
automatically.

GET READY. Log on to Windows Server 2008. When the logon process is completed, close
the Initial Configuration Tasks window and any other windows that appear.

1. Click Start. Then, click Administrative Tools > Windows Server Backup. The Windows
   Server Backup console appears.
2. In the actions pane, click Backup Schedule. The Backup Schedule Wizard appears,
   displaying the *Getting started* page
3. Click Next. The *Select backup configuration* page appears.
4. Select the Custom option and click Next. The *Select backup items* page appears.
5. Select the volume(s) you want to back up and click Next. The *Specify backup time*
   page appears, as shown in Figure 12-23.

Figure 12-23

The *Specify backup time* page of the Backup Schedule Wizard

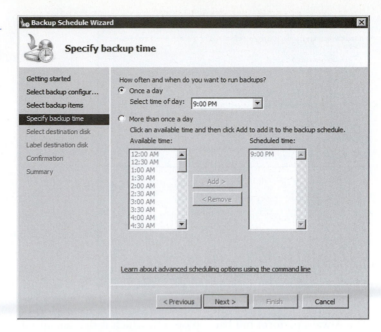

6. With the Once a day option selected, use the Select time of day dropdown list to specify when the backup should occur. Then, click Next. The *Select destination disk* page appears.

7. Select the disk you want to use for your backups. The Available disks box lists only the external disks connected to the computer. To use an internal disk, you must click Show All Available Disks and select the disk(s) you want to add to the list from the Show All Available Disks dialog box.

8. Click Next. A Windows Server Backup message box appears, informing you that the program will reformat the disk(s) you selected and dedicate it exclusively to backups. Click Yes to continue. The *Label destination disk* page appears.

9. Use the name specified on this page to label the backup disk. Then click Next. The *Confirmation* page appears.

10. Click Finish. The wizard formats the backup disk and schedules the backup job to begin at the time you specified.

11. Click Close. The wizard closes.

12. Close the Windows Server Backup console.

Windows Server Backup allows you to schedule only one backup job, so the next time you start the Backup Schedule Wizard, your only options are to modify or stop the current backup job.

Configuring Incremental Backups

Unlike older Windows backup packages and most commercial software packages, Windows Server Backup included with Windows Server 2008 does not support incremental backups as a general setting.

To perform an incremental backup, you have to select Configure Performance Settings from the actions pane in the Windows Server Backup console to open the Optimize Backup Performance dialog box, as shown in Figure 12-24.

Figure 12-24

The *Optimize Backup Performance* dialog box

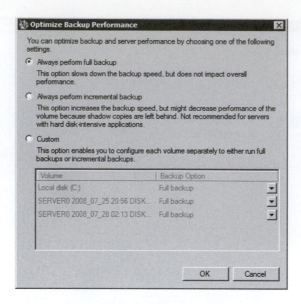

The Always perform full backup option, which is the default setting, causes the program to copy every file on the selected volume(s) to the backup medium every time you perform a backup. This means that the program copies all of the operating system and application files on the volume(s), files which never change, to the backup disk over and over, possibly occupying a great deal of space to no useful end.

Performing a Restore

Windows Server Backup enables you to restore entire volumes or selected files, folders, and applications, using a wizard-based interface in the Windows Server Backup console.

Once you have completed at least one backup job, you can use the Windows Server Backup console to restore all or part of the data on your backup disk. Administrators should perform test restores at regular intervals to ensure that the backups are completing correctly.

To perform a restore of selected files or folders, use the following procedure.

 PERFORM A RESTORE

GET READY. Log on to Windows Server 2008. When the logon process is completed, close the Initial Configuration Tasks window and any other windows that appear.

1. Click Start. Then, click Administrative Tools > Windows Server Backup. The Windows Server Backup console appears.

2. In the actions pane, click Recover. The Recovery Wizard appears, displaying the *Getting started* page, as shown in Figure 12-25.

Figure 12-25

The *Getting started* page of the
Recovery Wizard

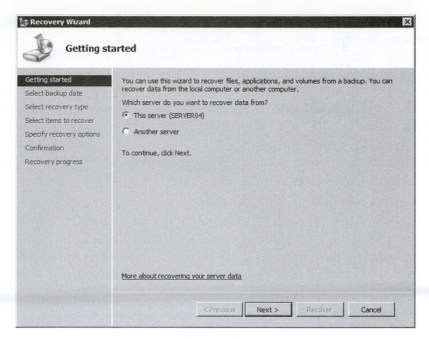

> 3. Leave the This server option selected and click Next. The *Select backup date* page appears, as shown in Figure 12-26.

Figure 12-26

The *Select backup date* page
of the Recovery Wizard

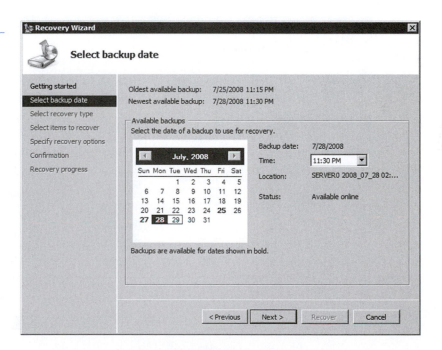

> 4. In the Available backups box, select the date of the backup you want to restore from and, if you performed more than one backup on that date, the time as well. Then, click Next. The *Select recovery type* page appears, as shown in Figure 12-27.

Figure 12-27

The *Select recovery type* page of the Recovery Wizard

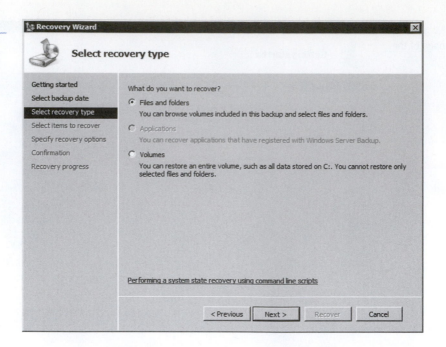

5. Leave the Files and folders option selected and click Next. The *Select items to recover* page appears, as shown in Figure 12-28.

Figure 12-28

The *Select items to recover* page of the Recovery Wizard

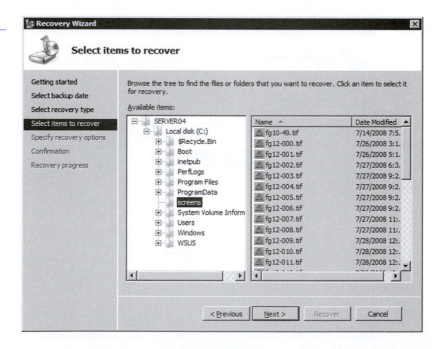

6. Expand the server folder and browse to the folder containing the files or subfolders you want to restore. Select the desired files and subfolders and click Next. The *Specify recovery options* page appears, as shown in Figure 12-29.

Figure 12-29

The *Specify recovery options* page of the Recovery Wizard

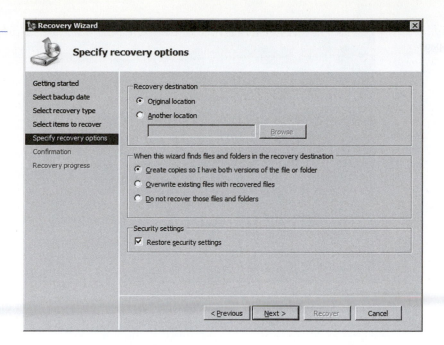

7. In the Recovery destination box, specify whether you want to restore the selections to their original location or to another location of your choice.

8. In the When the wizard finds files and folders in the recovery destination box, specify whether you want to copy, overwrite, or skip the existing files and folders.

9. In the Security settings box, specify whether you want to restore the access control lists of the selected files and folders. Then, click Next. The *Confirmation* page appears.

10. Click Recover. The wizard restores the selected files.

11. Click Close.

12. Close the Windows Server Backup console.

Restoring an Entire Server

If a disaster occurs in which all of a server's data is lost, or even just the volumes containing the boot and operating system files, the server cannot start. You can still do a full restore using a Windows installation disk.

To perform a full server restore, you must boot the system using a Windows Server 2008 installation disk and access the backup disk using the Windows RE (Recovery Environment) interface. To perform a full server restore on a new computer from a backup on an external hard disk, use the following procedure.

 PERFORM A FULL SERVER RESTORE

GET READY. Connect the external hard disk drive to the computer, if necessary. Then, insert a Windows Server 2008 installation disk into the computer's DVD drive and start the system.

1. Click Next to accept the default values in the language settings page. The *Install Windows* page appears, as shown in Figure 12-30.

Figure 12-30

The *Install Windows* page

2. Click Repair Your Computer. The System Recovery Options dialog box appears, as shown in Figure 12-31.

Figure 12-31

The *System Recovery Options* dialog box

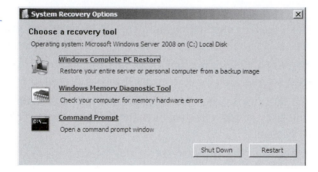

3. Click Windows Complete PC Restore. The Windows Complete PC Restore Wizard appears, as shown in Figure 12-32.

Figure 12-32

The Windows Complete PC Restore Wizard

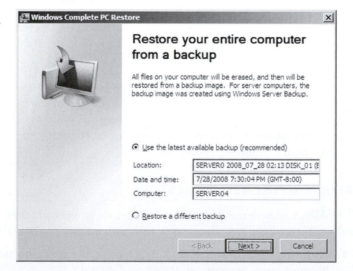

4. Click Next to restore from the latest available backup. The *Choose how to restore the backup* page appears.

5. Select the Format and repartition disks check box and click Next. The final page of the wizard appears.

6. Click Finish to begin the restore.

7. Restart the computer after removing the disk from the DVD drive.

Once the process is completed, the system restarts using the files restored from the backup.

 RECOVER A BACKUP CATALOG

GET READY. To recover a backup catalog using the Catalog Recovery Wizard:

1. Click Start, click Administrative Tools, and then click Windows Server Backup.

2. In the Actions pane of the snap-in default page, under Windows Server Backup, click Recover Catalog. This opens the Catalog Recovery Wizard.

3. On the *Specify storage type* page, if you do not have a backup that you can use to recover the catalog, and just want to delete the catalog, click I don't have any usable backups, click Next, and then click Finish. If you do have a backup that you can use, specify whether the backup is on a local drive or remote shared folder, and then click Next.

4. If the backup is on a local drive (including DVDs), on the *Select backup location* page, select the drive that contains the backup you want to use from the drop-down list. If you are using DVDs, make sure the last DVD of the series is in the drive. Click Next.

5. If the backup is on a remote shared folder, on the *Specify remote folder* page, type the path to the folder that contains the backup that you want to use, and then click Next.

6. You will receive a message that you will not be able to access backups taken after the backup that you are using for the recovery. Click Yes.

7. On the *Confirmation* page, review the details, and then click Finish to recover the catalog.

8. On the *Summary* page, click Close.

Once the catalog recovery is completed or you have deleted the catalog, you must close and then re-open Windows Server Backup to refresh the view.

Shadow Copy (Volume Snapshot Service or Volume Shadow Copy Service or VSS) is a technology in Microsoft Windows that allows you take a snapshot of data, even if it has a lock on a specific volume at a specific point in time, so that the file can be backed up. Today, most backup software uses VSS to make backups of files within Windows.

Shadow Copies of Shared Folders

Windows Server 2003 introduces a new feature called shadow copies of shared folders, which is also used in Windows Server 2008. Shadow copies, when configured, automatically create backup copies of the data stored in shared folders on specific NTFS drive volumes at scheduled times.

Shadow copies allow users to retrieve previous versions of files and folders on their own, without requiring IT personnel to restore files or folders from backup media. Of course, you need to have sufficient disk space to store the shadow copies, at least 100 MB of free space.

ENABLE AND CONFIGURE SHADOW COPIES:

GET READY. To enable and configure shadow copies of shared folders:

1. Click Start, click Administrative Tools, and then click Computer Management.

2. In the console tree, right-click Shared Folders, click All Tasks, and click Configure Shadow Copies.

3. In Select a volume, click the volume for which you want to enable Shadow Copies of Shared Folders, and then click Enable. See Figure 12-33.

4. You will see an alert that Windows will create a shadow copy now with the current settings and that the settings might not be appropriate for servers with high I/O loads. Click Yes if you want to continue or No if you want to select a different volume or settings.

5. To make changes to the default schedule and storage area, click Settings.

Figure 12-33

Enabling shadow copies

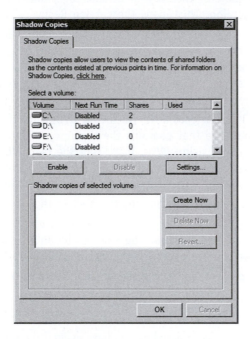

Once you enable shadow copies of shared folders and start creating shadow copies, you can use the Previous Version feature to recover previous versions of files and folders, or files and folders that have been renamed or deleted.

RESTORE A PREVIOUS VERSION OF A FILE OR FOLDER:

GET READY. To restore a previous version of a file or folder:

1. Locate the file or folder that you want to restore, right-click the file or folder, and click Properties. The Properties dialog box will appear.

2. Click the Previous Versions tab, click the version of the file that you want to restore, and then click Restore. A warning message about restoring a previous version will appear. Click Restore to complete the procedure. See Figure 12-34.

Restoring a previous version will delete the current version. If you choose to restore a previous version of a folder, the folder will be restored to its state at the date and time of the version you selected. You will lose any changes that you have made to files in the folder since that time. Instead, if you do not want to delete the current version of a file or folder, click Copy to copy the previous version to a different location.

Figure 12-34

Restoring a previous version

Recovering Active Directory Domain Services

THE BOTTOM LINE

Since Active Directory is essential for authentication, authorization, and auditing, backing up and restoring Active Directory is essential. While Active Directory is backed up with the System State, restoring it can be tricky.

Every company or organization that uses Active Directory should have at least two domain controllers. If you have two domain controllers and one fails, you just need to fix the computer (or at worst replace it), install Active Directory Domain Services, and add it back to the domain as a domain controller. With one server failing, users will still be able to access their resources since the remaining domain controller can provide services.

If someone deletes an individual user or group, you cannot restore it using Windows Backup. You can restore the entire contents of Active Directory as it stood at the time of the most recent backup. However, several commercial backup packages do support backing up and restoring individual Active Directory objects.

If you need to back up only the system state, you could use the Wbadmin.exe command:

```
wbadmin start SystemStateBackup
- backuptarget:drive_letter
```

To restore just the system state from a backup, use the following command:

```
wbadmin Start SystemStateRecovery -versionMM/DD/YYYY-HH:MM
```

The MM/DD/YYYY-HH:MM variable specifies the version identifier for the backup from which you want to restore the system state. To list the version identifiers of the available backups, use the following command, as shown in Figure 12-35:

```
wbadmin get versions
```

Figure 12-35

Displaying backup version
identifiers

If you have multiple domain controllers and you restore a system state of a domain controller, by default, you are doing a ***non-authoritative restore***, which means that the Active Directory database is restored in the exact state as it was at the time of the backup. However, since objects are date- and time-stamped, when Active Directory replication occurs, the other domain controller entries will overwrite the newly restored entries. Therefore, if you are trying to restore deleted objects, the replication process will cause the system to delete the newly restored objects.

If you choose to restore Active Directory so that you can recover deleted objects using a backup done with Windows Backup, you need to perform an ***authoritative restore***. To do an authoritative restore, you must restart the computer, press F8 to access the Advanced Boot Options, and select ***Directory Services Restore Mode***. After logging on using the Administrator account, you can then restore the system state using Wbadmin.exe. Once the restoration of the system state is complete, you can use the Ntdsutil.exe tool to specify the objects that you want restored authoritatively.

If you need to restore a Group policy object (GPO), you need to back up and restore GPOs using the Group Policy Management console. To back up a GPO, you right-click the GPO and select Back Up from the context menu. To restore a GPO, right-click the Group Policy Objects container and, from the context menu, select Manage Backups. The Manage Backups dialog box appears in which you can select the GPO you want to recover and click the Restore button.

SKILL SUMMARY

IN THIS LESSON YOU LEARNED:

- High availability is a system design protocol and associated implementation that ensures a certain degree of operational continuity during a given measurement period.

- A high-availability design must include backup and recovery design.

- Servers and the service they provide are often designed with service-level agreements (SLAs) that state how much a server or services must be available.

- A backup site is the ultimate business-continuity and disaster-recovery mechanism.

- NIC teaming is the process of grouping together two or more physical NICs into one single logical NIC that can be used for network fault tolerance and increased bandwidth through load balancing.

- An uninterruptible power supply or UPS is an electrical device consisting of one or more batteries to provide backup power when a power outage occurs.

- A power generator or a standby power generator is a backup electrical system that operates automatically within seconds of a power outage.

- A server farm or server cluster is a group of linked computers that work together as one computer. Depending on the technology used, clusters can provide fault tolerance (often referred to as availability), load balancing, or both.

- A failover cluster is often used for the back end servers such as a database (such as SQL server) or mail server (such as Exchange server).

- A load-balancing cluster is often used for the front-end that provide the web interface to the back-end servers.

- The most common failover cluster is the active-passive cluster in which both servers are configured to work as the same virtual server, but only one at a time.

- As networking technology has matured and bandwidth has increased, many companies and organizations are using geographically dispersed clusters in which cluster nodes are located at two different sites.

- Cluster nodes are kept aware of the status of the other nodes and services by the use of heartbeats sent through a dedicated network card.

- A backup or the process of backing up refers to making copies of data so that these additional copies may be used to restore the original after a data-loss event.

- The best method for data recovery is backup, backup, backup.

- Traditionally, magnetic tapes have been the most commonly used medium for bulk data storage, backup, and archiving.

- Recently, because hard drives can now provide increased capacity at lower cost, they have become a viable option for backups.

- Full backups backup all files and data that has been designated. For files, it shuts off an archive attribute bit to indicate that the file has been backed up.

- Full backups with incremental backups start with a full backup followed by several incremental backups.

- Full backup with differential backup starts with a full backup followed by several differential backups.

- One common backup rotation scheme is grandfather-father-son (GFS). The son backup is done once a day and those backups are rotated on a daily basis. At the end of the week, the daily backup is promoted to a weekly backup. The weekly or father backups are rotated on a weekly basis with one graduating to grandfather status each month.

- The Windows system state is a collection of system components that are not contained in a simple file that can be backed up easily.

- Windows includes Microsoft Windows Backup, which allows you to back up a system.

- Shadow copies allow users to retrieve previous versions of files and folders on their own, without requiring IT personnel.

- If you have multiple domain controllers and you restore a system state of a domain controller, by default, you are doing a non-authoritative restore, which means that the Active Directory database is restored in the exact state as it was at the time of the backup.

- If you choose to restore Active Directory to restore deleted objects using a backup done with Windows Backup, you need to perform an authoritative restore.

- To do an authoritative restore, you must restart the computer, press F8 to access the Advanced Boot Options, and select Directory Services Restore Mode.

■ Knowledge Assessment

Fill in the Blank

Complete the following sentences by writing the correct word or words in the blanks provided.

1. 99.99% availability means that there are only _____ minutes of downtime per month.

2. A _____ is used to relocate a server in case of a disaster.

3. A _____ is turned off and must be manually turned on or enabled; data usually needs to be restored.

4. You need to use a _____ until the backup generator goes on.

5. A _____ cluster has two computers, only one of which is providing services at any one time.

6. You would normally use _____ to provide redundancy of a web service used as a front-end server.

7. The _____ is a collection of system components that are not contained in a simple file that can be backed up easily.

8. To perform a restore of the system state, you use the _____ command.

9. To do a authoritative restore, you must press the _____ while Windows boots and select Directory Services Restore Mode.

10. A _____ allows users to retrieve previous versions of files and folders on their own.

True / False

Circle T if the statement is true or F if the statement is false.

T | F 1. The SLA states how much a server or services must be available.

T | F 2. A cold site is the most expensive type of backup site.

T | F 3. All nodes of a failover cluster must be located within the same subnet.

T | F 4. A cluster requires shared storage.

T | F 5. The best method for data recovery is backup, backup, backup.

T | F 6. Traditionally, magnetic tapes have been the most commonly used medium for bulk data storage.

T | F 7. Incremental backups backup all files since the last full backup.

T | F 8. A common backup rotation scheme is the Power Restore rotation.

T | F 9. To restore Active Directory, you need to do an authoritative restore.

T | F 10. Cluster nodes are kept aware of the status of the other nodes and services through heartbeats.

Review Question

1. Explain the primary difference between a failover cluster and a network load balancing cluster.

■ Case Scenarios

Scenario 12-1: Designing a Network Backup Solution

Alice is a consultant for a client who wants to install a new network backup system. The client's network has five servers containing company data, with a total capacity of 2000 GB. Roughly a third of the data consists of databases that are updated continually during business hours. The rest is archival data that seldom changes. The company works three shifts during the week, so there is a relatively small backup window of two hours, from 2:00 A.M. to 4:00 A.M. However, the IT department only works from 9:00 A.M. to 5:00 P.M. The company is closed on weekends. The client wants all new data to be protected every night. Alice is planning to purchase a magnetic tape drive for the client, as well as a comprehensive network backup software package. The tape drives Alice has been evaluating are as follows:

- A DDS 160 drive with a maximum capacity of 160 GB and a transfer speed of 6.9 MB/sec
- An SDLT 320 drive with a maximum capacity of 320 GB and a transfer speed of 16 GB/sec
- An LTO Ultrium drive with a maximum capacity of 800 GB and a transfer speed of 120 MB/sec

Specify what types of backup jobs Alice should perform each night and which of the tape drives would enable the company to back up its servers most conveniently.

Scenario 12-2: Recovering from a Disaster

You have configured a grandfather-father-son setup where a full backup is done each weekend and an incremental backup is performed Monday through Thursday. Once a month, a full backup is sent offsite. On Wednesday night, your server fails. What do you need to restore the backup?

Windows Server 2008, Enterprise Administrator (Exam 70-647)

OBJECTIVE DOMAIN	SKILL NUMBER	LESSON NUMBER
Planning network and application services		
Plan for name resolution and IP addressing.	1.1	1
Design for network access.	1.2	8
Plan for application delivery.	1.3	6, 10
Plan for Remote Desktop Services.	1.4	6
Designing core identity and access management components		
Design Active Directory forests and domains.	2.1	2
Design the Active Directory physical topology.	2.2	3
Design the Active Directory administrative model.	2.3	2
Design the enterprise-level group policy strategy.	2.4	3
Designing support identity and access management components		
Plan for domain or forest migration, upgrade, and restructuring.	3.1	4
Design the branch office deployment.	3.2	5
Design and implement public key infrastructure.	3.3	11
Plan for interoperability.	3.4	4
Designing for business continuity and data availability		
Plan for business continuity.	4.1	12
Design for software updates and compliance management.	4.2	7
Design the operating system virtualization strategy.	4.3	10
Design for data management and data access.	4.4	9

Index

327

Notes

Notes

Notes

Notes

Notes

Notes

Notes

Notes

Notes

Windows Server 2008 R2 System Requirements

If your CD/DVD is defective, please return it to Wiley. Please do not return it to Microsoft Corporation. Any customer service support provided, if at all, will be by Wiley. Please do not contact Microsoft Corporation for product support.

To use Windows Server 2008 R2 Service Pack 1, you need:*

COMPONENT	REQUIREMENT
Processor	Minimum: Single processor with 1.4 GHz (x64 processor) or 1.3 GHz (Dual Core)
	Note: An Intel Itanium 2 processor is required for Windows Server 2008 R2 with SP1 for Itanium-Based Systems. To use RemoteFX, a SLAT-capable processor is required on the host.
Memory	Minimum: 512 MB RAM
	Maximum: 8 GB (Foundation) or 32 GB (Standard) or 2 TB (Enterprise, Datacenter, and Itanium-Based Systems)
Disk Space Requirements	Minimum: 32 GB or greater
	Note: Computers with more than 16 GB of RAM will require more disk space for paging, hibernation, and dump files
Display	Super VGA (800 × 600) or higher resolution monitor
Other	DVD Drive, Keyboard and Microsoft Mouse (or compatible pointing device), Internet access (fees may apply)
	Note: To use RemoteFX, at least one qualified GPU is required on the host.

*Actual requirements will vary based on your system configuration, and the applications and features you choose to install. Processor performance is dependent upon not only the clock frequency of the processor, but the number of cores and the size of the processor cache. Disk space requirements for the system partition are approximate. Additional available hard disk space may be required if you are installing over a network.

INSTALLATION AND ACTIVATION

You do not need to enter a product key to evaluate any version of Windows Server 2008 R2 software, however activation is required within 10 days. Failing to activate the evaluation will cause the licensing service to shut down the machine every hour.

Notes